lonely planet

İstanbul

Tom Brosnahan

LONELY PLANET PUBLICATIONS
Melbourne • Oakland • London • Paris

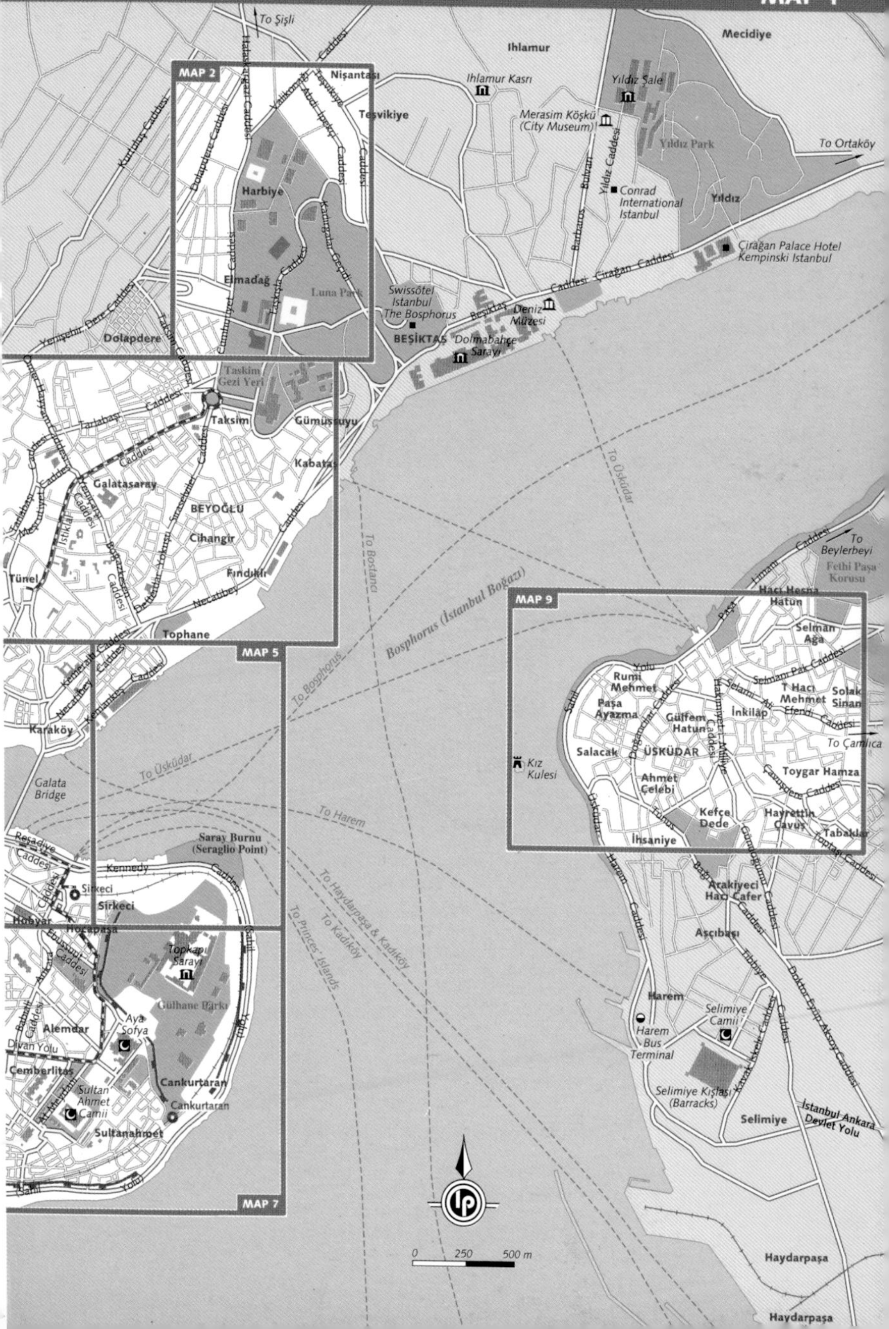

MAP 1

To Şişli

Ihlamur

Mecidiye

Ihlamur Kasrı

Yıldız Şale

Nişantaşı

Teşvikiye

MAP 2

Merasim Köşkü
(City Museum)

Yıldız Park

To Ortaköy

Harbiye

Yıldız Caddesi

Conrad
International
Istanbul

Yıldız

Elmadağ

Luna Park

Çırağan Palace Hotel
Kempinski Istanbul

Dolapdere

Swissôtel
Istanbul
The Bosphorus

Çırağan Caddesi

Taksim
Gezi Yeri

BEŞİKTAŞ

Deniz
Müzesi

Dolmabahçe
Sarayı

Taksim

Gümüşsuyu

Galatasaray

Kabataş

To Üsküdar

Fethi Paşa
Korusu

BEYOĞLU

To Beylerbeyi

Cihangir

Haçı Hesna
Hatun

Fındıklı

MAP 9

Selman
Aga

Tünel

To Bosphorus

To Boğaziçi

Bosphorus (Istanbul Boğazı)

Rumi
Mehmet

Solak
Sinan

Tophane

MAP 5

Paşa
Ayazma

T Hacı
Mehmet
Efendi

İnkilap

Karaköy

Gülfem
Hatun

To Çamlıca

Galata
Bridge

To Üsküdar

Kız
Kulesi

Salacak

ÜSKÜDAR

Ahmet
Çelebi

Toygar Hamza

To Harem

Reşadiye
Caddesi

Saray Burnu
(Seraglio Point)

Kefçe
Dede

Hayrettin
Çavuş

Tabaklar

Kennedy

Sirkeci

İhsaniye

Atakiyed
Haçı Cafer

Sirkeci

To Haydarpaşa & Kadıköy

To Kadıköy

To Prince's Islands

Aşçıbışı

Topkapı
Sarayı

Gülhane Park

Harem

Selimiye
Camii

Alemdar

Aya
Sofya

Harem
Bus
Terminal

Divan Yolu

Çankurtaran

Çemberlitaş

Selimiye Kışlası
(Barracks)

İstanbul-Ankara
Devlet Yolu

Sultan
Ahmet
Camii

Çankurtaran

Selimiye

Sultanahmet

MAP 7

0   250   500 m

Haydarpaşa

Haydarpaşa

İstanbul
2nd edition – April 1999
First published – April 1997

Published by
Lonely Planet Publications Pty Ltd ABN 36 005 607 983
90 Maribyrnong St, Footscray, Victoria 3011, Australia

Lonely Planet Offices
Australia Locked Bag 1, Footscray, Victoria 3011
USA 150 Linden St, Oakland, CA 94607
UK 10a Spring Place, London NW5 3BH
France 1 rue du Dahomey, 75011 Paris

Photographs
Many of the images in this guide are available for licensing from
Lonely Planet Images.
email: lpi@lonelyplanet.com.au

Front cover photograph
Blue Mosque, illuminated minarets (Kimberly Grant)

ISBN 0 86442 585 6

text & maps © Lonely Planet 1999
photos © photographers as indicated 1999

Printed by Colorcraft Ltd, Hong Kong

Contents

THE AUTHOR   3

THIS BOOK   4

FOREWORD   5

INTRODUCTION   9

FACTS ABOUT İSTANBUL   10

History 10
Geography 18
Climate 18
Ecology & Environment 18
Government & Politics 19
Economy 19
Population & People 20
Arts 21
Ottomon Mosques 27
Society & Conduct...............30
Religion 31

FACTS FOR THE VISITOR   33

When to Go......................33
Orientation 33
Maps 33
Tourist Offices 34
Documents 34
Embassies & Consulates 35
Customs............................36
Money 36
Post & Communications.......40
Internet Resources 42
Books................................42
Films 44
Newspapers & Magazines 44
Radio & TV 45
Photography & Video 45
Time 45
Electricity 46
Weights & Measures 46
Laundry 46
Toilets 46
Left Luggage 46
Health 46
Women Travellers 49
Gay & Lesbian Travellers 49
Disabled Travellers 50
Senior Travellers...................50
İstanbul for Children 50
Libraries 50
Dangers & Annoyances 51
Business Hours......................52
Public Holidays & Special
Events 53
Doing Business......................54
Work 55

GETTING THERE & AWAY   56

Air 56
Bus 59
Train 61
Car & Motorcycle 65
Hitching..............................66
Boat....................................67
Warning...............................68

GETTING AROUND   70

Atatürk Airport 70
Bus 71
Train 71
Metro 72
Tünel 72
Dolmuş 72
Taxi 72
Car 72
Boat....................................74
Walking 75
Organised Tours 76

THINGS TO SEE & DO   77

Highlights 77
Walking Tours 77
Sultanahmet.......................78
Eminönü 103
Beyoğlu 104
Hasköy...............................114
Western Districts 115
Yedikule.............................121

PLACES TO STAY   123

Sultanahmet.......................123
Taksim Square 129
Tepebaşi 130
Karaköy 131
Aksaray & Laleli 131
The Bosphorus 132
Near the Airport.................132

PLACES TO EAT 134

Sultanahmet 134
Topkapı Sarayı 137
Sirkeci & Eminönü 137
Kapalı Çarşı 140
Taksim Square 141
İstiklal Caddesi 141
Tepebaşi & Tünel 143
Kumkapi 143
The Bosphorus 145

ENTERTAINMENT 146

Music Festivals 146
Folk Dance & Music.............146
Classical Music & Ballet 146
Theatre 146
Cinema 147
Cafe-Bars 147
Nightclubs 148
Discos & Rock Clubs 149
Jazz Bars 149
Gay & Lesbian Venues 149
Night Cruises 149
Turkish Baths 150

SHOPPING 152

What & How to Buy 152
Where to Shop 156
Turkish Carpets 158

EXCURSIONS 165

The Bosphorus....................165
Touring the Bosphorus........167
Sights on the European
Shore..................................168
Sights on the Asian Shore ..176
Kızıl Adalar 182
Edirne 183
İznik & Bursa 189
İznik 189
Bursa 192
Gallipoli & Troy...................197
Gallipoli 197
Çanakkale 201
Troy...................................202

LANGUAGE 205

GLOSSARY 223

INDEX 225

MAP LEGEND back page

METRIC CONVERSION inside back cover

The Author

Tom Brosnahan

A native of Pennsylvania, Tom went to college in Boston, then set out on the road. His first two years in Turkey, during which he learned to speak fluent Turkish, were spent as a US Peace Corps Volunteer. He studied Middle Eastern history and the Ottoman Turkish language for eight years, but abandoned the writing of his PhD dissertation in favour of travelling and writing guidebooks.

So far his 30 books for various publishers have sold over two million copies in twelve languages. İstanbul city guide is the result of over a decade of experience and travel in Turkey.

Tom is also the co-author of Lonely Planet's Turkey, the Turkish phrasebook, Turkey travel atlas, Guatemala, Belize & Yucatán: La Ruta Maya, New England, Mexico, Central America and other LP guides.

FROM THE AUTHOR

Updated information for travellers to Turkey is available on Lonely Planet's website (www.lonelyplanet.com) and on my website (www.infoexchange.com). Please send us your tips, suggestions and comments so that we can improve our books and help other travellers. If you have a question for which this book and our websites do not provide the answer, I'll be happy to try to answer it through my website.

My thanks to Mr Selami Karaibrahimgil, director of the Turkish tourism office in New York City; Mr Mustafa Siyahhan of the Turkish Ministry of Tourism in Ankara; Mr Bülent Erdemgil, Press Counselor in the Turkish Embassy in Washington; Mr Ersan Atsür, Ms Ebru Akkale and the staff of Orion-Tour in İstanbul; Ms Mary Annn Whitten, USIS officer at the US Consulate in İstanbul; Ms Ann Nevens of the Hotel Empress Zoe in İstanbul; and Ms Ahrlene Flowers, Director of Corporate Public Relations for Four Seasons Hotels and Resorts.

This Book

From the Publisher

This edition of *İstanbul city guide* was edited at Lonely Planet in Melbourne by Bethune Carmichael and Elizabeth Swan, and proofed by Tom Smallman. Trudi Canavan designed the book and Maria Vallianos produced its cover. Trudi, Sarah Sloane and Paul Piaia took care of the mapping, and the illustrations were drawn by Trudi and Mick Weldon. Thanks to Quentin Frayne for editing the Language section, to Dan Levin for creating the soft fonts, and to Peter Ward of Peter Ward Book Exports for his assistance with bookshop information.

Acknowledgements

Many thanks to the travellers who used the last edition and wrote to us with helpful hints, useful advice and interesting anecdotes:

Eamonn, Petteri, Matthew Anderson, Paul Augenbroe, Tisha James Brock, Janet M Bryan, Gilly Carr, C & N Carter, Elizabeth Centeno, Kathleen Cherry, Dorothy Brier Cohen, Simona Decina, Karen Deetz, Deborah Filcoff, Robert G Finkel, Lawrence Forrester, Murat Germen, Jean L Hardy, Hilary Hepkiunsa, Karl Jeffery, Peter Jowett, Kristin Joynt, Ann Kennedy, Tone Larssen, Goerge Lechner, Caroline Lees, Kristina Lindberg, Jenny MacPherson, Wendy McCarty, Kathryn McClurg, Ann Mullen, Debby Nieuwenhuizen, Tracey Parker, Monica Pearl, Dick Richards, Carl Schwartzman, B & J Skerritt, Valerie Slemeck, Yolanthe Smit, Andrew Smith, Henrik Somogyvari, Fred Spengler, Sue Swarin, KJ Troy, John Udy, Elina Varmola, Philip Weld, Kian White, Roger AC Williams, Roger Williams, Genevieve Zalatorius.

Foreword

ABOUT LONELY PLANET GUIDEBOOKS

The story begins with a classic travel adventure: Tony and Maureen Wheeler's 1972 journey across Europe and Asia to Australia. Useful information about the overland trail did not exist at that time, so Tony and Maureen published the first Lonely Planet guidebook to meet a growing need.

From a kitchen table, then from a tiny office in Melbourne (Australia), Lonely Planet has become the largest independent travel publisher in the world, an international company with offices in Melbourne, Oakland (USA), London (UK) and Paris (France).

Today Lonely Planet guidebooks cover the globe. There is an ever-growing list of books and there's information in a variety of forms and media. Some things haven't changed. The main aim is still to help make it possible for adventurous travellers to get out there – to explore and better understand the world.

At Lonely Planet we believe travellers can make a positive contribution to the countries they visit – if they respect their host communities and spend their money wisely. Since 1986 a percentage of the income from each book has been donated to aid projects and human rights campaigns.

Updates Lonely Planet thoroughly updates each guidebook as often as possible. This usually means there are around two years between editions, although for more unusual or more stable destinations the gap can be longer. Check the imprint page (following the colour map at the beginning of the book) for publication dates.

Between editions up-to-date information is available in two free newsletters – the paper *Planet Talk* and email *Comet* (to subscribe, contact any Lonely Planet office) – and on our Web site at www.lonelyplanet.com. The *Upgrades* section of the Web site covers a number of important and volatile destinations and is regularly updated by Lonely Planet authors. *Scoop* covers news and current affairs relevant to travellers. And, lastly, the *Thorn Tree* bulletin board and *Postcards* section of the site carry unverified, but fascinating, reports from travellers.

Correspondence The process of creating new editions begins with the letters, postcards and emails received from travellers. This correspondence often includes suggestions, criticisms and comments about the current editions. Interesting excerpts are immediately passed on via newsletters and the Web site, and everything goes to our authors to be verified when they're researching on the road. We're keen to get more feedback from organisations or individuals who represent communities visited by travellers.

Lonely Planet gathers information for everyone who's curious about the planet – and especially for those who explore it first-hand. Through guidebooks, phrasebooks, activity guides, maps, literature, newsletters, image library, TV series and Web site we act as an information exchange for a worldwide community of travellers.

to enable travellers to make informed choices and to make the mechanics of a journey run smoothly. They also research historical and cultural background to help enrich the travel experience and allow travellers to understand and respond appropriately to cultural and environmental issues.

Authors don't stay in every hotel because that would mean spending a couple of months in each medium-sized city and, no, they don't eat at every restaurant because that would mean stretching belts beyond capacity. They do visit hotels and restaurants to check standards and prices, but feedback based on readers' direct experiences can be very helpful.

Many of our authors work undercover, others aren't so secretive. None of them accept freebies in exchange for positive write-ups. And none of our guidebooks contain any advertising.

Production Authors submit their raw manuscripts and maps to offices in Australia, USA, UK or France. Editors and cartographers – all experienced travellers themselves – then begin the process of assembling the pieces. When the book finally hits the shops, some things are already out of date, we start getting feedback from readers and the process begins again ...

HOW TO USE A LONELY PLANET GUIDEBOOK

WARNING & REQUEST

Things change – prices go up, schedules change, good places go bad and bad places go bankrupt – nothing stays the same. So, if you find things better or worse, recently opened or long since closed, please tell us and help make the next edition even more accurate and useful. We genuinely value all the feedback we receive. Julie Young coordinates a well travelled team that reads and acknowledges every letter, postcard and email and ensures that every morsel of information finds its way to the appropriate authors, editors and cartographers for verification.

Everyone who writes to us will find their name in the next edition of the appropriate guidebook. They will also receive the latest issue of *Planet Talk*, our quarterly printed newsletter, or *Comet*, our monthly email newsletter. Subscriptions to both newsletters are free. The very best contributions will be rewarded with a free guidebook.

Excerpts from your correspondence may appear in new editions of Lonely Planet guidebooks, the Lonely Planet Web site, *Planet Talk* or *Comet*, so please let us know if you *don't* want your letter published or your name acknowledged.

Send all correspondence to the Lonely Planet office closest to you:

Australia: Locked Bag 1, Footscray, Victoria 3011
USA: 150 Linden St, Oakland, CA 94607
UK: 10A Spring Place, London NW5 3BH
France: 1 rue du Dahomey, 75011 Paris

Or email us at: talk2us@lonelyplanet.com.au

For news, views and updates see our Web site: www.lonelyplanet.com

HOW TO USE A LONELY PLANET GUIDEBOOK

The best way to use a Lonely Planet guidebook is any way you choose. At Lonely Planet we believe the most memorable travel experiences are often those that are unexpected, and the finest discoveries are those you make yourself. Guidebooks are not intended to be used as if they provide a detailed set of infallible instructions!

Contents All Lonely Planet guidebooks follow the same format. The Facts about the Country chapters or sections give background information ranging from history to weather. Facts for the Visitor gives practical information on issues like visas and health. Getting There & Away gives a brief starting point for researching travel to and from the destination. Getting Around gives an overview of the transport options when you arrive.

The peculiar demands of each destination determine how subsequent chapters are broken up, but some things remain constant. We always start with background, then proceed to sights, places to stay, places to eat, entertainment, getting there and away, and getting around information – in that order.

Heading Hierarchy Lonely Planet headings are used in a strict hierarchical structure that can be visualised as a set of Russian dolls. Each heading (and its following text) is encompassed by any preceding heading that is higher on the hierarchical ladder.

Entry Points We do not assume guidebooks will be read from beginning to end, but that people will dip into them. The traditional entry points are the list of contents and the index. In addition, however, there is a complete list of maps and an index map illustrating map coverage.

There's also a colour map that shows highlights. These highlights are dealt with in greater detail in the Facts for the Visitor chapter, along with planning questions and suggested itineraries. Each chapter covering a geographical region begins with a locator map and another list of highlights. Once you find something of interest in a list of highlights, turn to the index.

Maps Maps play a crucial role in Lonely Planet guidebooks and include a huge amount of information. A legend is printed on the back page. We seek to have complete consistency between maps and text, and to have every important place in the text captured on a map. Map key numbers usually start in the top left corner.

Although inclusion in a guidebook usually implies a recommendation we cannot list every good place. Exclusion does not necessarily imply criticism. In fact there are a number of reasons why we might exclude a place – sometimes it is simply inappropriate to encourage an influx of travellers.

Introduction

Founded six centuries before Christ as Byzantium, refounded in 330 AD as Constantinople, and conquered by the Ottomans in 1453, İstanbul was the great eastern European imperial capital for almost 16 centuries.

Today İstanbul is Turkey's largest city, its busiest port, and the country's centre for business, banking, commerce, culture and the arts. Even though Ankara is Turkey's modern capital, İstanbul holds its heart. In this sprawling city you can tramp the streets where crusaders and janissaries once marched; admire mosques which are the most sublime architectural expressions of Islamic piety; peer into the sultan's harem; and hunt for souvenirs and bargains in the 4000 shops of the Kapalı Çarşı, or Grand Bazaar.

Known to its ancient inhabitants as simply 'The City', it remained enclosed within its mighty walls for 1500 years.

However, within the last half-century it has grown ferociously, spreading westward beyond the airport (23km from the city centre), northward almost to the Black Sea and eastward deep into Anatolia. This growth has mirrored the country's own as Turkey assumes its place as the economic powerhouse of the eastern Mediterranean.

The economic and tourism booms of the 1980s brought a new polish to the age-old metropolis. Hundreds of new hotels, restaurants, cafes, clubs and museums opened, transportation services were vastly improved and the city's cultural life took on a cosmopolitan energy and sophistication not seen here since the last years of the Ottoman Empire.

Whatever your interest – architecture, art, cuisine, history, nightlife, religion, shopping – İstanbul has it for you, at prices which are among the lowest in Europe.

Facts about İstanbul

HISTORY
Early Times

The Mediterranean region was inhabited as early as 7500 BC, during Palaeolithic (Old Stone Age) times. Turkey has some of the world's oldest 'cities', including Çatal Höyük, 50km south-east of Konya. These early Anatolian communities developed fine wall paintings, statuettes, domestic architecture and pottery during the Stone and Copper ages.

The Bronze Age, starting in 2600 BC, saw the rise of the Hittite civilisation in Central Anatolia, followed by those of the Phrygians, Urartians, Lydians and others.

Semistra, the earliest known settlement on the site of İstanbul, was probably founded around 1000 BC, a few hundred years after the Trojan War and in the same period that kings David and Solomon ruled in Jerusalem.

Semistra was followed by a fishing village named Lygos, which occupied Saray Burnu (Seraglio Point) where Topkapı Sarayı stands today. Later, around 700 BC, colonists from Megara (near Corinth) in Greece settled at Chalcedon (now Kadıköy) on the Asian shore of the Bosphorus.

In 512 BC, Darius, emperor of Persia, captured the town during his campaign against the Scythians. Following the retreat of the Persians in 478, the town came under the influence and protection of Athens, Sparta, Samos and other forces.

Around 400 BC, Xenophon led the remnants of the Ten Thousand (the Greek army in the service of Cyrus the Younger) back to Greece from the battle of Cunaxa by way of the Bosphorus.

Byzantium

The first settlement here to have historic significance was founded, according to legend, by a Megarian colonist named Byzas. Before leaving Greece, he asked the oracle at Delphi where he should establish his new colony.

The enigmatic answer was 'Opposite the blind'. When Byzas and his fellow colonists sailed up the Bosphorus, they noticed the colony on the Asian shore at Chalcedon. Looking west, they saw the superb natural harbour of the Golden Horn on the European shore. Thinking, as legend has it, 'Those people in Chalcedon must be blind', they settled in 657 BC on the opposite shore at Lygos, and their new town came to be called Byzantium after its founder.

The legend might as well be true. İstanbul's location on the waterway linking the Sea of Marmara and the Black Sea, and on the Thracian 'land bridge' linking Europe and Asia, is still of tremendous importance today, 26 centuries after the oracle spoke.

Byzantium submitted willingly to the armies of Alexander the Great, victor in the Battle of the Granicus (334 BC; near present-day Biga, north-west of Balıkesir). In 179 BC it was captured and became part of the Kingdom of Pergamum. When the last Pergamene king died in 133 BC, he willed his entire kingdom to Rome, and Byzantium became part of the Roman province of Asia.

Except for some tussles between Rome and the king of Pontus, Byzantium enjoyed peace and prosperity under Roman rule until it picked the wrong side in a civil war. When the Emperor Septimius Severus emerged victorious over his rival Pescennius Niger, he massacred Byzantium's citizens, razed its walls and burned the disloyal city.

Realising, however, the importance of the city's strategic position, he soon set about building a new, wider circuit of walls (which stretched roughly from the Yeni Cami to the Cankurtaran lighthouse) and named it Augusta Antonina.

Founding of Constantinople

Emperor Diocletian retired in 305 AD and left government of the Roman Empire to co-emperors Licinius in the east (Augusta Antonina) and Constantine in the west (Rome). This unstable arrangement resulted in a civil war, which was won by Constantine in 324 when he defeated Licinius at Chrysopolis (Üsküdar).

With his victory, Constantine became sole emperor (324-337) of a reunited empire. To solidify his power he summoned the First Ecumenical Council at Nicaea (İznik) in 325, which established the precedent of the emperor's supremacy in church affairs.

He also decided to move the capital of the empire to the shores of the Bosphorus. He built a new, wider circle of walls around the site of Byzantium and laid out a magnificent city within. The city was dedicated on 11 May 330 as New Rome, but was soon called Constantinople. The place which had been first settled as a fishing village over 1000 years earlier was now the capital of the Eurasian world, and would remain so for almost another 1000 years.

Constantine the Great died in Nicomedia (İzmit, Kocaeli) seven years after the dedication of his new capital. On his deathbed he formally adopted Christianity, though he had been governing its affairs for over a decade.

Much remains of Constantinople's 1123 years as a Christian city: churches, palaces, cisterns and the Hippodrome will draw your attention. Beneath the city's streets and buildings lies much more, revealed every time there's a modern excavation.

The city continued to grow. Emperor Theodosius II (408-450) came to the throne as a boy heavily influenced by his sister Pulcheria. Threatened by the forces of Attila the Hun, he ordered an even wider, more powerful circle of walls to be built around the city. Completed in 413, they were brought down by an earthquake in 447 and hastily rebuilt in a mere two months – the rapid approach of Attila and the Huns acting as a powerful stimulus. The Theodosian walls successfully held out invaders for the next 757 years, and still stand today.

Theodosius also built a new cathedral, the Sancta Sophia or Church of the Divine Wisdom (415), to replace an earlier church of the same name, which had been burned during a riot in 404.

Justinian & Theodora

During the 5th and 6th centuries, as the barbarians of Europe captured and sacked Rome, the new eastern capital grew in wealth and strength. Emperor Justinian (527-65) brought the Eastern Roman Empire to the height of its strength. A few years after taking the throne, he married Theodora, a devout, strong-willed former courtesan who is credited with having great influence over her husband. During the Nika riots of 532, the greatest threat to his reign, Justinian was reportedly ready to flee the capital, but the empress persuaded him to stand and fight, thus saving his throne.

Under Justinian, Byzantium's great general Belisarius reconquered Anatolia, the Balkans, Egypt, Italy and North Africa.

The emperor further embellished Constantinople with great buildings. His personal triumph was a new Sancta Sophia (today known as the Aya Sofya), built to replace Theodosius II's church, which had been burned in the Nika riots. When finished, in 537, this architectural masterpiece was the most splendid church in Christendom, and remained so for almost 1000 years, after which it became the most splendid mosque.

Justinian's ambitious building projects and constant wars of reconquest exhausted his treasury and his empire, however. Following his reign, the Byzantine Empire would never again be as large, powerful or rich.

Later Emperors

From 610 to 1025, a succession of warrior emperors kept the 'barbarians' at bay. The Arab armies of the nascent Islamic Empire reached the walls of Constantinople in 669, but couldn't penetrate them. Again in 717 they tried, and again failed. The powerful emperors of the Bulgarian Empire besieged the city in 814, 913 and 924, yet they never conquered it. Under Emperor Basil II (976-1025), the Byzantine armies drove the Arab

İstanbul Time Line

1000-657 BC	Ancient fishing villages on this site.
657 BC-330 AD	Byzantium, a Greek city-state, later subject to Rome.
330 AD	Constantine the Great founds Constantinople, the 'New Rome', capital of the Later, or Eastern, Roman (Byzantine) Empire.
410-447	Emperor Theodosius II builds a new, much wider ring of mighty walls around the city.
527-565	Reign of Justinian, the height of eastern Roman power and influence.
669-678	Arab Muslim armies lay siege to the city but cannot penetrate its walls.
717-718	Second Arab siege of Constantinople, also unsuccessful.
814-924	Armies of the Bulgarian Empire besiege the city three times unsuccessfully.
976-1025	Reign of Emperor Basil II, Byzantium's longest and most illustrious.
1071	Emperor Romanus IV Diogenes defeated and captured by the Selçuk Turks at Manzikert.
1204	Armies of the Fourth Crusade capture the city, sack it, and put a Latin emperor on the throne; Theodore I Lascaris founds the Empire of Nicaea to wait out the Latin occupation.
1261	Michael VIII Palaeologus, Emperor of Nicaea, recaptures Constantinople and re-establishes the Byzantine Empire.
1288	Osman Gazi, a Turkish warlord on the Byzantine frontier near Bursa, founds the Ottoman state.
1326-1331	Orhan Gazi, son of Osman, captures Bursa and Nicaea for the Ottomans; Bursa becomes the Ottoman capital.
1363	The Ottomans take Adrianople (Edirne) and make it their new capital.
1394	Sultan Beyazıt I builds Anadolu Hisarı and blockades Constantinople, but is forced to withdraw to do battle with Crusaders.
1453	Sultan Mehmet II (the Conqueror) builds Rumeli Hisarı and conquers Constantinople.

armies out of Anatolia and annihilated the Bulgarian forces.

After Basil, the empire was virtually ruled by the ambitious Empress Zoe (1028-50). She was 50 years old when she married the aged Emperor Romanus III Argyrus. He died mysteriously in his bath in 1034, and Zoe quickly married her youthful, virile companion who joined her on the throne as Michael IV. Eight years later, after Michael died from an illness contracted while on campaign, Zoe and her sister Theodora ruled as empresses in their own right, but they were no more able than men to dominate the fractious nobles. At the age of 64

Zoe wed an eminent senator who became the third Mr Zoe, Constantine IX Monomachus. He outlived the empress, but did no better a job at ruling. After his death, Zoe's sister Theodora ruled as empress again.

In 1071, Emperor Romanus IV Diogenes led his army to eastern Anatolia to do battle with the Selçuk Turks who had been forced out of Central Asia by the encroaching Mongols. However, at Manzikert (Malazgirt) the Byzantines were disastrously defeated, the emperor captured and imprisoned, and the former Byzantine heartland of Anatolia thus thrown open to Turkish in-

İstanbul Time Line

1520-1566	Reign of Sultan Süleyman the Magnificent, the apogee of Ottoman power and glory.
1566-1687	'The Rule of Women', when powerful princesses and queen mothers ruled Topkapı Palace in place of the dissolute and incompetent sultans.
1789-1807	Reign of Sultan Selim III, who adopted many European methods for the state and the military.
1826	Sultan Mahmut II destroys the corrupt jannisaries with a massacre in the Hippodrome.
1876	The 'Tanzimat' (Reform) movement culminates with the promulgation of the first Ottoman constitution.
1876-1909	Sultan Abdül Hamit II abrogates the constitution and rules the empire with an iron hand.
1909-1918	The 'Young Turks' depose Abdül Hamit II and rule as a virtual military junta.
1922-1923	The Grand National Assembly, led by Mustafa Kemal (Atatürk), abolishes the Ottoman sultanate and proclaims the Turkish Republic, with its capital at Ankara.
1973	The first Bosphorus Bridge, joining Europe and Asia, is opened on the 50th anniversary of the republic's founding.
1988	The Mehmet the Conqueror (Fatih) Bridge across the Bosphorus is opened.
1988 to the Present	İstanbul enjoys a renaissance as 'capital of the east'. The city government, following the lead of the Turkish Touring & Automobile Association, undertakes vast schemes to modernise and beautify the city and attract international business operations. New parks, museums and cultural centres are opened, old ones are restored and refurbished.

vasion and settlement. Soon the Selçuks had built a thriving empire of their own in central Anatolia, with their capital first at Nicaea, and later at Konya.

As Turkish power was consolidated in Anatolia to the east of Constantinople, the power of Venice – always a maritime and commercial rival to Constantinople – grew in the west.

The Crusades

The convoluted, treacherous imperial court politics of Constantinople have given us the word 'Byzantine'. Rarely blessed with a simple, peaceful succession, Byzantine rulers were always under threat from members of their own families as well as would-be tyrants and foreign powers.

In 1195 Alexius III deposed and blinded his brother, Emperor Isaac II. Isaac's oldest son, Prince Alexius, escaped to Rome and pleaded to the pope for help in restoring his father to the Byzantine throne. At the time, the Fourth Crusade was assembling in Venice to sail to Egypt and attack the Infidel. Unable to pay for passage in the Venetian ships, the crusaders were easily persuaded to forget about battling infidels and to conquer instead their co-religionists in the nearby port of Zara (today Zadar). It had once been a Venetian possession, but was lost, and Venice wanted it back.

When Prince Alexius offered to pay richly to be put on the throne, Enrico Dandolo, Doge of Venice, led the crusaders to his rival in Constantinople, arriving in 1203. Alexius III fled with the imperial treasury, and the crusaders restored Isaac II to the throne and made Prince Alexius his co-emperor. However, the new co-emperors had no money to pay their allies so they imposed a crushing tax burden on their people. Rising in revolt, the Byzantine people killed both of them. Within months, impatient for his money, Dandolo ordered the conquest of the city. On 13 April 1204 the crusaders succeeded in breaking through the walls; and then proceeded to sack and pillage the rich capital of their Christian ally.

When the smoke cleared, Dandolo took control of three-eighths of the city, including Aya Sofya, leaving the rest to his co-conspirator Count Baldwin of Flanders. The Byzantine nobility fled to what was left of their estates and fought among themselves in best Byzantine fashion for control of the shreds of the empire.

Count Baldwin had Aya Sofya converted to a Roman Catholic cathedral, and there had himself crowned Emperor of Romania, his name for his new kingdom.

Never a strong or effective state, Baldwin's so-called empire steadily declined until, just over a half-century later in 1261, it was easily recaptured by the soldiers of Michael VIII Palaeologus, formerly the Emperor of Nicaea, now emperor of a restored Byzantine Empire.

Birth of the Ottoman Empire

Two decades after Michael re-established Byzantine rule in its traditional capital, a Turkish warlord named Ertuğrul died in the village of Söğüt not far east of Nicaea. He left to his son Osman a small territory and a band of followers which in 1326 Osman would leave to his son, Orhan (1326-1361), as the nascent Ottoman Empire.

Orhan captured Bursa and made it his capital, then captured Nicaea (İznik) as

well, and sent his forces further afield, conquering Ankara to the east and Thrace to the west. His son Murat I (1361-1389) took Adrianople (Edirne) in 1362 and pursued his conquests to Kosovo, where he defeated the Serbs and Bosnians, though he was assassinated by a treacherous Serb.

Though temporarily checked by the armies of Tamerlane and by fratricidal civil war within the Ottoman ruling family, the empire continued to grow in power and size. By 1440 the Ottoman armies had laid siege to Constantinople and Belgrade (unsuccessfully), and had battled Christian armies for Transylvania.

The Conquest

What Europeans refer to as 'the fall of Constantinople' is to Turks 'the Conquest'.

By 1450, the Byzantine emperor had effective control over little more than Constantinople itself and a few small territories in what is now Greece.

When Sultan Mehmet II (1451-1481) came to the throne as a young man, his 150-year-old empire needed a firm hand. He provided it, establishing central governmental control and battling troublesome Turkish emirs into submission. To solidify his power, he decided on the obvious: the conquest of the great city his territories already surrounded.

Mehmet ordered construction of the fortress of Rumeli Hisarı to be completed in four months. Miraculously, it was. He also had Anadolu Hisarı, Beyazıt's fortress on the Asian shore, repaired. Between them, the two great fortresses could close the Bosphorus at its narrowest point, blockading the imperial capital from the north.

The Byzantines had closed the mouth of the Golden Horn with a heavy chain (on view today in İstanbul's Askeri Müzesi, or Military Museum) to prevent Ottoman ships from sailing in and attacking the city walls on the north side. Mehmet outsmarted them by marshalling his boats at a cove where Dolmabahçe Sarayı now stands and having them transported by night overland on rollers and slides up the valley (where the

İstanbul Hilton now stands) and down the other side into the Golden Horn at Kasım Paşa. As dawn broke, his fleet attacked the city, catching the Byzantine defenders completely by surprise. Soon the Golden Horn was under Ottoman control.

As for the mighty Theodosian land walls to the west, a Hungarian cannon founder named Urban had come to offer his services to the Byzantine emperor for the defence of Christendom. Finding that the emperor had no money, he went to Mehmet, who paid him richly to cast an enormous cannon capable of firing a huge ball up to 1.5km – or, more to the point, right through the city walls.

Despite the inevitability of the Conquest, Emperor Constantine XI Palaeologus refused surrender terms offered by Mehmet on 23 May 1453, preferring to wait in hope that Christendom would come to his rescue. On 28 May the final attack began, the mighty walls were breached between the gates now called Topkapı and Edirnekapı, the sultan's troops flooded in, and by the evening of the 29th they were in control of every quarter. The last emperor of Byzantium died in battle fighting on the walls.

Mehmet's triumphant entry into 'the world's greatest city' on the evening of 29 May is commemorated every year at the Topkapı (Cannon Gate).

The areas of the city that did not resist his troops were spared and their churches guaranteed to them. Areas that resisted were sacked for the customary three days, and the churches turned into mosques. As for Aya Sofya, the greatest church in Christendom, it was cleansed and converted immediately into a mosque.

Ottoman Greatness

Mehmet the Conqueror saw himself as the legitimate successor to the imperial throne of Byzantium by right of conquest. He began at once to rebuild and repopulate the city. He built a mosque, the Fatih (Conqueror) Camii, on one of the city's seven hills, repaired the city walls and made İstanbul, as it would soon be called, the

Süleyman I, sultan of the Ottoman Empire between 1520 and 1566, was also known as Süleyman the Magnificent or the Lawgiver.

administrative, commercial and cultural centre of his growing empire.

Süleyman the Magnificent was perhaps İstanbul's greatest builder. Blessed with the services of Mimar Sinan (circa 1497-1588), Islam's greatest architect, the sultan and his family, court and grand viziers crowded the city with great buildings. Süleyman's mosque, the Süleymaniye (1550), is İstanbul's largest. Many of the other 300 buildings attributed to Sinan are also in the capital.

During his reign (1520-66), Süleyman had the support of Hürrem Sultan, known in the west as Roxelana. Though allowed four legal wives and as many concubines as he could support by Islamic law, this sultan was devoted to Hürrem alone. A decisive and forceful woman, she mastered the art of palace intrigue. She even convinced the sultan to have İbrahim Paşa, Süleyman's lifelong companion and devoted grand vizier, strangled when he objected to her influence. Unfortunately, she also made sure that her drunken son, Selim the Sot, would succeed to the throne by having the able heir apparent, Prince Mustafa, strangled. Her machinations began the period known as the Rule of the Women (1566-1687).

Selim and his successors, under the influence of the powerful palace women, were encouraged to lose themselves in the pleasures of the harem and the bottle. Luckily for them all, external and military affairs were dealt with by a succession of exceptionally able grand viziers.

Among the most fascinating of the harem leaders was Kösem Sultan, the favourite of Sultan Ahmet III. She influenced the course of the empire through Ahmet, then through her sons Murat IV and İbrahim, and finally through her grandson Mehmet IV – a reign extending from 1617 to 1652. She was finally strangled at the command of the Valide Sultan Turhan Hatice, Mehmet IV's mother, who was jealous and perhaps not a little frightened of grandma's power.

Ottoman Decline

The motor which drove the Ottoman Empire was military conquest, and when the sultan's armies reached their geographical and technological limits, decline set in for good. In 1687 the Ottomans laid siege for the second time to Vienna, but failed again to take the city. With the Treaty of Karlowitz in 1699, the Austrian and Ottoman emperors divided up the Balkans, and the Ottoman Empire went on the defensive.

By this time Europe was well ahead of Turkey in politics, technology, science, banking, commerce and military development. Sultan Selim III (1789-1807) realised this and initiated efforts to catch up to Europe, but was overthrown in a revolt by *janissaries* (the sultan's personal bodyguards). The modernisation efforts were continued under Mahmut II. He founded a new army along European lines, provoked a riot among the janissaries, then sent his new force in to crush them, which it did. The bodies of janissaries filled the Hippodrome, and the ancient corps, once the glory of the empire, was no more.

Selim's efforts were too little, too late, however. During the 19th century, ethnic nationalism, a force more powerful even than western armies, penetrated the sultan's domains and proved his undoing.

Ethnic Nationalism

For centuries, the non-Turkish ethnic and non-Muslim religious minorities in the sultan's domains had lived side by side with their Turkish neighbours, governed by their own religious and traditional laws. The head of each community – chief rabbi, Orthodox patriarch etc – was responsible to the sultan for the community's well-being and behaviour.

Ottoman decline and misrule provided fertile ground for the growth of ethnic nationalism, however. The subject peoples of the Ottoman Empire rose in revolt, one after another, often with the direct encouragement and assistance of the European powers who coveted parts of the sultan's vast domains. After bitter fighting in 1832, the Kingdom of Greece was formed; the Serbs, Bulgarians, Romanians, Albanians, Armenians and Arabs would all seek their independence soon after.

As the sultan's empire broke up, the European powers (Britain, France, Italy, Germany, Russia) hovered in readiness to colonise or annex the pieces. They used religion as a reason for pressure or control, saying that it was their duty to protect the sultan's Catholic, Protestant or Orthodox subjects from misrule and anarchy.

The Russian emperors put pressure on the Turks to grant them powers over all Ottoman Orthodox Christian subjects, whom the Russian emperor would thus 'protect'. The result of this pressure was the Crimean War (1853-56), with Britain and France fighting on the side of the Ottomans against the growth of Russian power.

During the war, wounded British soldiers were brought to İstanbul for treatment. Florence Nightingale, a young nurse sent out to tend to them, was so appalled at the unsanitary conditions in the military hospitals. She and her fellow nurses established standards for care that served as the foundation for modern nursing.

Even during the war, the monarch in İstanbul continued in the imperial building tradition. Vast Dolmabahçe Sarayı and its mosque were finished in 1856, and the palaces at Beylerbeyi, Çırağan and Yıldız would be built before the end of the century. Though it had lost the fabulous wealth of the days of Süleyman the Magnificent, it was still regarded as the Paris of the East. It was also the terminus of the *Orient Express,* which connected İstanbul and Paris, the world's first great international luxury express train.

Abdül Hamit II & the Young Turks

In the midst of imperial dissolution, Mithat Paşa, a successful general and powerful grand vizier, brought the young crown prince Abdül Hamit II (1876-1909) to the throne along with a constitution in 1876. But the new sultan did away both with Mithat Paşa and the constitution, and established his own absolute rule.

Abdül Hamit modernised without democratising, building thousands of kilometres of railways and telegraph lines and encouraging modern industry. However, the empire continued to disintegrate with nationalist insurrections in Armenia, Bulgaria, Crete and Macedonia.

The younger generation of the Turkish elite – particularly the military – watched bitterly as their country fell apart, then organised secret societies bent on toppling the sultan. The Young Turk movement for western-style reforms gained enough power by 1908 to force the restoration of the constitution. In 1909, the Young Turk-led Ottoman parliament deposed Abdül Hamit and put his indecisive brother Mehmet V ('Vahdettin') on the throne.

In its last years, though a sultan still sat on the throne in İstanbul, the Ottoman Empire was ruled by three members of the Young Turks' Committee of Union & Progress: Talat, Enver and Jemal. Their rule was vigorous but harsh and misguided, and it only worsened an already hopeless situation. When WWI broke out, they made the fatal error of siding with Germany and

the Central Powers. With their defeat, the Ottoman Empire collapsed, İstanbul was occupied by the British, and the sultan became a pawn in the hands of the victors.

Republican İstanbul

The situation looked very bleak for the Turks as their armies were being disbanded and their country was taken under the control of the Allies, but a catastrophe provided the impetus for rebirth.

Ever since gaining independence in 1831, the Greeks had entertained the *Megali Idea* (Great Plan) of a new Greek empire encompassing all the lands which had once had Greek influence – in effect, the refounding of the Byzantine Empire, with Constantinople as its capital. On 15 May 1919, with western backing, Greek armies invaded Anatolia in order to make the dream a reality.

Even before the Greek invasion, however, an Ottoman general named Mustafa Kemal, the hero of Gallipoli, had decided that a new government must take over the destiny of the Turks from the powerless sultan. He

The son of a minor diplomat, Atatürk (Mustafa Kemal Paşa) turned an ageing empire into a forward-looking nation-state, and remains a national hero in Turkey today.

began organising resistance to the sultan's captive government on 19 May 1919.

The Turkish War of Independence, in which the Turkish Nationalist forces led by Mustafa Kemal fought off Greek, French and Italian invasion forces, lasted from 1920 to 1922. Victory in the bitter war put Mustafa Kemal in command of the fate of the Turks. The sultanate was abolished in 1922 and soon after, the Ottoman Empire. A republic was born on 29 October 1923.

The nation's saviour, proclaimed Atatürk (Father Turk) by the Turkish parliament, decided to move away, both metaphorically and physically, from the imperial memories of İstanbul, and also to establish the seat of the new republican government in a city that could not easily be threatened by foreign gunboats.

Robbed of its importance as the capital of a vast empire, İstanbul lost much of its wealth and glitter in succeeding decades. Its title 'Paris of the East' was assumed first by Beirut, then by Athens. But during the 1980s and 1990s Turkey's economic and tourism boom and İstanbul's vigorous municipal leadership has restored much of the city's historic importance. At the turn of yet another millennium Byzantium-Constantinople-İstanbul appears ready to again fulfil its role as the 'capital' of the eastern Mediterranean.

GEOGRAPHY

İstanbul is at latitude 41° north, and near longitude 29° east, putting it at about the same latitude as Beijing, Madrid, Naples, New York and Salt Lake City. The low hills on which the city is built border the Golden Horn, a freshwater estuary, and the Bosphorus, the saltwater strait connecting the Black and Marmara seas. The land of this region is excellent for producing fruit such as grapes, peaches and apricots, as well as vast crops of sunflowers.

CLIMATE

Turkey has seven climatic regions. İstanbul is situated in the Marmara region, which includes eastern Thrace and Edirne. It's a

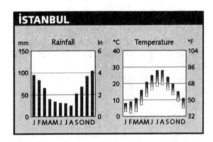

countryside of rolling steppeland and low hills with an average yearly rainfall of 668mm. Rainfall is highest (between 80 and 100mm per month) from November to February; July and August have the least rainfall. Humidity follows the same pattern, with the lowest humidity (under 30%) in July, August and September, and the highest (over 60%) – a bone-chilling damp – in December and January.

Temperatures in July and August peak at around 30°C (86°F), with lows around 20°C (68°F). In December and January, temperatures can fall as low as 2°C (36°F), with daily highs only about 9°C (48°F). April-May and September-October are the best times to visit, with daytime highs usually around 16°C to 25°C (61°F to 77°F), and lows from around 9°C to 18°C (48°F to 64°F).

ECOLOGY & ENVIRONMENT

İstanbul has been plagued by hyper-growth during the last few decades as villagers move to the cities by the tens of thousands in search of a better life.

Air and water pollution is a big problem, but important reclamation projects in recent years have cleaned up the Golden Horn and Bosphorus waters considerably – though they are still both polluted. Clean-burning Russian natural gas has replaced dirty lignite (soft coal) as the preferred winter heating fuel, and İstanbul's winter air is now cleaner than it has been at any time in this century, though it's still far from country-fresh.

There are some attempts to recycle glass and metal, and Bosphorus restaurants now seem to refrain from throwing food waste straight into the water. Sewage treatment plants are now under construction and vessels – including yachts – in Turkish waters are prohibited by law from emptying waste into the seas, though it still happens because of insufficient enforcement.

As for indoor pollution, cigarette smoking is a national passion. Although more and more areas are being declared nonsmoking zones, the rules are often ignored.

GOVERNMENT & POLITICS

Though the Turks are firm believers in democracy, the tradition of popular rule is relatively short. Real multiparty democracy came into being only after WWII, and has been interrupted several times by military control, though the military has always returned government to civilians.

İstanbul is actually two political entities: the city and the province. The city is organised as a *büyükşehir belediyesi,* or metropolitan municipality, with several large submunicipalities under the overall authority of a metropolitan city government. The boundaries of the province of İstanbul extend almost to Çorlu in the west and to Gebze in the east.

Until electoral reforms became law in the 1980s, municipal governments in Turkey were largely controlled by the national government. Now, however, İstanbullus elect their own local government, and complain that, whoever may be in power, the problems of corruption and cronyism persist.

The municipal elections of March 1994 were a wake-up call against politics as usual, however. The upstart religious-right Welfare Party (Refah Partisi) won municipal elections across the country, including those in İstanbul and Ankara. Their victory was seen in part as a protest vote against the corruption, ineffective policies and tedious political wrangles of the traditional parties.

In the national elections of December 1996, the Welfare Party polled more votes than any other party (23%), and eventually formed a government vowing moderation and honesty.

Emboldened by political power, however, Prime Minister Erbakan and other Refah politicians tested the boundaries of Turkey's traditional secularism. Erbakan made triumphant visits to Iran and other aggressively Islamist countries, and reputedly received financial subsidies from them. Local politicians made Islamist gestures and statements that alarmed the powerful National Security Council, the most visible symbol of the centrist military establishment's role as the caretaker of secularism and democracy.

In 1997 the Council let it be known that Refah's time was up. Prime Minister Erbakan was forced to resign and his party was dissolved for having flouted the constitutional ban against religion in politics. Most secular, democratically minded Turks were not sorry to see Refah go, but neither were they happy with the precedent of the military establishment, charged by Atatürk to protect democracy, forcing a democratically elected government from office.

Mr Recep Tayyip Erdogan, the Refah mayor of İstanbul elected in 1994, was ousted by the secularist forces in the national government in late 1998.

ECONOMY

Though Turkey has traditionally been a net exporter of food (one of only seven such countries in the world), its strong agricultural sector has now been superseded by even stronger commercial and manufacturing activity, much of which is centred in İstanbul. Turkey produces motor vehicles, appliances and consumer goods, and has undertaken many large engineering projects. The country's products are exported throughout the region: in the first half of 1995, exports grew by 29.5%, giving Turkey the fourth-highest export growth rate in the world. İstanbul's commercial centre is north of the historic city on the western side of the Bosphorus. Industrial plants are to the west and east of the city centre.

Tourism is now among the most important sectors of the Turkish economy. In

1998, nearly 10 million visitors came to Turkey, leaving billions of dollars behind.

POPULATION & PEOPLE

Turkey has a population exceeding 63 million, the great majority being Sunni Muslim Turks. Though İstanbul's population is given officially as some seven million, estimates of the true size of the urban agglomeration reach as high as 12 million.

Turks

The Turkic peoples originated in Central Asia, where they were a presence to be reckoned with as early as the 4th century AD. The Chinese called them *Tu-küe*, which is perhaps the root of our word 'Turk'. They were related to the *Hiung-nu*, or Huns.

The normally nomadic Turks ruled several vast but short-lived empires in Central Asia before being pushed westward by the Mongols. Various tribes of the Oğuz Turkic group settled in Azerbaijan, northern Iran and Anatolia, finally overrunning Constantinople in 1453, and going on to conquer much of eastern Europe.

Early Turks followed each of the great Asian and Middle Eastern religions, including Buddhism, Nestorian Christianity, Manichaeism and Judaism. During their western migrations they became more familiar with Islam, and it stuck.

Kurds

Turkey has a significant Kurdish minority estimated at 10 million or more. Some ethnologists believe that the Kurds, who speak an Indo-European language, are closely related to the Persians, and that they migrated here from northern Europe centuries before Christ. There are significant Kurdish populations in neighbouring Iraq, Iran and Syria as well. İstanbul numbers many Turkish Kurds among its citizens.

Though virtually all of Turkey's Kurds are Muslims and physically similar to the Turks, they jealously guard their language and cultural and family traditions.

Over the centuries the Kurds have struggled for autonomy from the various majority governments that have ruled them. In 1924 Kemal Ataturk banned any expression of Kurdishness in an attempt at assimilation. Major battles and atrocities ensued throughout the 20s and 30s and over the past few decades nearly 30,000 people have died.

For the last 15 years the leftist Kurdistan Workers Party (PKK) has responded to persecution with a guerilla war and acts of terrorism against the Turkish government. Civilian targets have also been hit in attacks throughout Turkey, especially in the southeast. At the same time the PKK's rival for control of the enclave, the Kurdistan Democratic Party, has recently sided with Ankara.

In 1997, 30,000 Turkish troops entered northern Iraq with the aim of rooting out the 4,000 PKK troops in hiding there. The operation continues with Turkish troops firmly entrenched and a rigorously enforced media blackout by the Turkish government.

Jews

İstanbul's Jewish community of 20,000 forms the majority of Turkey's Jewish population of some 24,000. The Turkish Jewish community is the remnant of a great influx which took place in the 16th century when the Jews of Spain (Sephardim) were forced by the Spanish Inquisition to flee their homes. They were welcomed into the Ottoman Empire, and brought with them knowledge of many European scientific and economic discoveries and advancements. Though in 1992 they celebrated 500 years of peaceful life among the Turks, many Turkish Jews have emigrated to Israel since the founding of the Jewish state in 1948.

Greeks

Turkey's community of ethnic Greeks was in the millions during the Ottoman Empire, but most fled to Greece or abroad during the cataclysm of WWI and the Turkish War of Independence. Many others left as part of the League of Nations' exchange of populations between Turkey and Greece after the war. The Cyprus conflict of the 1960s raised tensions between Turkey and Greece, causing another exodus of Turkish Greeks to Greece and Greek Turks to Turkey. It is estimated that ethnic Greeks in Turkey now number fewer than 100,000, most of whom live in İstanbul.

Armenians

The Armenians are thought by some to be descended from the Urartians (518-330 BC) of eastern Anatolia, but others think they arrived from the Caucasus area after the Urartian state collapsed.

Armenians have lived in eastern Anatolia for millennia, almost always as subjects of some greater state such as the Alexandrine Empire, or that of the Romans, Byzantines, Persians, Selçuks or Ottomans. They lived with their Kurdish and Turkish neighbours in relative peace and harmony under the Ottoman *millet* system of distinct religious communities. But when this system was destroyed by modern ethnic nationalism, their community was decimated by emigration, conflict, massacre and deportation.

Though many Armenians remained loyal to the Ottoman sultan, others organised guerrilla bands in pursuit of an independent Armenian state on Ottoman soil. They attacked official and civilian targets using methods now familiar from the exploits of other ethnic movements such as the Irish Republican Army, Palestine Liberation Organisation and Kurdistan Workers Party.

On 26 August 1896, Armenian revolutionaries seized the Ottoman Bank building in İstanbul, threatening to blow it up if their demands were not met. The authorities refused to deal with them and the terrorists were ultimately overpowered, but the outrage of terrorism (new at the time, though all too familiar to us now) set off a powerful anti-Armenian backlash, resulting in widespread massacres of innocent Armenians in İstanbul and elsewhere.

With the support of the Imperial Russian army, a short-lived Armenian Republic was proclaimed in north-eastern Anatolia in the closing years of WWI, and the victorious Armenians repaid defeated local Muslims with massacres in kind. But an offensive by the armies of Mustafa Kemal's Turkish nationalist Ankara government reclaimed the area for the nascent Turkish Republic.

On 3 December 1920, the Ankara government concluded a peace treaty with the Armenian government in Yerevan, by then a Soviet republic. By the end of the war, the Armenian population of Anatolia had been reduced to insignificant numbers. Today İstanbul has a small Armenian population with its own schools, churches and cultural organisations.

ARTS

Islam prohibits as idolatry the depiction of any being 'with an immortal soul' (meaning any human or animal). This prohibition determined the course of Islamic art: it would be rich in architecture, calligraphy, stained glass, manuscript illumination, glass-blowing, marquetry, metalwork and other geometric design, but would have little painting or sculpture as those arts are understood in non-Islamic countries.

Likewise, the Islamic tradition of sequestering women would hamper public performance of lively arts such as dance, theatre and music. These arts were highly refined within the households of the Ottoman nobility, but performances by family members were strictly private.

With the founding of the secular Turkish Republic in 1923, the Turkish art scene underwent a revolutionary change. All at once women were encouraged to perform in public, and artists of both genders were encouraged to create paintings, sculptures, plays, films and musical scores portraying the entire range of human activity and emotion. The government in Ankara oversaw the founding and subsidising of opera and dance companies, symphony and chamber music ensembles, and the establishment of fine arts academies and museums.

Today İstanbul is the cosmopolitan artistic centre of the Turkish Republic, with lively schools of painting, sculpture, film, music, literature, dance and theatre.

Calligraphy

Proportion of line and stroke, and felicity of design and execution are the strong points of Islamic calligraphy, an ancient and highly esteemed art. Its beauty is mostly lost on non-Muslims, unfamiliar with its aesthetic and with the religious formulas that are its most common subjects. Many of İstanbul's museums, including Topkapı Sarayı, the Türk-İslam Eserleri Müzesi (Museum of Turkish and Islamic Arts) and the Divan Ede-biyatı Müzesi (Museum of Divan Literature), have fine examples of calligraphers' art.

Literature

Literature before the republic was also bound up with Islam. Treatises on history, geography and science were cast in religious terms. Ottoman poets, borrowing from the great Arabic and Persian traditions, wrote sensual love poems of attraction, longing, fulfilment and ecstasy in the search for union with God.

By the late 19th century some Ottoman writers were adapting to European forms.

The Art of Writing

The Arabic alphabet has 28 characters. Mainly consonants are represented whereas the inclusion of vowels is optional, and are indicated by diacritics (dots or marks placed above or below a character). After the rise of Islam in the 7th century, Arabic writing developed into several calligraphic styles. These scripts fall into two categories: the Kufic or "dry" styles, and the cursive styles.

The Kufic Styles

After its creation in the 7th century, Kufic became the dominant script for religious subjects. Many ornamental forms of Kufic were developed and adapted for use on ceramics and architectural monuments, as well as in books.

 **Early Kufic** Kufic script combines square and angular lines with bold circular strokes, and is characterised by the contrast of short verticals with long, extended horizontals.

Persian Kufic The addition of slender vertical and oblique strokes gave dynamic form to the script. Popular on ceramics.

Foliate Kufic Decorative curls were added at the end of vertical strokes as decoration. Popular for architectural uses.

Knotted & Geometric Kufic The letters themselves were altered to form plaiting and braiding, or geometric patterns. Square Kufic was used extensively on buildings.

The Cursive Styles

Farsi (Talik) Used in Persia until the early 9th century, Farsi is once again a favoured calligraphic style.

With the foundation of the republic, the ponderous cadences of Ottoman courtly prose and poetry gave way to use of the vernacular. Atatürk decreed that the Turkish language be 'purified' of Arabic and Persian borrowings. This, and the introduction of the new Latin-based Turkish alphabet, brought literacy within the reach of many more citizens.

In the second half of the 20th century, Nazım Hikmet and Yashar Kemal have been translated into other languages and have met with critical and popular acclaim abroad. More recently, İstanbul novelist Orhan Pamuk has gained a worldwide following. *The White Tower* and *The Black Book* are his two best known works in English, while *New Life* is his most recent (1998).

Traditional Turkish Music

There are many kinds of Turkish music, almost all of them unfamiliar to foreign ears. Ottoman classical, religious (particularly Sufi Mevlevi) and some types of folk and popular music use a system of *makams* (modalities), an exotic-sounding series of notes similar in function to the familiar western scales of whole and half-tone intervals. Much Turkish music also uses

---

The Art of Writing

Nastaliq (Nestalik) Developed from Farsi in the 14th and 15th century, it was used for copying romantic and mystical epics. Unlike most other styles, which slant to the left, Nastaliq slants to the right.

Deewani (Divani) Also developed from Farsi, Deewani is highly cursive and structured and has no vowel marks.

Jali (Celi) An ornamental variety of Deewani.

Thuluth (Sülüs) formed in the 7th century during the Umayyad era, Thuluth script was fully developed by the late 9th century. The predominant ornamental script, it was a popular style for inscriptions, titles and epigrams, but was rarely used for writing the Holy Koran.

Req'aa (Rıka) A dense style with short horizontals that is easy to write. Developed as a simpler form of Thuluth, it is used for everyday writing.

Naskh (Nesih) A script with short horizontals, full curves and vertical uprights, Naskh was one of the first to develop. Easy to write and read, it gained popularity in the 10th century and was developed into an elegant script for use in writing the Koran, and is now the dominant script used for that purpose.

Numerous scripts have developed from these. One of the most intriguing and beautiful is zoomorphic art, which involves contorting letters and words to form animal shapes such as birds or tigers.

Trudi Canavan

Traditional Musical Instruments

Stringed Instruments

Kemençe A narrow, three-stringed fiddle with a short neck. It is held vertically, with the player sitting and the lower part of the fiddle resting on his/her knee, and played with a bow.

Saz The saz has a long, unfretted neck, four strings and a bulbous, melon-shaped body that has no sound hole.

Ud The lute, popular in the 15th and 16th centuries, evolved from the *ud*. The bellies of earlier uds were constructed of skin.

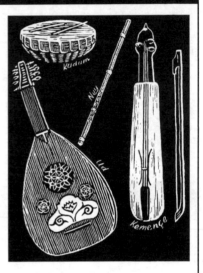

Wind Instruments

Ney A bamboo flute, difficult to master. It is the principal instrument in the Mevlevi music that accompanies the dance of whirling dervishes. Makes a breathy, plaintive sound.

Zurna A cylindrical wooden oboe with a double reed, often played with the *davul*.

Percussion Instruments

Davul A large, two-headed drum that is slung from the shoulders. The davul is a folk instrument usually played in combination with the zurna. The davul became fashionably exotic in the 18th century, and Mozart included sections reminiscent of it in his compositions.

Kaşık Wooden spoons, played either as the sole accompaniment for dancing or with wind or stringed instruments.

Kudum A small kettledrum, usually played in pairs, it is an essential element of Mevlevi music.

Turkish Crescent Otherwise known as a 'jingling Johnny', this instrument doubled as a standard carried by Ottoman soldiers. Crescent and hat-shaped ornaments bearing horsetail plumes and numerous bells are spaced along its length.

Trudi Canavan

quarter tones, which can be perceived as flat until the ear becomes accustomed to them.

Though Ottoman classical music sounds ponderous and lugubrious to the uninitiated, Turkish folk music as played in the countryside can be sprightly and immediately appealing. *Türkü*, of which you'll hear lots on the radio, falls somewhere in between: traditional folk music as performed by modern city-based singers.

The 1000-year-old tradition of Turkish troubadours *(aşık)*, still very much alive as late as the 1960s and 70s, is now all but dead in its pure form – killed off by radio, TV, video and audio cassettes. But the songs of the great troubadours – Yunus Emre, Pir Sultan Abdal (16th century) and more recently Aşık Veysel (who died in 1974) – are still popular.

Unfortunately, the Turkish music most easily comprehensible to foreign ears are the fairly vapid *taverna* styles, and the local popular songs based on European and US

models. Perhaps the best is Adnan Ergil's series of audio cassettes entitled *Turkish Folk Gitar*.

Popular Music

İstanbul's music scene (jazz, pop, rock) is lively and interesting. Though the music of Europe and the USA played a predominant role in Turkish musical life for most of this century, the phenomenal growth and sophisticated development of local Turkish artists

---

Turkish Top of the Pops

Rock music in Turkey is as faddy and ephemeral as anywhere else. The flavour of 1998, for example, was Tarkan, the teenybop idol of Turkish pop who rocketed to fame on the back of his *Acayıpsın* (*You're Weird*) album in 1994 and has been riding high ever since.

But alongside the shooting stars there are also many well-established artists whose back catalogues remain as popular as those of the Stones and Springsteen. Queen of 1990s pop was Sezen Aksu, a singer-songwriter whose memorable melodies were typified by the 1991 album *Gülümse* (*Smile*). Well enough established to take risks, she has since branched out with the more experimental *Işık Doğudan Yükselir* (*The Light Rises in the East*) which draws on Turkey's regional musical traditions.

Another long-established performer is protest singer Zülfü Livaneli, a singer and *saz* player who is also well known in Turkey as a columnist (for the daily newspaper *Milliyet*) with left-wing sympathies who was once narrowly defeated for the post of mayor of İstanbul. Since Livaneli's music often incorporates western instrumentation, it's fairly accessible to non-Turkish audiences. His songs are often covered by other musicians, not least by his daughter Aylin, and he has recorded with Greek musicians Maria Farandouri and Mikis Theodorakis in an effort to heal one set of Turkey's political wounds.

More alien to western ears is the style of music known as *arabesque* which, as its name implies, puts an Arabic spin on home-grown Turkish traditions. The mournful themes (if not the melodies) of this music have led to its being compared to Greek *rembetika* and until the advent of independent radio and TV in the 1990s, the authorities kept arabesque off the airwaves, even conjuring up their own, more cheerful version in an attempt to undermine its power.

Until recently it wasn't at all cool to like a style of music associated, as the *Virgin Guide to World Music* put it, 'with *gazinos* and the sound systems of taxis'. However, arabesque now attracts a homosexual following which sits rather oddly alongside its more traditional macho audience. Playing to arabesque's traditional audience is the hugely successful Kurdish singer İbrahim Tatlıses, a burly, moustached former construction worker from Şanlıurfa whose life seems positively dull compared to those of arabesque's artier practitioners.

In 1980, for example, Bülent Ersoy's music was banned following his sex-change operation. Once the ban was lifted, Ersoy started performing live again – only to be shot at by a member of the reactionary, neo-fascist Grey Wolves militia group for refusing to sing a nationalist anthem. Ersoy was last heard of arranging to have a baby with her new, much younger partner.

and recording studios (mostly in İstanbul) has recently pushed western music into a subsidiary role. Many western soloists and groups are popular in Turkey – everyone from the Spice Girls to Andrea Bocelli – but you will hear much more Turkish music.

Symphony & Chamber Music

The İstanbul Symphony Orchestra, visiting orchestras and chamber ensembles give concerts during the winter season and during the International İstanbul Music Festival in early summer. See the Entertainment chapter for details.

Opera & Ballet

The Devlet Opera ve Balesi (State Opera and Ballet Company), based in Ankara, gives performances in İstanbul throughout the winter season. From late June to mid-July, the International İstanbul Music Festival brings Turkish and foreign ensembles to perform in the city. A highlight is the performance of Mozart's *Abduction from the Seraglio* in Topkapı Sarayı, the scene of the action. See the Entertainment chapter for details.

Theatre

Prohibited to Muslims during Ottoman times, Turkish theatre shared in the explosion of creativity which followed the establishment of the Turkish Republic. Today İstanbul is the centre of Turkish drama. Though vibrant, Turkish theatre has been strongly challenged by the temptations of TV and video, which reduce audiences.

Turkish theatre troupes, some subsidised by government, stage traditional and contemporary dramas and comedies as well as the works of giants such as Brecht, Ibsen, Molière and Shakespeare.

For the foreign visitor, the major barrier to enjoying Turkish theatre is the obvious one of language.

Faïence

The making of coloured tiles is an ancient art form in the Middle East. Its high point was reached during the 16th and 17th centuries in Anatolia when the workshops of İznik (Nicaea) and Kütahya turned out exquisitely designed and crafted tiles to be used on the walls of palaces, mosques, Turkish baths, fountains and many other structures, both public and private. The best tiles from this period are now treasured antiquities, but the master tilemakers of Kütahya, and to a lesser extent İznik, continue the tradition, offering fine work for sale in İstanbul's Covered Market and other shopping areas.

Textiles

With portraiture prohibited during the Ottoman period, stylised and geometric design prevailed. Turkish textiles are among the world's finest, from the exquisitely designed sultans' caftans of the Topkapı Sarayı workshops to the vigorous, lively patterns of traditional Turkish carpets woven by village women. Several modern Turkish couturiers have ateliers with a worldwide following.

Painting

The Ottoman ruling class had a taste for Turkish miniature painting. In the 19th century, the upper class developed an inclination – and in a few cases a talent – for European-style painting. Freed by the new republic, Turkish painting had become vigorous enough by the 1970s and 1980s to support numerous different local schools of artists, whose work is shown by museums, galleries, collectors and patrons.

Architecture

Architecture was the glory of Islamic art, and it thrived during the Ottoman centuries when painting and sculpture were prohibited. The great buildings of the Ottomans, such as mosques (see the special section on Ottoman Mosques on the facing page), *medreses* (or theological schools), baths, caravanserais and palaces, are worthy descendants of the masterpieces produced by the Greeks, Romans, Persians, Arabs and Byzantines. A surprisingly large number of Byzantine buildings remain as well.

OTTOMAN MOSQUES

Design Evolution

Before Ottoman times (that is, before the 14th century), the most common form of mosque in Islam was the vaulted pier type, a large square or rectangular space sheltered by a flat roof supported by rows of square piers, as in Edirne's Eski Cami or Bursa's Ulu Cami.

When the Ottomans took Bursa and İznik in the early 14th century they were exposed to Byzantine architecture, particularly ecclesiastical architecture. From this exposure, blended with that of Sassanian Persia, sprang a completely new style: the inverted-T ground plan. The Nilüfer Hatun İmareti in İznik is the first known building made to this plan, constructed on the orders of Nilüfer Hatun, wife of Sultan Orhan and mother of Sultan Murad I.

In Bursa, the first Ottoman capital, the early Ottoman mosques – Yıldırım Beyazıt Camii, Yeşil Cami, Muradiye Camii – are of the inverted-T type: a two-storey facade fronted with a lofty porch behind which are administrative rooms on the ground floor and private apartments for the monarch on the upper floor. Behind this 'base of the inverted T' are two large domed prayer rooms (the leg of the inverted T) separated by an arch, with the *mihrab* (prayer niche indicating

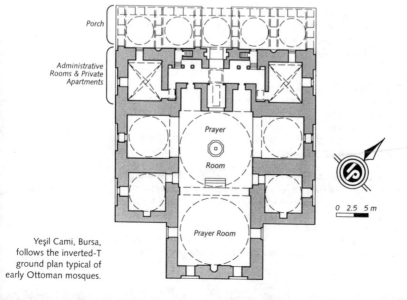

Yeşil Cami, Bursa, follows the inverted-T ground plan typical of early Ottoman mosques.

the direction of Mecca) in the far wall of the furthest prayer room. There may also be smaller domed rooms on the sides of the first prayer room.

After the conquest of Constantinople in 1453, Ottoman architects had full liberty to admire and examine the Aya Sofya (Sancta Sophia). They incorporated parts of its genius into the great Ottoman mosques, adapting the earlier design to Islamic usage.

Repopulating İstanbul

When the victorious armies of Mehmet the Conqueror poured through the great walls of vanquished Constantinople, they found a depopulated city. Foreseeing the inevitable fall of the Byzantine capital, many of its citizens had long since fled to Greece or Europe, and large tracts of the city were abandoned and derelict.

Mehmet the Conqueror, seeing himself as the legitimate successor to the Roman (Byzantine) emperors by right of conquest, sought to repopulate the great metropolis and make it a capital city worthy of his empire. One way in which he and his successors carried out this task was by building imperial mosques.

Mosque as Community Centre

When a sultan decided to build an imperial mosque, it quickly became the centre of a new quarter. Workers poured in, residences and workshops were built, and ancillary services such as shops quickly appeared. The building of a mosque took years, at the end of which time the quarter would be fully populated.

Each imperial mosque had a *külliye*, or collection of charitable institutions, clustered around it. These might include a hospital, insane asylum, orphanage, soup kitchen, hospice for travellers, religious school, library, baths and a cemetery in which the mosque's imperial patron, his family and other notables could be buried.

The Classic Ottoman Mosque

The classic Ottoman mosque as perfected by the great Mimar Sinan (circa 1497-1588), architect to Sultan Süleyman the Magnificent (1494-1566), has a large forecourt with an ablutions fountain at its centre and domed arcades on three sides. The courtyard and arcades can be used for prayers when the congregation is large and the weather is fine.

On the fourth side of the court is the mosque proper, with a two-storey porch. The main prayer hall is covered by a large central dome rising considerably higher than the two-storey facade and surrounded by smaller domes and semi-domes. A two-storey gallery at the back of the main prayer hall is for use by female worshippers, while men occupy the central space. The mihrab is in the far wall of the prayer hall. Many windows, often decorated with stained glass, let in abundant light.

Attached to the main prayer hall and entered from it is at least one minaret, a tall conical-capped tower with at least one balcony from which the muezzin can chant the call to prayer.

The mosque design developed during the reign of Süleyman the Magnificent proved so durable that it is still being used, with variations, for modern community mosques all over Turkey almost five centuries later.

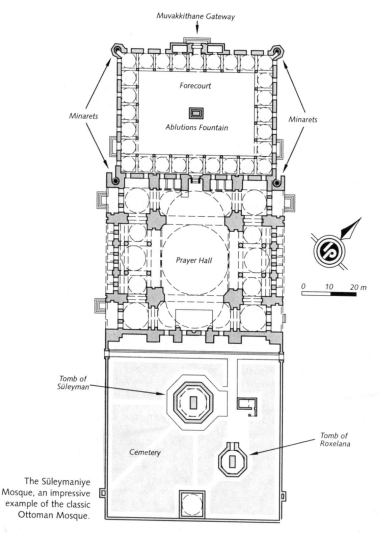

Muvakkithane Gateway

Forecourt

Minarets

Ablutions Fountain

Minarets

Prayer Hall

0   10   20 m

Tomb of Süleyman

Tomb of Roxelana

Cemetery

The Süleymaniye Mosque, an impressive example of the classic Ottoman Mosque.

Sculpture

İstanbul's wonders of sculpture are not modern works but the masterpieces created during the Hellenic, Hellenistic and Roman periods. See them in İstanbul's Archaeological Museums complex.

Cinema

Cinema appeared in Turkey just a year after the Lumière brothers presented their first cinematic show in 1895. At first it was only foreigners and non-Muslims who watched movies, but by 1914 there were cinemas run by and for Muslims as well.

The War of Independence inspired actor Muhsin Ertuğrul, Turkey's cinema pioneer, to establish a film company in 1922 and make patriotic films. Comedies and documentaries followed. Within a decade Turkish films were winning awards in international competitions, even though a mere 23 films had been made.

After WWII the industry expanded rapidly with new companies and young directors. Lütfi Akad's *Kanun Namına* (In the Name of the Law, 1952), Turkey's first colour film, brought realism to the screen in the place of melodrama and won first prize at the first Turkish film festival held a year later.

By the 1960s, Turkish cinema was delving deeply into social and political issues. Metin Erksan's *Susuz Yaz* (Dry Summer, 1964) won a gold medal at the Berlin Film Festival, and another award in Venice. Yılmaz Güney, the fiery actor-director, directed his first film *At, Avrat, Silah* (Horse, Woman, Gun) in 1966, and starred in Lütfi Akad's *Hudutların Kanunu* (The Law of the Borders) after he had written the script.

The 1970s brought the challenge of TV, dwindling audiences, political pressures, and unionisation of the industry. The quality of films continued to improve, and social issues such as Turkish workers in Europe were treated with honesty, naturalism and dry humour. By the early 1980s, several Turkish directors were well recognised in Europe and the USA. Among current directors, Tunç Başaran, Zülfü,

Halit Refiğ and Ömer Kavur are well worth watching.

İstanbul has a lively cinema culture centred in the movie houses along İstiklal Caddesi. See the Entertainment chapter for details.

SOCIETY & CONDUCT
Traditional Culture

In general, you may find your dealings with Turks to be more formal than you're used to at home.

Though Turks have abandoned the stiff formality of Ottoman society and adapted to the informality of 20th-century life, you'll still notice vestiges of the courtly Ottoman state of mind. Were you to learn Turkish, you'd find dozens of polite phrases – actually rigid formulas – to be repeated on cue in many daily situations: upon meeting or leaving someone, upon picking up a drink or sitting down to a meal or even emerging from a Turkish bath.

Hospitality is an honoured tradition in Turkey, from the shopkeeper who plies you with tea or coffee and sweets to the family that invites you to share their home and meals for the customary three days.

Commercialism has begun to corrupt traditional hospitality, however, producing the shady carpet merchant who lays on the friendliness with a trowel only to sell you shoddy goods at inflated prices, and the Turks who greet you with excessive informality, tailoring their behaviour to your expectations, usually in the hope of selling you something.

Don't, however, let this make you lose sight of true Turkish hospitality, which is wonderful.

Appearance & Conduct

Turks are very understanding of foreigners' different customs, but if you want to behave in accordance with local feelings, bear in mind a few things. It's looked upon as impolite to point your finger directly towards any person. Don't show the sole of your foot or shoe towards anyone (ie so they can see it). Don't blow your nose openly in

Turkish Body Language

Turks say 'yes' (evet, eh-VEHT) by nodding the head forward and down.

To say 'no' (hayır, HAH-yuhr), nod your head up and back, lifting your eyebrows at the same time. Or just raise your eyebrows: that's 'no'.

Another way of saying 'no' is yok (YOHK): literally, 'It doesn't exist (here)', or 'We don't have any (of it)' – the same head upward, raised eyebrows applies.

Remember, when a Turkish person seems to be giving you an arch look, they're only saying 'no'. They may also make the sound 'tsk', which also means 'no'. There are lots of ways to say 'no' in Turkish.

By contrast, wagging your head from side to side doesn't mean 'no' in Turkish; it means 'I don't understand'. So if a Turkish person asks you, 'Are you looking for the bus to Sultanahmet?' and you shake your head, they'll assume you don't understand English, and will probably ask you the same question again, this time in German.

If someone – a shopkeeper or restaurant waiter, for instance – wants to show you the stockroom or the kitchen, they'll signal 'Come on, follow me' by waving a hand downward and towards themselves in a scooping motion. Waggling an upright finger would never occur to them, except perhaps as a vaguely obscene gesture.

public, especially in a restaurant; instead, turn or leave the room and blow quietly. Don't pick your teeth openly, but cover your mouth with your hand. Don't do a lot of kissing or hugging with a person of the opposite sex in public. All of the above actions are considered rude.

Mosque Etiquette Always remove your shoes before stepping on the clean area just in front of the mosque door, or on the carpets inside. This is not a religious law but a practical one. Worshippers kneel and touch their foreheads to the carpets, and they like them to be clean. If there are no carpets, as in a saint's tomb, you can leave your shoes on.

Wear modest clothes when visiting mosques, as you would when visiting a church or synagogue. Don't wear tatty blue jeans, shorts (men or women) or gear that could be deemed outlandish. Women should have head, arms and shoulders covered, and wear modest dresses or skirts, preferably reaching to the knees. At some of the most visited mosques, attendants will lend you long robes if your clothing doesn't meet a minimum standard. The loan of the robe is free, though the attendant will probably indicate where you can give a donation to the mosque. If you donate, chances are that the money will actually go to the mosque.

The best time to visit mosques is midmorning on any day but Friday. Avoid entering mosques at prayer time, (ie at the call to prayer – dawn, noon, mid-afternoon, dusk and evening, or 20 minutes thereafter). Mosques are crowded with worshippers at noon on Friday, and sightseeing visits are inappropriate then.

When you're inside a mosque, even if it is not prayer time, there may be a few people praying. Don't disturb them in any way, don't walk directly in front of them, and don't take flash photos.

RELIGION

The Turkish population is 99% Muslim, mostly of the orthodox Sunni creed; there are groups of Alawites (Alevi) and Shiites in the east and south-east.

Principles of Islam

The Torah and Bible are sacred books to Muslims. Adam, Noah, Abraham, Moses, Jesus and other Jewish and Christian saints and prophets, their teachings and revelations, are accepted by Muslims, except for Jesus' divinity and his status as saviour. Jews and Christians are called 'People of the Book', meaning those with a revealed religion that preceded Islam.

However, Muslims believe that Islam is the 'perfection' of this earlier tradition, and Muhammed is the last and greatest of the prophets, in fact *the* Prophet. Muhammed is not a saviour, nor is he divine, nor even an object of worship or a figure of intercession. He is God's messenger, deliverer of the final, definitive message.

Muslims worship only God. In fact, *Muslim* in Arabic means, 'one who has submitted to God's will'; *Islam* is 'submission to God's will'. It's all summed up in the *ezan*, the phrase called out from the minaret five times a day and said at the beginning of Muslim prayers: 'God is great! There is no god but God, and Muhammed is his Prophet'.

The Koran

God's revelations to Muhammed are contained in the *Kur'an-i Kerim*, the Holy Koran. Muhammed recited the *suras* (verses or chapters) of the Koran in an inspired state. They were written down by followers, and are still regarded as the most beautiful, melodic and poetic work in Arabic literature, sacred or secular. The Koran, being sacred, cannot be translated. It exists truly only in Arabic.

The Islamic Commonwealth

Ideally, Islam is a commonwealth, a theocracy in which the religious law of the Koran is the only law. There is no secular law, and all courts are religious courts. In Turkey and several other Muslim countries, this belief has been replaced by modern secular law codes. By contrast, Saudi Arabia and Iran rely on Islamic law as the only law of the land.

Religious Duties & Practices

To be a Muslim, one need only submit in one's heart to God's will and perform a few simple religious duties:

One must say, understand and believe, 'There is no god but God, and Muhammed is his Prophet'.

One must pray five times daily: at dawn, noon, mid-afternoon, dusk and after dark.

One must keep the fast of Ramazan, if capable of doing so.

One must make a pilgrimage to Mecca once during one's life if possible.

Muslim prayers are set rituals. Before praying, Muslims wash hands and arms, feet and ankles, head and neck in running water; if no water is available, in clean sand; if there's no sand, the motions suffice. Then they cover their head, face Mecca and perform a precise series of gestures and genuflections. If they deviate from the pattern, they must begin again.

In daily life, a Muslim must not touch or eat pork, or drink 'wine' (interpreted as any alcoholic beverage), and must refrain from fraud, usury, slander and gambling. No 'being with an immortal soul' (ie human or animal), or its image or effigy, may be revered or worshipped in any way.

Though Islam has evolved a complex theology, and has been split (like Christianity) into many sects, these tenets are still the basic ones shared by all Muslims.

Facts for the Visitor

WHEN TO GO

Spring and autumn, roughly from April to June and from September to October, when the climate is perfect, are the best seasons to visit İstanbul. For more details see Climate in the Facts about İstanbul chapter, and the Public Holidays & Special Events section later in this chapter for information on religious festivals.

ORIENTATION

İstanbul is divided from north to south by the Bosphorus, the wide strait connecting the Black and Marmara seas, into European (Avrupa) and Asian (Asya) portions. European İstanbul is further divided by the Golden Horn (Haliç) into Old İstanbul (Eski İstanbul, sometimes called the Old City) to the south and Beyoğlu (BEY-oh-loo, formerly Pera and Galata) and other modern districts to the north.

The top sights are mostly in Old İstanbul so you can see them in a single day. Three days, however, is the minimum time necessary for a meaningful visit to this city. Five days is good, and gives you a chance for at least one day trip. With a week you can see most of the city's sights and take an overnight excursion; 10 days is even better if you plan to take an excursion further afield to Gallipoli, Troy or Cappadocia.

Old İstanbul

The Old City has gone by many different names: Byzantium, Constantinople, İstanbul (and 19th-century travellers called it Stamboul). It's in the Old City, stretching from Seraglio Point (Saray Burnu) on the Bosphorus to the mammoth land walls some 7km westward, that you'll find the great palaces and mosques, hippodromes and monumental columns, ancient churches and the Grand Bazaar, called the Covered Market (Kapalı Çarşı in Turkish). The best selection of bottom-end and middle-range

hotels is also found here, with a few top-end places as well.

Beyoğlu

North of the Golden Horn is Beyoğlu, the Turkish name for the Ottoman districts of Pera and Galata, or roughly all the land from the Golden Horn to Taksim Square. Here you'll find luxury hotels, airline offices, banks, the European consulates, hospitals and Taksim Square itself, the hub of 20th-century İstanbul.

Old İstanbul and Beyoğlu are connected by the Galata Köprüsü (Galata Bridge) at the mouth of the Golden Horn. Just east of the bridge are the docks for Bosphorus ferry boats.

Asian İstanbul

The Asian part of the city, on the eastern shore of the Bosphorus, is of less interest to tourists, being mostly dormitory suburbs such as Üsküdar (Scutari) and Kadıköy. Haydarpaşa station (Haydarpaşa Garı), between Üsküdar and Kadıköy, is the terminal for Anatolian trains.

The Bosphorus

The Bosphorus is lined with more suburbs, some of which are quite charming, and good for a day's excursion.

MAPS

Turkish government Tourism Information Offices hand out a useful *İstanbul City Plan* for free. There are editions in the languages of all major tourist groups visiting the city (English, French, German, Japanese etc).

For more detailed guidance, including all minor streets and ways, the *İstanbul A-Z Rehber-Atlas*, widely available in foreign-language and tourist-oriented bookshops for about US$10, is the cheapest and most reliable source.

Germany produces the Reise und Verkehrsverlag's *Euro-City* series, which includes a detailed atlas of İstanbul, and an equally detailed 1:7500 street plan in one sheet. They're on sale at some bookshops (see the Bookshop section in the Shopping chapter).

TOURIST OFFICES
Local Tourist Offices

There are Ministry of Tourism offices at Atatürk airport (☎ 212-663 6363, fax 663 0793) in the international arrivals area; at the north-western end of the Hippodrome in Sultanahmet (☎ 212-518 1802, fax 518 1802), open from 9 am to 5 pm daily; and at Sirkeci train station (☎ 212-511 5888).

In Beyoğlu, there is an office at the Karaköy Yolcu Salonu (Karaköy International Maritime Passenger Terminal) (☎ 212-249 5776); another in Elmadağ in the İstanbul Hilton Hotel arcade (☎ 212-233 0592), just off Cumhuriyet Caddesi, two long blocks north of Taksim Square on the right-hand side of the street (open from 9 am to 5 pm, closed on Sunday). Yet another office is in the regional Directorate of Tourism (☎ 212-243 2928, fax 252 4346), more or less opposite the British Consulate-General at Meşrutiyet Caddesi 57, Tepebaşı.

Tourist Offices Abroad

There are Turkish tourism offices in the following countries:

Australia
    (☎ 02-9223 3055, fax 9223 3204, email turkish@ozemail.com.au)
    Suite 101, 280 George St, Sydney NSW 2000
Canada
    (☎ 613-230 8654, fax 230 3683) Constitution Square, 360 Albert St, Suite 801, Ottawa ON K1R 7X7
France
    (☎ 1 45 62 78 68, fax 45 63 81 05) Turquie, Service d'Information, 102, avenue des Champs-Elysées, 75008 Paris
Germany
    Berlin: (☎ 30-214 3752, fax 214 3952) Informationsabteilung des Türkischen Generalkonsulats, Tauentzienstrasse 7, 10789
    Frankfurt: (☎ 69-23 30 81, fax 23 27 51) Informationsabteilung des Türkischen Generalkonsulats, Baselerstrasse 35-37, 60329

München: (☎ 89-59 49 02, fax 550 4138) Informationsabteilung des Türkischen Generalkonsulats, Karlsplatz 3/1, 80335
Israel
    (☎ 3-517 6157, fax 517 6303)
    Turkish Information Office 1 Ben Yehuda St, 63801 Tel Aviv
Italy
    (☎ 6-487 1190, fax 488 2425)
    Ambasciata di Turchia Ufficio Informazione, Piazza della Repubblica 56, 00185 Roma
Netherlands
    (☎ 20-626 6810, fax 622 2283)
    Turkish Embassy, Information Counsellor's Office, Herengracht 451, 1017 BS Amsterdam
UK
    (☎ 0171-629 7771, fax 491 0773, email eb25@cityscape.co.uk)
    170-173 Piccadilly, 1st floor, London W1V 9DD
USA
    (☎ 212-687 2194, fax 599 7568, www.turkey.org/turkey)
    821 UN Plaza, New York, NY 10017

DOCUMENTS
Visas

Traditional diplomatic practice holds that visa rules and fees should be reciprocal. Thus if the British government charges a Turk £10 for a visa to enter the UK, then the Turkish government should charge British passport holders £10 to enter Turkey.

Nationals of the following countries (among others) may enter Turkey for up to three months with only a valid passport (no visa is required): Australia, Belgium, Canada, Denmark, Finland, France, Germany, Greece, Holland, Iceland, Japan, Liechtenstein, Luxembourg, Monaco, New Zealand, Norway, Singapore, Sweden, Switzerland, Tobago, Trinidad, Vatican City. Make sure your passport has at least three months' validity remaining, or you may not be admitted.

Citizens of the Republic of South Africa may enter with a passport (no visa needed) for up to one month.

Nationals of Austria, Ireland, Israel, Italy, Portugal, Spain, UK and USA may enter for up to three months upon purchase of a visa sticker at their point of entry into

Turkey. Visas costs UK£10 for Britons and US$45 for Americans; exact cash (sterling or dollars, respectively), is required; no credit cards or travellers cheques are accepted.

Visa Extensions

Depending on your nationality, you may be permitted to extend your visa for a longer stay, or you may be required to obtain a residence permit *(ikamet tezkeresi)*, for which you may have to show proof of financial resources or of a legal job in Turkey. Most visitors wanting to extend their stay by a few weeks or months avoid bureaucratic tedium by taking a quick overnight trip to Greece (Thessaloniki or Rhodes), returning to Turkey the next day with a new three-month stamp in their passports.

With an ikamet tezkeresi, you may stay in Turkey for up to a year, with renewals possible from year to year. See the Work section later in this chapter.

Travel Insurance

Insurance to protect you against financial loss from trip cancellation, medical emergency or medical evacuation is available through travel agents. Before you buy it, check to see what is already covered by other policies you may have, such as home owner, renter, medical or motorist insurance. (See also Health Insurance in the Health section later in this chapter.)

Driving Licence & Permits

Drivers must have a valid driving licence. An International Driving Permit (IDP) is required for stays of more than three months, or if your licence is from a locality that a Turkish police officer is likely to find obscure.

Third-party insurance, such as a Green Card (valid for European and Asian Turkey), is obligatory; otherwise, you will be required to purchase a Turkish policy at the border.

Hostel Card

A Hostelling International (HI) card will get you almost nothing in Turkey. The very few HI-affiliated hostels usually offer virtually the same rates to all comers, and their rates are little different from those at comparable cheap hotels.

Student & Youth Cards

Holders of an International Student Identity Card (ISIC) will get discounts at some museums, historic buildings and archaeological sites. You'll also get at least a 10% discount on Turkish State Railways and Turkish Maritime Lines fares – of little good within İstanbul proper.

EMBASSIES & CONSULATES
Turkish Embassies

Turkey has the following embassies:

Australia
  (☎ 02-6295 0227, fax 6239 6592)
  60 Mugga Way, Red Hill 2603 ACT
Bulgaria
  (☎ 02-980 2270, fax 981 9358)
  Blvd Vasil Levski No 80, 1000 Sofia
Canada
  (☎ 613-789 4044, fax 789-3442)
  197 Wurtemburg St, Ottawa, Ontario KIN 8L9
Greece
  (☎ 01-724 5915, fax 722 9597)
  Vasilissis Georgiou B 8, 10674 Athens
UK
  (☎ 0171-393 0202, fax 393 0066)
  43 Belgrave Square, London SW1X 8PA
USA
  (☎ 202-659 8200, fax 659 0744)
  1714 Massachusetts Ave NW, Washington, DC, 20036

Embassies & Consulates in İstanbul & Ankara

Embassies *(büyükelçiliği)* are in Ankara, the national capital. İstanbul has consulates *(konsosloluğu)* from many countries:

Australia (Avustralya)
  Ankara: (☎ 312-436 1240, fax 445 0284)
  Avustralya Büyükelçiliği, Nene Hatun Caddesi 83, Gaziosmanpaşa
  İstanbul: (☎ 212-257 7050, fax 257 7054)
  Avustralya Konsosloluğu, Tepecik Yolu 58, 80630 Etiler, open from 8.30 am to 12.30 pm weekdays

Canada (Kanada)
  Ankara: (☎ 312-436 1275/9, fax 446 4437)
  Kanada Büyükelçiliği, Nenehatun Caddesi
  75, 06700 Gaziosmanpaşa
  İstanbul: (☎ 212-272 5174, fax 272 3427)
  Kanada Fahri Konsolosluğu (Honorary
  Consulate), Büyükdere Caddesi 107/3,
  Bengün Han, 3rd floor, Gayrettepe

France (Fransa)
  Ankara: (☎ 312-468 1154, fax 467 1489)
  Fransız Büyükelçiliği, Paris Caddesi 70,
  Kavaklıdere
  İstanbul: (☎ 212-243 1852, fax 249 9168)
  Fransız Başkonsolosluğu, İstiklal Caddesi 8,
  Taksim

Germany (Almanya)
  Ankara: (☎ 312-426 5451/65, fax 426 6959)
  Alman Büyükelçiliği, Atatürk Bulvarı 114,
  Kavaklıdere
  İstanbul: (Map 3; ☎ 212- 251 5404, fax 249
  9920) Alman Başkonsolosluğu, İnönü
  Caddesi 16-18, Gümüşsuyu, Taksim

Greece (Yunanistan)
  Ankara: (☎ 312-436 8861, fax 446 3191)
  Yunan Büyükelçiliği, Ziya-ur-Rahman Sokak
  (Karagöz Sokak) 9-11, Gaziosmanpaşa
  İstanbul: (Map 3; ☎ 212-245 0596, fax 252
  1365) Yunan Başkonsolosluğu, Turnacıbaşı
  Sokak 32, Ağahamam, Kuloğlu, Beyoğlu

Israel (İsrail)
  Ankara: (☎ 312-446 3605, fax 426 1533)
  İsrail Büyükelçiliği, Mahatma Gandi Caddesi
  85, 06700 Gaziosmanpaşa
  İstanbul: (☎ 212-225 1040, fax 225 1048)
  İsrail Konsolosluğu, Valikonağı Caddesi
  73/4, Nişantaşı

Italy (İtalya)
  Ankara: (☎ 312-426 5460, fax 426 5800)
  İtalyan Büyükelçiliği, Atatürk Bulvarı 118,
  Kavaklıdere
  İstanbul: (☎ 212-243 1024, 251 3294, fax
  252 5879) İtalyan Başkonsolosluğu, Palazzo
  di Venezia, Tomtom Kaptan Sokak 15, 80073
  Galatasaray

Netherlands (Holanda)
  Ankara: (☎ 312-446 0470, fax 446 3358)
  Holanda Büyükelçiliği, Uğur Mumcu
  Caddesi 16, Gaziosmanpaşa
  İstanbul: (Map 3; ☎ 212-251 5030, fax 251
  9289) Holanda Başkonsolosluğu, İstiklal
  Caddesi 393, Tünel, Beyoğlu

New Zealand (Yeni Zelanda)
  Ankara: (☎ 312-467 9054, fax 467 9013)
  Yeni Zelanda Büyükelçiliği, İran Caddesi,
  Kavaklıdere
  İstanbul: (☎ 212-275 2989, fax 275 5008,

211 0473) Maya Akar Center, 24th floor,
  Büyükdere Caddesi 100/102, Esentepe 80280

Spain (İspanya)
  Ankara: (☎ 312-438 0392/3/4, fax 439 5170)
  İspanyol Büyükelçiliği, Abdullah Cevdet
  Sokak 9, Çankaya
  İstanbul: (☎ 212-225 2153, fax 262 6530)
  İspanyol Başkonsolosluğu, Valikonağı
  Caddesi 33, Başaran Apt, Harbiye

UK (İngiltere, Birleşik Krallığı)
  Ankara: (☎ 312-468 6230, fax 468 6643)
  İngiliz Büyükelçiliği, Şehit Ersan Caddesi
  46/A, Çankaya
  İstanbul: (Map 3; ☎ 212-293 7540, fax 245
  4989) İngiliz Başkonsolosluğu, Meşrutiyet
  Caddesi 34, Tepebaşı, Beyoğlu

USA (Amerika Birleşik Devletleri, Amerika)
  Ankara: (☎ 312-468 6110, fax 467 0019)
  Amerikan Büyükelçiliği, Atatürk Bulvarı
  110, Kavaklıdere
  İstanbul: (Map 3; ☎ 212-251 3602, fax 252
  3218) Amerikan Başkonsolosluğu,
  Meşrutiyet Caddesi 104-108, Tepebaşı,
  Beyoğlu

CUSTOMS

İstanbul's Atatürk airport uses the red and
green channel system, spot checking passengers' luggage at random. Things of
exceptional value (jewellery, unusually expensive electronic or photographic gear etc)
are supposed to be declared, and may be
entered in your passport to guarantee that
you will take the goods out of the country
when you leave.

Antiquities

*It is illegal to buy, sell, possess or export
antiquities.* Only true antiquities well over
a century old are off limits, not newer items
or the many artful fakes (but will the
customs officer know genuine from fake?).
Penalties for breaking the antiquities law
are severe, and may land you in jail.

MONEY
Currency

The unit of currency is the Turkish *lira*, or
TL. The lira is fully convertible and floats
freely in world currency markets. It is
subject to a continuing 'slippage' or gradual
devaluation against stronger currencies
such as the US dollar, German mark and

pound sterling. Coins come in 1000, 2500, 5000, 10,000, 25,000 and, as time goes on, ever higher denominations. Banknotes come in 10,000, 20,000, 50,000, 100,000, 250,000, 500,000, one million, five million and 10 million lira denominations.

With all those zeroes, it's often difficult to make sure you're trading the correct notes. Beware! Shopkeepers and taxi drivers may sometimes try to give you a 50,000-lira note in place of a 500,000, or 100,000 note instead of one million.

When the government undertakes the inevitable elimination of some zeroes on the currency, the confusion will be far greater, as old lira notes with all the zeroes will remain in circulation with new notes for a time. Take your time and be sure of amounts.

Exchange Rates

With inflation at 100% in Turkey, the value of the lira drops daily. An exchange rate table is therefore not provided: it would be prehistoric by the time you arrive.

Exchanging Money

An ATM card (see the section on ATMs later) is the best way to get Turkish liras.

Wait until you arrive in Turkey to change your home currency (cash or travellers cheques) into Turkish liras. Exchange bureaus in other countries (eg the UK, USA) usually offer terrible rates of exchange for Turkish liras.

As Turkish liras are fully convertible, there is no black market.

Don't change large amounts of money all at once. With constant devaluation, tomorrow you'll almost certainly get even more liras for your money.

Cash US dollars and German marks are easily changed anywhere, and are often accepted as payment without being changed. Other major currencies such as pounds sterling, French francs and Japanese yen are easily changed as well, as are many other EC currencies, though the rates may not be as good as when changing marks or dollars. Instead of bringing Australian, Canadian or New Zealand dollars or Irish punts, for example, it's better to have US dollars, German marks or pounds sterling. You will always need your passport when changing travellers cheques in Turkey, and you may need it when you change cash as well.

Travellers cheques – even for major currencies – are more of a hassle to change than cash; many exchange offices and banks balk at taking them, and some refuse outright, forcing you to search for a place that will accept them.

The best rates of exchange are in non-touristic districts at exchange bureaus, not banks. Many tourist shops, travel agencies, expensive restaurants and most hotels accept foreign currency, though they often give bad rates of exchange.

Exchange Offices İstanbul has an ever-growing number of currency exchange bureaus (döviz bürosu). They offer faster service than banks, longer opening hours, and may not charge a commission. The rates are worse at offices heavily used by tourists, such as those in Sultanahmet. Better rates are offered outside the Grand Bazaar, in Taksim, Şişli, Eminönü and other areas where Turks change money.

Exchange Receipts Save your currency exchange receipts (bordro). You may need them to reconvert Turkish liras at the end of your stay.

Price Adjustments Government entities such as the Ministry of Culture (which administers many of the country's museums) and the Turkish State Railways may set prices at the beginning of the year, and then adjust them every three or four months – if at all – throughout the year. Thus a museum admission fee or train fare might cost you US$6 in January, but only US$4 or even US$3 later in the year. For this reason, many prices in this guide must be looked upon as approximate.

Private enterprises tend to adjust prices more frequently and many in the travel industry such as airlines, rental car firms and the more expensive hotels quote prices not in liras but in US dollars or in German marks.

Travellers Cheques Banks, shops and hotels often see it as a burden to change travellers cheques (including Eurocheques), and may try to get you to go elsewhere. You may have to insist. The more expensive hotels, restaurants and shops will more readily accept the cheques, as will car rental and travel agencies, but not at good rates of exchange. Generally, it's better to change cheques to Turkish liras at a bank, although some banks charge fees.

ATMs Automated teller machines (ATMs, cashpoints) are common in İstanbul. Virtually all offer instructions in English, French, German and Turkish, and will pay out Turkish liras when you insert your bank debit (cash) card. This is the fastest and cheapest way to get Turkish money.

ATMs will also pay cash advances on most major credit cards (especially Visa). The limit on cash advances is generally the equivalent of about US$250 per day. Remember that you will pay a steep rate of interest on the cash advance from the day you use the ATM until the day you pay off your credit-card bill.

One way to avoid paying interest is to pay a generous amount of money into your debtless credit-card account before leaving on your trip, creating a balance in your favour. You can then draw down this balance as you travel. So long as you don't spend beyond your deposit (including both credit-card charges and cash advances), there should be no interest to pay as you will have no debt to the bank.

All of the major Turkish banks – Akbank, Garanti Bankası, Türkiye İş Bankası, Pamukbank, Yapı Kredi and Ziraat Bankası – and some smaller banks have ATMs connected to the major card systems such as Cirrus, Maestro, Plus Systems etc. Akbank, Pamukbank and Yapı Kredi claim to have the most machines connected to Plus Systems. I've found Yapı Kredi ATMs to be the most convenient and reliable, with Akbank as second choice.

The specific machine you use must be reliably connected to the major ATM networks' computers via telephone lines. Look for stickers with the logos of services affixed to the machine. If the connection is not reliable, you may get a message saying that the transaction was refused by your bank (which may not be true), and your card will be returned to you. Try another machine.

Credit Cards Big hotels and the more expensive shops will accept your major credit cards. Car rental agencies certainly will. Make sure in advance because not all establishments accept all cards. The commonly used cards are Access, American Express, Diners Club, Eurocard, MasterCard and Visa, with Visa heading the pack.

Turkey suffers from a great deal of credit-card fraud, and you may find that the bank that issued your credit card will not permit charges from Turkey. I discovered this to my dismay when a Visa card issued by a large New England (USA) bank failed to be approved anywhere in Turkey, even though the bank had assured me that they had no such policy. (An agent later let slip that they never approved charges from some countries including Thailand, Turkey, Vietnam and others.) Thus, even if you check with your bank, you may not be told the truth.

Costs

All costs in this guide are given in US dollars only, as prices in Turkish liras would be hopelessly out of date before the book even emerged from the printer.

In recent years, inflation has been over 100% per annum, and the Turkish lira has been subjected to a slow, creeping devaluation, which offsets this inflation and keeps actual costs low for foreign visitors. Indeed, you may find some of the prices given in this guide to be higher than the amounts you'll actually pay. The situation is volatile, and prices may fluctuate from month to month.

Turkey is Europe's low-price leader, and you can visit İstanbul for as little as US$25 to US$40 (average) per person per day staying in a hostel or pension, getting around by city bus and shared taxi (*dolmuş*), and eating one restaurant meal daily. For US$40 to US$55 per person per day you can stay in one and two-star hotels with private baths, and eat most meals in average restaurants. For US$55 to US$85 per day you can move up to three and four-star hotels, take taxis everywhere, and dine in restaurants all the time. If you have over US$100 per person to spend, you can travel luxury class, although staying and eating at the top hotels and having a car and driver at your disposal each day can easily drive the cost of an İstanbul stay up to US$250 to $400 per person per day.

Outside İstanbul and the major resorts, costs are substantially lower.

Here are some average costs for İstanbul:

Single/double room in small pension	US$20 to US$40
Single/double room with bath in one-star hotel	US$40 to US$70
Loaf of bread	US$0.35
Bottle of beer (from a shop)	US$1
Litre of petrol/gasoline (US gallon)	US$0.70 to US$0.90 US$2.56 to US$3.31
100 km by express train (1st class)	US$2 to US$2.50
Local telephone call	US$0.15
Turkish Daily News	US$0.80

Tipping

Restaurants Some places will automatically add a service charge (*servis ücreti*) of 10% or 15% to your bill, but this does not absolve you from the tip, oddly enough. The service charge goes into the pocket of the *patron* (owner). Turks will give around 5% to the waiter directly, and perhaps the same amount to the maître d'hôtel.

If service is included, the bill may say *servis dahil* (service included). Still, a small tip is expected. In any situation, 5 to 10% is fine. Only in the fancy, foreign-operated hotels will waiters expect those enormous 15 to 20% US-style tips. In the very plain, basic restaurants you needn't tip at all,

though the price of a soft drink or a cup of coffee is always appreciated. Watch what others do.

Hotels In the cheapest hotels there are few services and tips are not expected. In the better hotels, a porter will carry your luggage and show you to your room. For doing this he'll expect US$1 or US$2.

Taxis Turks don't tip taxi drivers, though they often round up the metered fare to a convenient amount. A driver of a dolmuş gets only the standard fare.

Turkish Baths If staff in a non-tourist bath approach you as you are leaving, share out 20% of the bath fees among them. In the touristy baths, don't tip – you've already paid too much.

Bargaining

Though most shop items bear price stickers, when you shop for souvenirs or expensive items, particularly in the bazaars and markets, you must expect to bargain.

Traditionally, when a customer enters a Turkish shop to make a significant purchase, he or she is offered a comfortable seat and a drink (coffee, tea or a soft drink). There is some getting acquainted chitchat, then some discussion of the goods (carpets, apparel, jewellery etc) in general, then of the customer's tastes, preferences and requirements. Finally, a number of items in the shop are shown for the customer's inspection.

The customer asks a price; the shop owner gives it; the customer looks doubtful and makes a counter-offer 25 to 50% lower. This procedure goes back and forth several times before a price is arrived at. If no price is agreed upon, the customer has absolutely no obligation and may walk out at any time.

To bargain effectively you must not be in a hurry, and you must know something about the items in question and their market price. The best way to do this is to look at similar goods in several shops, asking prices but not making counter-offers. Shopkeepers will give you a quick education about their wares by showing you what's good about them, and telling you what's bad about their competitors'. Soon you will discover which shops have the best quality for the lowest asking prices, and you can proceed to bargain.

If you don't have sufficient time to shop around, follow the age-old rule: find something you like at a price you're willing to pay, buy it, enjoy it, and don't worry about whether or not you got the world's lowest price.

Discounts

When haggling, you can often get a discount by offering to buy several items at once, or to pay in US dollars, German marks, or another strong major currency.

Taxes & Refunds

As in many European countries, Turkey has a value-added tax (VAT), the *katma değer vergisi* (KDV).

If you buy an expensive item such as a carpet or leather garment and take it out of the country soon afterwards, in principle you are entitled to a refund of the KDV, which may be as high as 15% or 20% of the purchase price. Not all shops participate in the scheme, so you must ask if it is possible to get a *KDV iade özel fatura* (keh-deh-VEH ee-ah-DEH err-ZEHL fah-too-rah, or special VAT refund receipt). Ask for this during the haggling rather than after you've bought.

The receipt can – in principle – be converted to cash at a bank in the international departures lounge at the airport (if there is a bank open, which there may not be), or at your other point of exit from Turkey; or, if you submit the form to a customs officer as you leave the country, the shop will (one hopes) mail a refund cheque to your home after the government has completed its procedures. Don't hold your breath.

To increase your chances of actually getting the refund, make a photocopy or two of the KDV iade özel fatura in advance and, when you're leaving Turkey, take

along a stamped envelope addressed to the shop where you bought the goods. Have your KDV form stamped by the customs officer at the airport to show that you've exported the goods, then mail it right from the airport to the shop. Enclose a note requesting refund of the tax and giving the address to which the refund cheque should be sent. In some cases it can take as long as four months for the cheque to arrive.

POST & COMMUNICATIONS
Post

Post offices, marked by black-on-yellow signs, are traditionally known as PTTs (peh-teh-TEH, *posta, telefon, telgraf*), even though the post office no longer operates the telephone network.

İstanbul's central post office *(merkez postane)* is several blocks west of Sirkeci train station on Mevlana Caddesi. It's open daily from 8 am to 8 pm, though many services such as poste restante have more restricted hours and close for lunch. The *yurtdışı* slot is for mail to foreign countries, *yurtiçi* is for mail to other Turkish cities, and *şehiriçi* is for mail within İstanbul.

There are PTT branches in Taksim Square next to McDonald's on Cumhuriyet Caddesi; on İstiklal Caddesi in Galatasaray; and in the north-western corner of the Covered Market near the Havuzlu Lokantası on Gani Çelebi Sokak.

Parcels To mail packages out of the country you must have your package opened for customs inspection, and you may have to endure a bit of frustrating officialdom. You may be directed by postal officials to the special Paket Postahane (Parcel Post Office) near Karaköy. Have paper, box, string, tape and marker pens with you when you go.

If you want to make certain that a parcel will get to its destination intact and quickly, send it by Federal Express (Fedex), United Parcel Service (UPS), DHL, express mail *(acele posta servisi)* or at least by registered mail *(kayıtlı)*.

Telephone

Though targeted for privatisation, Türk Telekom is still, at the time of this writing, a government controlled monopoly.

You pay for calls with a *telekart* debit card or a major credit card, depending upon the phone. Older phones may require a *jeton* (zheh-TOHN, token), or perhaps several. Calls are measured in usage units, each of which costs about 15c; a local call of several minutes duration costs one usage unit. Telekarts come in denominations of 30, 60, 100, 180 and 250 usage units. In general a 30-unit card is sufficient for local calls; 60 for a short, domestic intercity call; 100 for a domestic intercity call of moderate length or a short international call; and the higher-value cards for longer domestic or international calls.

Turkey's country code is ☎ 90. European İstanbul's area code is ☎ 212; the area code for Asian İstanbul is ☎ 216. Local numbers have seven digits.

Long-Distance Calls Rates for local and intercity domestic calls are moderate, but international calls can be quite expensive, almost £1 per minute to the UK, US$2 per minute to the USA, and even higher to Australia. Reduced rates are in effect from midnight to 10 am, and on Sunday. Beware of hotel surcharges, which can double your bill. Perhaps the best strategy is to make a quick call, give the other person the telephone number and a time at which you can be reached, and have them call you back.

Press '0' (zero) to make an intercity call within Turkey, or '00' to make an international call.

In theory, you can call one of the numbers below toll-free from Turkey to access your home telephone company, which may have cheaper rates. In practice, the call often doesn't go through:

Australia	☎ 00 800-61 1177
Canada – Teleglobe	☎ 00 800-1 6677
France – Telecom	☎ 00 800-33 1177
Germany – PTT	☎ 00 800-49 1149
Ireland	☎ 00 800-353 1177
Italy	☎ 00 800-39 1177

Japan – IDC Direct	☎ 00 800-81 0086
IDC	☎ 00 800-81 0080
KDD	☎ 00 800-81 1177
Netherlands – PTT	☎ 00 800-31 1177
UK – BTI	☎ 00 800-44 1177
Mercury	☎ 00 800-44 2277
USA – AT&T	☎ 00 800-1 2277
MCI	☎ 00 800-1 1177
SPRINT	☎ 00 800-1 4477

Fax

Most businesses including hotels, car rental companies and airlines have fax machines. If you must make reservations in advance, this is the fastest, cheapest and most reliable way. Usually you can send a fax in English, German or French and the recipients will have someone translate it and reply in the same language.

Email & Internet Access

The Internet snakes its way through Turkey, but access points are often heavily used and thus slow or temporarily inaccessible, especially in the morning and evening on workdays. The best time to log on is before breakfast, especially on Sunday.

You can check your email at several backpackers hostels and cafes in Cankurtaran, south of Sultanahmet, including the Orient Youth Hostel and the Mavi Guesthouse (see the Places to Stay chapter) and the Backpackers Cafe (☎ 212-636 6343, email backpackers@turk.net, Yeni Akbıyık Caddesi 22), among others. In Beyoğlu, Yağmur Cybercafe (☎ 212-292 3020, email anu@citlembik.com.tr) is near the American Consulate-General, in the Çitlembik Apartıman building (2nd floor), Şeyh Bender Sokak 18, Asmalımescit, Beyoğlu.

CompuServe (modem 212-234 5168) and America Online (modem 212-234 5158) have nodes in İstanbul. You will need to download and install supplementary CCL files in your CompuServe or AOL software to access these networks, and pay a surcharge while you're online. Contact those companies for information.

In four and five-star hotels, most telephone connections are made using the American-style small clear plastic RJ11 plug. In cheaper hotels the phones often use a larger white or beige three-prong Turkish plug. Many electrical shops sell these plugs and also phone cords with RJ11 plugs on them, so if you're handy with a screwdriver you can easily make your own phone line adaptor for a laptop computer.

INTERNET RESOURCES

Lonely Planet's award-winning Web site is at www.lonelyplanet.com. You can read what other travellers have to say about their experiences in Turkey in the postcards section of Lonely Planet's Web site at: www.lonelyplanet.com/letters/meast/tur–pc .htm. Also check my site at www.infoexchange.com for supplemental and updated Turkey information.

The *Turkish Daily News* has a good Web site at www.turkishdailynews.com. The daily *Milliyet* also provides news in both English and Turkish: www.milliyet.com/e/index.html.

The Turkish government maintains a Web site with links to other sites of Turkish interest at www.turkey.org/turkey.

There are sites at www.istanbul.com, www.istanbul.org and www.istanbul.net. Like most Turkish tourism sites they are heavy on slow-loading graphics and complicated layout, and light on useful information.

BOOKS

Everyone from Mark Twain to Agatha Christie has written about İstanbul. The books mentioned below have not been published in all countries by the same publisher, and titles may even change from country to country. Bookshops and libraries index books by author and title, which should help you find the ones you want.

Lonely Planet

As well as this guide to İstanbul, a good companion is Lonely Planet's *Turkish phrasebook*. Lonely Planet also covers the entire country in detail in *Turkey*, which is complemented by LP's *Turkey travel atlas*. And if you're taking the children, Maureen Wheeler's *Travel with Children* will help to make the trip an interesting and enjoyable one for all the family.

Guidebooks

The classic in-depth walking guide to the great buildings of İstanbul is *Strolling Through İstanbul* by Hilary Sumner-Boyd & John Freely.

For the literary-minded, *Istanbul – a traveller's companion* by Laurence Kelly is a delight. The editor has combed through the writings of two millennia and collected the choicest bits of history, biography, diary and travellers' observations relating to Byzantium, Constantinople and İstanbul.

Travel

The published diaries and accounts of earlier travellers in Turkey provide fascinating glimpses of Ottoman life. Of the many Europeans who lived in Ottoman İstanbul and wrote about it, the most interesting and revealing is Lady Mary Wortley Montagu, who published her *Letters* in 1789, followed in 1837 by Miss Julia Pardoe with her *City of the Sultan and Domestic Manners of the Turks*.

One of the more familiar 19th-century accounts of a visit to imperial İstanbul is Mark Twain's *Innocents Abroad*.

Jeremy Seal's *A Fez of the Heart* is the account of the author's recent journeys throughout Turkey in search of Turks who still wear the fez. It's a witty, entertaining inquiry into resurgent Islam and what it means to be a 'modern' Turk.

History

The city's two millennia of history have inspired countless writers to describe Byzantium, Constantinople and İstanbul, and the events that took place there. Procopius (died circa 565), Byzantine chronicler and one-time prefect of Constantinople, left us his scurrilous *Secret History* of court life in the capital during the reign of Justinian.

Kritovoulos's *History of Mehmet the Conqueror* is a chronicle of the conquest of

Constantinople, by an astute Byzantine observer of the time.

Peter Gilles (Petrus Gyllius) left us his *Antiquities of Constantinople*, published in an English edition in 1729.

For a fascinating look into the final years of the Ottoman Empire and early years of the Turkish Republic, read İrfan Orga's *Portrait of a Turkish Family*.

The premier writer on İstanbul today is undoubtedly Mr Çelik Gülersoy, director of the Turkish Touring & Automobile Association, who has written and published dozens of books on various İstanbul subjects, from the many palaces and markets to the caiques, or row boats, which were the city's taxis in Ottoman times. They are on sale in many bookshops in the city, but are usually not available abroad.

General

Anthropology For a good overview of life during the great days of the empire, look in a library for *Everyday Life in Ottoman Turkey* by Raphaela Lewis.

Carpets *Oriental Carpets: A buyer's guide,* by Essie Sakhai, contains everything you need to know about buying carpets. It includes full-colour photographs of each style of carpet as well as information on the origins of design, how they are made and tips on what buyers should look for.

Cuisine The definitive guide to Turkish cookery is *Eat Smart in Turkey*, by Joan & David Peterson. More than just an aid in deciphering menus, recognising foodstuffs in the marketplace, and enjoying Turkish cooking, this book provides amusing and informative historical notes on Turkish dishes as well. If your bookshop doesn't have it, you can order it from the publisher, Ginkgo Press Inc (☎ 1 608-233 5488, fax 233 0053, email joanp@ginkgopress.com, www.ginkgopress.com), PO Box 5346, Madison, WI 53705 USA.

Fiction Everybody knows about Agatha Christie's *Murder on the Orient Express.*

Though it has some scenes in Turkey, most of the train's journey was through Europe and the Balkans. In any case, it helps to make vivid the 19th-century importance of the Turkish Empire.

Many modern 'harem' novels trade on the romance (real or wildly imagined) of the sultan's private household. Most are facile. The exception is *The Bride of Suleiman* by Aileen Crawley, a historically faithful and absorbing fictionalised account of the relationship between Hürrem Sultan ('Roxelana') and her husband Süleyman the Magnificent, greatest of the Ottoman sultans.

Bookshops

Books published in Turkish are relatively cheap, those published in Turkey for a foreign audience considerably more expensive, but books imported from abroad are very expensive and vary widely from bookshop to bookshop. A book which sells for US$20 at home may cost US$35 or US$40 in Turkey.

Galeri Kayseri (☎ 212-512 0456, fax 511 7380), Divan Yolu 58, has the best choice of books in Sultanahmet. Also in Sultanahmet is the International Book House, Klodfarer Caddesi, Ragıp Uluca Apt 27/1, which stocks Lonely Planet guides.

İstiklal Caddesi near Tünel Square has numerous good bookshops.

Robinson Crusoe (☎ 212-293 6968), İstiklal Caddesi 389, Tünel, has two floors of books and a good selection, including many in European languages.

Dünya Aktüel (☎ 212-249 1006), İstiklal Caddesi 469, Tünel, has Turkish, French and English books and periodicals.

ABC Kitabevi (☎ 212-293 1629), in Tünel Square, has mostly language-learning aids. The nearby Metro Kitabevi (☎ 212-249 5827), İstiklal Caddesi 513 facing Tünel Square, sells guidebooks and maps.

Pandora (☎ 212-243 3503, email h.sonmez @info-ist.comlink.apc.org, www.ftz.org/ info-ist/pandora), Büyükparmakkapı Sokak 3, Taksim, off İstiklal Caddesi, has books in English on Turkish history and literature, as well as Lonely Planet guidebooks.

Librairie de Péra (☎ 212-245 4998), Galip Dede Caddesi 22, Tünel, is an antiquarian shop with old books in Turkish, Greek, Armenian, Arabic, French, German, English etc.

Eren (☎ 212-251 2858), Sofyalı Sokak 34, Tünel, has old and new history and art books and maps.

Firnas Bookstore (☎ 212-244 5446), at No 5 in the Avrupa Pasajı between Meşrutiyet Caddesi and Sahne Sokak off Galatasaray Square, stocks dictionaries of many languages and some travel guides.

Beyoğlu Net Kitabevi, İstiklal Caddesi 79/81, 80060 Beyoğlu, stocks Lonely Planet guides.

In Nişantaşı, north-east of Taksim, look for the excellent Remzi Kitabevi (☎ 212-234 5475), at Rumeli Caddesi 44, with a wide selection of English-language books on all subjects. It also has a superb branch in the Akmerkez shopping centre (☎ 212-282 0245). Karum (☎ 212-241 7988), Akkavak Sokak 19/21, Nişantaşı, has a good selection of art books.

Sahaflar Çarşısı, the Old Book Bazaar, is great fun for browsing. It's just west of the Covered Market, sandwiched between Çadırcılar Caddesi and the Beyazıt Camii. Among the shops here, one of the best is the Üniversiteli Kitabevi (☎ 212-511 3987, fax 345 9387), at No 5, with a modern outlook and the most current books published in Turkey. The Zorlu Kitabevi (☎ 212-511 2660, fax 526 0495), at No 22, specialises in books about İstanbul, old documents and maps. Look also at the Dilmen Kitabevi (☎ 212-527 9934), Şahaflar Çarşıı 20, which has titles in English on Turkey and Turkish history.

The No Name Book Exchange has lots of English-language books to swap. It's upstairs in the Bergama Export Building (through the carpets) across the hall from the Hotel Hipodrom and near the Mosaic Museum.

FILMS

Perhaps the most famous movie about Turkey is *Midnight Express*, a politically motivated, anti-Turkish diatribe in which a convicted drug smuggler is magically transformed into a suffering hero. Controversial director Oliver Stone created this visually striking and emotionally chilling early work by playing fast and loose with the facts, a practice he expanded upon in *Mississippi Burning* and *JFK*. Virtually all of the 'Turkish' actors in the movie are of Greek or Armenian ancestry. Surprisingly, an entire generation of intelligent cinemagoers never questioned its overt racism and political purpose.

The classic suspense-comedy *Topkapi*, with Peter Ustinov and Melina Mercouri, is much more fun to watch, as is the James Bond thriller *From Russia With Love*, set in Istanbul.

For years various producers have been discussing a film biography of Atatürk – a dramatic story if ever there was one – but actors and directors approached about the film are often put under extreme pressure by anti-Turkish elements not to participate. In addition, anything but positive coverage of the national hero is sure to meet with the disapproval of the Turkish government, not to mention a large proportion of the populace.

NEWSPAPERS & MAGAZINES

Local daily newspapers are produced by up-to-date computerised methods in lurid colour. Of prime interest to visitors is the *Turkish Daily News*, an English-language daily newspaper published in Ankara and sold for US$0.80 in most Turkish cities where tourists go. It is the cheapest source of English language news in print.

The big international papers such as the *International Herald Tribune, Le Monde, Corriere della Sera, Die Welt* etc are on sale in tourist spots as well, but are much more expensive (US$2 for the *Herald Tribune*). Check the date on any international paper before you buy it. If it's more than a day or two old, look elsewhere.

Large-circulation magazines including *The Economist, Newsweek, Time, Der Spiegel* and the like, are also sold in tourist spots.

If you can't find the foreign publication

you want, go to a big hotel's newsstand or check at a foreign-language bookshop.

RADIO & TV

TRT (Türkiye Radyo ve Televizyon) is a quasi-independent government broadcasting service modelled on the BBC. Western classical and popular music, along with Turkish classical, folk, religious and pop music, are played regularly on both AM (medium-wave) and FM channels.

TRT Tourism (Holiday) Radio broadcasts travel-oriented features in English, French and German on 101.6 Mhz FM in İstanbul daily from 7.30 am to 12.45 pm and 6.30 to 10 pm. Listen for news from 8.30 am to 12.30 pm and at 9.30 pm. TRT's Radio 3 (FM) also presents short news broadcasts in English at 9 am, noon, 2, 5, 7 and 10 pm.

The BBC World Service is often receivable on AM as well as on short-wave. The Voice of America broadcasts in English on AM, relayed from Rhodes, each morning. The rest of the medium-wave band is a babel of Albanian, Arabic, Bulgarian, Greek, Hebrew, Italian, Persian, Romanian and Russian.

TRT broadcasts on four TV channels from breakfast time till midnight. Independent Turkish-language stations carry the familiar Los Angeles-made series and films dubbed in Turkish. Occasionally you'll catch a film in the original language. In addition to the Turkish channels, many of the larger and more expensive hotels have satellite hook-ups to receive European channels, with programs mostly in German, but often including the European service of the US Cable News Network (CNN), NBC Super-Channel, and/or the BBC and a Japanese channel.

PHOTOGRAPHY & VIDEO

Many museums and historical sites impose a fee for photography above the one for admission, and a fee for video above that for photography. This seems counterproductive, as photos and videos taken home by tourists provide some of the best possible publicity for Turkey at the tourists' (not the museums') expense.

Payment of such a fee normally entitles you to only take photos without the help of flash and/or tripod; to use these 'professional' accessories you must obtain official written permission from the Ministry of Culture or the official body in charge of the museum or site, a difficult, tedious and time-consuming process.

Film is moderately expensive in Turkey (24 Kodacolor prints cost about US$8, plus developing). Both major and minor-brand colour print film is readily available and easily developed in Turkey, as are the E-6 process slide (diapositive, transparency) films such as Ektachrome, Fujichrome and Velvia. Kodachrome slide film is difficult to find, and cannot be developed in Turkey. Photo shops are concentrated in the narrow streets just west of Sirkeci train station, and more thinly sprinkled throughout the city.

If you are from North America, remember that Turkey uses the European PAL TV-video system, not the NTSC system.

Don't take photos of military subjects. It's also polite to ask (sign language will suffice) before taking pictures of people who are not obviously used to such exposure.

For camera repair, one reader recommends Mr Nazmi Kılıçer (☎ 212-511 4259, 527 7935), Babiali Caddesi, Başmusahip Sokak 19/1, Gün Han, 34410 Cağaloğlu, İstanbul. Although he is a Hasselblad specialist, he repairs all sorts of cameras.

TIME

İstanbul time is East European Time, two hours ahead of Coordinated Universal Time (UTC, alias GMT), except in the warm months, when clocks are turned ahead one hour. Daylight saving (summer) time usually begins at 1 am on the last Sunday in March, and ends at 2 am on the last Sunday in September. When it's noon in İstanbul, the time elsewhere is:

city	winter	summer
Auckland	10 pm	9 pm
London	10 am	10 am

Los Angeles	2 am	2 am
New York	5 am	5 am
Paris, Rome	11 am	11 am
Perth, Hong Kong	6 pm	5 pm
Sydney	8 pm	7 pm

ELECTRICITY

Electricity in İstanbul is supplied at 220V, 50Hz, as in Europe. Plugs (fiş, FEESH) are of the European variety with two round prongs. Electricity shops have adaptors for European and North American plugs, though it's not a bad idea to bring your own to avoid wasting time finding a Turkish electrical shop.

WEIGHTS & MEASURES

Turkey uses the metric system. For those who are used to imperial or US measurements, see the metric conversion table inside the back cover.

LAUNDRY

If you don't do your own laundry, ask for prices at your hotel. By the way, the word çamaşır (laundry) also means 'underwear' in Turkish. This can be confusing at times.

In Sultanahmet, alternatives to washing your own are:

Active Laundry
Dr Emin Paşa Sokak 14, off Divan Yolu Caddesi beneath the Arsenal Youth Hostel. It charges US$1.50 per kilogram to wash, US$0.50 to dry, and is open daily.
Hobby Laundry
Caferiye Sokak 6/1, in the Yücelt Interyouth Hostel and across the street from Aya Sofya, Sultanahmet. Posted hours are from 9 am to 8 pm every day, actual hours may be different. The charge is US$1.50 per kilogram to wash (minimum 2kg) and about US$0.50 per kilogram to dry, although 'dry' means dampish. Attendants take your clothes and operate the machines.

İstanbul has numerous dry-cleaning shops (kuru temizleme), usually open daily (except Sunday) from 8 am to 7 pm. Bring items in early for same-day service. Two blocks westward uphill from the southern end of the Hippodrome in Sultanahmet is

Doğu Expres (☎ 212-526 0725), Peykhane Sokak 61 (also called Üçler Sokak).

TOILETS

In most public conveniences you must pay a fee of US$0.10 to US$0.20. Turkish toilets are equipped with facilities for washing the user's bottom (always with the left hand): a tap, or spigot, with a can on the floor nearby, or, much more conveniently, a little copper tube pointing right to the spot where it's needed. As washing is the accustomed method of hygiene, toilet paper – used by Turks mostly for drying – is considered a dispensable luxury and may not be provided. If you want to use paper, it's a good idea to carry it with you at all times.

You may also meet with the traditional flat 'elephant's feet', or squat, toilet, a porcelain or concrete rectangle with two oblong foot-places and a sunken hole. Though daunting, it has much to recommend it: it is said that the squatting position aids in the swift and thorough accomplishment of your daily duty; and since only your shod feet contact the vessel, it is more sanitary than bowl toilets.

Serviceably clean public toilets can be found near the big tourist attractions. In other places, it depends. Look first. Every mosque has a toilet, often smelly and very basic, but it may be better than nothing, depending upon the urgency of Nature's call.

LEFT LUGGAGE

Airports do not have left luggage rooms (baggage checks) for security reasons, but most Turkish bus and railway stations do. The word is emanet or emanetçi. Fees vary, but are not high. Though most emanetçis are honest, it would be unwise to leave anything of great value with them, whether your luggage is locked or unlocked.

HEALTH

İstanbul has the best medical services in Turkey, including hospitals under American, French and German administration.

For minor problems, it's customary to ask at a chemist/pharmacy *(eczane,* edj-zahn-NEH) for advice. Sign language usually suffices to communicate symptoms, and the pharmacist will prescribe treatment on the spot. Drugs requiring prescription in western countries are often sold over the counter (except for the most dangerous or addictive ones). Most pharmacies have both male and female staff, so if you need to explain embarrassing problems you can usually find a sympathetic soul of your own gender. See the Language chapter later in this book for a short list of medical terms; for a more comprehensive list get a copy of Lonely Planet's *Turkish phrasebook.*

Though Turkey manufactures many medicines, avoid the risk of running out of a drug taken regularly by bringing your own supply. If your medicine is available in Turkey, it may be less expensive than at home. Make sure you know the generic name of your medicine; the commercial name may not be the same.

Predeparture Preparations

Health Insurance Travel agencies sell policies to protect you against loss from trip cancellation, illness, robbery and theft, and to cover medical evacuation while abroad. The coverage tends to be expensive for what you get, but less expensive than having to pay for one of these woes yourself should it happen. The international student travel policies handled by STA or other student travel organisations are often good value. Some policies offer lower and higher medical expenses options, but the higher one is chiefly for cover in countries like the USA, which have extremely high medical costs.

Medical Kit It is wise to carry a small, straightforward medical kit with analgesics and bandages, but the many pharmacies/chemists in İstanbul have most of what you're likely to need.

Vaccinations You need no special inoculations before entering Turkey unless you're coming from an endemic or epidemic area. If you plan to travel extensively in Turkey, especially off the beaten track, you should consider getting vaccinations against hepatitis A and B, and typhoid fever, and make sure that your tetanus/diphtheria and polio vaccinations are up to date (boosters are necessary every 10 years).

Your local health authorities are supposed to have up-to-date information on recommended inoculations for all parts of the world, but often they don't. It might be good to compare what they say with information provided by the following authoritative sources:

Australia
Travellers' Medical & Vaccination Centre. In Melbourne call ☎ 03-9602 5788, 9347 7132. In Sydney call ☎ 02-9221 7133.

Hit the Internet

Lonely Planet provides up-to-date information for travellers on health issues on the Internet. For all you need to know about predeparture planning, keeping healthy, women's health and diseases and ailments, check out www.lonelyplanet.com/health/health.htm. Lonely Planet's site can also direct you to other relevant on-line health information.

The US Public Health Service's Centers for Disease Control & Prevention in Atlanta, Georgia, can also provide current health information through the three Internet sites it maintains.

The CDC site is at www.cdc.gov/travel/travel.html. Look for the Middle East section. You may also be interested in the item called Information Networks & Other Information Sources.

There's more information available by file transfer protocol (ftp) at ftp.cdc.gov, and at the CDC Gopher site at gopher://gopher.cdc.gov/ under Traveler's Health.

FACTS FOR THE VISITOR

UK
> Medical Advisory Service for Travellers Abroad (MASTA) at the London School of Hygiene & Tropical Medicine (☎ 0891-224 100), London, UK. You answer a set of questions on your destination and means of travel. Following assessment, MASTA will send you a health brief with a list of precautions to take. The phone line is open 24 hours a day; charges are UK£0.37 off-peak and UK£0.49 peak.

USA
> Public Health Service, Centers for Disease Control & Prevention (☎ /fax 404-332 4559). Its Web site at www.cdc.gov/travel/travel.html also has detailed information, or you can get the files via file transfer protocol (ftp) from ftp.cdc.gov, or via gopher at gopher.cdc.gov/ under Traveler's Health.

Food & Water

Travellers in Turkey experience a fair amount of travellers' diarrhoea ('the Sultan's Revenge'). Most people suffer some consequences from a drastic change of diet and water, as each area (and cuisine) has its own 'normal' bacteria.

Dining Precautions In restaurants serving ready cooked food (see the Places to Eat chapter later in this book), choose dishes that look freshly prepared and sufficiently hot. As for grilled meats, if they look pink, send them back for more cooking (no problem in this). See the Language chapter later in this book for a list of the cooking terms you'll need to know.

Beware of milk products and dishes containing milk that have not been properly refrigerated. If you want a rice pudding (sütlaç) or some such dish with milk in it, choose a shop that has lots of them in the window, meaning that a batch has been made recently. In general, choose things from bins, trays, cases, pots etc that are fairly full rather than almost empty. Eating some fresh yoghurt every day helps to keep your digestive system in good condition.

Drinking Precautions Tap water in İstanbul is chlorinated, but is still not guaranteed to be safe (locals don't drink it), and bottled water tastes better. Spring water is sold everywhere in .33L, 1.5L and 3L clear plastic bottles.

Alternatives to spring water include maden suyu, naturally fizzy mineral water, and maden sodası (or just soda), artificially carbonated mineral water. Packaged fruit juice (méyva suyu), soft drinks, beer and wine are reliably pure, except in rare cases.

Illnesses

Food Poisoning Symptoms are headaches, nausea and/or stomach ache, diarrhoea, fever and chills. If you get food poisoning, go to bed and stay warm. Drink lots of fluids, preferably hot tea without sugar or milk. Chamomile tea, papatya çay, can ease a queasy stomach.

Until the bout of food poisoning has run its course (from 24 to 30 hours), drink nothing but plain tea (no milk or sugar), and eat nothing but dry toast (kızartmış ekmek) or rusks (kurutmuş ekmek) and maybe a little yoghurt. The day after, you'll feel weak, but the symptoms should have passed except perhaps for residual diarrhoea. If you take it easy and eat only bland, easily digested foods for a few days, you'll be fine.

Travellers' Diarrhoea The standard treatments for travellers' diarrhoea, as recommended by the US Public Health Service, include antibiotics, bismuth subsalicylate (Pepto-Bismol), and difenoxine (Lomotil) or loperamide (Imodium). Each of these medicines has side effects; you should consult a physician before taking any of them, and you should not take any medicine as a preventative – only take them if you actually become ill. Antibiotics, for example, can cause the side effect of sun sensitivity (rashes and swelling).

Doctors, Dentists & Hospitals

Contact your country's consulate in İstanbul or embassy in Ankara for advice about suitable doctors, dentists, hospitals and other medical care.

Half of all the physicians in Turkey are women. If a woman visits a male doctor, it's customary to have a companion present

Two girls from the Balat neighbourhood.

A patriotic juice seller hits the spot.

Pigeon-food seller with accomplices.

For a shoe shine guaranteed to impress.

Washing feet under the watchful eye of an old man in a hat, within Fatih Camii.

Locals enjoy watching the tourist watching the locals watching the tourist ...

Early morning fishing on Galata Bridge.

during any physical examination or treatment as there is not always a nurse available to serve in this role.

İstanbul has several private hospitals that provide good quality care at government-controlled prices. These include:

Alman Hastanesi
(☎ 212-293 2150) Sıraselviler Caddesi 119, Taksim; it's a few hundred metres south of Taksim on the left-hand side. Has a German administration

American Hospital
(☎ 212-231 4050, fax 234 1432) Güzelbahçe Sokak 20, Nişantaşı; about 2km north-east of Taksim. Has a US administration and a dental clinic

Avrupa Hastanesi (European Hospital)
(☎ 212-288 3008) Mehmetçik Caddesi, Cahit Yalçın Sokak, Mecidiyeköy; about 5km north-east of Taksim

Florence Nightingale Hospital
(☎ 212-231 2021) Abidei Hürriyet Caddesi 290, Çağlayan, Şişli; about 4km north of Taksim

Intermed Check-up Centre
(☎ 212-225 0660) Teşvikiye Caddesi, Bayar Apt 143, Nişantaşı; about 2km north of Taksim

International Hospital
(☎ 212-663 3000) İstanbul Caddesi 82, Yeşilyurt; on the shore near the airport

La Paix ('Lape') Hastanesi
(☎ 212-246 1020), Büyükdere Caddesi 22-24, Şişli; has a French administration

WOMEN TRAVELLERS

As in most Muslim countries, western women often attract the sort of attention they never would at home. Since Turkey is basically friendly and welcoming, much of this attention will be perfectly pleasant. Inevitably, however, some of it won't be. Though serious assault is far less common in İstanbul than in London, Paris or New York, harassment such as rude noises and touching are more common.

Much of this is cultural misunderstanding bred by European and American films and different cultural norms: what a foreign woman may see as a simple courtesy or pleasantry – such as a smile upon greeting – a Turkish man may well take as an invitation to greater intimacy.

In general, keep your dealings with Turkish men very formal, polite and proper, not friendly. Avoid casual eye contact. Ignore noises or advances on the street. If you are approached by a Turkish man in circumstances that upset you, try saying *Ayıp!* (ah-YUHP) which means 'Shame on you!'.

Whatever happens, try not to get paranoid and don't let these hassles ruin your trip. Provided you dress modestly and behave appropriately with local attitudes in mind, most men will treat you hospitably, with kindness and respect.

The Aile Salonu

Women are welcomed in all public establishments, but the overwhelmingly male clientele of many places makes some Turkish women uncomfortable. Therefore, many restaurants have rooms set apart for use only by women, couples or mixed groups. Called the *aile salonu* (family room), it is the place for single women to go to escape unwanted attention. Look for the sign *Aile Salonumuz Vardır* ('We Have a Family Room') in the front windows of cheap and mid-range restaurants. Sitting in the aile salonu is optional, of course. If you'd rather sit in the main dining room, feel free to do so.

GAY & LESBIAN TRAVELLERS

Though not uncommon in a culture that traditionally separated men and women in society, overt homosexuality is not socially or legally acceptable in Turkey. While not strictly illegal, laws prohibiting 'lewd behaviour' are often used to suppress it. Even so, it exists openly at a small number of gay bars and clubs in major cities and resorts. Be discreet. For more information, surf to www.qrd.org/qrd/www/world/europe /turkey.

For reliable and useful information on gay and lesbian contacts, see *Spartacus International Gay Guide*, published by Bruno Gmünder Verlag (☎ 49-30-615 00 30), PO Box 11 07 29, D 10837 Berlin, Germany. See also Gay & Lesbian Venues in the Entertainment chapter.

DISABLED TRAVELLERS

Turkey has severely limited accessibility for disabled travellers. Though local people will go out of their way to help a disabled traveller get around, with few exceptions the arrangements will be ad hoc.

Airlines and the top hotels and resorts have some provisions for wheelchair access, and ramps are beginning to appear (ever so slowly) in a few other places. But generally you should expect difficulties.

For good information on accessible travel, contact the Royal Association for Disability & Rehabilitation (RADAR; ☎ 0171-250 3222), 12 City Forum, 250 City Rd, London EC1V 8AF, UK.

SENIOR TRAVELLERS

Seniors (altın yaş, golden age) are welcomed and age is respected in Turkey. Seniors sometimes receive discounts at hotels. Upon presentation of a passport, seniors may be granted reduced-price admission to some museums and historical and other touristic sites.

İSTANBUL FOR CHILDREN

For loads of practical advice on hassle-free family travel, Lonely Planet's Travel with Children by Maureen Wheeler is a valuable resource.

Your child (çocuk) or children (çocuklar) will be well received in Turkey, and given the high Turkish birthrate, they'll have lots of company.

The market for childhood products and services is not as elaborately developed in Turkey as in Europe or America, but Turks are handy at improvising anything which may be needed for a child's safety, health or enjoyment. Public parks sometimes have basic play equipment.

The larger hotels and resorts can arrange for daycare (kreş) and baby-sitting services.

Child safety seats are available from all large and many small car rental companies at an extra daily charge. It's best to request a child seat in advance, when you reserve your car.

Disposable nappies, or baby diapers, (bebek bezi), are readily available for infants (bebek). The best brand is Ultra Prima, sold in pharmacies/chemists according to the baby's weight in kilograms. A packet of 24 costs about US$6.

Ultra-pasteurised milk is sold everywhere. Some baby foods in individual jars may also be found, but it's usually better to rely on the willingness and ingenuity of hotel and restaurant staff to make up special dishes for small children. If you have an infant, you might also want to carry a small portable food mill to purée vegetables, fruits and meats.

Children's Activities

The mysterious, eerie darkness of Yerebatan Saray (the Cistern Basilica) in Sultanahmet Square usually fascinates kids. Another sure winner is to climb aboard any ferryboat going from Eminönü across the Bosphorus to the Asian shore. The trip takes only 15 or 20 minutes each way. Kids will love the boat ride and you'll love the fine city views. Boats leave frequently and cost less than US$1 for a round trip.

The fortress of Rumeli Hisar, on the European shore of the Bosphorus and a 30-minute ride north of the city centre, is a real medieval castle with crenellated walls, cylindrical towers and ancient cannons. It's closed Monday. See the Things to See & Do chapter for details.

The Military Museum, just north of Taksim Square and the İstanbul Hilton, has displays showing centuries of Turkish military history, including lots of old swords and suits of armour.

Take the Tünel, İstanbul's little century-old underground train, from Karaköy at the northern end of Galata Bridge, up to the southern end of İstiklal Caddesi (Map 3). From there, a restored Victorian-era tram goes along İstiklal to Taksim Square.

LIBRARIES

The American Library (☎ 212-251 2675), next to the US Consulate at Meşrutiyet Caddesi 108, Tepebaşı, has been scaled back to a reference library due to government budget cuts. It's open Monday to Friday from noon to 4 pm.

The British Council Library (☎ 212-252 7474 extension 115, 118 or 119), İstiklal Caddesi 151-253, Beyoğlu, two flights up in the Örs Turistik İş Merkezi building, is open Tuesday to Friday from 10.30 am to at least 5.30 pm (later some nights) and on Saturday from 9.30 am to 2.30 pm.

The Women's Library (Kadın Eserleri Kütüphanesi ve Bilgi Merkezi Vakfı; ☎ 212-534 9550), just east of St Stephen's Church (the cast iron church) on the southwest side of the Golden Horn, is open from 9 am to 5.30 pm; closed Sunday. Housed in a historic building, the library acts as a women's resource centre, with a program of cultural and special events of interest to women. An English-speaking volunteer is present most Tuesday afternoons.

DANGERS & ANNOYANCES

İstanbul is quite a safe city compared to others of its size. If you live in a large European or US city, you may feel safer here than at home.

Police

Blue-clad officers, both men and women, are part of a national force designated by the words *Polis* or *Emniyet* (security). Under normal circumstances you will have little to do with them. If you do encounter them, they will judge you partly by your personal appearance. If you look tidy and 'proper', they'll be on your side. If you're dressed carelessly, they may not be as helpful.

Other blue-clad officers with peaked caps are market inspectors *(belediye zabıtası)* who make sure a loaf of bread weighs what it should, that 24-carat gold is indeed 24 carats, and that scales and balances don't cheat the customer. You won't have much to do with them.

Theft & Robbery

Theft is not much of a problem, and robbery (mugging) even less, but don't let Turkey's relative safety lull you. Take normal precautions.

Keep close track of your wallet or other valuables on crowded buses and trains and in markets. Don't leave valuables in your hotel room, or at least not in view, and don't walk into unknown parts of town when nobody else is around. There are isolated reports of bags being quietly slashed in the Covered Market, and of distract-bump-and-grab thefts in similar crowded places.

See the Entertainment chapter for information on a common nightclub rip-off.

Lese-Majesty

There are laws against insulting, defaming or making light of Atatürk, the Turkish flag, the Turkish people, the Turkish Republic etc. Any difficulty will probably arise from misunderstanding. At the first sign that you've inadvertently been guilty of lese-majesty, be sure to make your apologies, which should be readily accepted.

Earthquakes

Turkey sometimes has bad ones. The big quakes only seem to hit every eight or 10 years, though. It's up to Allah.

The Imperial Auto

As a pedestrian, give way to cars and trucks in all situations, even if you have to jump out of the way. The sovereignty of the pedestrian is recognised in law but not out on the street. If a car hits you, the driver (if not the law courts) will blame *you*. This does not apply, however, on a recognised crossing controlled by a traffic officer or a traffic signal, where if you've got a 'walk' light, you've got the right of way. Watch out, all the same. Know that every Turkish driver considers you, a pedestrian, merely an annoyance composed of so much worthless protoplasm. A dispute with a driver will get you nowhere and may escalate into an even bigger problem of assault and battery.

Traffic Accidents

It's worth mentioning that Turkey has one of the world's highest motor vehicle accident rates. Drive very defensively. A massive safety campaign is under way, but its full effects will not be felt for some years.

Racial Discrimination

The Ottoman Empire was not a colonial power, and so the country's ethnic diversity is not of a wide scope. Turkey's racial mix is mostly among sub-groups of the Caucasian group, with admixtures (sometimes ancient) of Asian races.

Although blacks sent as slaves from Africa sometimes rose through the imperial palace hierarchy to positions of very great importance in the government, most who did so were eunuchs, and thus they left no legacy of prominent families.

With a relatively homogeneous population and no great history of foreign travel or colonisation, most Turks have little or no experience in dealing with people of other races. Racial prejudice and discrimination root easily in such soil.

If you are of Asian ancestry, Turks will probably assume that you are a Japanese tourist even if you carry an American or Australian passport; you may have an amusing time convincing them that you are a 'real' American or Aussie.

If you are of African ancestry, you should anticipate some hassles. The least of it will be people staring at you on the street simply because they have seen few black people and are curious. The worst of it may be finding that hotels with plenty of vacant rooms are mysteriously and suddenly 'full' when you request lodging. This may happen more frequently in the cheapest places, less frequently or hardly at all in the more expensive places. There is no organised or institutionalised racism, so any instances of it will depend on the actual persons involved. The best plan is usually to withhold your patronage from such people and to find a more fair and open-minded establishment to patronise.

Cigarette Smoke

If you're offended by cigarette smoke, you will have some unpleasant moments in Turkey. Though the local cancer prevention society fields a brave effort to stop smoking, this is the land of aromatic Turkish tobacco, and smoking is a well and truly a national passion. The movement for non-smoking areas in public places is gaining ground, but it will be a long battle. Smoking is not permitted on city buses, intercity buses, airplanes, in museums and mosques, and in similar public spaces.

Noise

İstanbul is an intense, crowded, noisy city. Among the most persistent and omnipresent noises is that of the call to prayer, amplified to ear-splitting levels. In the good old days before microphones and amplifiers, it must have been beautiful to hear the clear, natural voices of the muezzins calling from a hundred minarets, even before dawn, when the first call is given. Now you hear a cacophony of blaring noise five or more times a day. If there's a minaret right outside your hotel window, you'll know it.

When considering a hotel room, ask *Sakin mi?* (sah-KEEN mee, 'Is it quiet here?').

Air Pollution

In summer there is pollution from cars, but it's no worse than in other big cities. In winter the air is dirtier, but far better than it used to be in the days before clean Russian natural gas replaced lignite (soft brown coal) as the heating fuel of choice. The heating season lasts from 15 October to 1 April.

BUSINESS HOURS

Some small one-person shops in traditional markets may close for 20 minutes or so at prayer time so the owner can worship. Otherwise, Turkish opening hours are:

Banks
> Monday to Friday from 8.30 am to noon and 1.30 to 5 pm.

Covered Markets
> İstanbul's Grand Bazaar and Egyptian (Spice) Market are open Monday to Saturday from 8 am to 6.30 pm.

Grocery Shops & Markets
> Monday to Saturday from 6 or 7 am to 7 or 8 pm. Most markets close on Sunday, though one or two grocers open in each neighbourhood.

Mosques

The large imperial mosques are open all the time. If a mosque is locked, there is usually a *bekçi* (guardian) with a key somewhere nearby. Avoid visiting mosques at prayer time (or within 20 minutes after the call to prayer). Avoid visiting on Friday, the Muslim holy day, particularly at noon, when congregations fill the mosques to hear the weekly sermons.

Museums

The largest museums do not close for lunch, though smaller ones and those off the beaten path may be open from 8.30 or 9.30 am to noon or 12.30 pm, then close for lunch, reopening at 1 or 1.30 pm and remaining open until 5 or 5.30 pm, perhaps later in the summer. Most museums are closed on Monday, with these exceptions:

Dolmabahçe Sarayı, Beylerbeyi Sarayı and some of the imperial lodges *(kasrs)* – closed Monday and Thursday

Topkapı Sarayı – closed Tuesday

Kariye Müzesi (Chora Church) – closed Wednesday

Maritime Museum – closed Wednesday and Thursday

Offices

Government and business offices may open at 8 or 9 am, close for lunch, and reopen around 1.30 pm, remaining open until 4 or 5 pm. However, during the holy month of Ramazan (see Religious Holidays, below) the workday is shortened.

Post Offices

The central post office in Eminönü is open daily from 8 am to 8 pm for stamp sales, telephone jeton and card sales. However, poste restante and parcel services may only be open from 8.30 am to noon and 1.30 to 5 or 6 pm. Smaller post offices have limited hours: from 8.30 am to 12.30 pm and 1.30 to 5.30 pm, and may be closed part of Saturday, and all day Sunday. Telephone centres may be open until midnight.

Restaurants

Most restaurants serve food continuously from 11 am to 11 pm or later. Many open early (6 or 7 am) for breakfast. The exceptions are a few restaurants in bazaars, business and financial districts, which primarily serve lunch to office workers.

Shops

Monday to Saturday from 9 am to noon and 1.30 or 2.30 to 6 or 7 pm or even later; many don't close for lunch.

Tourist Offices

Usually Monday to Friday from 8.30 am to noon or 12.30 pm, and 1.30 to 5.30 pm, longer in summer.

PUBLIC HOLIDAYS & SPECIAL EVENTS

The official Turkish calendar is the Gregorian (western) one, as in Europe. Friday is the Muslim holy day, but it is not a holiday. The day of rest, a secular one, is Sunday.

For important music and film events see Music Festivals and Cinema in the Entertainment chapter.

Religious Holidays

Religious festivals, two of which (Şeker Bayramı and Kurban Bayramı) are public holidays, are celebrated according to the Muslim lunar Hijri calendar. As the lunar year is about 11 days shorter than the Gregorian one, Muslim festivals occur 11 days earlier each year.

Muslim days, like Jewish ones, begin at sundown. Thus a Friday holiday will begin on Thursday at sunset and last until Friday at sunset.

For major religious and civic holidays there is also a half-day vacation for preparation, called *arife*, preceding the start of a festival; shops and offices close about noon, and the festival begins at sunset.

Ramazan During the Holy Month, called Ramadan in other Muslim countries, a good Muslim lets *nothing* pass the lips during daylight hours: no eating, drinking, smoking, or even licking a postage stamp.

The fast is broken traditionally with flat *pide* bread. Lavish dinners are given and may last far into the night. Before dawn, drummers circulate through town to awaken the faithful so they can eat before sunrise.

Although many İstanbullus observe the fast, most restaurants and cafes are open as usual to serve non-Muslims and locals who are not observing the fast. It's polite to avoid ostentatious public smoking, eating, drinking and drunkenness during Ramazan.

The 27th day of Ramazan is *Kadir Gecesi*, the Night of Power, when the Koran was revealed and Muhammed was appointed to be the Messenger of God.

Ramazan runs from 8 December 1999 to 6 January 2000, 27 November to 26 December 2001, and 16 November to 15 December 2002.

Şeker Bayramı Called Eid es-Seghir in Arabic countries, this is a three-day festival at the end of Ramazan. *Şeker* (shek-EHR) is sugar or candy. During this festival children traditionally go door to door asking for sweet treats, Muslims exchange greeting cards and pay social calls, and everybody enjoys drinking lots of tea in broad daylight after fasting for Ramazan. The festival is a three-day national holiday when banks and offices are closed, and hotels, buses, trains and aeroplanes are heavily booked.

Kurban Bayramı The most important religious holiday of the year, Kurban Bayramı (Sacrifice Holiday, Eid al-Adha) commemorates Abraham's near-sacrifice of his son on Mt Moriah (Genesis 22; Koran, Sura 37). It starts on 28 March 1999, 16 March 2000, 5 March 2001 and 22 February 2002. Plan ahead – almost everything closes.

Right after the early morning prayers on the actual day of Bayram, the head of the household sacrifices a sheep. A feast is prepared, with much of the meat going to charity.

Plan ahead – again, almost everything closes, including banks. Transport and resort hotels may be packed.

Annual Holidays & Events

1 January
  New Year's Day
23 April
  National Sovereignty Day (first republican parliament met in Ankara in 1920) and Children's Day
19 May
  Youth & Sports Day (Atatürk's landing in Samsun to begin the War of Independence)
29 May
  Conquest of Constantinople in 1453, with ceremonies at the city walls between the Topkapı and Edirnekapı gates

June
  Oiled wrestling in Edirne (2nd week); International İstanbul Music Festival (early June-early July)
30 August
  Victory Day (victory over invading Greek armies at Dumlupınar in 1922)
29 October
  Republic Day (proclamation of the republic in 1923)
10 November
  Date of Atatürk's death (1938); not a holiday, but special ceremonies are held.

DOING BUSINESS

Despite the many public-sector holdovers of the étatist period from the 1930s to the 1970s, Turkey has a vibrant private-sector business community and newly prominent stock market. Several large Turkish holding companies are among the Fortune 500.

Turkish offices have a gloss of western-style business manners and practices, but doing business here can be different from what you may be used to in Western Europe or North America. Most risks are greater, but as a rapidly developing country, the rewards may be greater as well. Government, traditionally a capricious and stubborn obstacle to business development, has been actively more cooperative with business endeavours since the late president Turgut Özal introduced reforms and innovations.

Even so, government cooperation cannot be assumed until the project is completed and actively operating. In part, this is because of frequent changes in the endless succession of fairly weak ruling coalitions, and the subsequent uncertainty among the ministries regulating business and financial activity. An astute Turkish business partner is usually essential; finding a suitably ethical one is important.

For guidance in personal interaction with Turks, read *Turkish Culture for Americans*, by Hasan Dindi, Maija Gazur, Wayne M Gazur & Ayşen Kırkköprü-Dindi, and published by International Concepts Ltd, 5311 Holmes Place, Boulder, Colorado 80303-1243 USA.

For More Information

The first person to contact is the commercial attaché at the nearest Turkish embassy or consulate. The attaché can put you in touch with local trade and business groups in your home country, and can suggest useful government contacts in Turkey.

The Scientific & Technical Research Council of Turkey (Türkiye Bilimsel ve Teknik Araştırma Kurumu, TÜBİTAK, www.tubitak.gov.tr) has many links to business, government and university Web sites.

In North America, the American Turkish Council (☎ 202-783 0483, fax 783 0511, email atctr@aol.com), 1010 Vermont Ave, NW, Suite 300, Washington, DC 20005-4902 will help you to set up business contacts. ATC hosts the major annual conference of government, business, cultural and military leaders each winter in Washington, DC.

WORK

You can extend your time in Turkey by getting a job. Most people who do this teach English at one of the many private colleges or schools in İstanbul or Ankara. Others work at one of the publication offices such as the *Turkish Daily News*.

It's best to obtain a work visa *(çalışma vizesi)* from the Turkish embassy or consulate (in person or by mail; it takes from three weeks) in your home country before you leave. Submit the completed visa form, your passport, two photos of yourself, your proof of employment (a contract or letter from your employer) and the required fee. Your passport will be returned with the visa stamped inside.

If you're not at home and you want a work visa, apply for it before you arrive in Turkey. The Turkish consulate in Komotini in Greece, a day's bus ride from İstanbul, is familiar with such requests. It usually grants the visa within a few hours. If you plan to make a special trip, check to make sure the consulate will be open and issuing work visas when you arrive. Your own consulate or a Greek consulate may be able to tell you (see Embassies & Consulates earlier in this chapter).

Once you arrive in Turkey on a work visa, you must obtain an İkamet Tezkeresi, a combined work and residence permit, from the Yabancılar Polisi (Foreigners' Police) in Cağaloğlu behind the İstanbul Valiliği building on Ankara Caddesi. Your employer may do this for you. If not, apply with your passport, two more photos and the US$40 processing fee. They should have your 'pink book', as it's sometimes called, ready in two or three days. The pink book, which takes over from the visa in your passport, is renewable every year, as long as you show proof of continued employment.

If you can't provide proof of employment (that is, if you're working illegally), you may still be able to get a three-month residence permit if you can show bank deposits in Turkey totalling more than about US$200. You may or may not be able to renew a three-month permit – it's at the whim of the officer.

When all else fails, leave the country for a day or two for Greece, Bulgaria or Cyprus, and get a new 90-day tourist visa as you return to Turkey. However, this may only be possible a few times as the immigration officer will become suspicious of an unbroken series of Turkish stamps in your passport.

FACTS FOR THE VISITOR

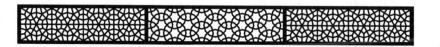

Getting There & Away

AIR

İstanbul's Atatürk airport is Turkey's largest and busiest. See the Getting Around chapter for details on the airport, and ground transportation to and from it.

Check-In Procedures

In the summer months – and particularly July, August and September – Atatürk airport is often overwhelmed with travellers. Allow a *minimum* of 75 to 90 minutes at the airport for security clearance, check-in and passport control for any international flight, or *at least* 45 minutes for a domestic flight. Signs and announcements are not always provided or understandable, so you need to keep asking to make sure you end up at the proper gate.

Departure Tax

Turkey's airport departure tax of approximately US$12 is usually included in the price of your air ticket.

Security

Pack anything which can be construed as a weapon (a pocket knife or screwdriver, for example) in the luggage you will check in (ie, *not* in your carry-on luggage).

As you approach the airport perimeter, your bus or taxi may be stopped and spot-checked by police. On a bus, your passport and ticket may be inspected.

As you enter the terminal, your luggage must go through an x-ray machine. Before you leave the terminal to board your flight, police will frisk you for weapons and your hand baggage will be x-rayed again, and/or searched. If you have neglected to pack potential weapons in your checked luggage, declare them, don't wait until the officer finds them.

As you approach the aircraft, all passengers' checked luggage will be lined up, and you will be asked to point out your bag. It will then be put on board. This is to prevent someone from checking in a bag with a bomb inside it, then not boarding the plane. If you forget to point out your bag to the baggage handler, it may not be loaded on board and may be regarded with distrust, or even destroyed. At the least it will delay the flight while the crew searches for its owner.

Other Parts of Turkey

Turkish Airlines Türk Hava Yolları (THY, Turkish Airlines; symbol: TK), the state-owned airline waiting reluctantly for privatisation, has the major route network in Turkey. When you fly THY, ask about the 10% discount for couples or parent(s) with child(ren) travelling together, and discounts for youth (aged from 12 to 24 years), seniors (60 years and over), and those on a honeymoon or wedding anniversary.

THY flights serve these cities and towns: Adana, Ağrı, Ankara, Antalya, Balıkesir, Batman, Bodrum, Dalaman, Denizli, Diyarbakır, Edremit, Elazığ, Erzincan, Erzurum, Eskişehir, Gaziantep, Isparta, İstanbul, İzmir, Kahramanmaraş, Kars, Kayseri, Konya, Malatya, Muş Samsun, Siirt, Sinop, Sivas, Şanlıurfa, Tokat, Trabzon and Van. Hubs are İstanbul and Ankara; to go from Dalaman to Diyarbakır, for example, you will connect at İstanbul or Ankara.

İstanbul Airlines İstanbul Hava Yolları (symbol: IL) operates a few flights between its namesake city and Adana, Ankara, Antalya, Bodrum, Dalaman, Erzurum, Gaziantep, İzmir, Kars, Trabzon and Van, as well as on international routes to Europe. The domestic flights are essentially feeder operations for the international routes, so most flights operate only once or twice per week.

Prices are usually lower than those of THY. You can make reservations through the reservations centre in İstanbul at Firuzköy Yolu No 26, Avcılar (☎ 212-509 2121, fax 593 6035) and buy tickets at the airport. Discounts include 10% for families, youth fares (12 to 24 years), and seniors over 60 years of age.

Other Countries

Turkish Airlines has daily flights to/from Europe's major cities, New York and Chicago, the Middle East, North Africa and South Africa, Central Asia, Bangkok, Singapore, Osaka and Tokyo.

İstanbul Airlines has weekly or more frequent flights between Turkey and dozens of European cities in Austria, Belgium, Denmark, Eire, France, Germany, Holland, Italy, Spain, Turkish Cyprus and the UK.

Greece Olympic Airlines and Turkish Airlines share the Athens-İstanbul route, offering at least two flights per day in summer. Fares for the 70-minute flight are US$255 one way, US$386 for a round-trip excursion (fixed-date return) ticket.

Western Europe Both Turkish Airlines and İstanbul Airlines fly to Turkey from many points in Europe. Most Turkish Airlines' flights go to the airline's hub in İstanbul, while İstanbul Airlines flies nonstop from Europe to cities such as Adana, Antalya, Dalaman and İzmir. İstanbul Airlines' fares tend to be lower than those of the major carriers, but flights are less frequent, perhaps only once a week.

The normal one-way fare from London to İstanbul is UK£250 (US$425) and up, but there are fixed-date return (excursion) fares as low as UK£175 (US$300). British Airways and Turkish Airlines fly the route nonstop, and most other European airlines do it with one stop.

Don't neglect the European and Turkish charter lines such as Condor (German) and Air Alfa (Turkish), which fly to Turkey from more than a dozen European centres, often for round-trip fares as low as US$225.

Recently some European and Turkish tour operators have been selling complete tours priced below normal airfares. They make up the difference by lodging tour participants in hotels attached to shopping centres, and by depositing participants in shops during each day's touring, then collecting huge commissions on any purchases. These tours can be great bargains if you take advantage of the cheap flight and perhaps some of the hotels, but avoid the shopping, or go shopping on your own, away from the tour.

Middle East Middle Eastern flights by Turkish Airlines include the following weekly nonstop flights to/from İstanbul: two from Bahrain, three from Beirut, two from Dubai, five from Kuwait, four from Tehran, three from Tripoli as well as four from Tunis.

Details of the most popular services to İstanbul from various Middle Eastern cities follow.

Amman Turkish Airlines and Royal Jordanian share the traffic, with about three flights per week. The nonstop 2½-hour flight costs US$310 one way. A round-trip excursion ticket costs about US$388.

Cairo EgyptAir and Turkish Airlines have at least one flight per day between them, charging from US$355 to US$398 one way. It costs from US$408 to US$450 for a round-trip excursion ticket on the nonstop, two-hour flight.

Damascus Syrian Arab Airlines and Turkish Airlines make the 2½-hour flight two days per week and charge from US$240 to US$278 one way, from US$300 to US$326 for a round-trip excursion.

Nicosia (Turkish Side) Turkish Airlines operates nonstop flights connecting Cyprus' Ercan airport (ECN) in Nicosia (Lefkoşa in Turkish) with Adana (four flights weekly), Ankara (five flights weekly), Antalya (one flight weekly), İstanbul (daily, twice daily in summer, US$200 round-trip excursion) and İzmir (four flights weekly).

İstanbul Airlines flies nonstop from Nicosia to Antalya and İstanbul.

Tel Aviv El Al and Turkish Airlines have daily nonstop flights to/from İstanbul for US$333 one way and US$369 for a round-trip excursion. Turkish Airlines also has nonstop flights at least weekly between Tel Aviv and Ankara, Antalya and İzmir.

Azerbaijan & Georgia Turkish Airlines runs flights from İstanbul nonstop to Baku, and nonstop to Tblisi, four days per week.

The USA Turkish Airlines operates daily nonstop flights in summer on the New York-İstanbul route, and a daily service from Chicago (nonstop three days per week). Delta Air Lines also flies nonstop daily. All of the major European airlines offer one-stop service.

Coach-class New York-İstanbul excursion fares sometimes dip below US$500 in the wintertime, and even Los Angeles-İstanbul fares can get as low as US$570 or so; November and early January are particularly cheap times to travel. Summer excursion fares are more like US$650 to US$950.

Australia There are direct flights from Australia to İstanbul offered by Malaysian Airlines (via Kuala Lumpur and Dubai) and Singapore Airlines (via Singapore and Dhahran) with round-trip fares for about A$1800. Cheaper are Middle Eastern Airlines, Gulf Air and EgyptAir with round-trip fares for about A$1600. There are also connecting flights via Athens, London, Rome, Amsterdam or Singapore on Thai International, British Airways, Olympic, Alitalia, KLM, Turkish Airlines and Qantas.

All these airlines regularly have specials (usually during the European low season of mid-January to the end of February and the start of October to mid-November) with most offering fares for A$1400 or less. Usually these specials must be booked and paid for reasonably quickly.

If you can get a cheap fare to London, you might do well once you're there to look for a cheap flight to Turkey.

Airline Offices

Most of the offices are on Cumhuriyet Caddesi between Taksim Square and Harbiye, in the Elmadağ district, but Turkish Airlines has offices around the city. Travel agencies can also sell tickets and make reservations. Some addresses follow:

Aeroflot
   (☎ 212-243 4725, fax 252 3998)
   Mete Caddesi 30, Taksim
Air France
   (☎ 212-254 4356, 254 3196, fax 254 4334)
   corner of Cumhuriyet & Tarlabaşı Caddesis, Taksim;
   (☎ 212-663 0600) Atatürk airport
Alitalia
   (☎ 212-231 3391, 232 7065, fax 230 6304)
   Cumhuriyet Caddesi 12/4, Elmadağ;
   (☎ 212-663 0577) Atatürk airport
American Airlines
   (☎ 212-237 2003, fax 237 2005)
   Cumhuriyet Caddesi 47/2, Elmadağ
British Airways
   (☎ 212-234 1300, fax 234 1308)
   Cumhuriyet Caddesi 10, Elmadağ;
   (☎ 212-663 0574) Atatürk airport
Delta Airlines
   (☎ 212-231 2339, fax 231 2346)
   in the Hilton arcade;
   (☎ 212-663 0752) Atatürk airport
El Al
   (☎ 212-246 5303, fax 230 3705)
   Rumeli Caddesi 4/1, Nişantaşı;
   (☎ 212-663 0810) Atatürk airport
Iberia
   (☎ 212-237 3104, fax 250 5478)
   Topçu Caddesi 2/2, Elmadağ;
   (☎ 212-663 0826) Atatürk airport
İstanbul Airlines
   (☎ 212-231 7526, fax 246 4967)
   Harbiye Ticket Office, Cumhuriyet Caddesi 289;
   (☎ 212-663 0664, fax 663 2712)
   Atatürk airport, international routes;
   (☎ 212-574 4271, fax 663 2713)
   domestic routes
Japan Air Lines
   (☎ 212-241 7366, fax 234 2209)
   Cumhuriyet Caddesi 141/6, Elmadağ

GETTING THERE & AWAY

KLM
(☎ 212-230 0311, fax 232 8749)
Abdi İpekçi Caddesi 8, Nişantaşı, north-east of Harbiye;
(☎ 212-663 0603) Atatürk airport
Lot
(☎ 212-240 7927, fax 246 7626)
Cumhuriyet Caddesi 91/2, Elmadağ
Lufthansa
(☎ 212-288 1050, fax 275 6961)
Maya Akar Center, Büyükdere Caddesi 100-102, Esentepe;
(☎ 212-663 0594) Atatürk airport
Malev
(☎ 212-248 8153, fax 230 2034)
Cumhuriyet Caddesi 141, Elmadağ;
(☎ 212-663 6400) Atatürk airport
Olympic Airways
(☎ 212-246 5081, fax 232 2173)
Cumhuriyet Caddesi 203, Elmadağ;
(☎ 212-663 0820) Atatürk airport
Qantas Airways
(☎ 212-240 5032, fax 241 5552)
Cumhuriyet Caddesi 155/1, Elmadağ
Sabena
(☎ 212-254 7254, fax 240 1513)
Topçu Caddesi 2/1, Taksim;
(☎ 212-663 0824) Atatürk airport
SAS
(☎ 212-246 6075, fax 233 8803)
Cumhuriyet Caddesi 26/A, Elmadağ;
(☎ 212-663 0818) Atatürk airport
Singapore Airlines
(☎ 212-232 3706, fax 248 8620)
Halaskargazi Caddesi 113, Harbiye;
(☎ 212-663 0710) Atatürk airport
Swissair
(☎ 212-231 2850, fax 240 1513)
Cumhuriyet Caddesi 6, Elmadağ;
(☎ 212-663 6778) Atatürk airport
Turkish Airlines
(☎ 212-663 6363, fax 240 2984)
reservations;
(☎ 212-252 1106)
Taksim Square Ticket Office, Cumhuriyet Caddesi, in the Taksim Gezi Yeri shops

BUS
Other Parts of Turkey

The bus and the *dolmuş* (minibus) are the most widespread and popular means of transport in Turkey. Buses go literally everywhere, all the time. Virtually every first-time traveller in Turkey comments on the convenience of the bus system.

The bus service runs the gamut from plain and inexpensive to comfortable and moderately priced. It is so cheap and convenient that many erstwhile long-distance hitchers opt for the bus. The six-hour, 450km trip between İstanbul and Ankara, for example, costs only US$15 to US$24, depending on the bus company.

Though bus fares are open to competition among companies, and even to haggling for a reduction, the cost of bus travel in Turkey usually works out to be around US$2.25 to US$2.75 per 100km – a surprising bargain.

Main Intercity Bus Terminal The International İstanbul Bus Trminal (☎ 212-658 0505, fax 658 2858), Uluslararası İstanbul Otogarı, called simply the 'otogar', is in the western district of Esenler, just south of an expressway and about 10km west of Sultanahmet or Taksim. With 168 ticket offices, restaurants, mosques and shops, it is a town in itself, and one of the world's largest bus terminals. For Turkish travellers, this is the domestic equivalent of London-Heathrow or New York-JFK.

Buses depart the otogar for virtually all cities and towns in Turkey and to neighbouring countries including Azerbaijan, Bulgaria, Greece, Iran, Romania, Saudi Arabia, Syria, and other destinations in eastern Europe and the Middle East. The top national lines, giving premium service at somewhat higher prices, are As Turizm (office 117), Bosfor Turizm (127), Pamukkale (43), Ulusoy (128) and Varan (15). Other lines are smaller regional or local lines which may have more frequent service and less polished service at lower prices.

Except in busy holiday periods, you can usually just come to the otogar, spend 30 minutes shopping for tickets, and be on your way to your destination at a good price within the hour. There is no easy way to find the best bus company and the best fare; you've got to go from one office to another asking for information and looking at the buses parked at the *perons* (gates) at the back.

Metro, municipal buses and taxis connect the otogar with the city centre and the

GETTING THERE & AWAY

airport. See the Getting Around chapter for details.

Harem Bus Terminal There is another bus terminal on the Asian shore of the Bosphorus at Harem (☎ 216-333 3763), 2km north-west of Haydarpaşa train station. If you're arriving from the east, by all means get out at Harem and take the car ferry to Sirkeci; it'll save you two hours' crawl through traffic to the main otogar, then the Metro ride back to the centre. If you're heading east you can save some time and hassle by taking the Harem car ferry from Sirkeci and getting the bus there. But the selection of buses, seats, routes and companies is nowhere near as big at Harem as at the main otogar in Esenler.

Bus Ticket Offices Travel agencies on Divan Yolu by the Hippodrome and in Cankurtaran will sell you bus tickets, often at inflated prices.

Some bus companies have city ticket offices near Taksim Square on Mete and İnönü Caddesis. Pamukkale (☎ 249 2791) is at Mete Caddesi 16; Nev Tur (☎ 249 7961), with buses to Cappadocia, is nearby. Down the hill along İnönü are Varan (☎ 249 1903, 251 7481), at İnönü Caddesi 29/B, a premium line with routes to major Turkish cities and to several points in Europe (including Athens); Kamil Koç (☎ 257 7223), İnönü Caddesi 31; As Turizm and Hakiki Koç lines (☎ 245 4244); and Ulusoy (☎ 249 4373), İnönü Caddesi 59.

Fares & Travel Times Here are some examples of bus fares and travel times to/from İstanbul. Fares vary among companies, and sometimes can be reduced by haggling or by showing a student card. Departures to major cities and resorts are very frequent.

destination	distance (km)	duration (hours)	price (US$)
Alanya	840	17	23
Ankara	450	6	15-24
Antakya	1115	20	23-31
Antalya	725	12	16-20
Artvin	1352	24	34-40
Ayvalık	570	9	16-21
Bodrum	830	14	24
Bursa	230	4	9
Çanakkale	340	6	9-12
Denizli (for Pamukkale)	665	13	13-20
Edirne	235	2½	6
Erzurum	1275	18	18-30
Fethiye	980	12-14	18-23
Gaziantep	1136	14	21
Göreme (Cappadocia)	725	11	12-18
İzmir	610	8	12
Kaş	1090	14	20
Konya	660	10	16
Kuşadası	700	10	15
Marmaris	900	14	18-24
Side	790	12	19-24
Trabzon	1110	18	20-30

Other Countries

Turkish bus companies operate frequent passenger services between Europe and Turkey, but the bus trip takes days, the flight only hours; and a cheap airfare is usually cheaper than the bus fare from western or central Europe, especially when you add the cost of bus-trip meals and incidentals.

Greece The buses to İstanbul depart from the Peloponnese railway station (OSE Hellenic Railways Organisation, Plateia Peloponisu) in Athens.

Varan Turizm (☎ 1-513 5768) operates daily buses to and from İstanbul via Thessaloniki, as does Ulusoy Turizm (☎ 1-524 0519, fax 524 3290), also at the Peloponnese railway station. The trip takes about 20 hours and costs about US$65 from Athens and US$40 one way from Thessaloniki.

Elsewhere in Europe Going by bus is often faster and more comfortable than the now-neglected trains, and comparable in price.

Several Turkish bus lines, including Ulusoy and Varan/Bosfor, offer service between İstanbul and some central European cities such as Frankfurt, Munich and Vienna; the trip may take 30 to 45 hours. One-way tickets range from US$85 to

US$140 – so there's little savings over a cheap air ticket. Round-trip fares are discounted about 20%. The major discomfort on the trip may be cigarette smoke.

TRAIN

Turkish State Railways (TC Devlet Demiryolları, TCDD or DDY) runs services to many parts of the country on lines laid out by German companies which were supposedly paid for by the kilometre. Some newer, more direct lines have been laid during the republican era, shortening travel times for the best express trains.

Alas, TCDD trains are the poor cousins in Turkey's transport mix. In the past few decades millions have been poured into highways and airports, but very little into the railway network. Passenger equipment has a distinctly 1960s look to it, with many holes, patches and cigarette burns since then.

Other Parts of Turkey

It's not a good idea to plan a train trip all the way across Turkey in one stretch as the country is large, and the cross-country trains are slower than the buses. For

---

The Orient Express

The fabled *Orient Express*, which first ran between Paris and Constantinople in 1883, was removed from the timetables and the rails in 1977 and replaced by the İstanbul Express to Munich.

In the 1960s and 1970s, there was little romance left on the famed *Orient Express* route from Paris (Gare de l'Est) via Lausanne, Milan, Venice, Trieste, Belgrade, Sofia and Edirne to İstanbul. The trains were not well kept, and were always many hours – even days – late.

When armed conflict does not make rail travel through the Balkans impossible, the *Orient Express* lives on in special excursion trains with various names, but the fares for these deluxe tours cost between US$2500 and US$5500 one way. These packages include transportation from European points to İstanbul aboard restored railway coaches, with lectures and optional side-trips. By the way, the train which now bears the name *Venice-Simplon Orient Express* goes nowhere near İstanbul on its run between London and Venice.

From its first journey in 1882, the **Orient Express** carried many important and famous passengers – from opera singers to spies to kings travelling incognito. Tickets were expensive: a return ticket for two was equivalent to the yearly rent of a home in the classier suburbs of London. Sleeping cars like the one above were first built for the train in 1882.

example, the *Vangölü Ekspresi* from İstanbul to Lake Van (Tatvan), a 1900km trip, takes almost two full days – and that's an express! The bus would take less than 24 hours, the plane under two hours. Train travel between Ankara and İstanbul is fast and pleasant, however.

Whenever you take an intercity train in Turkey, you'd do well to take only *mavi tren* (blue train), *ekspres* or *mototren* trains. These are fairly fast, comfortable, and often not too much more expensive than the bus. On *yolcu* (passenger) and *posta* (mail) trains, however, you could grow old and die before reaching your destination.

Note that Turkish train schedules indicate *stations*, not cities; the station name is usually, but not always, the city name. Thus you may not see İstanbul on a schedule, but you will see Haydarpaşa and Sirkeci, the Asian and European stations in İstanbul.

Top Trains Here are the top trains serving İstanbul. All trains are daily unless otherwise noted, and all schedules and fares are subject to change.

Anadolu Ekspresi This nightly couchette and coach train between **Ankara** and **İstanbul** (Haydarpaşa) via Eskişehir hauls Pullman (US$6.50) and couchette *(kuşetli)* (US$8) cars. It departs Ankara and İstanbul at 10 pm and arrives in the other city at 7 am.

Ankara Ekspresi Sleeping compartments on this nightly all-sleeping-car express between **Ankara** and **İstanbul** (Haydarpaşa) cost US$25/40 a single/double. It departs Ankara and İstanbul at 10.30 pm and arrives in the other city at 7.35 am.

Başkent Ekspresi The Capital Express, pride of the Turkish State Railways, departs **İstanbul** and **Ankara** at 10.30 am and makes the run to the opposite city in seven hours, the fastest train of all. It's an air-con, super-1st-class day train between İstanbul (Haydarpaşa) and Ankara with Pullman seats, video and meals served at your seat, airline-style. The fare is US$12, or US$9 for students.

Boğaziçi Ekspresi The Bosphorus Express is a comfortable if faded 1st-class, Pullman-car train costing US$6.50 between **İstanbul** (Haydarpaşa) and **Ankara**, departing each city at 1.55 pm, and arriving in the other at 10 pm.

Doğu Ekspresi Though this train departs from **İstanbul** (Haydarpaşa) on time at 11.55 pm, it is usually late thereafter on its long trip via **Ankara, Sivas, Erzincan** and **Erzurum** to **Kars** near the Armenian border. It is a long (about 45 hours) and not particularly pleasant trip, but it is certainly cheap, costing only US$18/13 in 1st/2nd class. There are coaches only, no sleeping accommodation. See also Yeni Doğu Ekspresi, later.

Fatih Ekspresi Named for Mehmet the Conqueror (Fatih), this is a night train departing **İstanbul** (Haydarpaşa) and **Ankara** at 11.30 pm, arriving in the opposite city at 7.10 am, otherwise similar to the *Başkent* in comfort, speed and price.

Güney/Vangölü Ekspresi This train departs **İstanbul** (Haydarpaşa) each evening at 8 pm, and departs **Ankara** (5.55 am), **Kayseri** (2.32 pm), **Sivas** (6.48 pm), **Malatya** (1.20 am) before coming to **Elazığ Junction**. East of the junction, the train continues as the *Vangölü* (Lake Van) *Ekspresi* to **Tatvan** (arrives 2.30 pm), or the *Güney* (Southern) *Ekspresi* to **Diyarbakır** (8.25 am) and **Kurtalan** (east of Diyarbakır, arrives 12.05 pm), depending upon the day.

For the *Vangölü* eastbound, board in İstanbul on Monday, Wednesday or Saturday, or in Ankara, Kayseri or Sivas on Tuesday, Thursday or Sunday.

For the *Güney*, board in İstanbul on Tuesday, Thursday, Friday or Sunday, or in Ankara, Kayseri or Sivas on Monday, Wednesday, Friday or Saturday.

These trains haul sleepers and 2nd-class coaches. A one-way 1st/2nd-class ticket from Ankara costs US$12/9 to Tatvan, US$10/7 to

Diyarbakır. The fare in a sleeping car is from US$20/37/52 for one/two/three people.

İç Anadolu Mavi Tren This coach and couchette train departs İstanbul at 11.50 pm via Kütahya (6.10 am), Afyon (8.02 am) and Konya (noon) to Karaman (1.40 pm), for US$10; couchette US$12.

İstanbul-Ankara Mavi Tren 'Blue Trains' are comfortable expresses with 1st-class Pullman-style seats only. The İstanbul-Ankara Mavi Tren departs each city at 1 pm, arrives in the other at 8.11 pm. The one-way fare is US$9. The *Ek Mavi I* departs at noon and arrives at 7.35 pm; the *Ek Mavi II* departs at 9 pm and arrives at 6.20 am.

Marmara Ekspresi Take one of the several daily fast car ferries *(hızlı feribot)* from İstanbul's Yenikapı docks to Bandırma to catch the Marmara Ekspresi, a motor-train which departs Bandırma each afternoon at 3 pm, reaching İzmir (Basmane) by 9.15 pm, for US$3. The return train departs İzmir (Basmane) at 8 am, arriving in Bandırma at 2.12 pm, connecting with a fast car ferry to İstanbul (Yenikapı).

Meram Ekspresi The Meram departs İstanbul (Haydarpaşa) daily at 7.30 pm via Kütahya (1.55 am) and Afyon (4 am), arriving in Konya at 8.10 am. The İstanbul-Konya fare is US$8/5 in 1st/2nd class; for sleeping compartments, total fares are US$20/38/56 for singles/doubles/triples.

Pamukkale Ekspresi The night-time Pamukkale Express departs from İstanbul (Haydarpaşa) daily at 6.30 pm, via Kütahya (12.46 am), Afyon (2.20 am), Isparta (6.14 am), Burdur (7.40 am), Eğirdir (8.03 am), arriving in Denizli at 9.10 am. İstanbul-Denizli fares are US$8/5 in 1st/2nd class; for sleeping compartments, total fares are US$20/38/56 for singles/doubles/triples.

Toros Ekspresi This train departs from İstanbul (Haydarpaşa) on Tuesday, Thursday and Sunday at 8.25 am and heads for the south-east, stopping in Eskişehir (Enveriye, 1.55 pm), Afyon (5.40 pm), Konya (10.10 pm), Adana (4.50 am) and finally Gaziantep (11.40 am). On the return trip, it departs Gaziantep at 2.40 pm, Adana at 9.45 pm, Konya at 4.55 am, Afyon at 9.02 am, and Eskişehir at 12.35 pm, to arrive in İstanbul (Haydarpaşa) at 5.54 pm. Fares from İstanbul are US$7 to Konya, US$10 to Adana, and US$13 to Gaziantep. A sleeping car between İstanbul and Gaziantep costs US$20/25/28 a single/double/triple, total fare.

Vangölü Ekspresi See *Güney/Vangölü Ekspresi*, earlier.

Yeni Doğu Ekspresi The newer, faster cousin of the Doğu Ekspresi (see earlier), the Yeni Doğu runs from İstanbul (Haydarpaşa) to Kars in about 33 hours, departing İstanbul's Haydarpaşa station on Tuesday, Thursday and Saturday at 1.30 pm, arriving in Ankara at 9 pm and departing thence at 9.10 pm for Sivas (6.40 am), Erzurum (6.10 pm) and Kars (10.20 pm). On its return, the train departs Kars at 8.30 am, Erzurum at 12.40 pm, Sivas at 11.45 pm and Ankara at 10.20 am, arriving in İstanbul (Haydarpaşa) at 5.30 pm. Tickets between Ankara and Erzurum cost US$10 for a 1st-class seat, or US$18/30 for a single/double berth in a sleeping car. To go all the way from İstanbul to Kars costs only US$20/15 in a 1st/2nd-class seat, or US$30/55 in a single/double sleeping compartment.

Buying Tickets Most seats on the best trains, and all sleeping compartments, must be reserved. As the best trains are popular, particularly the sleeping-car trains, you should make your reservation and buy your ticket as far in advance as possible. A few days will usually suffice, except at holiday times (see Public Holidays & Special Events in the Facts for the Visitor chapter). Weekend trains, between Friday evening and Monday morning, seem to be the busiest.

If you can't buy in advance, check at the station anyway. There may be cancellations, even at the last minute.

Though Turkish State Railways now has a computerised reservations system, it is usually impossible to book sleeping-car space except in the city from which the train departs. You can buy tickets at the station, at some post offices (PTTs) in the major cities, and at some travel agencies.

Classes of Travel Most of the best trains, and the short-haul *mototrens* (motor-trains) and rail-buses now have only one class of travel. Coaches on the top trains (*Başkent* and *Fatih Ekspresi, Mavi Tren*) usually have Pullman reclining seats; the normal expresses usually have European-style compartments with six seats. The very slow trains and those in the east often have 1st and 2nd-class coaches with compartments.

Sleeping accommodation is of three classes. A *kuşetli* (couchette) wagon has six-person compartments with seats which rearrange into six shelf-like beds at night; you sleep with strangers. *Örtülü kuşetli* means the couchettes have bedding (sheets, pillows, blanket), and there may be only four beds per compartment, so two couples travelling together can get an almost private compartment. A *yataklı* wagon has European-style sleeping compartments capable of sleeping up to three people. Price depends upon the number of occupants: per person cost is lowest when three share, highest if you want a compartment all to yourself.

Discounts & Passes Inter-Rail passes are valid on the Turkish State Railways' entire network; Eurail passes are not valid on any of it.

Full fare is called *tam*. Round-trip (return) fares, called *Gidiş-Dönüş*, are discounted by 20%. Student (*öğrenci* or *talebe*) fares discounted by 20 to 30% are offered on most routes (show your ISIC). If you are under 26 years of age or over 55, you can buy a Tren-Tur card which allows you one month's unlimited rail travel. Ask at Sirkeci station in İstanbul, or at the Ankara Garı. Families (*aile*), meaning a married couple travelling with or without children, are entitled to a 20 to 30% discount; disabled persons get 30% off, press card holders 50% off.

Cancellation Penalties If you decide not to travel and you seek a refund for your rail ticket up to 24 hours before the train's departure, you must pay a cancellation fee of 10% of the ticket price. Within 24 hours of departure the fee rises to 25%. After the train has departed the fee is 50%.

Other Countries

Few travellers choose to travel to Turkey by train these days. The *Orient Express* is long gone (although its name lives on in excursion train tours nowhere near İstanbul). Excursion airfares are often lower than international rail fares, and the flight takes only hours, not days. Even the bus is usually faster than the train.

All trains from Europe terminate at Sirkeci Garı (SEER-keh-jee, ☎ 212-527 0051), next to Eminönü in the shadow of Topkapı Palace. The station has a small post office and currency exchange booth, as well as a restaurant and cafe, and a tourism office (☎ 212-511 5888).

The northern facade of the building was where passengers entered to board the fabled *Orient Express* to Paris. The new main (west) station door is a boring modern structure.

Greece The daily Thessaloniki-İstanbul passenger train takes 16 to 18 hours to cover the 850km. Almost a century ago, under the Ottoman Empire, it took 13½ hours. The bus covers the distance in greater comfort in about half the time.

Central Europe At this writing there are no direct trains between Western or central Europe and Turkey. To travel from Munich to İstanbul, for example, you must change trains in Vienna and again in Belgrade; or Budapest and Niš, a journey of close to 40 hours. There is a daily direct train service between Budapest and İstanbul (*Balkan Express*, 31 hours) and Bucharest and İstanbul (*Bucharest-İstanbul Express*, 17 hours).

CAR & MOTORCYCLE

Don't plan to get around İstanbul by private vehicle. The traffic is horrendous, the driving cavalier and the signage insufficient. If you arrive in Turkey by car or motorcycle, plan to park your vehicle in a safe place for the duration of your stay in İstanbul, taking it out only for excursions out of the city.

If you plan to rent a car for excursions to Thrace, Edirne, Gallipoli and/or Troy, you might want to pick it up at the airport. This saves you the hassle of fighting your way out of the city centre. It's easy to get on the highway westward from the airport.

If you plan to go south to İznik, Bursa and other parts of Anatolia, you may want to have the car delivered for pick-up at the Yenikapı Hızlı Feribot İskelesi (Yenikapı fast ferryboat dock). That way you can get right on the ferry, and you won't have to fight the city's inscrutable traffic patterns and rocket-powered drivers.

Other Parts of Turkey

Road Conditions The quality of Turkish highways is passable. The Türkiye Cumhuriyeti Karayolları (Turkish Republic Highways Department or TCK) undertakes ambitious improvements constantly, but despite its efforts most roads still have only two lanes, perhaps with overtaking lanes on long uphill grades. Otoyols (expressways/ motorways) run from the Bulgarian border near Edirne to İstanbul and Ankara.

The expressways are often busy but not impossible; the lesser highways can be busy or pleasantly traffic-free. City streets are usually thronged.

In the cities *düzensizlik* (disorder) is universal. In addition to the customary and very appropriate *Allah Korusun* ('May God Protect Me') emblazoned somewhere on every Turkish car, bus and truck, imagine the additional motto *Önce Ben* ('Me First').

Highway Safety Turkey has one of the world's highest motor vehicle accident rates, with about 7000 deaths a year, and tens of thousands of injuries. The government, media and several private groups have undertaken a vigorous driver education safety campaign, urging motorists to tame the 'Trafik Canavarı' (Motoring Monster) within them, to drive considerately and at a safe speed; but it may be years before the campaign has an effect.

Though terrors in the city, Turkish drivers are not particularly discourteous out on the highway, but they are impatient and incautious. They drive at high speed and have an irrepressible urge to overtake you. To survive on Turkey's highways, drive very defensively, avoid driving at night, and *never* let emotions affect what you do.

Fuel Fuel stations are everywhere, operated by some familiar international companies (BP, Shell, Mobil) and unfamiliar Turkish ones (Türk Petrol, Petrol Ofisi). Many never close, others stay open long hours, so refuelling is usually no problem. All the same, it's a good idea to have a full tank when you start out in the morning across the vast spaces of central and eastern Anatolia.

Most accept credit cards in payment, though they may not be able to get approval for your charge due to insufficient telephone lines.

Benzin (petrol/gasoline) comes as *normal, süper* and *kurşunsuz* (the last being unleaded). Normal costs about US$0.80 per litre (US$3 per US gallon); süper, about US$0.82 per litre (US$3.10 per US gallon); kurşunsuz, about US$0.87 per litre (US$3.30 per US gallon). *Dizel* (diesel) costs about US$0.55 per litre (US$2.08 per US gallon).

Some stations give a free car wash when you fill your tank.

Spares & Repairs Turkey's equivalent of the Automobile Association (UK) and American Automobile Association (USA) is the Türkiye Turing ve Otomobile Kurumu (TTOK), the Turkish Touring & Automobile Association (☎ 212-282 8140, fax 282 8042), Oto Sanayi Sitesi Yanı, Seyrantepe, 4 Levent, İstanbul. It is useful for driving aids (maps, lists of repair shops, legal necessities) as well as for repairs and advice on repairs.

Spare parts for most cars may be available, if not readily so, outside the big cities. European models (especially Renaults, Fiats and Mercedes-Benz) are preferred, though ingenious Turkish mechanics contrive to keep all manner of huge US models – some half a century old – in daily service.

If you have a model with which Turkish mechanics are familiar, repairs can be swift and very cheap. Don't be afraid of little roadside repair shops, which can often provide excellent, virtually immediate service, though they (or you) may have to go somewhere else to get the parts. The Sanayi Bölgesi (industrial zone) on the outskirts of every city and town has a row of repair shops.

It's always good to get an estimate of the repair cost in advance. Ask *Tamirat kaç para?* ('How much will repairs cost?'). For tyre repairs find an *oto lastikçi* (tyre repairer). Repair shops are closed on Sunday, but even so, if you go to the repair shop district of town (every town has one: ask for the *sanayi bölgesi*) and look around, you may still find someone willing and able to help you.

Traffic Police *Trafik Polisi* in black-and-white cars (usually Renaults) and blue uniforms set up checkpoints on major highways in order to make sure that vehicle documents are in order, that you are wearing your seat belt, and that vehicle safety features are in working condition. They busy themselves mostly with trucks and buses, as that is where lie the greatest possibilities for supplemental income. They'll usually wave you on, but you should slow down and prepare to stop until you get the wave.

If you are stopped, officers may ask for your car registration, insurance certificate and driving licence. They may ask you to turn on your headlights (high and low beam),

hoot your horn, switch on your turning signals and windscreen wipers etc, to see that all are working properly. They'll certainly ask your nationality, and try to chat, because one of the reasons you (an 'exotic' foreigner) have been stopped is to break the monotony of checking trucks. If they seem to be requesting money, refuse to understand.

Other Countries

The major routes from Europe to İstanbul are usually heavily trafficked by trucks and buses. It's not a pleasant drive. The final stretch from Edirne to İstanbul is a breeze on the *otoyol* (multi-lane divided toll highway).

Normally, you cannot rent a car in Europe and include Turkey (or many other eastern European countries) in your driving plans. If you want to leave your car in Turkey and return for it later, the car must be put under customs seal, usually a tedious process.

You don't really need an International Driving Permit (IDP) when you drive in Turkey, despite what some travel books say. Your home driving licence, unless it's something unusual (say, from Burkina Faso), will be accepted by traffic police and by car rental firms. If you'd feel more secure against bureaucratic hassle by carrying an IDP, you can get one through your automobile club in your home country. Always carry your normal licence as well.

Do not drive someone else's car into Turkey. The car will be entered in the driver's passport as imported goods, and must be driven out of the country by the same visitor within the time period allowed.

No special car documents are required for visits of up to three months. For stays longer than three months, or for any other information regarding car travel in Turkey, contact the Turkish Touring & Automobile Association (see under 'Spares & Repairs' earlier for details).

HITCHING

Long-distance hitching in Turkey, though possible, is uncommon. When you hitch *(otostop)*, Turkish custom requires that you

GETTING THERE & AWAY

offer to pay for your ride. The bus and minibus network is so elaborate and cheap that most people opt for that, figuring that if bus fares must be paid, bus comforts might as well be enjoyed. Women in particular should not hitch in Turkey.

The signal used in hitching is not an up-turned thumb. In Turkey, you face the traffic, hold your arm out towards the road, and wave your hand and arm up and down as though bouncing a basketball.

If you hitch in from another country, don't be the one driving the car when crossing the border, or it will be registered in your passport and you will have to take it out or pay a huge duty when you leave. Also, if contraband (drugs etc) is found hidden in the car, customs officers will assume that it's yours.

BOAT

Luxury cruise ships frequently dock at İstanbul during Aegean or Mediterranean cruises, and fast ferryboats bring people here from other parts of Turkey.

Other Parts of Turkey

Turkish Maritime Administration (Türkiye Denizcilik İşletmeleri), also called Turkish Maritime Lines (TML) operates car and passenger ferries from İstanbul eastward along the Black Sea coast and southward through the Aegean to İzmir, as well as car and passenger ferry services in the Sea of Marmara.

Car Ferry Car and passenger ferries save you days of driving. Even if you have no car, they offer the opportunity to take mini-cruises along the Turkish coasts. Room on these ships is usually in hot demand, so reserve as far in advance as possible through one of TML's agents (see later), or directly with the İstanbul Karaköy office by fax.

İstanbul to İzmir The İstanbul-İzmir car ferry service operates each weekend throughout the year, departing İstanbul's Sarayburnu dock each Friday at 3 pm, arriving in İzmir on Saturday at 9 am. Departure

from İzmir is on Sunday at 2 pm, arriving in İstanbul on Monday at 9 am.

One-way fares (per person) range from Pullman seats for US$35 to deluxe cabin berths for US$150; a two-berth, B-class cabin would cost US$160 a double. Should you want to use your cabin as a hotel room on Saturday night in İzmir, the cost ranges from US$45 a double for the cheapest cabin to US$165 a double for deluxe, with a two-berth, B-class cabin costing US$95.

Meals are extra, at US$7 for breakfast, US$15 for lunch and US$15 for dinner. The fare for a car is US$60 one way, less than half that for a motorcycle.

İstanbul to Trabzon Car ferries operate each week from early June to mid-September, departing from İstanbul on Monday at 2 pm, stopping briefly in Sinop, arriving in Samsun on Tuesday at 6.30 pm and departing at 8.30 pm, arriving in Trabzon on Wednesday at 9.30 am.

The boat continues to Rize, returning to Trabzon and departing on the return voyage to İstanbul at 4.30 pm on Wednesday. The returning ferry stops briefly at Giresun, Samsun and Sinop, arriving back in İstanbul on Friday at 2 pm.

Per-person fares between İstanbul and Trabzon are US$35 for a Pullman seat, US$50 to US$160 for cabin berths; meals cost US$7 for breakfast, US$15 for lunch or dinner extra. Cars cost US$56; motorcycles, US$25.

Catamaran & Fast Car Ferries Fast catamaran passenger and car ferries connect İstanbul's Yenikapı seabus port with Yalova (near İznik and Bursa) and Bandırma where you can catch a train to İzmir. See the relevant sections for details.

There is also a traditional (meaning slow) car ferry service every half-hour between Gebze (Eskihisar docks), on the coast east of Üsküdar, and Topçular, east of Yalova on the Sea of Marmara's southern shore. A similar car ferry shuttles between Hereke and Karamürsel, further east. The drive (or bus ride) east around the Bay of İzmit is long, boring, congested and the scenery's ugly. Take one of these ferries instead.

Other Countries

Comfortable car ferry services operate between Italian and Greek ports and several Turkish ports. However, there are no direct connections with İstanbul.

Turkish Maritime Lines Turkish Maritime Lines (Denizyolları, or TML) operates comfortable car and passenger ferries departing from Venice on Wednesday afternoon, arriving in İzmir midday on Saturday; departing İzmir on Saturday evening, and arriving in Venice on Tuesday at noon.

Per-person one-way Venice-İzmir fares range from US$215 to US$240 for a Pullman seat to US$600 for a berth in a luxury cabin; the fare for each of two berths in an air-conditioned, B-class cabin with shower and toilet is US$390 in the busy summer months; three meals and port tax are included in these examples. A car costs US$260 one way.

Another TML service operates in summer, departing Brindisi, Italy around noon on Tuesday, Wednesday, Friday and Saturday, arriving in Çeşme, on the following evening around suppertime; departing Çeşme late in the evening on Wednesday, Thursday, Saturday and Sunday, arriving in Brindisi at breakfast time two days later.

Per-person, one-way Brindisi-Çeşme fares range from US$155 for a Pullman seat to US$402 for a berth in a luxury cabin; the fare for each of two berths in an air-con, B-class cabin with shower and toilet is US$236 in the busy summer months; three meals and port tax are included in these examples. A car costs US$228 one way.

For more information, contact TML at the following addresses:

Brindisi
(☎ 0831-568 633) Corso Garibaldi SpA, 19 72100 Zacmari, Brindisi, Italy

İstanbul
(☎ 212-249 9222, fax 251 9025) Türkiye Denizcilik İşletmeleri, Rıhtım Caddesi, Karaköy, İstanbul, Turkey
İzmir
(☎ 232-421 1484, fax 421 1481) Türkiye Denizcilik İşletmeleri Acenteliği, Yeniliman, Alsancak, İzmir, Turkey
London
(☎ 0171-923 3230, fax 923 3118), Alternative Holidays Ltd, 146 Kingsland High St, London E8 2NS, UK; (☎ 0181-211 7779, fax 211 8891) Pasha Travel Ltd, 9 Grand Parade, Green Lane, Haringay, London N4 1JX, UK
Venice
(☎ 041-522 9544, fax 520 4009) Bassani SpA, Via 22 Marzo 2414, 30124 Venezia, Italy

Med Link Lines Med Link Lines operates two ferries, the *Poseidon* and the *Maria G* on the route Brindisi-Igoumenitsa-Patras-Çeşme from June to September. Fares tend to be lower than on TML, and there are reductions for students travelling in Deck, Pullman or C-class cabins (four to eight beds).

Departures from Brindisi are on Tuesday, Wednesday and Saturday, from Çeşme on Monday, Thursday, Friday and Sunday.

For information, contact MLL at:

Brindisi
(☎ 0831-52 76 67, fax 56 40 70) Discovery Shipping Agency, 49 Corso Garibaldi, 72100 Brindisi, Italy
Çeşme
(☎ 232-712 7230, fax 712 8987) Karavan Shipping, Belediye Dükkanları 3, by the harbour, Çeşme, Turkey
Cologne
(☎ 221-257 3781, fax 257 3682) Viamare see-touristik, Apostelnstrasse 9, 50667 Köln, Germany
Igoumenitsa
(☎ 0665-26 833, fax 26 111) Eleni Pantazi, 8 December St No 27, Igoumenitsa, Greece
Patras
(☎ 061-62 30 11, fax 62 33 20) George Giannatos, Othonos Amalias St 15, Patras, Greece

WARNING

Information in this chapter is particularly vulnerable to change: prices for international travel are volatile, routes are introduced and cancelled, schedules change, special deals come and go, and rules and visa requirements are amended. Airlines and governments seem to take a perverse pleasure in making price structures and regulations as complicated as possible. You should check directly with the airline or a travel agent to make sure you understand how a fare (and ticket you may buy) works. In addition, the travel industry is highly competitive and there are many lurks and perks.

The upshot of this is that you should get opinions, quotes and advice from as many airlines and travel agents as possible before you part with your hard-earned cash. The details given in this chapter should be regarded as pointers and are not a substitute for your own careful, up-to-date research.

GETTING THERE & AWAY

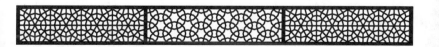

Getting Around

Even though several wide boulevards have been cut through the city's medieval street pattern, and modern expressways now fly past its medieval walls, they are often insufficient to move the glut of traffic quickly. For much of the day, transport by road creeps. Transport by sea is far more pleasant and speedy, although it serves only a handful of routes. Transport by rail is useful, though limited.

ATATÜRK AIRPORT

İstanbul's Atatürk airport, 23km west of the Hippodrome, presently has three terminals: international *(Dış Hatlar)*, domestic *(İç Hatlar)*, and Terminal C, used mostly for charter and small-airline flights. A new, larger and much-needed international terminal is under construction.

From the international terminal to the domestic terminal, take the infrequent Havaş shuttle, or a rip-off taxi for US$3, or make the eight-minute walk. Terminal C is about a 10-minute walk from the domestic terminal, or a US$3 taxi ride.

TO/FROM THE AIRPORT
Airport to City

The fastest way to get into town from the airport is by taxi (from 20 to 30 minutes, US$10 to US$20); the fare depends upon what part of the city you're headed for and whether it's night or day.

A far cheaper but less speedy alternative is the Havaş airport bus (from 35 to 60 minutes, US$3.50), which departs from the domestic terminal, then goes to Taksim Square. Buses leave every half-hour from 5.30 to 10 am, every hour from 10 am to 2 pm, every half-hour from 2 to 8 pm, and every hour from 9 to 11 pm; there are no buses between 11 pm and 5.30 am.

For even less, find two or three other thrifty travellers and share a taxi (US$5 total; make sure the driver runs the meter) from the airport to the Yeşilköy *banliyö*

tren istasyonu, the suburban railway station in the neighbouring town of Yeşilköy. From here, battered trains (US$0.50) run every half-hour or less to Sirkeci station. Get off at Cankurtaran for Sultanahmet hotels, or at Sirkeci (end of the line) for Beyoğlu.

City to Airport

You must check in *at least* 45 minutes before departure time for domestic flights. For international flights, you should be in line at the check-in counter at least 1½ hours before take-off as it can take a half-hour just to get through the first security check and into the terminal building. After check-in, you must go through passport control, customs and another security check before boarding. If the aircraft is large, the officials will have to process about 400 passengers at once.

If you're staying in Old İstanbul, you can get on a suburban train ('Halkalı', US$0.50) at Sirkeci, Cankurtaran or Yenikapı, and get out at Yeşilköy, then take a taxi (US$5) to the airport.

There are also frequent minibus dolmuşes from the corner of Şehit Muhtarbey and Aydede caddesis just north of Taksim Square (US$1.50).

Several private services run minibuses to the airport, advertising their services at budget hotels in and around Sultanahmet. Fares range from US$4 to US$6 per person. Reserve your seat in advance for pick-up from your hotel. Allow lots of time for the trip: the minibus may spend an hour circulating through the city collecting all the passengers before heading out to the airport (30 to 45 minutes).

If you're staying in Beyoğlu, the cheapest and most convenient way to the airport is the Havaş bus (US$3.50) which departs from in front of the DHL office on Cumhuriyet Caddesi just north of the Mc-Donald's in Taksim Square. The trip takes 45 minutes to an hour. There are also dolmuşes to the airport (Hava Limanı) from the Yeşilköy-Ataköy-Florya-Hava Limanı dolmuş stand on Şehit Muhtar Bey Caddesi two blocks north of Taksim.

A taxi to the airport costs US$10 to US$20.

BUS
International Bus Terminal
The international İstanbul bus terminal (Uluslararası İstanbul Otogarı; ☎ 212-658 0505, fax 658 2858) is the city's main bus terminal for both domestic and international routes. Called simply the 'otogar', it's in the western district of Esenler, just south of the expressway and about 10km west of Sultanahmet or Taksim.

To reach the city centre, take the Metro east toward Aksaray or Yenikapı. In Aksaray, leave the station, turn right and go through the underpass to cross the road, then take the side turn-off beside the mosque to the main road and tramway stand for Sultanahmet. Board the other tram to Sultanahmet, Sirkeci and Eminönü. At Yenikapı, board the suburban train (*banliyö treni*) and get out at Cankurtaran for Sultanahmet hotels, or at the Sirkeci terminal for points north (ie Beyoğlu and Taksim).

Harem Bus Terminal
There is a much smaller, older, more confusing bus terminal on the Asian shore of the Bosphorus at Harem (☎ 216-333 3763), south of Üsküdar and north of Haydarpaşa train station. If you're arriving by bus from the east, get out at Harem and take the car ferry to Sirkeci/Eminönü.

City Buses
Destinations and intermediate stops on city bus routes are shown on a sign on the right (kerb) side of the bus. Red-and-beige IETT buses are run by the city, and you must have a ticket (US$0.50) before boarding; some long routes require that you stuff two tickets into the box. You can buy tickets from the white booths near major stops or from some nearby shops (look for 'IETT otobüs bileti satılır'). Stock up in advance. Özel Halk

Otobüsü are blue-and-silver private buses regulated by the city, running the same routes; they accept either city bus tickets or cash.

Akbil Fare Savings
If you plan to stay in the city a week or more and to use the buses, trams and ferries frequently, you may want to buy an Akbil pass, a computerised debit fare card. Get one at the Akbil Satış Noktası (Akbil Sales Point) at transfer points (Sirkeci, Eminönü, Aksaray, Taksim, etc) for US$2.75. Decide how much in fares you want to load (from US$2 and up), and it'll be recorded electronically on your card. Press the card's metal button into the fare machine on a bus, ferry or tram and the fare is automatically deducted. The advantage is that Akbil fares are 22 to 30% lower than cash or ticket fares.

TRAIN
Sirkeci Station
All trains from Europe terminate at Sirkeci Garı (SEER-keh-jee, ☎ 212-527 0051), right next to Eminönü in the shadow of Topkapı Palace. Right outside the station's west door is the tram up the hill to Sultanahmet, Beyazıt, Laleli and Aksaray.

If you're headed for Taksim Square, go out the station door and turn right. Walk towards the sea and you'll see the Eminönü bus ranks to your left, with departures to many parts of the city. For a dolmuş to Taksim, go to the Yeni Cami at the southern end of the Galata Bridge and look for the Kentbank building on the mosque's south-eastern side. The dolmuş rank is behind the Kentbank.

Haydarpaşa Station
Haydarpaşa Garı (☎ 216-336 0475, 348 8020), on the Asian shore of the Bosphorus south of Üsküdar, is the terminal for trains to and from Anatolia and points east and south.

Ferries (US$0.50, 20 minutes) run every 15 to 30 minutes between Karaköy (at the northern end of the Galata Bridge) and Haydarpaşa station.

Ignore anyone who suggests that you take a taxi to Haydarpaşa. The ferry is cheap, convenient, pleasant and speedy. Taxis across the Bosphorus are expensive and slow.

Haydarpaşa has a left luggage room (*emniyet*), a restaurant serving alcoholic beverages, numerous snack shops, bank ATMs and a small PTT.

METRO

İstanbul's Metro system will be under construction for a decade more, but several useful lines are already in service. The fare is US$0.50.

The main tramway line goes from the western side of Aksaray north-westward along Adnan Menderes Bulvarı (formerly Vatan Caddesi) through the Bayrampaşa and Sağmalcılar districts to the bus terminal in Esenler, then turns south-westward to pass the airport, terminating at Ataköy on the Sea of Marmara, where it meets the Sirkeci-Halkalı suburban train line.

A street tram runs from Eminönü to Gülhane and Sultanahmet, then along Divan Yolu to Çemberlitaş, Beyazıt (for the Covered Bazaar) and Aksaray, then southwest to Zeytinburnu.

The suburban train line (*banliyö treni*) follows the Sea of Marmara shore southwestward from Seraglio Point to the south-western suburbs. At Ataköy it links to the main Metro line. The suburban trains are decrepit but serviceable and cheap.

In Beyoğlu, a restored early 20th-century tram runs along İstiklal Caddesi between Taksim and Tünel squares, but is too small and infrequent to be of great use.

The 7.8km-long Taksim-Dördüncü Levent underground line is nearing completion.

TÜNEL

İstanbul's little underground train, the Tünel, runs between Karaköy and the southern end of İstiklal Caddesi called Tünel Meydanı (Tünel Square). The fare is US$0.35. There are only two stations on the line, the upper and lower, so there's no getting lost. Trains run every five or 10 minutes from 7 am to 11 pm.

DOLMUŞ

A dolmuş is a shared taxi or minibus. It waits at a specified departure point until it has a full complement of passengers, then follows a given route to its destination. Fares are slightly more than the bus, but a dolmuş is almost as comfortable as a taxi, yet considerably cheaper. Useful routes are mentioned in the text.

TAXI

İstanbul has 60,000 yellow taxis. All have digital meters and are required to run them. Still, some drivers may try to take advantage of you by demanding a flat fare, or by refusing to run the meter so they can gouge you at the end of the run. Some drivers also take advantage of the many zeros on Turkish currency to charge you 10 times what the meter reads.

The base rate (drop rate, flag fall) is about US$1 during the daytime (*gündüz*); the night-time (*gece*) rate is 50% higher. A daytime trip between Aksaray and Sultanahmet costs about US$1.25; between Taksim and Karaköy about US$2.25; between Taksim and Sultanahmet about US$4, between Sultanahmet and the airport about US$10 to US$12.

Older meters have tiny red lights marked with these words to show which rate is being used. Newer meters, with LCD displays, flash 'gündüz' or 'gece' when they are started.

CAR

It makes no sense to drive in İstanbul. If you have a car, park it (if you can find a spot) and use public transport, except perhaps for excursions out of the city. If you plan to rent a car, do so when you're ready to leave İstanbul or, better yet, at some smaller town well away from the chaos of city driving.

Rental

Renting a car is expensive, but gives you freedom. If you share the cost among several people, renting can be reasonable.

Minimum age is generally 19 or 21 years for the cheapest cars, 24 for some larger cars, and 27 for the best. You must pay with a major credit card, or you will be required to make a large cash deposit.

Avis has the most extensive and experienced network of agencies and staff, and the highest prices. Some firms will be happy to deliver your car to another place, or arrange for pick-up, at no extra charge; others will charge you.

You should not be afraid to try (with caution) one of the small local agencies. Though there is no far-flung network for repairs and people in these places have little fluency in English, they are friendly, helpful and charge from 10 to 20% less than the large firms, particularly if you're willing to haggle a bit.

The most popular rental cars are the Fiat 124 (Serçe), a small four-passenger car with limited space and power; Fiat 131 (Şahin), more powerful and comfortable; Fiat 131SW (Kartal), still more powerful and comfortable; and Fiat Mirafiori (Doğan), big enough for five. Of the Renaults, the 12TX is similar to the Fiat 131, but more economical with fuel; the Renault 9 is larger and more powerful, the 12 STW, better still. All of these cars have standard gear shift. Only the most expensive cars (big Fords, Mercedes etc) have automatic transmission and air-conditioning.

Costs Rental cars are moderately expensive in Turkey, partly due to huge excise taxes paid when the cars are purchased. Total costs of a rental arranged on the spot in Turkey during the busy summer months, for a week with unlimited kilometres, including full insurance and tax, might be from US$300 to US$600. Ask your travel agent to shop around, or to set up a fly-drive arrangement.

If you rent from abroad before arriving in Turkey, the Collision Damage Waiver (CDW) is usually included in the all-inclusive price quoted to you. The CDW is not a bad thing to have, because a renter is liable not merely for damage, but for rental revenue lost while the car is being repaired or, in the case of a stolen car, until the car is recovered.

The normal CDW does not cover damage to the car's glass (windscreen, side windows, head and tail lamps, etc) nor to its tyres – yet another charge of US$3 to US$5 per day is required to pay for this. If you do not pay this charge and encounter these misfortunes, it's usually best and cheapest to arrange for repair or replacement yourself, en route.

Note that many travellers do not need the personal injury insurance proffered by the rental company. Your health insurance from home may cover any medical costs of an accident.

When you look at a rental company's current price list, keep in mind that the daily or weekly rental charge is only a small portion of what you will actually end up paying, unless it includes unlimited kilometres. The charge for kilometres normally ends up being higher, per day, than the daily rental charge. By the way, the 15% Value Added Tax (KDV) should be included in the rental, insurance and kilometre prices quoted to you. It should not be added to your bill as an extra item.

Any traffic fines you incur will be charged to you. Normally, the company charges your credit card.

Safety & Accidents Child safety seats are usually available from the larger companies for about US$5 per day if you order them at least 48 hours in advance.

If your car incurs any accident damage, or if you cause any, do not move the car before finding a police officer and asking for a *kaza raporu* (accident report). The officer may ask you to submit to a breath-alcohol test. Contact your car rental company within 48 hours. Your insurance coverage may be void if it can be shown that you were operating under the influence of alcohol or other drugs, were speeding, or if you did not submit the required accident report within 48 hours.

Rental Agencies The well-known international car-rental firms have desks at

GETTING AROUND

Atatürk airport and in the city centre, mostly near Taksim Square and the Elmadağ district just a few blocks to the north.

Avis
Atatürk airport international arrivals hall (☎ 212-663 0858), and domestic arrivals hall (☎ 212-663 6400, fax 663 0724)
Reservations centre (☎ 212-257 7670, fax 263 3918)
Beyazıt office (☎ 212-516 6109, fax 516 6108) Ordu Caddesi, Haznedar Sokak 1
Budget
Atatürk airport international arrivals hall (☎ 212-663 0858, fax 663 0724)
Reservations Centre (☎ 212-296 3196, fax 296 3188) Cumhuriyet Caddesi 12, Seyhan Apartımanı, 4th floor, office 10, just north of Taksim Square
Office (☎ 212-253 9200, fax 237 2919, www.budgettr.com, email budget @escortnet.com) Cumhuriyet Caddesi 19/A, Gezi Apartımanı
Europcar/Inter-rent
Atatürk airport international arrivals hall (☎ 212-663 0746, fax 663 6830)
Esin Turizm (☎ 212-254 7788, emergency 663 0746, fax 237 3158), Topçu Caddesi, Uygun İş Merkezi 2, 80090 Talimhane, a few short blocks north of Taksim Square and only steps west of Cumhuriyet Caddesi
Hertz
Ekin Turizm (☎ 212-234 4300, fax 232 9260) Cumhuriyet Caddesi 295, Harbiye
Sun Rent a Car
Sun Tours (☎ 216-318 9040, fax 321 4014), Kısıklı Caddesi, Nurbaba Sokak 1, 81190 Üsküdar. Auto Europe's representative; a local firm with a good reputation and offices in major cities and resorts

BOAT

Without doubt the nicest – and cheapest – way to travel any considerable distance in İstanbul is by ferry. The familiar white İstanbul ferries have been replaced on many routes by fast, modern catamarans called *deniz otobüsü* which cost several times as much (see below).

The major ferry docks are at the mouth of the Golden Horn (Eminönü, Sirkeci and Karaköy) and at Kabataş, 3km north-east of the Galata Bridge, just south of Dolmabahçe Mosque and Palace. Short ferry rides (under 30 minutes) cost US$0.50, most longer ones (up to an hour) US$1.30.

Buy your token or ticket from the agent in the booth; if you buy them from the men who stand around outside the ferry docks hawking them, you may pay four times the fare.

Ferries to Üsküdar

Ferries depart from Eminönü every 15 minutes between 6 am and midnight for Üsküdar, even more frequently during rush hour. From Kabataş, just south of Dolmabahçe Palace, ferries run to Üsküdar every 30 minutes on the hour and half-hour from 7 am to 8 pm. A similarly frequent ferry service operates between Beşiktaş and Üsküdar.

Karaköy to Haydarpaşa/Kadıköy

To get to the Asia train station at Haydarpaşa, or for a little cruise around Seraglio Point and across the Bosphorus (good for photos of Topkapı Palace, Aya Sofya and the Blue Mosque), catch a ferry from Karaköy; they depart every 15 minutes (every 20 minutes on weekends). Some go only to Kadıköy, 1km south of Haydarpaşa, so check your boat's itinerary. The round-trip to Haydarpaşa and/or Kadıköy (US$1) takes about an hour.

Bosphorus Excursion Ferries

The ferry most tourists use is the Eminönü-Kavaklar Boğaziçi Özel Gezi Seferleri (Eminönü-Kavaklar Bosphorus Special Touristic Excursions) up the Bosphorus. These ferries depart from Eminönü daily at 10.35 am, 12.35 and 2.10 pm each weekday, stop at Beşiktaş on the European shore, Kanlıca on the Asian shore, Yeniköy, Sarıyer and Rumeli Kavağı on the European shore, and Anadolu Kavağı on the Asian shore (the turn-around point). Times are subject to change.

The ferries go all the way to Rumeli Kavağı and Anadolu Kavağı (1¾ hours), but you may want to go only as far as Sarıyer, then take a dolmuş or bus back down, stopping at various sights along the

The most romantic and scenic way to arrive in İstanbul is by water.

way. Arrival at Sarıyer, on the European shore about three quarters of the way up the Bosphorus, is at 11.50 am, 1.50 and 3.30 pm respectively. Departures from Sarıyer for the trip back down the Bosphorus are at 2.20, 3.10 and 5.50 pm on weekdays.

Trips are added on Sunday and holidays, with boats departing from Eminönü at 10 and 11 am, noon, 1.30 and 3 pm.

The weekday round-trip fare is US$5, half-price on Saturday and Sunday. Prices are printed on all tickets. Hold onto your ticket; you need to show it to re-board the boat for the return trip. The boats fill up early in summer – on weekends particularly – so buy your ticket and walk aboard at least 30 or 45 minutes prior to departure to get a seat.

Cross-Bosphorus Ferries

At several points along the Bosphorus, passenger ferries run between the European and Asian shores, allowing you to cross easily from one side to the other. If you can't catch one of these ferries, you can often hire a boater to motor you across the Bosphorus for a few dollars.

Southernmost are the routes from Eminönü, Kabataş and Beşiktaş in Europe to Üsküdar in Asia. For details see Sights on the Asian Shore in the Excursions chapter.

Another ring route is from Kanlıca to Anadolu Hisar on the Asian shore, then across the Bosphorus to Bebek on the European shore. Departures from Kanlıca are at 8.30, 9.30, 10.30 and 11.30 am, and 12.30, 2.30, 4, 5.15 and 6.15 pm. The voyage to Bebek takes 25 minutes and costs US$0.50.

Other ring ferries run from İstinye on the European side to Beykoz and Paşabahçe on the Asian side. Yet another ring ferry operates from Sarıyer and Rumeli Kavağı in Europe to Anadolu Kavağı in Asia, with 17 ferries a day (at least one every hour) from 7.15 am to 11 pm.

Catamaran

Called *deniz otobüsü* (seabus), fast catamarans run on commuter routes between the European and Asian shores of İstanbul, and up the Bosphorus. Major docks are on the European side are at Yenikapı and Kabataş, with less frequently served docks at Eminönü, Karaköy and several Bosphorus docks such as İstinye and Sarıyer. On the Asian side, major docks are at Bostancı and Kartal, and minor docks at Büyükada and Heybeliada.

Fares for the catamarans are several times higher than those for ferries. Except for the route up the Bosphorus, you may find that you rarely use the intracity catamarans on touristic excursions.

WALKING

Given the city's overburdened public transport system, walking can often be faster and more rewarding. The street scenes are never dull, and the views from one hill to the next can be extraordinary. While walking, watch out for broken pavement, bits of pipe sticking a few centimetres out of the pavement, and all manner of other obstacles.

Don't expect any car driver to stop for you, a pedestrian, in any situation. Drivers seize the right of way virtually everywhere, and they become furiously annoyed with pedestrians who assert ridiculous and specious claims to right of way and safety. The infant, the lame, the aged, the infirm and all the rest flee before the onslaught of the automobile. Step lively or you're road-kill.

ORGANISED TOURS

The quality of any tour depends greatly on the competence, character and personality of your particular guide; but it's difficult to pick a tour by guide rather than company, so you must go by the tour company's reputation.

The best course of action is to ask about at your hotel for recommendations. Other foreign visitors may be able to give you tips about which companies to use and which to avoid.

Watch out for the following rip-offs: a tour bus that spends the first hour or two of your 'tour' circulating through the city to various hotels, picking up tour participants; a tour that includes an extended stop at some particular shop (from which the tour company or guide gets a kickback); a tour that includes a lunch which turns out to be mediocre.

Most of the time, it is a lot cheaper and quicker to see things on your own by bus, dolmuş, or even taxi. Tours can cost from US$20 to US$40 per person. If you can get a group of three or four people together, you may be able to hire a taxi and driver for the entire day for less than what you'd pay for tours.

Travel Agencies

Sultanahmet has many small travel agencies, all of them selling air and bus tickets and tours, sometimes at a big markup; shop around for the best deals. Most also offer speedy (but expensive) foreign-exchange facilities and can arrange minibus transport to the airport.

The fancier travel agencies and airline offices are in the districts called Elmadağ and Harbiye, north of Taksim Square along Cumhuriyet Caddesi between the Divan Oteli and İstanbul Hilton Hotel.

A travel agent/tour operator which gives good service with English-speaking staff is Orion-Tour (☎ 212-248 8437, fax 241 2808, email oriontour@compuserve.com, www .orion-tour.com), Halaskargazi Caddesi 284/3, Marmara Apartımanı, Şişli, about 2km north of Taksim. Orion (pronounced OR-yohn in Turkish) can arrange for flights, cruises (including private or group yacht charters), transfers to and from the airport, city tours of İstanbul and other major cities, and private or group tours anywhere in Turkey.

Things to See & Do

HIGHLIGHTS
The heart of historical İstanbul is Sultanahmet, the district centred on the Byzantine Hippodrome in the oldest part of the city. The top sights are grouped within a few minutes stroll of one another:

- Topkapı Sarayı (Topkapı Palace)
- Aya Sofya (Sancta Sophia)
- Sultan Ahmet Camii (Blue Mosque)
- Hippodrome (Atmeydanı)
- Türk-Islam Eserleri Müzesi
  (Museum of Turkish & Islamic Arts)
- Yerebatan Saray (Cistern Basilica)

In addition, a short walk brings you to Gülhane Park and the archaeological museums complex adjoining Topkapı Sarayı:

- Arkeoloji Müzesi (Archaeological Museum)
- Eski Şark Eserler Müzesi (Museum of the Ancient Orient)
- Çinili Köşk (Tiled Kiosk)

Other top sights in the old city are a walk or a short bus, tram or taxi ride away:

- Kapalı Çarşı (Grand Bazaar or Covered Market)
- Süleymaniye Camii
  (Mosque of Süleyman the Magnificent)
- Kariye Müzesi (Chora Church)
- City Walls

In Beyoğlu, on the north side of the Golden Horn, don't miss a stroll past the grand old 19th-century buildings along İstiklal Caddesi, once the Grande Rue de Péra, or a visit to Dolmabahçe Sarayı on the shores of the Bosphorus.

The Bosphorus itself is a must-see for a day excursion. Take a cruise north at least halfway to the Black Sea for a look at Rumeli Hisar fortress and Beylerbeyi Sarayı.

WALKING TOURS
Most of the city's principal sights can be seen on six walking tours. Plan to walk to reach sights east of Atatürk Bulvarı, and to use buses, taxis, trams and suburban trains to reach sights west of Atatürk Bulvarı. Sights in this chapter have been arranged to help you follow these walking tours.

Sultanahmet
The sights around Sultanahmet Square are all within an easy walk of one another. Plan at least two days to see them all: Topkapı Sarayı is closed Tuesday; Aya Sofya, the Türk-Islam Eserleri Müzesi and the Arkeoloji Müzesi are all closed Monday; Sultan Ahmet Camii, the Hippodrome and Yerebatan Saray are all open daily.

Sultan Ahmet Camii (The Blue Mosque).

Minor sights include the Halı ve Kilim Müzesi (Carpet & Kilim Museum), Büyüksaray Mozaik Müzesi (Great Palace Mosaic Museum), Küçük Aya Sofya Camii ('Little' Aya Sofya Mosque), Haseki Hürrem Hamamı (Baths of Lady Hürrem), Sultan III Ahmet Çeşmesi (Fountain of Ahmet III), Soğukçeşme Sokak and Gülhane Park.

Uzunçarşı & Tahtakale
This tour, covered in the Shopping chapter, begins at the Kapalı Çarşı and takes you down 'Longmarket Street' into the Tahtakale market district, where you can buy anything and everything, mundane or exotic, legal or illegal. Bonuses here are the

exquisite Rüstem Paşa Camii, the Yeni Cami and the Mısır Çarşısı (Egyptian, or Spice, Market).

Divan Yolu

Walk from Sultanahmet (Hippodrome) west on Divan Yolu to the Kapalı Çarşı (closed Sunday), İstanbul University, Süleymaniye Camii, and the Laleli and Şehzadebaşı districts.

The entrance to İstanbul University.

Eminönü

Eminönü, the transport nerve centre of the city, has two fine mosques, the Rüstem Paşa and the Yeni, and lots of markets. You may wish to do this walk in conjunction with Uzunçarşı & Tahtakale.

Beyoğlu

From Taksim Square, stroll along İstiklal Caddesi, the former Grande Rue de Péra and now a lively pedestrian precinct. Follow the street through Galatasaray and Tünel squares, then head downhill to the Galata Tower and Karaköy (Galata) on the Golden Horn. If you're staying in Old İstanbul, you can follow this route in reverse by crossing the Galata Bridge and ascending the hill by the Tünel, a little two-station underground train from Karaköy to Tünel Square. Tünel Square is then the starting point for your walk along İstiklal Caddesi, although you may want to backtrack downhill to the Galata Tower, which stands in the midst of a historic neighbourhood.

An old Frankish house in Beyoğlu.

Kariye & Edirnekapı

The Kariye Müzesi (once the Chora Church), with its fabulous Byzantine mosaics, is set apart from the other major sights in the north-western corner of Old İstanbul. After you've visited the church (closed Wednesday), plan to spend 1½ to two hours walking in the neighbourhood to see the Byzantine city walls, Mihrimah Sultan Camii, and Tekfur Sarayı (the Palace of Constantine Porphyrogenetus).

Byzantine mosaic in the Kariye Müzesi.

SULTANAHMET (MAP 7)

Named after Sultan Ahmet Camii, this district is the heart of historic İstanbul.

Topkapı Sarayı

Topkapı Sarayı (see the Topkapı Sarayı map between pages 80 and 82) was the residence of the sultans for almost three centuries. Mehmet the Conqueror built the first palace shortly after the Conquest in 1453, and lived here until his death in 1481. Sultan after sultan played out the drama of the Ottoman sovereign here until the 19th century. Mahmut II (1808-39) was the last emperor to occupy the palace. After him, the sultans preferred to live in new European-style palaces – Dolmabahçe, Çirağan, Yıldız – which they built on the Bosphorus.

Foreigners called Topkapı the *Seraglio*, an Italian word. Mozart's famous opera *Abduction from the Seraglio* is performed in the palace every summer in late June-early July during the International İstanbul Music Festival.

Topkapı Sarayı (☎ 212-512 0480) is open from 9 am to 4.30 pm (later in summer); closed on Tuesday. Admission to the palace costs US$5, US$4 for students; entry to the Harem costs an additional US$1.50. You may also choose to pay US$0.25 as a donation to the İstanbul Kültür ve Sanat Vakfı (Istanbul Culture & Arts Foundation).

I suggest that you head straight for the **Harem** when you enter the palace, note the tour times posted on the board by the entry, buy your ticket, and return in time to catch the next tour. In summer this may not work; the crowds are so thick and the tour groups so numerous that individual travellers sometimes miss out – group tours sometimes book all of the Harem tours in advance.

It will take you more than half a day to explore Topkapı Sarayı. In the busy summer months, if you start early (at 9.30 am) you can avoid the worst of the crowds.

Court of the Janissaries Topkapı grew and changed with the centuries, but its basic four-courtyard plan remained the same. As you pass through the Bab-i

---

The Janissaries

The word 'janissary' comes from the Turkish *yeni çeri*, 'new levies'. These soldiers were personal servants of the sultan, fed and paid regularly by him, and subject to his will. They were full-time soldiers, an innovation in an age when most soldiers – and all soldiers in Europe – were farmers in spring and autumn, homebodies in winter, and warriors only in summer.

In a process termed *devşirme*, which was begun shortly after the conquest of Constantinople, government agents went out from İstanbul into the towns and villages of the Balkans rounding up 10-year-old boys from Christian families for the sultan's personal service. Having one's son taken was undoubtedly a blow to the family, who would probably lose his love and labour forever; but it was the road to ultimate advancement. The boy would be instructed in Turkish, converted to Islam, and enrolled in the sultan's service.

The imperial service was a meritocracy. Those of normal intelligence and capabilities went into the janissary corps, the sultan's imperial guard. The brightest and most capable boys went into the palace service, and many eventually rose to the highest offices, including that of grand vizier. This ensured that the top government posts were always held by personal servants of the sultan. These top government and military officers would often remember their birthplaces, and would lavish benefits such as public works projects (mosques, bridges, schools etc) upon them.

By the early 19th century, the janissary corps had become unbearably corrupt and self-serving, and a constant threat to the throne. The reforming sultan Mahmut II, risking his life, his throne and his dynasty, readied a new, loyal, European-style army, then provoked a revolt of the janissaries in the Hippodrome and brought in his new army to wipe them out, ending their 350-year history in 1826.

Hümayun (Great or Imperial Gate) behind Aya Sofya, you enter the first court *(birinci avlu)*, the Court of the Janissaries. In June 1998, archaeologists discovered painted walls and other structures from the Great Palace of the Byzantine emperors in this court. Excavations and preservation efforts are under way.

On your left is the former **Aya İrini Kilisesi**, or Church of Divine Peace (☎ 212-520 6952). There was a Christian church here from earliest times and, before that, a pagan temple. The early church was replaced by the present one during the reign of the Byzantine emperor Justinian, in the 540s, so the church you see is as old as Aya Sofya. When Mehmet the Conqueror began building his palace, the church was within the grounds. It was used as an arsenal for centuries, then as an artillery museum, and now, more fittingly, as a concert hall.

The former Darphane, or Ottoman Mint, just past Aya İrini, has been renovated and is now the İstanbul City Museum.

Janissaries, merchants and tradespeople could circulate as they wished in the Court of the Janissaries, but the second court was restricted. The same is true today as you must buy another admission ticket to enter the second court. The ticket windows are on your right as you approach the entrance. Just past them is a little fountain where the imperial executioner used to wash the tools of his trade after decapitating a noble or rebel who had displeased the sultan. The head of the unfortunate was put on a pike and exhibited above the gate you're about to enter.

Ortakapı & Second Court The Ortakapı (Middle Gate, Gate of Greeting or Bab-üs Selâm) led to the palace's second court, used for the business of running the empire. Only the sultan and the *valide sultan* (queen mother) were allowed through the Ortakapı on horseback. Everyone else, including the grand vizier, had to dismount. The gate was constructed by Süleyman the Magnificent in 1524, utilising architects and workers he had brought back from his conquest of Hungary.

To the right after you enter are models and a map of the palace, and beyond them an exhibit of imperial carriages made for the sultan and his family in Paris, Torino and Vienna.

Within the second court is a beautiful, park-like setting. Topkapı is not a palace on the European plan – one large building with outlying gardens – but rather a series of pavilions, kitchens, barracks, audience chambers, kiosks and sleeping quarters built around a central enclosure, much like a fortified camp.

The great **palace kitchens**, on your right, hold a small portion of Topkapı's vast collection of Chinese celadon porcelain, valued for its beauty but also because it was reputed to change colour if touched by poisoned food. Beyond the celadon are the collections of European and Ottoman porcelain and glassware. The last of the kitchens, the Helvahane in which all the palace sweets were made, is now set up as a kitchen, and you can easily imagine what went on in these rooms as the staff prepared food for the 5000 inhabitants of the palace.

On the left (west) side of the Second Court is the ornate **Kubbealtı** ('beneath the cupola') or Imperial Council Chamber, also called the Divan Salonu, beneath the squarish Adalet Kulesi tower which is among the palace's most distinctive architectural features. The Imperial Divan (council) met in the Divan Salonu to discuss matters of state while the sultan eavesdropped through a grill high on the wall.

North of the Kubbealtı is the armoury *(silahlar)* exhibit of fearsome Ottoman and European weaponry.

Harem The entrance to the Harem, open by guided tour only from 9.30 am to 4.30 pm (3.30 pm in winter), is beneath the Adalet Kulesi (Tower of Justice), the palace's highest point.

Legend vs Reality Fraught with legend and romance, the Harem is usually imagined as a place where the sultan could engage in debauchery at will. In fact, these were the

Decorated domed ceiling, Topkapı Sarayı (Topkapı Palace)

Imperial tuğra, Middle Gate

Jewelled water jug, Treasury

Decorative water fountain

Hünkâr Sofası (The Emperor's Chamber), Topkapı Sarayı (Topkapı Palace)

TOPKAPI SARAYI (Topkapı Palace)

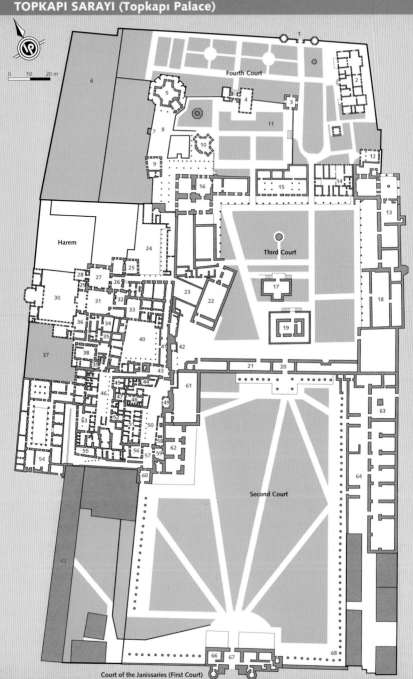

Fourth Court

6

5

4

3

8

11

10

9

16

15

14

12

Harem

24

13

25

Third Court

28
29

27

26

17

30

31

32

33

23

22

18

36

34

19

35

40

41

37

38

39

42

21

20

43

45

44

61

46

47

149

63

53

52

51

50

55

56

57

58

59

62

60

54

64

Second Court

65

66 67

68

Court of the Janissaries (First Court)

0   10   20 m

TOPKAPI SARAYI (Topkapı Palace)

SECOND COURT

61 Inner Treasury (Enderun Hazinesi; Arms & Armour)
62 Divan Salonu
63 Restored Confectionery (Helvahane)
64 Palace Kitchens (Porcelain & Glass Exhibits)
65 Imperial Stables (Has Ahırları)
66 Bookshop
67 Middle Gate (Ortakapı, Bab-üs Selâm)
68 Imperial Carriages

THIRD COURT

13 Imperial Treasury (Hazine)
14 Museum Directorate
15 Treasury Barracks (Hazine Koğuşu; Calligraphy, Illumination & Miniatures)
16 Sacred Safe Keeping Rooms (Mukaddes Emanetler Dairesi; Prophet's Relics)
17 Library of Ahmet III
18 Dormitory of the Expeditionary Force (Seferli Koğuşu); Imperial Caftans
19 Audience Chamber (Arz Odası)
20 Gate of Felicity (Bab-üs Saade)
21 White Eunuchs Quarters (Akağalar)
22 Mosque/Library (Ağalar Camii)

FOURTH COURT

1 Gate of the Privy Gardens (Has Bahçe Kapısı)
2 Mecidiye Köşkü; Konyalı Restaurant
3 Doctor's Room (Hekimbaşı Odası)
4 Mustafa Paşa (Sofa) Köşkü
5 Baghdad Kiosk (Bağdat Köşkü)
6 Lower Gardens of the Imperial Terrace; Fig Garden; Elephant Garden (Sofa-i Hümayun Alt Bahçeleri; İncir Bahçesi; Fil Bahçesi)
7 Canopy for Breaking the Fast (İftariye Kameriyesi ve Mehtaplık)
8 Marble Terrace & Pool (Mermer Teras ve Havuz)

9 Circumcision Room (Sünnet Odası)
10 Erivan Kiosk (Revan Köşkü)
11 Tulip Garden
12 Sofa or Terrace Mosque (Sofa Camii)

HAREM

23 Harem Mosque
24 Favourites Courtyard & Apartments (Gözdeler Mabeyn Taşlığı ve Daireleri)
25 Double Kiosk with Stained Glass
26 Beautifully Tiled Antechamber
27 Privy Chamber of Murat III
28 Library of Ahmet I; Dining Room of Ahmet III (Fruit Paintings)
29 Ahmet III Dining Room
30 Terrace of Osman III
31 Emperor's Chamber (Hünkar Sofası)
32 Room with Hearth (Ocaklı Oda); Room with Fountain (Çeşmeli Oda)
33 Consultation Place of the Genies
34 Valide Sultan's Hamam
35 Sultan's Hamam
36 Chamber of Abdül Hamit I
37 Harem Garden
38 Valide Sultan's Quarters (Valide Sultan Taşlığı)

39 Sultan Ahmet Köşkü
40 Courtyard of the Valide Sultan
41 Golden Road (Altınyol)
42 Birdcage Gate (Kuşhane Kapısı)
43 Main Gate (Cümle Kapısı) with Gilded Mirrors & Sentry Post; Second Guard Room
44 Chief Black Eunuch's Room (Kızlarağası)
45 Concubines' Corridor (Cariyeler Koridoru)
46 Concubines' & Consorts' Courtyard (Cariye & Kadinefendi Taşlığı)
47 Harem Kitchen
48 Imperial Princes' School
49 Harem Chamberlain's Room
50 Black Eunuchs' Courtyard (Ağalar Taşlığı)
51 Black Eunuchs' Dormitories (Ağalar Koğuş)
52 Women's Hamam
53 Women's Dormitory
54 Harem Hospital
55 Laundry Room
56 Black Eunuchs' Mosque
57 Guard Room/Hall with Şadırvan
58 Harem Eunuchs' Mosque
59 Tower of Justice (Adalet Kulesi)
60 Carriage Gate & Dome with Cupboards (Dolaplı Kubbe)

Rehearsal for Mozart's *Abduction from the Seraglio.*

TOM BROSNAHAN

imperial family quarters, and every detail of Harem life was governed by tradition, obligation and ceremony.

Every traditional Muslim household had two distinct parts: the *selamlık* (greeting room) where the master greeted friends, business associates and tradespeople; and the *harem* (private apartments), reserved for himself and his family. The Harem, then, was something akin to the private apartments in Buckingham Palace or the White House.

The women of the Harem had to be foreigners, as Islam forbade enslaving Muslims, Christians or Jews (although Christians and Jews could be enslaved in the Balkans: see the The Janissaries boxed text). Girls, too, were bought as slaves (often having been sold by their parents at a good price) or were received as gifts from nobles and potentates. A favourite source of girls was Circassia, north of the Caucasus Mountains in Russia, as Circassian women were noted for their beauty, and parents were often glad to give up their 10-year-old girls in exchange for hard cash.

Upon entering the Harem, the girls would be schooled in Islam and Turkish culture and language, the arts of make-up, dress, comportment, music, reading and writing, embroidery and dancing. They then entered a meritocracy, first as ladies-in-waiting to the sultan's concubines and children, then to the sultan's mother and finally, if they were the best, to the sultan himself.

Ruling the Harem was the valide sultan, the mother of the reigning sultan. She often owned large landed estates in her own name and controlled them through black eunuch servants. She was allowed to give orders directly to the grand vizier. Her influence on the sultan, on the selection of his wives and concubines and on matters of state, was often profound.

The sultan was allowed by Islamic law to have four legitimate wives, who received the title of *kadın* (wife). If a wife bore him a child, she was called *haseki sultan* if it was a son; *haseki kadın* if it was a daughter. The Ottoman dynasty did not observe primogeniture, so in principle the throne was available to any imperial son. Each lady of the Harem contrived mightily to have her son proclaimed heir to the throne, thus assuring her own role and power as the new valide sultan.

As for concubines, Islam permits as many as a man can support in proper style. The Ottoman sultans had the means to support many, sometimes up to 300, though they were not all in the Harem at the same time. The domestic thrills of the sultans were usually less spectacular, however. Mehmet the Conqueror, builder of Topkapı, was the last sultan to have four official wives. After him, sultans did not officially marry, but instead kept four chosen concubines without the legal encumbrances, thereby saving themselves the embarrassments and inconveniences suffered by another famous Renaissance monarch, King Henry VIII of England.

The Harem was much like a village with all the necessary services. About 400 or 500 people lived in this section of the palace at any one time. Not many of the ladies stayed in the Harem all their lives: the sultan might grant them their freedom, after which they would often marry powerful men who wanted the company of these supremely graceful and intelligent women, not to mention their connections with the palace.

The *kızlarağası* (kuhz-LAHR-ah-ah-suh, chief black eunuch), the sultan's personal representative in administration of the Harem and other important affairs of state, was the third most powerful official in the empire, after the grand vizier and the Şeyhul İslâm (supreme Islamic judge).

Many of the 300-odd rooms in the Harem were constructed during the reign of Süleyman the Magnificent (1520-66), but much more was added or reconstructed thereafter. In 1665 a disastrous fire destroyed much of the complex, which was rebuilt by Mehmet IV and later sultans.

Touring the Harem Although the Harem is built into a hillside and has six levels, the standard tour takes you through or past only

Life in the Cage

As children, imperial princes were brought up in the Harem, taught and cared for by its women and servants.

In the early centuries of the empire, Ottoman princes were schooled as youths in combat and statecraft by direct experience: they practised soldiering, fought in battles and were given provinces to administer. But as the Ottoman dynasty did not observe primogeniture (succession of the firstborn), the death of the sultan regularly resulted in a fratricidal blood-bath as his sons battled it out among themselves for the throne. In the case of Beyazit II (1481-1512), his sons began the battles even before the sultan's death, realising that to lose the battle for succession meant death for themselves. The victorious son, Selim I (1512-1520), not only murdered his brothers but even forced Sultan Beyazit to abdicate, and may even have had him murdered as he went into retirement.

Fratricide was not practised by Ahmet I (1603-17), who could not bring himself to murder his mad brother Mustafa. Instead, he kept him imprisoned in the Harem, beginning the tra-dition of *kafes hayatı* (cage life). This house arrest, adopted in place of fratricide by later sultans, meant that princes were prey to the intrigues of the women and eunuchs, corrupt-ed by the pleasures of the Harem, ignorant of war and statecraft, and thus usually unfit to rule if and when the occasion arose. Luckily for the empire in this latter period, there were able grand viziers to carry on.

In later centuries the dynasty abandoned kafes hayatı and adopted the practice of having the eldest male in the direct line assume the throne.

---

a few dozen rooms on one level, but these are among the most splendid. The tour route may vary from time to time as this room or that is closed for restoration, and others are finished and opened to view.

Most Harem tours are given in Turkish and English, and in other languages in summer. Plaques in Turkish and English have been placed here and there in the Harem. They tend to be more informative than the guide's brief commentary.

Following is a description of the tour at the time of writing.

You enter the Harem by the carriage gate, through which Harem ladies would enter their carriages. Inside the gate is the **Dolaplı Kubbe**, or Dome with Cupboards, decorated with fine İznik faïence (tin-glazed earthen-ware tiles); the green and yellow colours are unusual in İznik tiles. Beyond it is the **Hall with Şadırvan** (*Şadırvan*: ablutions foun-tain), a guardroom with more fine-coloured tiles. To the left is a doorway to the **Black**

Eunuchs' Mosque, on the right the doorway to the **Adalet Kulesi**, or Tower of Justice which rises above the Imperial Divan, or council chamber.

In principle, groups of no more than 20 are allowed to climb to the top of the Adalet Kulesi at 11 am and 2 pm in conjunction with the harem tour, but in practice you will be whisked right by the door. When you reach the door, mention to your guide that you'd like to go up in the tower; the guide will insist that it be done at the end of the tour, but at the end of the tour will ignore you, so after the tour is over insist that the door be opened. A guard will be assigned to escort you up to the top, past the gilded grill through which the sultan eavesdropped on the meetings of his ministers of state. The view from the top is splendid.

Beyond the Hall with Şadırvan is the narrow **Black Eunuchs' Courtyard**, decorat-ed in Kütahya tiles from the 17th century. Behind the marble colonnade on the left are the **Black Eunuchs' Dormitories.** In the early days white eunuchs were used, but black eunuchs sent as presents by the Ottoman governor of Egypt later took control. As many as 200 lived here, guarding the doors and waiting on the women.

Near the far end of the courtyard on the left, a staircase leads up to the rooms in which imperial princes were given their primary schooling. On the right is the Chief Black Eunuch's room. Neither of these was open to the public at this writing.

At the far end of the courtyard, safely protected by the eunuchs, is the **Cümle Kapısı** (Main Gate) into the Harem proper, and another **guard room** with two gigantic gilded mirrors. From this, the **Cariyeler Koridoru** (Concubines' Corridor) on the left leads to the **Cariye ve Kadınefendi Taşlığı** (Concubines' & Consorts' Courtyard). A concubine *(cariye)* came by gift or purchase; the more talented and intelligent rose in the palace service to hold offices in the administration of the Harem *(kadınefendi)*; the less talented waited on the more talented.

The **Valide Sultan's Quarters & Courtyard**, the very centre of power in the Harem, include a large salon, a small bedroom, a room for prayer and other small chambers. Mannikins dressed in period costumes help you to visualise the scene as the valide sultan oversaw and controlled her huge 'family'. After his accession to the throne, a new sultan came here to receive the allegiance and congratulations of the people of the Harem.

The sultan, as he walked these corridors, wore slippers with silver soles. As no woman was allowed to show herself to the sultan without specific orders, the clatter of the silver soles warned residents of the sultan's approach allowing them to disappear from his sight. This rule no doubt solidified the valide sultan's control, as *she* got to choose which girls would be presented to the sultan. She chose the most beautiful, talented and intelligent of the Harem girls to be her personal servants, and thus introduced them to her son the sultan.

From the valide sultan's quarters the tour passes the chamber of Abdül Hamit I on the left, then the private hamams and toilets of the valide sultan and the sultan on the right, to the **Hünkâr Sofası,** or Emperor's Chamber, decorated in Delft tiles. This grand room was where the sultan and his ladies gathered for entertainments, often with musicians in the balcony. Designed perhaps by Sinan during the reign of Murat III (1574-95), it was redecorated in Baroque style by Osman III (1754-57). The smaller part of the room remains Baroque; the larger part has had its 16th-century decor restored.

The tour enters a small, oddly shaped room lavishly decorated with 16th-century İznik tiles. In fact this is the remaining half of a small room which was sacrificed to build the adjoining **Privy Chamber of Murat III** (1578), one of the most sumptuous rooms in the palace. Virtually all of the decoration is original, and is probably the work of Sinan. Besides the gorgeous İznik tiles and a fireplace, there is a three-tiered fountain to give the sound of cascading water and, perhaps not coincidentally, to make it difficult to eavesdrop on the sultan's conversations.

Adjoining the Privy Chamber to the west are the **Library of Ahmet I** (1609), with small fountains by each window to cool the summer breezes as they enter the room. Perhaps Ahmet I retired here to inspect plans of his great building project, the Sultan Ahmet Camii. The adjoining **Dining Room of Ahmet III** (1706), with wonderful painted panels of flowers and fruit, was built by Ahmet I's successor.

East of the Privy Chamber of Murat III is the **Double Kiosk**, two rooms dating from around 1600. Note the painted canvas dome in the first room, and the fine tile panels above the fireplace in the second. Fireplaces and braziers – which give off toxic carbon monoxide – were the palace's winter heating system.

North and east of the Double Kiosk is the **Gözdeler Mabeyn Taşlığı ve Daireleri** (Favourites' Courtyard & Apartments). The Turkish word for 'favourite', *gözde,* literally means 'in the eye' (of the sultan).

A long, plain corridor leads east to the **Altınyol** (Golden Road), a passage leading south. A servant of the sultan's would toss gold coins to the women of the Harem here, hence the name.

The tour re-enters the guardroom with the huge gilded mirrors, then exits through the **Kuühane Kapısı** (Birdcage Gate) into the palace's third courtyard. If you want to ascend the Tower of Justice, this is where you corner the guide and insist.

Third Court If you enter the Third Court through the Harem, and thus by the back door, you should head for the main gate into the court. Get the full effect of entering this holy of holies by going out through the gate, and back in again.

This gate, the **Bab-üs Saade**, or Gate of Felicity, also sometimes called the Akağalar Kapısı (Gate of the White Eunuchs), was the entrance into the sultan's private domain. As is common with oriental potentates, the sultan preserved the imperial mystique by appearing in public very seldom. The Third Court was staffed and guarded by white eunuchs, who allowed only a few, very important people in. As you enter the Third Court, imagine it alive with the movements of imperial pages and white eunuchs scurrying here and there in their palace costumes. Every now and then the chief white eunuch or the chief black eunuch would appear, and all would bow deferentially. If the sultan walked across the courtyard, all activity stopped until the event was over.

An exception to the imperial seclusion was the ceremony celebrating a new sultan's accession to the throne. After girding on the sword of Osman, which symbolised imperial power, the new monarch would sit enthroned before the Bab-üs Saade and receive the obeisance, allegiance and congratulations of the empire's high and mighty.

Before the annual military campaigns in summertime, the sultan would also appear before this gate bearing the standard of the Prophet Muhammed to inspire his generals to go out and win one for Islam.

During the great days of the empire, foreign ambassadors were received on days when the janissaries were to get their pay. Huge sacks of silver coins were brought to the Kubbealtı. High court officers would dispense the coins to long lines of the tough, impeccably costumed and faultlessly disciplined troops as the ambassadors looked on in admiration.

Today the Bab-üs Saade is the backdrop for the annual performance of Mozart's *Abduction from the Seraglio* during the International İstanbul Festival in late June and early July.

Arz Odası Just inside the Bab-üs Saade is the Arz Odası, or Audience Chamber, constructed in the 16th century, but refurnished in the 18th century. Important officials and foreign ambassadors were brought to this little kiosk to conduct the high business of state. An ambassador, frisked for weapons and held on each arm by a white eunuch, would approach the sultan. At the proper moment, he knelt and kowtowed; if he didn't, the eunuchs would urge him ever so forcefully to do so.

The sultan, seated on the divans whose cushions are embroidered with over 15,000 seed pearls, inspected the ambassador's gifts and offerings *(pişkeş)* as they were passed through the small doorway *(pişkeş kapısı)* on the left. Even if the sultan and the ambassador could converse in the same language (sultans in the later years knew French, and ambassadors often learned Turkish), all conversation was with the grand vizier. The sultan would not deign to speak to a foreigner, and only the very highest Ottoman officers were allowed to address the monarch directly.

Seferli Koğuşu Right behind the Arz Odası is the pretty little **Library of Ahmet III** (1718). Walk to the right as you are leaving the Arz Odası, and enter the rooms of the Seferli Koğuşu (Dormitory of the Expeditionary Force), which now house the rich collections of imperial robes, kaftans and uniforms (Padişah Elbiseleri) worked in silver and gold thread. Textile design reached its highest point during the reign of Süleyman the Magnificent, when the imperial workshops produced cloths of exquisite design and work.

Hazine Next along on the same side are the chambers of the Hazine (Imperial Treasury), packed with an incredible number and variety of objects made from or decorated with gold, silver, rubies, emeralds, jade, pearls and diamonds. Look for the tiny figurine of a sultan sitting under a canopy, his body one enormous pearl. Next to him, a black eunuch's pantaloons are also one pearl.

The Kaşıkçının Elması, or Spoonmaker's Diamond, is an 86-carat rock surrounded by several dozen smaller stones. First worn by Mehmet IV at his accession to the throne in 1648, it is the world's fifth-largest diamond. There's also an uncut emerald weighing 3.26kg, and the golden dagger set with three large emeralds which was the object of Peter Ustinov's criminal quest in the movie *Topkapi*.

Also be sure to see the gold throne given by Nadir Shah of Persia to Mahmud I (1730-54). Other thrones are almost as breathtaking.

Next door to the Imperial Treasury is the **Hayat Balkonu**, or the Balcony of Life. From here the breeze is cool and there's a marvellous view of the Bosphorus and the Sea of Marmara.

Hırka-i Saadet Opposite the Imperial Treasury is another set of wonders, the holy relics in the Hırka-i Saadet, or Suite of the Felicitous Cloak, nowadays called the Mukaddes Emanetler Dairesi (Sacred Safekeeping Rooms). These rooms, sumptuously decorated with İznik faïence, constitute a holy of holies within the palace. Only the chosen could enter the Third Court, but entry into the Hırka-i Saadet rooms was for the chosen of the chosen, and even then only on ceremonial occasions.

Notice, in the entry room, the carved door from the Kaaba in Mecca and, hanging from the ceiling, gilded rain gutters from the same place. Don't miss the harmonious dome above.

To the right (north) a room contains the cloak of the Prophet Muhammed and other relics. Sometimes an imam is seated here, chanting passages from the Koran. The 'felicitous cloak' itself resides in a golden casket in a special alcove along with the battle standard. During the empire, this suite of rooms was opened only once a year so that the imperial family could pay homage to the memory of the Prophet on the 15th day of the holy month of Ramazan. Even though anyone, prince or commoner, faithful or infidel, can enter the rooms now, you should respect the sacred atmosphere by observing decorous behaviour.

On the opposite side (south) of the entry room are more relics: a letter from Muhammed to the governor of El Aksa mosque in Jerusalem, a hair of the Prophet's beard and a print in clay of his foot; Caliph Omar's sword and the Koran that was read by Caliph Osman when he was murdered; Joseph's turban; and even Moses' walking stick!

Other Exhibits Between the Treasury and the Hırka-i Saadet is the Hazine Koğuşu, or Treasury Barracks, with exhibits of Turkish and Islamic bibliographic arts, including calligraphy and illumination; and portraits of the sultans (Padişah portreleri).

Other exhibits in the Third Court include the **Ağalar Camii**, or Mosque of the Eunuchs, another little **library**, Turkish miniature paintings, imperial monograms, seals and arms, calligraphy, and portraits of the sultans. In the room with the seals, notice the graceful, elaborate *tuğra* (TOO-rah, monogram) of the sultans. The tuğra, placed at the top of any imperial proclamation, contains elaborate calligraphic rendering of the names of the sultan and his father, eg 'Abdül Hamit Khan, son of Abdül Mecit Khan, Ever Victorious'.

Fourth Court Four imperial pleasure domes occupy the north-easternmost part of the palace, sometimes called the gardens, or Fourth Court. The **Mecidiye Köşkü** was built by Abdül Mecit (1839-61) according to 19th-century European models. Beneath it is the Konyalı Restaurant, which fills up by noon. If you want to dine here, arrive by 11.30 am, or after 2 pm.

In the other direction (north-east) is the **Mustafa Paşa Köşkü**, or Kiosk of Mustafa Pasha, sometimes called the Sofa Köşkü. Also here is the room of the *hekimbaşı*, or chief physician to the sultan, who was always one of the sultan's Jewish subjects.

During the reign of Sultan Ahmet III (1703-30), known as the Tulip Period because of a rage for these flowers which spread through the upper classes, the gardens around the Sofa Köşkü were filled with tulips. Little lamps would be set out among the hundreds of varieties at night. A new variety of the flower earned its creator fame, money and social recognition. Tulips had been grown in Turkey from very early times, having come originally from Persia. Some bulbs were brought to Holland during the Renaissance. The Dutch, fascinated by the possibilities in the flower, developed and created many varieties, some of which made their way back to Turkey and began the tulip craze there.

Up the stairs at the end of the tulip garden are two of the most enchanting kiosks. Sultan Murat IV (1623-40) built the **Revan Köşkü**, or Erivan Kiosk, in 1635 after reclaiming the city of Yerevan (now in Armenia) from Persia. He also constructed the **Bağdat Köşkü**, or Baghdad Kiosk, in 1638 to commemorate his victory over that city. Notice the İznik tiles, the inlay and woodwork, and the views all around.

Just off the open terrace with the wishing well is the **Sünnet Odası**, or Circumcision Room, used for the ritual that admits Muslim boys to manhood. (Circumcision is usually performed when the boy is nine or 10.) The outer walls of the chamber are graced by particularly beautiful tile panels.

Has Ahırları Though closed for renovation, the Has Ahırları (Imperial Stables) are entered from the Second Court, just to the north-west of the middle gate (Ortakapı). Go down the cobbled slope.

Leaving the Palace As you leave the palace proper through the Ortakapı, you can walk to your right and down the slope along Osman Hamdi Bey Yokuşu to the archaeological museums, or straight to Aya Sofya. I'll assume, for the moment, that you're heading for Aya Sofya, only a few steps away.

Sultan III Ahmet Çeşmesi

Heading for Aya Sofya from Topkapı Sarayı, take a look at the ornate little structure on your left just after you pass beneath the Bab-i Hümayun, or imperial gate. It's the Fountain of Ahmet III, built in 1728 by the sultan who so favoured tulips. It replaced a Byzantine fountain at the same spring.

The ornate Bab-i Hümayun was the gate by which the sultan would enter Aya Sofya for prayers. It led to the Hünkar Mahfili, or Imperial Loge, which you'll see once inside the mosque.

Soğukçeşme Sokak

Soğukçeşme Sokak, or Street of the Cold Fountain, runs between the Topkapı Sarayı walls and Aya Sofya. This street of Ottoman-style houses was entirely restored by the Turkish Touring & Automobile Association. The houses clinging to the palace walls are the Ayasofya Pansiyonları, or Aya Sofya Pensions. At the far (western) end of the street is the entrance to the Restaurant Sarnıç, or Cistern Restaurant, in a restored Byzantine cistern, and across the street from it the Konuk Evi, a new hotel and garden restaurant built in the old İstanbul manner. (See the Places to Stay and Places to Eat chapters.)

Aya Sofya

The Church of the Divine Wisdom (Sancta Sophia in Latin, Hagia Sofia in Greek, Aya Sofya in Turkish; see the accompanying Aya Sofya map) was not named after a

AYA SOFYA (Sancta Sophia)

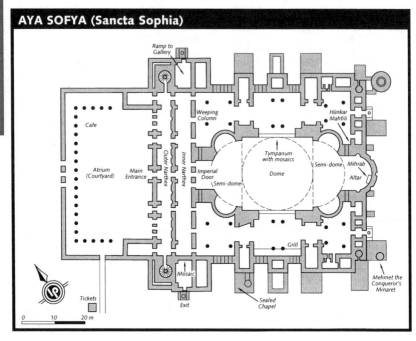

saint; its name means Holy (sancta, hagia) Wisdom (sophia). Aya Sofya (☎ 212-522 1750) is open daily except Monday from 9 am to 4 pm (later in summer); the galleries with their mosaics are open from 9 am to 3.30 pm, till 4.30 pm in summer. Admission costs US$5, students half-price.

Emperor Justinian (527-65) had the church built as yet another effort to restore the greatness of the Roman Empire. It was constructed on the site of Byzantium's acropolis, which had also been the site of an earlier Aya Sofya destroyed in the Nika riots of 532. Justinian's church was completed in 537 and reigned as the greatest church in Christendom until the conquest of Constantinople in 1453.

A lot can happen to a building in 14 centuries, especially in an earthquake zone, and a lot has certainly happened to Aya Sofya. Ignore, if you can, the clutter of buttresses and supports, kiosks, tombs and outbuildings which hug its massive walls, and the renovations which are filling the interior with scaffolding.

In Justinian's time, a street led uphill from the west straight to the main door. Today the ticket kiosk is at the south-west side. To experience the church as its architects, Anthemius of Tralles and Isidorus of Miletus, intended, walk to the Atrium (courtyard) before the main entrance. Here are the sunken ruins of a Theodosian church (404-15), and the low original steps. Enter through the main entrance slowly, one step at a time, looking ahead: at first there is only darkness broken by the brilliant colours of stained-glass windows. As your eyes adjust to the dark, two massive doorways appear within, in the Outer Narthex and Inner Narthex, and far beyond them in the dim light, a semi-dome blazing with gold mosaics (presently obscured by scaffolding) portraying the Madonna & Child – she as Queen of Heaven. Take a few steps and stop just inside the threshold of the main entrance: the far mosaic is clear and beautiful, and the apse beneath it makes a harmonious whole.

Look up from where you are standing now in the Outer Narthex to see a brilliant mosaic of Christ as Pantocrator (Ruler of All) above the third and largest door (the Imperial Door in the Inner Narthex), visible except for the august expression on the face.

Stand in the doorway between the Outer and Inner Narthexes and the face of the Pantocrator becomes visible. Look deep into the church again, and you'll see that the semi-dome of the Madonna & Child is topped by another semi-dome, and above that is the famous, gigantic main dome of the church; at the same time, you are facing the Pantocrator in all His majesty.

Walk through the second door into the Inner Narthex and towards the immense Imperial Door, and you are surprised to see that the 'gigantic main dome' is in fact only another semi-dome: halfway to the Imperial Door, a row of windows peeks out above the larger semi-dome and betrays the secret. As you approach the Imperial Threshold the real, magnificent main dome soars above you and seems to be held up by nothing. Justinian, on entering his great creation for the first time almost 1500 years ago, exclaimed, 'Glory to God that I have been judged worthy of such a work. Oh Solomon! I have outdone you!'

During its years as a church (almost 1000), only imperial processions were permitted to enter through the central, Imperial Door. You can still notice the depressions in the stone by each door just inside the threshold where imperial guards stood. It was through the Imperial Door that Mehmet the Conqueror came in 1453 to take possession for Islam of the greatest religious edifice in the world. Before he entered, historians tell us, he sprinkled earth on his head in a gesture of humility. Aya Sofya

remained a mosque until 1935, when Atatürk proclaimed it a museum.

There are bigger buildings, and bigger domes, but not without modern construction materials such as reinforced concrete and steel girders. The achievement of the architects is unequalled. The sense of air and space in the nave, the 30 million gold *tesserae* (mosaic tiles) which covered the dome's interior, and the apparent lack of support for the dome made the Byzantines gasp in amazement. Indeed, it almost was impossible, because the dome lasted only 11 years before an earthquake brought it down in 559.

The dome, a daring attempt at the impossible, is supported by 40 massive ribs constructed of special hollow bricks made in Rhodes from a unique light, porous clay, resting on huge pillars concealed in the interior walls. (Compare them to the Sultan Ahmet Camii's four huge free-standing pillars to appreciate the genius of Aya Sofya.) To appreciate the acoustics, stand beneath the centre of the dome and clap your hands, though the effect is now dampened somewhat by the scaffolding.

Over the centuries it was necessary for succeeding Byzantine emperors and Ottoman sultans to rebuild the dome several times, to add buttresses and other supports and to steady the foundations. Current restoration research shows that the original 6th-century mosaic work was extremely fine, but that later 14th-century repairs were done quickly and poorly.

The Ottoman chandeliers, hanging low above the floor, combined their light with rows of glass oil lamps lining the balustrades of the gallery and even the walkway at the base of the dome. Imagine them all lit to celebrate some great state occasion, with the smell of incense and the chants of the Orthodox liturgy reverberating through the huge interior space!

Justinian ordered the most precious materials for his church. Note the matched marble panels in the walls, and the breccia columns. The Byzantine emperor was crowned while seated in a throne placed

THINGS TO SEE & DO

Dandolo the Doge

Enrico Dandolo (circa 1108-1205), buried in Aya Sofya, came from the prominent Venetian family that supplied Venice with four doges, numerous admirals and a colonial empire. Dandolo became doge in 1192. During the Fourth Crusade of 1203-04, he diverted the crusader armies from their goal of an assault on the infidels to an assault on the friendly but rival Christian city of Constantinople. Venice got the better part of the rich spoils, as well as numerous Byzantine territories. Dandolo ruled three-eighths of conquered Constantinople, including Sancta Sophia, until his death in 1205, when he was buried here. Look for his tomb, marked by a marble slab inscribed DANDOLO in the floor of the south gallery toward its eastern wall.

Tradition tells us that Dandolo's tomb was broken open after the Conquest of the city in 1453, and his bones thrown to the dogs.

within the Omphalion, the square of inlaid marble in the main floor. The nearby raised platform was added during the Ottoman period, as was the *mihrab* (prayer niche), which shows the faithful the direction in which Mecca lies. The large alabaster urns were added by Sultan Murat III (1574-95) so that worshippers could perform their ritual ablutions here before prayer.

The large 19th-century medallions inscribed with gilt Arabic letters, the work of master calligrapher Mustafa İzzet Efendi, give the names of God (Allah), Muhammed and the early caliphs Ali and Abu Bakr.

The curious, elevated kiosk, screened from public view, is the **Hünkar Mahfili** or Imperial Loge. Ahmet III (1703-30) had it built so he could come, pray and go unseen, preserving the imperial mystique.

In the side aisle to the left of the Imperial Door is the 'weeping column', with a copper facing pierced by a hole. Legend has it that those who put their finger in the hole and make a wish will see it come true if the finger emerges moist.

Mosaics Justinian filled his church with fine mosaics. The Byzantine church and state later endured a fierce civil war (726-87) over the question of whether images were biblically correct or not. The debated passage was Exodus 20:4:

Thou shalt not make unto thee any graven image, or any likeness of anything that is in heaven above, or that is in the earth beneath, or that is in the water under the earth: Thou shalt not bow down thyself to them, nor serve them.

Though the Bible seems clear, images (icons, mosaics, statues) were very popular, and the iconoclasts ('image-breakers') were ultimately defeated. It's interesting to speculate whether iconoclastic Islam, militant and triumphant at this time, had any influence on Byzantine theology.

When the Turks took Constantinople there was no controversy. The Koran repeatedly rails against idolatry, as in Sura 16:

We sent a Messenger into every nation saying, Serve God and give up idols.

Islamic art is supposed to have no saints' portraits, no pictures of animals, fish or fowl, nor anything else with an immortal soul, and the mosaics had to go. Luckily they were covered with plaster rather than destroyed, and some have been uncovered successfully.

From the floor of Aya Sofya, 9th-century mosaic portraits of St Ignatius the Younger (800s), St John Chrysostom (around 400) and St Ignatius Theodorus of Antioch are visible high up at the base of the northern tympanum (semicircle) beneath the dome. Even better mosaics are in the galleries, reached by a switchback ramp at the northern end of the Narthex, and reserved for female worshippers in Byzantine times.

The striking Deesis, in the south gallery (where the best mosaics are found), dates from the early 14th century. Christ is at the centre, with the Virgin Mary on the left, and John the Baptist on the right.

At the eastern (apse) end of the south gallery is the famous mosaic portrait of the Empress Zoe (1028-50). When her portrait was done she was 50 years old and newly married (by her dying father's command) to the aged Romanus III Argyrus. Upon Romanus' 'mysterious' death in his bath in 1034, she had his face excised and that of her youthful, virile new husband, Michael IV, put in its place. Eight years later, with Michael dead from an illness contracted on campaign, Zoe and her sister Theodora ruled as empresses in their own right, but did it so badly that it was clear she had to marry again. At the age of 64, Zoe wed an eminent senator who became the third Mr Zoe, Constantine IX Monomachus, whose portrait remains only because he outlived the empress. The inscription reads, 'Constantine, by the Divine Christ, Faithful King of the Romans'.

As you leave the Narthex and enter the passage to the outside, turn and look up to see the Madonna & Child, one of the church's finest late 10th-century mosaics, above the door. Constantine the Great, on the left, offers Mary the city of Constantinople; Emperor Justinian, on the right, offers her Aya Sofya.

As you exit the museum, the şadırvan fountain to the right was for Muslim ablutions. Immediately to your left is the church's baptistry, converted after the Conquest to a tomb for sultans Mustafa and Ibrahim. Other tombs are clustered behind it: those of Murat III, Selim II, Mehmet III and various princes. The minarets were added by Mehmet the Conqueror (1451-81), Beyazıt II (1481-1512) and Selim II (1566-74).

Haseki Hürrem Hamamı

Every mosque had a steam bath nearby. Aya Sofya's is across the road to the left (east) of the park with the fountain. It's the Haseki Hürrem Hamamı, or Baths of Lady Hürrem, designed by Sinan and built in 1556 on the site of earlier Byzantine baths. It's now a carpet gallery and shop, the Turkish Handwoven Carpets Sale Centre (☎ 212-511 8192), open daily except Tuesday from 9.30 am to 5 pm; admission is free.

Designed as a 'double hamam' with identical baths for men and women, the centre wall dividing the two has now been breached by a small doorway. Both sides have the three traditional rooms: first the square *frigidarium* for disrobing (on the men's side, this has a pretty marble fountain and stained-glass windows); then the long *tepidarium* for washing, and finally the octagonal caldarium for sweating and massage. In the caldarium, note the four *eyvan* niches and the four semi-private washing rooms. The *göbektaşı* (hot platform) in the men's bath is inlaid with coloured marble.

The carpet shop, by the way, offers guaranteed quality and fixed prices, but some readers of this book have found its prices surprisingly high.

Sultan Ahmet Camii (Blue Mosque)

There used to be palaces just south of Aya Sofya where the Sultan Ahmet Camii (Mosque of Sultan Ahmet or the Blue Mosque) now stands. The Byzantine emperors built several of them, stretching from near Aya Sofya all the way to the site of the mosque. You can see a mosaic from one of these palaces, still in place, in the Büyüksaray Mozaik Müzesi.

Sultan Ahmet I (1603-17) set out to build a mosque that would rival and even surpass the achievement of Justinian. He came close to his goal. The Sultan Ahmet Camii is a triumph of harmony, proportion and elegance, and its architect, Mehmet Ağa, achieves the sort of visual experience on the exterior that Aya Sofya has on the interior.

As with Aya Sofya, you must approach the Sultan Ahmet Camii properly in order to appreciate its architectural mastery. Don't walk straight from Aya Sofya to the Sultan

Ahmet Camii through the crowd of touts. Rather, go out to the middle of the Hippodrome and approach the mosque from its front.

Walk towards the mosque and through the gate in the peripheral wall. Note the small dome atop the gate: this is the motif Mehmet Ağa uses to lift your eyes to heaven. As you walk through the gate, your eyes follow a flight of stairs up to another gate topped by another dome; through this gate is yet another dome, that of the şadırvan in the centre of the mosque courtyard. As you ascend the stairs, semi-domes come into view, one after another: first the one over the mosque's main door, then the one above it, and another, and another. Finally the **main dome** crowns the whole, and your attention is drawn to the sides, where forests of smaller domes reinforce the effect, completed by the **minarets**, which lift your eyes heavenward.

The layout of the Sultan Ahmet Camii is classic Ottoman design. The forecourt contains an ablutions fountain in its centre. The portico around three sides could be used for prayer and meditation, or for study during warm weather.

The Sultan Ahmet Camii is such a popular tourist sight that admission is controlled so as to preserve its sacred atmosphere. Only worshippers are admitted through the main door; tourists must use the north door and are not admitted at prayer times. At the north door an attendant will take your shoes; if your clothing is immodest by local standards, you'll be lent a robe. There's no charge for this, but you may be asked to make a donation for the mosque.

Though the stained-glass windows are replacements, they still create the luminous effects of the originals. The semi-domes and the dome are painted in graceful arabesques. The 'blue' of the mosque's English nickname comes from the **İznik tiles** that line the walls, particularly in the gallery (which is not open to the public).

You can see immediately why the Sultan Ahmet Camii, constructed between 1606 and 1616, over 1000 years after Aya Sofya,

is not as daring as Aya Sofya. Four massive pillars hold up the less ambitious dome, a less elegant but sturdier solution to the problem.

Note also the Imperial Loge, covered with marble latticework, to the left; the piece of the sacred Black Stone from the Ka'aba in Mecca, embedded in the mihrab; the grandfather clock, useful as prayers must be made at exact times; and the high, elaborate chair *(mahfil)* from which the imam (teacher) gives the sermon on Friday. The *mimber*, or pulpit, is the structure with a curtained doorway at floor level, a flight of steps and a small kiosk topped by a spire. From this mimber, of fine marble skilfully carved, the destruction of the janissary corps was proclaimed in 1826.

Mosques built by the great and powerful usually included numerous public-service institutions. Clustered around the Sultan Ahmet Camii were a *medrese* (theological school); an *imaret* (soup kitchen) serving the poor; a hamam so that the faithful could bathe on Friday, the holy day; and shops, the rent from which supported the upkeep of the mosque. The tomb *(türbe)* of the mosque's great patron, Sultan Ahmet I, is on the north side facing the fountain park (open for visits daily except Monday and Tuesday from 9.30 am to 4.30 pm). Buried with Ahmet are his brothers, Sultan Osman II and Sultan Murat IV.

Halı ve Kilim Müzesi Up the stone ramp on the Sultan Ahmet Camii's north side is the Halı ve Kilim Müzesi (Carpet & Kilim Museum, ☎ 212-528 5332), with displays of some of the country's finest. It's open daily except Sunday and Monday from 9 am to 4 pm; admission costs US$1.

Büyüksaray Mozaik Müzesi When archaeologists from the University of Ankara and the University of St Andrew's (Scotland) dug at the back (east) of the Sultan Ahmet Camii in the mid-1950s, they uncovered a mosaic pavement dating from early Byzantine times, circa 500 AD. It is now preserved in the Büyüksaray Mozaik

Müzesi, or Great Palace Mosaic Museum. The pavement, filled with wonderful hunting and mythological scenes and emperors' portraits, was a triumphal way that led from the Byzantine emperor's Great Palace, which stood where the Sultan Ahmet Camii now stands, down to the harbour of Boucoleon. The dust and rubble of 1500 years have left the excavated pavement considerably lower than ground level.

Other 5th-century mosaics were saved providentially when Sultan Ahmet had shops built on top of them. A row of shops, called the **Arasta**, was intended to provide rent revenues for the upkeep of the mosque. Now they house numerous souvenir vendors and the exit from the museum.

The museum is open daily except Tuesday from 9 am to 5 pm, for US$1. To find the entrance, go halfway along the Arasta, turn east through a passage, and then right (south).

After you've paid your admission fee, descend to the walkways around the sunken mosaics. The intricate work is impressive, with hunters, beasts, maidens and swains. Note the ribbon border with heart-shaped leaves surrounding the mosaic. In the westernmost room is the most colourful and dramatic picture, that of two men in leggings carrying spears and holding off a raging tiger.

The Hippodrome

The Hippodrome, or Atmeydanı (Horse Grounds), was the centre of Byzantium's life for 1000 years and of Ottoman life for another 400 years. It was the scene of countless political and military dramas during the long life of this city.

History In Byzantine times, the rival chariot teams of 'Greens' and 'Blues' had seperate political connections. Support for a team was akin to membership of a political party, and a team victory had important affects on policy. A Byzantine emperor might lose his throne as the result of a postmatch riot.

Ottoman sultans kept an eye on activities in the Hippodrome. If things were going badly in the empire, a surly crowd gathering here could signal the start of a disturbance, then a riot, then a revolution. In 1826, the slaughter of the debased and unruly janissary corps was carried out here by the reformer Sultan Mahmut II. Almost a century later, in 1909, there were riots here which caused the downfall of Abdül Hamit II and the repromulgation of the Ottoman constitution.

Though the Hippodrome might be the scene of their downfall, Byzantine emperors and Ottoman sultans outdid one another in beautifying it. Many of the priceless statues carved by ancient masters have disappeared. The soldiers of the Fourth Crusade sacked Constantinople, a Christian ally city, in 1204, tearing all the bronze plates from the stone obelisk at the Hippodrome's southern end in the mistaken belief that they were gold. The crusaders also stole the famous *quadriga*, or team of four horses cast in bronze, a copy of which now sits atop the main door of the Basilica di San Marco in Venice (the original is in the museum inside).

Monuments Near the northern end of the Hippodrome, the little gazebo in beautiful stonework is actually **Kaiser Wilhelm's fountain**. The German emperor paid a state visit to Abdül Hamit II in 1901 and presented this fountain to the sultan and his people as a token of friendship. According to the Ottoman inscription, the fountain was built in the Hijri (Muslim lunar calendar) year of 1316 (1898-99 AD). The monograms in the stonework are those of Abdül Hamit II and Wilhelm II, and represent their political union.

The impressive granite obelisk with hieroglyphs is called the **Obelisk of Theodosius**, carved in Egypt around 1450 BC. According to the hieroglyphs, it was erected in Heliopolis (now a Cairo suburb) to commemorate the victories of Thutmose III (1504-1450 BC). The Byzantine emperor, Theodosius, had it brought from Egypt to Constantinople in 390 AD. He then had it erected on a marble pedestal engraved with scenes of himself in the midst of various imperial pastimes. Theodosius' self-promoting marble billboards have weathered badly over the centuries. However, the magnificent obelisk, spaced above the pedestal by four bronze blocks, is as crisply cut and shiny as when it was carved from the living rock in Upper Egypt some 3500 years ago.

South of the obelisk is a strange **spiral column** coming up out of a hole in the ground. It was once much taller and was topped by three serpents' heads. Originally cast to commemorate a victory of the Hellenic confederation over the Persians, it stood in front of the temple of Apollo at Delphi from 478 BC until Constantine the Great had it brought to his new capital city around 330 AD. Though badly bashed up in the Byzantine struggle over the place of images in the church, the serpents' heads survived until the early 18th century. Now all that remains of them is one upper jaw, housed in İstanbul's Archaeological Museum.

The level of the Hippodrome rose over the centuries, as civilisation piled up its dust and refuse here. The obelisk and serpentine column were cleaned out and tidied up by the British troops who occupied the city after the Ottoman defeat in WWI.

No-one is quite sure who built the large **rough-stone obelisk** at the southern end of the Hippodrome. All we know is that it was repaired by Constantine VII Porphyrogenetus (913-59), and that its sheath of bronze plates were ripped off during the Fourth Crusade.

Türk ve İslam Eserleri Müzesi

The Palace of İbrahim Paşa (1524) is on the western side of the Hippodrome. Now housing the Türk ve İslam Eserleri Müzesi, or Turkish & Islamic Arts Museum (☎ 212-522 1888), it gives you a glimpse into the opulent life of the Ottoman upper class in the time of Süleyman the Magnificent. İbrahim Paşa was Süleyman's close friend, son-in-law and grand vizier. His wealth, power and influence on the monarch

became so great that others wishing to influence the sultan became envious. After a rival accused İbrahim of disloyalty, Süleyman's favourite, Haseki Hürrem Sultan (Roxelana), convinced her husband that İbrahim was a threat. Süleyman had him strangled.

The museum is open from 9 am to 4.30 pm daily; closed on Monday. Admission costs US$2.50. Labels are in Turkish and English. A video show on the 1st floor gives you a quick summary of Turkish history, and explains the sultan's tuğra (monogram) and *ferman* (imperial edict). The coffee shop in the museum is a welcome refuge from the press of crowds and touts in the Hippodrome.

Highlights among the exhibits, which date from the 8th and 9th centuries up to the 19th century, are the decorated wooden Koran cases from the high Ottoman period; the calligraphy exhibits, including fermans with tuğras; Turkish miniatures; and illuminated manuscripts. You'll also want to have a look at the *rahles*, or Koran stands, and the many carpets from all periods.

The lower floor of the museum houses ethnographic exhibits. At the entry is a black tent *(kara çadır)* like those used by nomads in eastern Turkey. Inside the tent is an explanation of nomadic customs, in English. Inside the museum building are village looms on which carpets and kilims are woven, and an exhibit of the plants and materials used to make natural textile dyes for the carpets. Perhaps most fascinating are the domestic interiors, including those of a *yurt* (Central Asian felt hut), a village house from Yuntdağ, and a late 19th-century house from Bursa. One display shows women shopping for cloth; another, a scene of daily life in an İstanbul home of the early 20th century.

The buildings behind and beside İbrahim Paşa's palace are İstanbul's law courts and legal administration buildings.

Gülhane Park & Sublime Porte

Walk downhill from Yerebatan Saray along Alemdar Caddesi with Aya Sofya on your right. Just past a big tree in the middle of the road, the street turns left, but just in front of you is the arched gateway to Gülhane Parkı.

Before entering the park, look to the left. That bulbous little kiosk built into the park walls at the next street corner is the **Alay Köşkü**, or Parade Kiosk, from which the sultan would watch the periodic parades of troops and trade guilds, which commemorated great holidays and military victories.

Across the street from the Alay Köşkü (not quite visible right from the Gülhane gate) is a gate leading into the precincts of what was once the grand vizierate, or Ottoman prime ministry, known in the west as the Sublime Porte. Today the buildings beyond the gate hold various offices of the İstanbul provincial government.

Gülhane Park was once the palace park of Topkapı. Crowds pack it at weekends to enjoy its green shade, its small zoo (the camels and Angora goats are the most interesting exhibits), live music, street food and the musty **Tanzimat Müzesi** (☎ 212-512 6384), open daily from 9 am to 5 pm. 'Tanzimat' (Reorganisation) was the name given to the political and societal reforms planned by Sultan Abdül Mecit in 1839 and carried out through the middle of the 19th century.

At the far (north) end of the park, up the hill, is a flight of steps used as seats, and a small tea garden – a secret corner good for a few quiet moments.

Archaeological Museums

İstanbul's **Arkeoloji Müzeleri** (Archaeological Museum Complex), between Gülhane Park and Topkapı, can be reached most easily by walking down the slope from Topkapı's Court of the Janissaries. Admission to the complex (closed Monday) costs US$2.50.

The complex is divided into nine separate exhibit areas, which are never all open at the same time due to insufficient staff. The schedule changes from time to time, but presently the Arkeoloji Müzeleri (☎ 212-520 7740) is open most days from 9 am to 4.30 pm (last ticket sold at 4 pm), but the Eski Şark Eserler Müzesi, or Museum of

the Ancient Orient, is only open from Tuesday to Friday, and the Çinili Köşk, or Tiled Kiosk, only on Tuesday afternoon.

These museums were the palace collections, formed during the 19th century and added to greatly during the republic. While not immediately as dazzling as Topkapı, they contain a wealth of artefacts from the 50 centuries of Anatolia's history.

The **Eski Şark Eserler Müzesi**, or Museum of the Ancient Orient, contains the gates of ancient Babylon from the time of Nebuchadnezzar II (604-562 BC), clay tablets bearing Hammurabi's famous law code (in cuneiform, of course), ancient Egyptian scarabs, and artefacts from the Assyrian and Hittite empires. It is a rich collection.

The Ottoman Turkish inscription over the door of the **Arkeoloji Müzesi** reads 'Eser-i Atika Müzesi', or Museum of Ancient Works. The neoclassical building houses an extensive collection of Hellenic, Hellenistic and Roman statuary and sarcophagi. Signs are in Turkish and English.

A Roman statue in the archaic style of the daemonic god Bes greets you as you enter. Turn left to see the ancient monolithic basalt sarcophagus of King Tabnit of Egypt. Its former occupant is in a neighbouring glass case. Nearby, the famous marble Alexander sarcophagus is now known not to have been Alexander's, but is nonetheless an impressive work of art.

In a long room behind the entrance hall is a mock-up of the facade of the Temple of Athena at Assos (Behramkale). Erected in 525 BC, it was the first and only temple of the Archaic Period designed in the Doric order. The frieze depicted hunting and banquet scenes, and battles of the centaurs. Some bits of the original frieze have been incorporated here; other bits are in the Louvre and in Boston.

On the mezzanine level above the Temple of Athena is an exhibition called 'İstanbul Through the Ages', tracing the city's entire history, concentrating on its most famous buildings and public spaces: Archaic, Hellenistic, Roman, Byzantine and Ottoman.

To the right of the entrance hall are the statuary galleries. In ancient Greece and Rome, sculpture was an important element in the decoration of building facades and public spaces. Artisans at Anatolia's three main sculpture centres – Aphrodisias, Ephesus and Miletus – turned out thousands of beautiful works, the best of which have been collected here and arranged by period: Archaic, Persian, Hellenistic and Roman.

The museum's 2nd and 3rd floors were closed for renovation at the time of writing.

The **Çinili Köşk**, or Tiled Kiosk, of Sultan Mehmet the Conqueror is the oldest surviving nonreligious Turkish building in İstanbul, constructed in 1472 not long after the Conquest. Though once completely covered in fine tile work, only the tile work on the facade remains. The kiosk, once an imperial residence, now houses an excellent collection of Turkish faïence including many good examples of İznik tiles from the period in the 17th and 18th centuries when that city produced the finest coloured tiles in the world.

South of the Hippodrome

Take a detour into the district's back streets for a look at a feat of Byzantine engineering and two exquisite small mosques.

Facing south, with the Sultan Ahmet Camii on your left, go to the end of the Hippodrome and turn left, then right, onto Aksakal Sokak. Soon you'll be able to recognise the filled-in arches of the Byzantine **Sphendoneh** on your right. The Sphendoneh supported the southern end of the Hippodrome.

Follow the curve of the street around to the right and onto Kaleci Sokak. The next intersecting street is Mehmet Paşa Sokak; turn left to find the **Küçük Aya Sofya Camii**, or 'Little' Aya Sofya. However, if the mosque is not open, look around or signal to a boy on the street and the guardian will come with the key.

Justinian and Theodora built this little church sometime between 527 and 536. Inside, the layout and decor are typical of an early Byzantine church, though the building was repaired and expanded several times during its life having been converted into a mosque after the Conquest. Repairs and enlargements to convert the church to a mosque were added by the chief white eunuch Hüseyin Ağa around 1500. His tomb is to the left as you enter. The medrese cells are arranged around the mosque's forecourt (compare it to the Sokollu Mehmet Paşa Camii, the next attraction on this walk), which is now a park with a teahouse.

Go north on Mehmet Paşa Sokak, back up the hill to the neighbouring **Sokollu Mehmet Paşa Camii**. This one was built during the height of Ottoman architectural development in 1571 by the empire's greatest architect, Sinan. Though named after the grand vizier of the time, it was really sponsored by his wife Esmahan, daughter of Sultan Selim II. Besides its architectural harmony, typical of Sinan's greatest works, the mosque is unusual because the medrese is not a separate building but actually part of the mosque structure, built around the forecourt (compare it to the similar plan of the Mihrimah Camii, described in the Edirnekapı section later in this chapter).

If the mosque is not open, wait for the guardian to appear. When you enter, notice the harmonious form, the coloured marble and the spectacular İznik tiles – some of the best ever made. The mosque contains four fragments from the sacred Black Stone in the Kaaba at Mecca: one above the entrance framed in gold, two in the mimber and one in the mihrab. Interestingly, the marble pillars by the mihrab revolve if the foundations have been disturbed by an earthquake – an ingenious early warning device.

Surrounding the mosque are several ruined religious buildings, including a Halveti dervish *tekke* (lodge), and an Uzbek tekke for Nakşibendi dervishes.

Walk back up the hill on Suterazisi Sokak to return to the Hippodrome.

South-east of the Sultan Ahmet Camii near the shore is the **Hamamzade İsmail Dede Efendi Evi Müzesi** (☎ 212-516 4314),

YEREBATAN SARAY

GEOFF STRINGER

Built in 532 AD the Yerebatan Saray, or Basilica Cistern, is the largest surviving Byzantine cistern in İstanbul.

In fact it's not a basilica at all, but an enormous water storage tank constructed by Emperor Justinian the Great (527-65), who was incapable of thinking in small terms. Columns, capitals and plinths from ruined buildings were among those used in its construction.

The cistern, also known as the Sunken Palace, is 70m wide and 140m long and its roof is supported by 336 columns. Two columns in the north-western corner are supported by two blocks carved into Medusa heads. The cistern was used to support part of the city during lengthy sieges. The water was pumped and delivered through nearly 20km of aqueducts from a reservoir near the Black Sea.

The cistern once held 80,000 cubic metres of water but it became a dumping ground for all sorts of junk, as well as corpses. Since it was built the cistern has undergone a number of facelifts most notably in the 18th century and then between 1955-60. The cistern was then cleaned and renovated between 1985-88 by the İstanbul Municipality.

Today, water still drips through the ceiling and you can see coloured lights, listen to recorded western classical music, wander a maze of walkways and spot carp in the water.

Located diagonally across the street from the Aya Sofya, Yerebatan Saray is open from 9 am to 4.30 pm (5.30 pm in summer) and admission costs US$3.50, US$3 for students. The exit from Yerebatan Saray is through a gift shop onto Alemdar Caddesi.

Yerebatan Saray in Eminönü. A total of 336 columns support the roof of this vast and eerie underground reservoir.

EDDIE GERALD

The remains of Byzantine mosaics glow on the walls of Aya Sofya.

Akbıyık, Ahırkapı Sokak 17, the restored house of Dede Efendi (1778-1846) a famous Ottoman musical composer of the Mevlevi (whirling) dervish order. The well-restored house (which is open Tuesday, Wednesday, Saturday and Sunday only, from 11 am to 5 pm, for US$0.50) gives you a good idea of living conditions among the Ottoman intelligentsia of the 18th and 19th centuries.

Across the street, the modest **Akbıyık Camii** dates from 1453, and is thus one of the oldest mosques in the city.

DIVAN YOLU (MAPS 6 & 7)

Divan Yolu, the Road to the Imperial Council, is the main thoroughfare of the Old City. Starting from the Hippodrome and Yerebatan Saray on the city's first of seven hills, it heads due west, up another hill, past the Kapalı Çarşı, through Beyazıt Square and past İstanbul University to Aksaray Square. Turning north a bit, it continues to the Topkapı (Cannon Gate) in the ancient city walls. In its progress through the city, its name changes from Divan Yolu to become Yeniçeriler Caddesi, Ordu Caddesi and Turgut Özal (formerly Millet) Caddesi.

This thoroughfare, dating from the early times of Constantinople, was laid out by Roman engineers to connect the city with the Roman roads heading west. The Milion, the great marble milestone from which all distances in Byzantium were measured, is on the south side of the tall shaft of stones which rises above Yerebatan Saray. The street held its importance in Ottoman times, as Mehmet the Conqueror's first palace was in Beyazıt Square, and his new one, Topkapı, was under construction.

Start from Aya Sofya and the Hippodrome and go up the slope on Divan Yolu. The little **Firuz Ağa Camii** on the left, built in 1491, was commissioned by the chief treasurer to Beyazıt II (1481-1512). The style is the simple one of the early Ottomans: a dome on a square base with a plain porch in front.

Just behind Firuz Ağa Camii is the **Palace of Antiochus** (5th century), now mere ruined foundations.

The first major intersection on the right is that with Babıali Caddesi. Turn right onto this street until you reach Nuruosmaniye Caddesi; a block to the right is **Cağaloğlu Square**, once the centre of İstanbul's newspaper and book publishing industry. Most of the newspaper publishers have moved to large, modern buildings outside the city walls, though some of the smaller book publishers survive here. The **Cağaloğlu Hamamı** is just off the square, on the right (see the Entertainment chapter for details).

If instead you turn left (south) from Divan Yolu, you'll be on Klodfarer Caddesi, named after the Turcophile French novelist Claude Farrère. It leads to a small park beneath which lies the 4th-century Byzantine Philoxenes cistern now called **Binbirdirek**, or 'A Thousand-and-One Columns'. A door in the only building on the park grounds opens onto stairs leading down to the cistern, which, regrettably, has been ruined: ugly, intrusive concrete floors have been built to hold shops, but shopkeepers have refused to rent them because of the dampness. It's a total tragedy. The echoing, gloomy space has been violated and spoiled and lots of money wasted at the same time.

Back on Divan Yolu, the impressive enclosure right at the corner of Babıali Caddesi is filled with **tombs** of the Ottoman high and mighty, including several sultans. The first to be built was for Sultan Mahmut II (1808-39), the reforming emperor who wiped out the janissaries and revamped the Ottoman army. Several of Mahmut's successors, including sultans Abdülaziz (1861-76) and Abdül Hamit II (1876-1909), are here as well. The tombs are usually open for visits from 10 am to 5 pm (donation requested).

Right across Divan Yolu from the tombs is a small stone **library** built by the Köprülü family in 1659. The Köprülüs rose to prominence in the mid-17th century and furnished the empire with viziers, generals and grand admirals for centuries. They administered the empire during a time when the scions of the Ottoman dynasty fell well below the standards of Mehmet the Conqueror and Süleyman the Magnificent.

Running south downhill near the library is Piyer Loti Caddesi, named after another French Turcophile author. Follow this street for a short distance and look for the large Eminönü Belediye Başkanlığı (Eminönü Municipal Presidency) building on the right. To the right of the main entrance is a doorway with **Şerefiye Sarnıcı** (Cistern of Theodosius) carved into its lintel. Wander in, have the guard turn on the lights and you can see what Binbirdirek and Yerebatan Saray looked like before being tarted up for tourism.

Back on Divan Yolu, at the corner of Türbedar Sokak is the **Basın Müzesi** (Press Museum), Divan Yolu 84, open from 10 am to 5.30 pm (closed Sunday), without charge. The old printing presses will interest some, the lively *Müze Café* will interest more as it serves cappuccino (US$1.75), Turkish coffee, tea (US$0.50), *sahlep* (US$1.25), pastries, soups and salads.

Stroll a bit further along Divan Yolu. On the left, the curious tomb with wrought-iron grillework on top is that of Köprülü Mehmet Paşa (1575-1661). Across the street, that strange building with a row of streetfront shops is actually an ancient Turkish bath, the **Çemberlitaş Hamamı** (1580; see the Entertainment chapter).

The derelict, time-worn column rising from a little plaza is one of İstanbul's most ancient and revered monuments. Called **Çemberlitaş** (The Banded Stone or Burnt Column), it was erected by Constantine the Great (324-37) to celebrate the dedication of Constantinople as capital of the Roman Empire in 330. This area was the grand Forum of Constantine, and the column was topped by a statue of the great emperor himself. In an earthquake zone erecting columns can be a risky business. This one has survived, though it needed iron bands for support within a century after it was built. The statue crashed to the ground in a quake almost 1000 years ago.

The little **mosque** nearby is that of Atik Ali Paşa, a eunuch and grand vizier of Beyazıt II.

Beyond Çemberlitaş along Divan Yolu, on the right (north) side is the cemetery of the Atik Ali Paşa mosque. Past the impressive tomb of Grand Vezir Koca Sinan Paşa and to the right is the *İlesam Lokalı*, a club formed by the enigmatically named Professional Union of Owners of the Works of Science & Literature. Touted as a 'traditional mystic water pipe and tea garden', it almost lives up to its billing. Tables and chairs are set out in the shady cemetery, and low benches covered with kilims in the medrese courtyard. Try a water pipe *(nargile,* US$1) or a glass of tea or cup of coffee. Some of the other patrons may speak some English.

Just on the other side of Bileyciler Sokak from İlesam is a similar place, the *Erenler Nargile Salonu*, in the courtyard of the Çorlulu Ali Paşa Medresesi and to the right. Most of the other people in this lofty türbe-like structure will either be absorbed in the racing forms or in watching a horserace on television. If a race is running, better leave them to it or you risk becoming *persona non grata.*

The Kapalı Çarşı & Nuruosmaniye Camii

İstanbul's Kapalı Çarşı, known in English as the Covered Market or Grand Bazaar (see the accompanying Kapalı Çarşı map), consists of 4000 shops, as well as mosques, banks, police stations, restaurants and workshops lining kilometres of streets. It's open daily except Sunday from 8.30 am to 6.30 pm. Today the main streets are touristy, with touts badgering bus tour groups, but many of the back streets and *hans* (warehouse and workshop courtyards) still serve a local clientele as they have for centuries. Guard your bag and wallet here as purse-snatchers and bag and pocket-slashers are not unknown, especially in the midst of crowds.

Starting from a small *bedesten* (warehouse) built in the time of Mehmet the

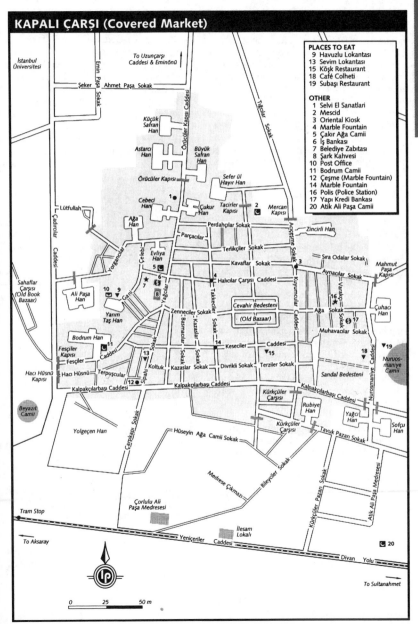

KAPALI ÇARŞI (Covered Market)

PLACES TO EAT
9 Havuzlu Lokantası
13 Sevim Lokantası
15 Köşk Restaurant
18 Café Colheti
19 Subaşı Restaurant

OTHER
1 Selvi El Sanatları
2 Mescid
3 Oriental Kiosk
4 Marble Fountain
5 Çakır Ağa Camii
6 İş Bankası
7 Belediye Zabıtası
8 Şark Kahvesi
10 Post Office
11 Bodrum Camii
12 Çeşme (Marble Fountain)
14 Marble Fountain
16 Polis (Police Station)
17 Yapı Kredi Bankası
20 Atik Ali Paşa Camii

0   25   50 m

Conqueror, the bazaar grew to cover a vast area. Roofs and walls were extended so that commerce could be conducted comfortably in all weather. The wealthy built hans at the edges of the bazaar so that caravans could bring goods from all parts of the empire, unload and trade right in the bazaar's precincts. A system of locked gates and doors was provided so that the entire market could be closed up tight at the end of the business day.

Though tourist shops now crowd the bazaar, it is also still a place where an İstanbullu (citizen of İstanbul) may come to buy a few metres of printed cloth, a gold bangle for a daughter's birthday gift, an antique carpet or a fluffy sheepskin. Whether you want to buy or not, you should see the bazaar (closed on Sunday).

Turn right off Yeniçeriler Caddesi (the continuation of Divan Yolu) at the Çemberlitaş and walk down Vezir Hanı Caddesi to the big **Nuruosmaniye Camii** built in Ottoman Baroque style between 1748 and 1755 by Mahmut I and his successor Osman III. Though meant to exhibit the sultans' 'modern' taste, the Nuruosmaniye (Light of Osman) has very strong echoes of Aya Sofya: the broad, lofty dome, colonnaded mezzanine galleries, Roman-arch- topped windows, and the broad band of calligraphy around the interior. Twelve hundred years after it was built, Aya Sofya was still 'the one to beat'.

Turn left through the mosque gate to the peaceful, green courtyard with its constant flow of pedestrian traffic heading to and from the bazaar.

Out the other side of the courtyard, you're standing in Çarşıkapı Sokak before the Çarşıkapı (Bazaar Gate), with its gold-toned Ottoman armorial emblem, restored in 1998.

Enter the gate to **Kalpakçılarbaşı Caddesi**, the bazaar's main east-west street. The bazaar was traditionally ordered according to trade or goods, a plan which was reflected in the street names: Mirror-makers St, Pearl Merchants St, Fez-makers St. The plan has long since been abandoned, with a few exceptions. **Kuyumcular Caddesi**, the second street on the right as you walk along Kalpakçılarbaşı Caddesi, is still Jewellers St, aglitter with tonnes of gold and gems.

The Sandal Bedesteni, once the city's auction place for used and antique goods, is now filled with shops and a decent cafe.

The Kürkçüler Çarşısı (Furriers Bazaar) now houses shops selling mostly leather garments.

At the centre of the bazaar is the Cevahir Bedesteni (Jewellery Warehouse; signs read 'Old Bazaar'), the original core of the bazaar dating from the 15th century, which can be closed off with its own set of doors. Shops here hold the best of the bazaar's antiques, old coins and jewellery, and silver new and old. The atmospheric **Zincirli Han** at the far (north) end of Kuyumcular Caddesi, on the right, holds workshops where custom jewellery is made.

Sahaflar Çarşısı Exit the bazaar by walking to the western end of Kalpakçılarbaşı Caddesi. Once outside, turn right onto Çadırcılar Caddesi, then left through a doorway and you'll enter the Sahaflar Çarşısı, or Old Book Bazaar. Go up the steps and along to the shady little courtyard. Actually, the wares in the shops are both new and old; mostly new, though, and mostly in Turkish.

The book bazaar dates from Byzantine times, but today many of its booksellers are members of the Halveti dervish order founded by Hazreti Mehmet Nureddin-i Cerrahi-i Halveti. Their *sema* (religious ceremony) includes chanting from the Koran, praying, and rhythmic dancing and breathing to the accompaniment of classical Turkish liturgical music. As with all dervish orders, the sema is an attempt at close knowledge of and communion with God. The Mevlevi dervishes attempt it by their whirling dance, the Halveti through their circular dance and hyperventilation. Dervishes, unlike Christian monks, live and work in the 'secular' world, and confine their overt dervish activities to periodic meetings.

Out the north gate of the Sahaflar Çarşısı is a small daily flea market. On Sunday the flea market has traditionally expanded to fill neighbouring Beyazıt Square. Signs erected by the city forbid street selling, but they are cheerfully ignored by one and all.

Uzunçarşı Caddesi The Kapalı Çarşı is the southern anchor of a vast market district which spills northward downhill to the Golden Horn, ending at Eminönü's Mısır Çarşısı (Egyptian, or Spice, Bazaar). Mahmutpaşa Yokuşu curves downhill on the district's eastern side, and features hundreds of clothing shops, but aptly named Uzunçarşı Caddesi ('Longmarket Street') goes right through the heart of the market. This makes for a very interesting walk, as much as for an introduction to Turkish society and traditional commerce as for shopping possibilities.

Longmarket St lives up to its name: one long market of woodturners' shops, bakeries for *simits* (sesame rolls), stores selling luggage, guns and hunting equipment, second-hand clothing and hundreds of other products. This is the market district of Tahtakale, where almost anything, legal or illegal, can be purchased.

Uzunçarşı Caddesi ends at the exquisite Rüstem Paşa Camii, perhaps the most beautiful small mosque in the city, which is described in the Eminönü section.

Beyazıt & İstanbul University

The Sahaflar Çarşısı is right next to **Beyazıt Camii** (built 1501-06), or Mosque of Sultan Beyazıt II (Map 6). Beyazıt used an exceptional amount of fine stone in his mosque – marble, porphyry, verd antique and rare granite. The mihrab is simple except for the rich stone columns framing it.

This was the second imperial mosque to be built in the city after Mehmet the Conqueror's Fatih Camii (see the Western Districts section later in this chapter), and was the prototype for the great imperial mosques, which would come after it. In effect, it is the link between Aya Sofya, which obviously inspired its design, and the great mosques such as the Süleymaniye, which are realisations of Aya Sofya's design fully adapted to Muslim worship.

The main street here, which started out as Divan Yolu, is now called Yeniçeriler Caddesi. It runs past Beyazıt Square, officially called Hürriyet Meydanı (Freedom Square), though everyone knows it simply as Beyazıt. Under the Byzantines, this was the largest of the city's many forums, the Forum of Theodosius, built by that emperor in 393.

The plaza is backed by the impressive portal of İstanbul University. The grand gates, main building and tall tower of the university were originally built as the Ottoman War Ministry, which explains their grandiose and martial aspect. After the Conquest, Mehmet the Conqueror built his first palace here, a wooden structure, which burnt down centuries ago. After Mehmet built Topkapı, he used the Old Palace as a home for ageing harem women.

The small building at the western side of the square, once the medrese of the Beyazıt Camii, is now the **Beyazıt Hat Sanatları Müzesi**, or Beyazıt Calligraphy Museum, open from 9 am to 4 pm (closed Sunday and Monday), for US$0.50 admission. Though you may not be fascinated by Ottoman calligraphy, the building, once a theological college, is certainly worth a look.

Süleymaniye Camii

The Süleymaniye Camii (Map 4), or Mosque of Sultan Süleyman the Magnificent, directly north of (behind) the university, is İstanbul's largest mosque. Facing the university portal in Beyazıt, go to the left along Takvimhane Caddesi to reach the mosque and its tombs, which are open every day.

The Süleymaniye Camii crowns one of İstanbul's hills, dominating the Golden Horn and providing a magnificent landmark for the entire city. This, the grandest of all Turkish mosques, was built between 1550 and 1557 by the greatest, richest and most powerful of Ottoman sultans, Süleyman I (1520-66), 'The Magnificent'.

Süleyman, the patron of Mimar Sinan, Turkey's greatest architect, was a great builder who restored the mighty walls of Jerusalem (an Ottoman city from 1516) and built countless other monuments throughout his empire. Though the smaller Selimiye Camii in Edirne is generally counted as Sinan's masterpiece, the Süleymaniye is without doubt his grandest work.

Most visitors enter the mosque precincts by a side door. Though this is the most convenient entrance coming from Beyazıt, the effect of entering from the north-west side and through the courtyard, seeing the four towering minarets and the enormous billowing domes, is far better.

Inside, the mosque is breathtaking in its size and pleasing in its simplicity. There is little decoration except for some very fine İznik tiles in the mihrab, gorgeous stained-glass windows done by one İbrahim the Drunkard, and four massive columns, one from Baalbek, one from Alexandria and two from Byzantine palaces in İstanbul. The painted arabesques on the dome are 19th-century additions, recently renewed. Sinan, ever challenged by the technical accomplishments of Aya Sofya, took the floor plan of that church, and here perfected his adaptation to the requirements of Muslim worship.

The *külliye* (mosque complex; see the boxed text on Ottoman Mosques in the Facts for the Visitor chapter) of the Süleymaniye is particularly elaborate, with the full complement of public services: soup kitchen, hostel, hospital, theological college etc. Near the south-east wall of the mosque is the cemetery, with the *türbeler* (tombs) of Süleyman and his wife Haseki Hürrem Sultan (known in the west as Roxelana). The tile work in both is superb. In Süleyman's tomb, little jewel-like lights in the dome are surrogate stars. In Hürrem's tomb, the many tile panels of flowers and the delicate stained glass produce a serene, feminine effect.

Places to Eat There are several little eateries in the row of souvenir shops outside the mosque enclosure to the south-west, including the **Beydağı** and **Kanaat Lokantası** restaurants.

For upmarket meals, try **Darüzziyafe** (☎ 212-511 8414, *Şifahane Caddesi 6*), in the imaret opposite the mosque's main portal. Constructed as part of the külliye, the building has a courtyard surrounded by porches and centred on a fountain. The court is used for dining in fine weather, and several rooms opening onto it have changing art exhibits. The menu is Ottoman with mid-range prices, such as soup for US$2.50, meze plates for US$3, main courses for US$5 to US$8, and full meals for US$10 to US$18. Check your bill for errors.

Şehzadebaşı Caddesi

Bozdoğan Kemeri Walk along Süleymaniye Caddesi (see Map 4), which goes south-west from the mosque, and turn right onto Şehzadebaşı Caddesi. You can see remnants of the high Bozdoğan Kemeri, or Aqueduct of Valens, on the left side of the street. It's not certain that the aqueduct was constructed by the Emperor Valens (364-78), though we do know it was repaired in 1019, and in later times by several sultans. After the reign of Süleyman the Magnificent, parts of it collapsed, but restoration work began in the late 1980s.

Şehzade Camii On the south side of the aqueduct, beyond the Saraçhane Parkı, is the Şehzade Camii, the Mosque of the Prince. Süleyman had it built between 1544 and 1548 as a memorial to his son Mehmet, who died in 1543. It was the first important mosque to be designed by Mimar Sinan, who spent the first part of his long career as a military architect. Among the many important people buried in tile-encrusted tombs here are Prince Mehmet, his brothers and sisters, and Süleyman's grand viziers, Rüstem Paşa and İbrahim Paşa. The mosque is currently under restoration, which may last for years.

Fatih Anıtı Parkı Across busy Atatürk Bulvarı from the Şehzade Camii and

Saraçhane Parkı is Fatih Anıtı Parkı, the Conqueror Monument Park, so named after the obvious monument to the mounted Mehmet II.

South of the park across Macar Kardeşler Caddesi are a few bits of marble ruin and foundation, all that remains of the gigantic Byzantine Church of St Polyeuchtos. The church, built during the reign of Justinian by one of the immensely powerful noble families which the emperor sought to control, is thought to have been a physical symbol of the nobles' challenge to Justinian's authority. Larger and grander than Aya Sofya, it was the nobles' way of one-upping the head of state. Earthquakes ruined it utterly, however, while Justinian's great church still exists to this day.

Gazanfer Ağa Medresesi If you have a few minutes to spare, have a look at the former medrese of Gazanfer Ağa (1599), now the **İstanbul Karikatür ve Mizah Müzesi** or Cartoon & Humour Museum. It's on the north side of the Aqueduct of Valens, on the west side of Atatürk Bulvarı. Turkish cartoon artistry has been lively and politically important since Ottoman times, as the changing exhibits show. The pleasant sunny courtyard, with its fountain, grapevines, cafe and toilets, is an excellent place for a rest-stop in warm weather. Hours are from 10 am to 6 pm daily; admission is free.

Laleli & Aksaray

Continue west along Ordu Caddesi (Army or 'Horde' Ave), the extension of Yeniçeriler Caddesi and notice the huge broken marble columns decorated with stylised oak-knot designs on the left-hand side of the roadway. These were part of the decoration in the Forum of Theodosius. There was a monumental arch hereabouts.

A bit further along, on the right, are more university buildings, and beyond them the hotel district of Laleli. Stay on Ordu Caddesi and, just past the big Merit Hotel, you'll come to the **Laleli Camii**, an Ottoman Baroque mosque built in 1759-63 by Sultan Mustafa III. The ornate Baroque architec-

ture houses a sumptuous interior. Underneath the mosque are shops and a plaza with a fountain, the former producing rent for the upkeep of the mosque.

Continue down the hill on Ordu Caddesi and you will enter the confused clamour of Aksaray Square, once an open grassy plaza, but now a chaos of traffic. The **Valide Camii** on the square's north-west side is an ornate, late Ottoman work built in 1871 by Valide Sultan Pertevniyal, mother of Sultan Abdülaziz. It once looked like a white wedding cake among the drab structures of Aksaray, but exhaust fumes have sullied it and traffic flyovers block a full view.

EMİNÖNÜ (MAP 4)

No doubt you've already seen Eminönü. The view of the Galata Bridge, crowded with ferries and dominated by the Yeni Cami (YEHN-nee jahm-mee), or New Mosque (it's also called the Pigeon Mosque because of the ever present flocks of these birds), often features in advertisements and magazine articles about İstanbul. The Yeni Cami sits comfortably and serenely in the midst of the bustling Eminönü district as traffic, both vehicular and pedestrian, swirls around it. Visitors to İstanbul find themselves passing through Eminönü frequently.

Eminönü is the inner city's transportation hub. Bosphorus and Marmara ferries dock here, Galata Bridge traffic passes through, and Sirkeci train station is nearby.

Galata Bridge

In Byzantine times the Golden Horn provided a perfect natural harbour for the city's commerce. Suppliers of fresh vegetables and fruits, grain and staple goods set up shop in the harbour. Until a decade ago, their successors in İstanbul's wholesale vegetable, fruit and fish markets performed the same services, in the same area to the west of the Galata Bridge in Eminönü. With the drive to clean up and beautify the Golden Horn, the wholesale markets have been moved to the outskirts of the city.

Until June 1992 the Galata Bridge, which crosses the mouth of the Golden Horn, was a 19th-century structure which floated on pontoons. Ramshackle fish restaurants, tea-houses and hookah joints filled the dark recesses beneath the roadway, while an intense stream of pedestrian and vehicular traffic passed above.

The pontoon bridge blocked the natural flow of water and kept the Golden Horn from flushing itself of pollution, so it was replaced by a new bridge which allows the water to flow. (The old bridge was moved farther up the Golden Horn and reinstalled without its flow-blocking pontoons.)

Still picturesque and interesting is the retail market district surrounding the Mısır Çarşısı (Egyptian Market). But before wandering into this maze of market streets, take a look inside the Yeni Cami.

Yeni Cami

Only in İstanbul would a 400-year-old mosque be called 'New'. The New Mosque was begun in 1597, commissioned by Valide Sultan Safiye, mother of Sultan Mehmet III (1595-1603). The site was earlier occupied by a community of Karaite Jews, radical dissenters from orthodox Judaism. When the valide sultan decided to build her grand mosque here, the Karaites were moved to Hasköy, a district farther up the Golden Horn that still bears traces of their presence.

The valide sultan lost her august position when her son the sultan died, and the mosque was completed six sultans later in 1663 by Valide Sultan Turhan Hatice, mother of Sultan Mehmet IV (1648-87).

In plan, the Yeni Cami is much like the Sultan Ahmet Camii and the Süleymaniye Camii, with a large forecourt and a square sanctuary surmounted by a series of half-domes crowned by a grand dome. The interior is richly decorated with gold, coloured tiles and carved marble. The mosque and its tiles were created after the period when Ottoman architecture was at its peak. The tilemakers of İznik were turning out slightly inferior products by the late 17th century. Compare these tiles to the ones in the Rüstem Paşa Camii, which are from the high period of İznik tile work.

Rüstem Paşa Camii

The Rüstem Paşa Camii, or Mosque of Rüstem Pasha, is at the Uzunçarşı Caddesi and Hasırcılar Caddesi intersection, a few blocks north-west of the Mısır Çarşısı. From the Yeni Cami, turn left into Tahmis Caddesi, then right into Hasırcılar Caddesi. The mosque is easy to miss because it's not at street level: look for a stone doorway and a flight of steps leading up. There is also a small marble fountain and plaque.

At the top of the steps is a terrace and the mosque's colonnaded porch. You'll notice at once the panels of İznik faïence set into the mosque's façade. The interior is covered in similarly gorgeous tiles, so take off your shoes (women should also cover head and shoulders), and venture inside. This particularly beautiful mosque was built by Sinan for Rüstem Paşa, son-in-law and grand vizier of Süleyman the Magnificent. Ottoman power, glory, architecture and tile work were all at their zenith when the mosque was built in 1561.

Tahtakale

After your visit to the mosque, you might want to spend some more time wandering the streets of this fascinating market quarter. Tahtakale, as it's called, is synonymous with buying and selling anything and everything, including the bizarre and the illegal. Informal moneychangers here will give you the best rate for your foreign currency, but be careful of con men and petty thieves.

BEYOĞLU (MAPS 3 & 4)

Across the Galata Bridge from Eminönü lies Beyoğlu. Dolmuşes depart for Taksim Square from in front of the Borsa Lokantası just inland from the ferry docks opposite the pedestrian overpass; or you can cross the Galata Bridge to Karaköy and take the underground train to Tünel Square to begin your walking tour. However, the easiest

Pera in History

Sometimes called the New City, Beyoğlu is 'new' only in a relative sense. There was a settlement on the northern shore of the Golden Horn, near Karaköy Square, before the birth of Christ. By the time of Theodosius II (408-50), it was large enough to become an official suburb of Constantinople. Theodosius built a fortress here, no doubt to complete the defence system of his great land walls, and called it Galata, as the suburb was then the home of many Galatians.

The word 'new' actually applies more to Pera, the quarter above Galata, running along the crest of the hill from the Galata Tower to Taksim Square. This was built up only in later Ottoman times.

In the 19th century, the European powers were waiting eagerly for the 'Sick Man of Europe' (the decadent Ottoman Empire) to collapse so that they could grab territory and spheres of influence. All the great colonial powers – the British, Russian, Austro-Hungarian and German empires, France and the kingdom of Italy – maintained lavish embassies and tried to cajole and pressure the Sublime Porte into concessions of territory, trade and influence.

The embassy buildings, as lavish as ever, still stand in Pera. Ironically, most of the great empires which built them collapsed along with that of the Ottomans. Only the British and French survived to grab any of the spoils. Their occupation of Middle Eastern countries under League of Nations 'mandates' has given us the Middle East we have today.

way to tour Beyoğlu is to start from its busy nerve-centre, Taksim Square.

Beyoğlu (BEY-oh-loo), the 'new' section of İstanbul on the northern side of the Golden Horn, is not really new. There's been a settlement here almost as long as there has been a city on Saray Burnu (Seraglio Point). But new ideas, brought from Europe by traders and diplomats, walked into Ottoman daily life down the streets of Pera and Galata.

The Europeans who lived in Pera brought new fashions, machines, arts and manners, and rules for the diplomatic game. Old İstanbul, on the south bank of the Golden Horn, was content to continue living in the Middle Ages with its oriental bazaars, great mosques and palaces, narrow streets and traditional values. But Pera was to have telephones, underground trains, tramways, electric light and modern municipal government.

Eventually the sultans followed Pera's lead, and the upper classes followed the sultans. From the reign of Abdül Mecit

(1839-61) onwards, no sultan lived in Mehmet the Conqueror's palace at Topkapı. Rather, they built opulent European-style palaces in Pera and along the shores of the Bosphorus to the north.

Beyoğlu holds the architectural evidence of the Ottoman Empire's frantic attempts to modernise and reform itself, and the evidence of the European powers' attempts to undermine and subvert it. As the Ottomans struggled to keep their sprawling, ramshackle empire together, the European diplomats in the great embassies of Pera were jockeying for domination of the entire Middle East. They wanted to control its holy places, its sea lanes through the Suez Canal to India, and especially its oil, already important at that time.

Taksim Square

A 'taksim' in Turkish is a dividing-point. Taksim Square takes its name from a reservoir in the city's old water-conduit system. The main water line from the Belgrade Forest, north of the city, was laid to this point in 1732 by Sultan Mahmut I (1730-54). Branch lines then led from the taksim to other parts of the city.

Today Taksim Square is the point where the metal rivers of cars divide and merge as they flow through the city.

The prominent modern building at the eastern end of the plaza is the **Atatürk Kültür Merkezi**, or Atatürk Cultural Centre (sometimes called the Opera House). In the summertime, during the International İstanbul Music Festival, tickets for the various concerts are on sale in the ticket kiosks here, and numerous performances are staged in the centre's halls.

At the western end of the square is the **Cumhuriyet Anıtı**, or Republic Monument, one of the Turkish Republic's earliest monuments, executed by Canonica, an Italian sculptor, in 1928. Atatürk, his assistant and successor İsmet İnönü and other revolutionary leaders appear prominently on the monument set in a circular garden circumnavigated by the İstiklal Caddesi tram. The monument's purpose was not only to commemorate revolutionary heroes, but also to break down the Ottoman-Islamic prohibition against the making of 'graven images' (there is no figurative painting or sculpture of living beings in traditional Islamic art).

To the south of the square is the luxury Marmara Hotel. To the north is the **Taksim Gezi Yeri**, Taksim Park or Promenade, with the Inter-Continental Hotel at its northern end.

Beneath the square is the southern terminal of the city's newest Metro line which runs north along Cumhuriyet Caddesi to more business and residential districts.

Before leaving Taksim on your walking tour of old Pera along İstiklal Caddesi, consider taking a detour north, south or east of the square.

North of Taksim

From the roundabout, Cumhuriyet Caddesi (Republic Ave) leads north past sidewalk cafes and restaurants, banks, travel agencies, airline offices, nightclubs and the Divan, İstanbul Hilton and Hyatt Regency hotels to the districts of Harbiye, Nişantaşı and Şişli (Map 2). Harbiye holds the Turkish war college and its interesting military museum. Nişantaşı is an upmarket shopping and cafe district. Şişli is a district of offices, shops and apartments.

Askeri Müzesi A kilometre north of Taksim in Harbiye is the Askeri Müzesi, or Military Museum, (☎ 212-248 7115). It's open from 9 am to noon and from 1 to 5 pm (it's closed on Tuesday); admission costs US$1.50. Concerts by the Mehter, the medieval Ottoman Military Band, are held at 3 and 4 pm (none on Monday or Tuesday).

The museum, within the war college complex, has two parts. Entering from Cumhuriyet Caddesi, you'll come first to the new section. On the ground floor are displays of weapons, a 'heroes' gallery (*şehit galerisi*) with artefacts from fallen Turkish soldiers of many wars, displays of Turkish military uniforms through the ages, and many glass cases holding battle standards, both Turkish and captured. The captured ones include Byzantine, Greek, British, Italian, Austro-Hungarian and Imperial Russian. Perhaps the most interesting of the exhibits, are the *sayebanlar*, or imperial pavilions. These luxurious cloth shelters, heavily worked with fine silver and gold thread, jewels, precious silks and elegant tracery, were the battle headquarters for sultans during the summer campaign season.

The upper floor of the new section has fascinating displays of Ottoman tents, more imperial pavilions, and a room devoted to Atatürk who was, of course, a famous Ottoman general before he became founder and commander-in-chief of the republican army, and first president of the Turkish Republic.

To reach the old section of the Military Museum, walk out of the new section, turn right, and walk down the hill past displays of old cannon, then turn right again, and climb the steps into the museum. Signs along the way read 'To the Other Departments'. The cannons, by the way, include

Gatling guns cast in Vienna, bearing the sultan's monogram.

The old section is where you really feel the spirit of the Ottoman Empire. It has exhibits of armour (including cavalry), uniforms, field furniture made out of weapons (chairs with rifles for legs etc), and a Türk-Alman Dostluk Köşesi (Turco-German Friendship Corner) with mementos of Turkish and German military collaboration before and during WWI.

Amazingly, there is also a portion of the great chain which the Byzantines stretched across the mouth of the Golden Horn to keep out the sultan's ships during the battle for Constantinople in 1453; and a tapestry woven by Ottoman sailors (who must have had lots of time on their hands) showing the flags of all of the world's important maritime nations.

Perhaps the best reason to visit the Military Museum is for a short **concert by the Mehter**. According to historians, the Mehter was the world's first true military band. Its purpose was not to make pretty music for dancing, but to precede the conquering Ottoman paşas into vanquished towns, impressing upon the defeated populace their new, subordinate status. Marching in with steady, measured pace, turning all together to face the left side of the line of march, then the right side, looking formidable in their long moustaches, tall janissary headdresses, brilliant instruments and even kettledrums, they were the musical representatives of Ottoman conquest.

East of Taksim

Walk downhill along İnönü Caddesi for 10 minutes to grandiose Dolmabahçe Sarayı on the shores of the Bosphorus (Map 1).

Dolmabahçe Sarayı Dolmabahçe was built between 1843 and 1856, when the homeland of the once-mighty Ottoman padişah had become the 'Sick Man of Europe'. His many peoples, aroused by a wave of European nationalism, were in revolt; his wealth was mostly under the control of European bankers; his armies, while still considerable, were obsolescent and disorganised. The western, European, Christian way of life had triumphed over the eastern, Asian, Muslim one. Attempting to turn the tide, 19th-century sultans turned to European models, modernising the army and civil service, granting autonomy to subject peoples, and adopting – sometimes wholesale – European ways.

Sultan Abdül Mecit decided he wanted a grandiose palace which would give the lie to talk of Ottoman decline. For a site he chose the *dolma bahçe* (filled-in garden) where his predecessor Sultan Ahmet I (1607-17) had filled in a little cove in order to build an imperial pleasure kiosk surrounded by gardens. Other wooden buildings succeeded the original kiosk, but all burned to the ground in 1814. Abdül Mecit's imperial architects, Nikogos and Karabet Balyan, erected a sumptuous, extravagant, overdecorated Ottoman-European fantasy designed more to precipitate the empire's bankruptcy than to dispel rumours of it.

Admission The palace is divided into two sections (*bölüm*), the **Selamlık** (ceremonial suites) and the **Harem-Cariyeler** (Harem & Concubines' Quarters). You must take a guided tour, which lasts about an hour, to see either section. Only 1500 people are allowed into each section each day, so it's not a bad idea to reserve your space on a tour in advance. The palace (☎ 212-227 3441) is open from 9 am to 4 pm, closed Monday and Thursday. Entrance to the Selamlık costs US$8, to the Harem-Cariyeler the same; a ticket good for both sections costs US$14. The charge for a camera is US$8, for a video camera US$16. Thus, for a couple with a camera and video to see the entire palace costs a cool US$52. Save the camera fee and check your camera at the door as the palace interior is too dark to photograph (even with fast film) and flash and tripod are not allowed. Rather, take your photos from the small garden near the clock tower, or the park on the south side of the mosque.

The tourist entrance to the palace is near the ornate clock tower, north of the mosque.

Touring the Palace The tours pass through opulent public and private rooms, into a harem with steel doors, past numerous Sèvres vases and Bohemian chandeliers, and up a staircase with a crystal balustrade. One room was used by the fat Sultan Abdülaziz who needed an enormously large bed. The magnificent throne room, used in 1877 for the first meeting of the Ottoman Chamber of Deputies, has a chandelier that weighs over 4000kg.

Don't set your watch by any of the palace clocks, all of which are stopped at 9.05 am, the moment at which Kemal Atatürk died in Dolmabahçe on the morning of 10 November 1938. You will be shown the small bedroom he used during his last days. Each year on 10 November, at 9.05 am, the entire country observes a moment of silence in commemoration of the republic's founder.

Dolmabahçe's **Kuşluk ve Sanat Galerisi**, or Aviary & Art Gallery, is on the inland side of the palace and can be entered from Dolmabahçe Caddesi from 9.30 am to 4 pm (closed Monday and Thursday). This less interesting section of the palace was the aviary, with its bird house and cages (now restored), and a pretty garden restaurant has now been added. The art gallery is a single corridor, over 100m long, lined with paintings by 19th and 20th-century Ottoman artists (many of them from the nobility).

Around Taksim Square

To the south-west, two streets meet before entering the square. Sıraselviler Caddesi goes south and İstiklal Caddesi goes south-west (see Map 3).

Nestled in the small triangle formed by these two streets, rising above the shops and restaurants which hide its foundations, is the **Aya Triyada Kilisesi**, or Greek Orthodox Church of the Holy Trinity, dating from 1882. It's open daily for services, and you can visit. Walk along İstiklal Caddesi and turn left.

Now head down İstiklal Caddesi for a look at the vestiges of 19th-century Ottoman life. The restored turn-of-the-century tram runs from Taksim via Galatasaray to Tünel for US$0.35. It's fun, but it runs too seldom to be very useful, and is always crowded.

İstiklal Caddesi

Stretching between Taksim Square and Tünel Square, İstiklal Caddesi (Independence Ave; Map 3) was formerly the Grande Rue de Péra. It was the street with all the smart shops, several large embassies and churches, many impressive residential buildings and a scattering of teashops and restaurants. Renovation has restored much of its appeal. It's now a pedestrian way, which in Turkey means not that there are no cars, but that there are fewer cars.

As you stroll along İstiklal, try to imagine it during its heyday a century ago, peopled by frock-coated merchants and Ottoman officials, European officers in uniform, lightly veiled Turkish women, and European women in the latest fashions.

Just out of Taksim Square, the first building on the right is the former French plague hospital (1719), now the **French Consulate General** and cultural centre.

As you stroll along, take detours down the narrow side streets with intriguing names such as Büyükparmakkapı Sokak, 'Gate of the Thumb St'; Sakızağacı Sokak, 'Pine-Gum Tree St'; and Kuloğlu Sokak, 'Slave's Son St'. The Places to Eat and Entertainment chapters have lots of suggestions for cafes, restaurants and clubs in this area.

A few streets before coming to Galatasaray Square, turn left onto Turnacıbaşı Sokak. At its end is the **Tarihi Galatasaray Hamamı**, or Historic Galatasaray Turkish Bath. The bath is one of the city's best, with lots of marble decoration, comfy little cubicles for resting and sipping tea after the bath, pretty fountains and even a shoeshine service.

Down behind the hamam are Faik Paşa and Çukurcuma caddesis, lined with **antique shops** (see the Antiques section in the Shopping chapter).

Galatasaray Square The square's prominent feature is its namesake, the Galatasaray Lycée, established in 1868 by Sultan Abdülaziz who wanted a place where Ottoman youth could listen to lectures in both Turkish and French. Across İstiklal Caddesi from the school is the Galatasaray post office.

Çiçek Pasajı Just north of Galatasaray, turn right into the Çiçek Pasajı (chee-CHEHK pah-sah-zhuh, Flower Passage; see Places to Eat on the Map 3 key). This is the inner court of the 19th-century 'Cité de Pera' building, which symbolised Pera's growth as a 'modern' European-style city. For years the courtyard held a dozen cheap little restaurant-taverns. In good weather beer barrels were rolled out onto the pavement, marble slabs were balanced on top, wooden stools were put around, and enthusiastic revellers filled the stools as soon as they hit the ground.

In the late 1980s parts of the Cité de Péra building collapsed. In rebuilding, the venerable Çiçek Pasajı was 'beautified', its makeshift barrel heads and stools replaced with comfortable, solid wooden tables and benches, and the broken pavement with smooth tiles, all topped by a glass canopy to keep out foul weather. The clientele is better behaved now, and its smattering of adventurous tourists has become a significant proportion. The Çiçek Pasajı is still OK for an evening of beer drinking, food and conversation, but prices are relatively high.

Pick a good place, pull up a stool and order a mug of beer, *beyaz* (pale) or *siyah* (dark). For something stronger, ask for *Bir kadeh rakı* (BEER kah-deh rah-KUH, 'a shot of rakı'). As for food, printed menus, even if you can find them, mean little here. If you already know a few Turkish dishes you like, order them, but ask prices first. Otherwise, the waiter will lead you to the kitchen so you can see what's cooking. As you eat and drink, at least three nearby revellers will want to know where you are from; when you tell them, the response is always *Çok iyi*, 'Very good!'

Many regulars have now abandoned the Çiçek Pasajı to the tourists and their attendant carpet and leather-apparel touts, opting instead to dine at little *meyhanes* (taverns) deeper in the market (see the İstiklal Caddesi section in the Places to Eat chapter).

Balık Pazar Walk out of the courtyard to neighbouring Sahne Sokak, turn right, then look for a little passage off to the left. This is the Avrupa Pasajı (European Passage), a small gallery with marble paving and shops selling upmarket goods. In Pera's heyday it was elegant, a state which recent restoration has done much to recreate.

Sahne Sokak is the heart of Beyoğlu's Balık Pazar (or Fish Market), though it's actually a general-purpose market with a good number of fish merchants. Small stands sell *midye* (skewered mussels) fried in hot oil, and *kokoreç* (grilled lamb intestines packed with more lamb intestines). I recommend the mussels, but get a skewer that's been freshly cooked.

Farther up Sahne Sokak, Duduodaları Sokak leads off to the left and down to the British Consulate General. Continuing along Sahne Sokak, near this junction on your right is the entrance to the **Üç Horan Ermeni Kilisesi**, the Armenian Church of Three Altars. You can visit if the doors are open.

Past the Armenian church, Sahne Sokak changes its name to Balık Sokak. Leading off to the right is Nevizade Sokak, lined with meyhanes where the old-time life of the Çiçek Pasajı continues, untrammelled by the glossy overlays of tourist İstanbul. Feel free to wander in and have a meal and a drink (see the İstiklal Caddesi section in the Places to Eat chapter).

Unless you want to continue down the slope among the fishmongers on Balık Sokak, turn back and then right into Duduodaları Sokak, and stroll down this little street past fancy food shops, butchers', bakers' and greengrocers' shops to the British Consulate General.

At the end of the market street you will emerge into the light. Straight ahead of you is Meşrutiyet Caddesi, and on the corner here are the huge gates to the **British Consulate General**, an Italian palazzo built in 1845 to plans by Sir Charles Barry, architect of London's Houses of Parliament.

Walk past the British Consulate General along Meşrutiyet Caddesi, which makes its way down to the Pera Palas Oteli and the US Consulate General. Watch for an iron gate and a small passage on the left, leading into a little courtyard, the Hacopulo Pasajı, with a derelict lamp post in the centre. Enter the courtyard, turn right up the stairs, and you'll discover the Greek Orthodox **Church of Panaya Isodyon**. It's tidy and quiet, hidden away in the midst of other buildings. The custodian is usually happy to let you have a look inside.

When you've seen the church, go down the stairs *behind* it (not the stairs you came up). Turn right, and just past the church property on the right-hand side you will see the entrance to the **Yeni Rejans Lokantası**, or New Regency Restaurant. Founded apparently by three White Russian dancing girls who fled the Russian Revolution, the restaurant is still operated by their Russian-speaking descendants.

This area of Beyoğlu was a favourite with Russian emigrés after the 1917 revolution. The Yeni Rejans, by the look of it, was a cabaret complete with orchestra loft and grand piano. Lunch and dinner are still served daily, except on Sunday. Though in vogue with İstanbul's intelligentsia, service is far from good and prices are quite high for what you get.

When you go out the restaurant door, go down the steps, turn right, and then left along the narrow alley called Olivia Han Pasajı, which brings you back to İstiklal Caddesi.

Back on İstiklal Caddesi Across the avenue notice the large Italian Gothic church behind a fence. The Franciscan **Church of San Antonio di Padua** was

founded here in 1725; the red brick building dates from 1913.

Cross over to the church, turn right, and head down İstiklal Caddesi once more. Past the church is Eskiçiçekçi Sokak on the left, then Nuruziya Sokak. The third street, a little cul-de-sac, ends at the gates of the **Palais de France**, once the French embassy to the Ottoman sultan. The grounds are extensive and include the chapel of St Louis of the French, founded here in 1581, though the present chapel building dates from the 1830s. You can get a better look at the palace and grounds another way: read on.

A few steps along İstiklal Caddesi brings you to the pretty **Netherlands Consulate General**, built as the Dutch embassy in 1855 by the Swiss Fossati brothers, formerly architects to the Russian tsar. The first embassy building here dates from 1612. Past the consulate, turn left down the hill on Postacılar Sokak. The **Dutch Chapel**, on the left, is now the home of the Union Church of İstanbul, a multinational English-speaking Protestant congregation.

The narrow street turns right, bringing you face to face with the former Spanish embassy. The little chapel, which was founded in 1670, is today still in use, though the embassy is not.

The street then bends left and changes names to become Tomtom Kaptan Sokak. At the foot of the slope, on the right, is the **Palazzo di Venezia**, once the embassy for Venice, now the Italian consulate. Venice was one of the great Mediterranean maritime powers during Renaissance times, and when Venetian and Ottoman fleets were not madly trading with one another, they were locked in ferocious combat.

To the left across the open space is a side gate to the Palais de France. Peek through the gates for another, better view of the old French embassy grounds, then slog back up that hill to İstiklal Caddesi.

Continuing along İstiklal Caddesi, the **Church of St Mary Draperis**, built in 1678 and extensively reconstructed in 1789, is behind an iron fence and down a flight of steps.

Past the church, still on the left-hand side, is the grand **Russian Consulate General**, once the embassy of the tsars, built in 1837 to designs by the Fossati brothers. After designing several embassies, they were employed by the sultan to do extensive restorations of Aya Sofya.

Turn right (north-west) off İstiklal Caddesi along Asmalımescit Sokak, a narrow, typical Beyoğlu street that holds some fusty antique shops, food shops, suspect hotels and little eateries. After 50m the street intersects Meşrutiyet Caddesi. To the left of the intersection is the American Library & Cultural Center (once the Constantinople Club), and just beyond it the **Palazzo Corpi** (1880), a pretty marble palace built by an Italian shipping magnate and later rented, then sold, to the USA for use as the US embassy to the Sublime Porte. It is now the US Consulate General, and heavily fortified.

To the right of the consulate is the grand old **Pera Palas Oteli** (see the boxed text below), built for passengers arriving on the *Orient Express*.

Once you've taken a turn through the Pera Palas, and perhaps had a drink in the bar or tea in the salon (not for the budget-minded), walk back up Asmalımescit Sokak toward İstiklal Caddesi.

Christ Church Back on İstiklal Caddesi, you will notice, on your left, the **Royal Swedish Consulate**, once the Swedish embassy. Across İstiklal, the large pillared building called the Narmanlı Han was formerly the Russian embassy.

Beside the Swedish consulate, turn left downhill on Şahkulu Bostanı Sokak. At the base of the slope turn left, then right, onto Serdari Ekrem Sokak to find the Anglican sanctuary of Christ Church (☎ 212-244 4828) at No 82. Designed by CE Street (who did London's Law Courts), its cornerstone was laid in 1858 by Lord Stratford de Redcliffe, known as 'The Great Elchi' *(elçi:* ambassador) because of his paramount influence in mid-19th century Ottoman affairs. The church, dedicated in 1868 as the Crimean Memorial Church, is the largest of the city's Protestant churches. It had fallen into disrepair, but was restored and renamed in the mid-1990s. Ring the bell and with luck the caretaker will admit you for a look round.

Back up on İstiklal Caddesi, the road curves to the right into Tünel Square.

Tünel

İstanbul's short underground railway, the Tünel, was built by French engineers in 1875. It allowed European merchants to get from their offices in Galata to their homes in Pera without hiking up the steep hillside. Until the 1970s, the carriages were of dark wood with numerous coats of bright lacquer, and the Turkish signs within read

---

Pera Palas Oteli

The Pera Palas was built by Georges Nagelmackers, the Belgian entrepreneur who founded the Compagnie Internationale des Wagons-Lits et Grands Express Européens in 1868. Nagelmackers, who had succeeded in linking Paris and Constantinople by luxury train, found that once he got his esteemed passengers to the Ottoman imperial capital, there was no suitable place for them to stay.

The hotel opened in the 1890s and advertised itself as having 'a thoroughly healthy situation, being high up and isolated on all four sides', and 'overlooking the Golden Horn and the whole panorama of Stamboul'.

With its spacious salons, atmospheric bar, precious and pricey pastry shop, and birdcage lift, the Pera Palas is a living memory of what life was like in İstanbul a century ago.

'It is Requested that Cigarettes not be Smoked in the Cars'. A modernisation program replaced them with rubber-tyred Paris Metro-type steel trains in which the signs read 'No Smoking'.

The fare is US$0.35. Trains run as frequently as necessary during rush hours, about every five or 10 minutes at other times.

In Tünel Square, stop for a rest at **Cafe Gramofon** (☎ 212-293 0786), which echoes the style of the restored trams with its turn-of-the-century decor. Sandwiches, pastries, light meals and drinks are served all day every day.

Walk back to İstiklal Caddesi to begin the descent toward Karaköy along Galipdede Caddesi to see a whirling dervish monastery, the Galata Tower and more glimpses of Beyoğlu daily life.

Galata Mevlevihanesi On the left of Galipdede Caddesi you'll find the **Divan Edebiyatı Müzesi** or Museum of Divan Literature (☎ 212-245 4141), originally a Galata Mevlevihanesi (Whirling Dervish Hall), a meeting place for Mevlevi (whirling) dervishes, and preserved as such.

The museum is open daily except Tuesday from 9.30 am to 5 pm. Admission costs US$0.75. The dervishes still whirl here, on the last Sunday afternoon of each month.

In Ottoman times, the Galata Mevlevihanesi was open to all who wished to witness the *sema* (ceremony), including foreign, non-Muslim visitors.

This modest tekke was restored between 1967 and 1972, but the first building here was erected by a high officer in the court of Sultan Beyazıt II in 1491. Its first *şeyh* (sheik, or leader) was Muhammed Şemai Sultan Divani, a grandson of the great Mevlana. The building burned in 1766, but was repaired that same year by Sultan Mustafa III.

In the midst of the city, this former monastery is an oasis of flowers and shady nooks. As you approach the building, notice

The Whirling Dervishes

The whirling dervishes took their name from the great Sufi mystic and poet, Celaleddin Rumi (1207-73), called *Mevlana* (Our Leader) by his disciples. Sufis seek mystical communion with God through various means. For Mevlana, it was through a *sema* (ceremony) involving chants, prayers, music and a whirling dance. The whirling induced a trancelike state which made it easier for the mystic to seek spiritual union with God.

The Mevlevi *tarikat* (order), founded in Konya during the 13th century, flourished throughout the Ottoman Empire and survives in Konya even today. Like several other orders, the Mevlevis stressed the unity of humankind before God regardless of creed.

Dervish orders were banned in the early days of the republic because of their ultraconservative religious politics. The Galata Mevlevi Tekkesi (Galata Whirling Dervish Hall) is now a museum of *hattat* (Arabic calligraphy) and *Divan* (Ottoman) poetry. However, the Mevlevi dervishes (now a 'cultural' organisation), still whirl here on the last Sunday of each month. Ask at the museum (☎ 212-245 4141) for details.

The bustling atmosphere of the Kapalı Çarşı (Grand Bazaar)

Cafe in the garden of the Archaeological Museum, Eminönü

Sunlight filters into the serene interior of the Süleymaniye Camii.

Old meets new at the Bozdoğan Kemeri.

Galata Kulesi, built by Genoese colonists.

The majestic Dolmabahçe Sarayı, part of a vain attempt to arrest the decline of the Ottoman Empire.

the graveyard on the left and its stones with graceful Ottoman inscriptions. The shapes atop the stones reflect the headgear of the deceased, each hat denoting a different religious rank. Note also the tomb of the sheik by the entrance passage, and the şadırvan.

Inside the tekke, the central area was for the whirling sema, while the galleries above were for visitors who had come to observe. Separate areas were set aside for the orchestra and for female visitors (behind the lattices).

Don't neglect the exhibits of calligraphy, writing instruments and other paraphernalia associated with this highly developed Ottoman art.

Galipdede Caddesi

Leaving the Galata Mevlevihanesi, turn left down Galipdede Caddesi, which is lined with shops selling books, Turkish and European musical instruments, plumbing and cabinet-making supplies. The hillside is covered with winding streets, passageways, alleys of stairs and European-style houses built mostly in the 19th century. There are also older 'Frankish' houses giving a glimpse of what life was like for the European emigrés who came to make their fortunes centuries ago.

A few minutes walk along Galipdede Caddesi will bring you to Beyoğlu's oldest landmark, the Galata Tower.

Galata Kulesi & Neve Shalom Synagogue

The cylindrical Galata Kulesi or Galata Tower (☎ 212-245 1160) was the high point in the Genoese fortifications of Galata, and has been rebuilt many times. Today it holds a forgettable restaurant/ nightclub as well as a memorable **panorama balcony**, open to visitors daily from 9 am to 9 pm, for US$1.75 (US$1 on Monday).

In the shadow of the tower are woodworking shops, turners' lathes, workshops making veneer and other materials for interior decoration, and a few dusty antique stores (see the Antiques section in the Shopping chapter).

During the 19th century, Galata had a large Sephardic Jewish population, but most of this community has now moved to more desirable residential areas. The Neve Shalom Synagogue, a block north-west of the Galata Kulesi towards Şişhane Square on Büyük Hendek Sokak, was the site of a brutal massacre by Arab gunmen during the summer of 1986. Now restored, it is used by İstanbul's Jewish community for weddings, funerals and other ceremonies.

From the Galata Kulesi, continue downhill on the street called Yüksek Kaldırım to reach Karaköy.

Karaköy (Galata)

In order to avoid 'contamination' of their way of life, both the later Byzantine emperors and the Ottoman sultans relegated European traders to offices and residences in Galata, now called Karaköy (Map 4). Under the later Byzantines, Genoese traders took over the town. Today Karaköy still harbours some shipping and commercial offices and banks, as well as small traders.

As you approach the Galata Bridge from Karaköy, the busy ferry docks and also the docks for Mediterranean cruise ships are to your left. To your right is a warren of little streets filled with hardware stores and plumbing-supply houses. Scattered throughout this neighbourhood are Greek and Armenian churches and schools and a large Ashkenazi synagogue, reminders of the time when virtually all of the empire's businesspeople were non-Muslims.

At the far end of the square north of the Galata Bridge, right at the lower end of Yüksek Kaldırım, Voyvoda Caddesi (also called Bankalar Caddesi) leads up a slope to the right towards Şişhane Square. This street was the banking centre during the days of the empire, and many merchant banks still have headquarters or branches here. The biggest building was that of the Ottoman Bank, now a branch of the Turkish Republic's Central Bank. On 26 August 1896, Armenian revolutionaries seized the Ottoman Bank building and threatened to blow it up if their demands were not met. They were not, and the terrorists surrendered, but anti-Armenian riots following the incident caused many Armenian casualties.

Karaköy has busy bus stops, dolmuş queues and the lower station of the Tünel. To find the Tünel station descend into the hubbub of the square from Yüksek Kaldırım Caddesi, and turn into the next major street on the right, Sabahattin Evren Caddesi. The Tünel is a few steps along this street, on the right, in a concrete bunker.

HASKÖY (MAP 1)

About 6km north-west of Karaköy on the Golden Horn and in Hasköy, the early 19th-century imperial hunting lodge at Aynalıkavak is rarely visited by foreign tourists, which makes it all the more appealing. Also here is a fine museum chronicling İstanbul's industrial history.

Aynalıkavak Kasrı

İstanbul's imperial lodges, or *kasrs*, are less outwardly impressive than its many palaces. However, they are designed on a more human scale; kasrs were built not to impress visitors but to please the monarchs themselves.

Several centuries ago an imperial naval arsenal was established at Kasımpasa, south-east of Hasköy, and near it a *tersane* (shipyard). The collection of imperial hunting lodges and pleasure kiosks at Hasköy became known as the Tersane Sarayı, after the shipyard. A wooden palace was built on this site by Sultan Ahmet III (1703-30), and restored by Selim III (1789-1807). What you see today is mostly the work of Sultan Mahmut II (1808-39).

With its Lale Devri (Tulip Period, early 18th-century) decoration and Ottoman furnishings, the pavilion is a splendid if dusty place giving a vivid impression of the lifestyle of the Ottoman ruling class at the turn of the 19th century, when Hasköy was a thriving Jewish neighbourhood. Some rooms – much the most comfortable – are furnished in eastern style, others in the less

commodious European style then penetrating the sultan's domains.

Selim III composed poetry and music in one of its eastern rooms; futon-like beds were tucked away into cabinets during the day. The *bekleme salonu* (waiting room) has the only extant Tulip Period ceiling. One of the European-style rooms is filled with sumptuous mother-of-pearl furniture. There's also a small **Museum of Turkish Musical Instruments** on the lower level.

The pavilion's gardens and grounds provide a welcome respite from the city's concrete landscape.

Aynalıkavak Kasrı (☎ 212-250 4094) is open daily except Monday and Thursday from 9.30 am to 4 pm; admission costs less than US$1, with reductions for students.

Getting There & Away The only practical way to reach Aynalıkavak is by taxi (US$3 from Beyoğlu). Tell the driver to take you to the Hasköy Polis Karakolu (police station) or the Şükrü Urcan Spor Tesisleri (athletic facilities), which are well known. A minute's walk south-east of the Hasköy police station along Kasımpaşa-Hasköy Yolu brings you to Aynalıkavak Kasrı.

Rahmi M Koç Müzesi

The Rahmi M Koç Industrial Museum (☎ 212-256 7153), Hasköy Caddesi 27, Sütlüce, was founded by the current head of the Koç industrial group, one of Turkey's most prominent conglomerates, to exhibit artefacts from İstanbul's industrial past. It's open from 10 am to 5 pm, closed Monday. Admission costs US$2.50.

Exhibits include engines and anything having to do with them: Bosphorus ferryboat parts and machinery, Hotchkiss guns, ship and train models, cars (how about that 1936 Austin roadster!), jet engines, soda machines and even much of the fuselage of 'Hadley's Harem', a US B-24D Liberator bomber which crashed off Antalya in August, 1943.

The *Café du Levant* (☎ *212-250 8938)*, on the museum's grounds, is a surprisingly elegant French bistro serving lunch and dinner at moderate prices daily except Monday.

The museum is near the northern end of the old Galata Bridge on Kumbarahane Caddesi about 1km north-west of Aynalıkavak Kasrı.

WESTERN DISTRICTS (MAP 1)

From early times the heart of this ancient city has been near the tip of Saray Burnu. As the city grew over the centuries, its boundaries moved westward. That process continues.

West of Atatürk Bulvarı in Old İstanbul, out towards the city walls, are many more interesting things to see, including the Fatih Camii, Kariye Müzesi (once the Chora Church), Tekfur Sarayı (Palace of Constantine Porphyrogenetus), a number of other mosques, the mammoth city walls, and Yedikule, the Fortress of the Seven Towers. These sights are listed below by district: Fatih, Fener, Edirnekapı, Balat, Eyüp and Yedikule. Unless you're an Olympic hiker, you'll want to ride to these rather than walk, though walking among the sights of Fener is pretty easy, and there's a good walking tour of the sights at Edirnekapı.

Fatih

Named after Mehmet the Conqueror (*fatih* means conqueror), Fatih is north-west of Şehzadebaşı and the Aqueduct of Valens. Catch any bus that has either 'Fatih' or 'Edirnekapı' listed on its itinerary board; from Taksim, get an Aksaray dolmuş but get out at Saraçhane by the aqueduct (*su kemeri*).

Fatih Camii The Mosque of the Conqueror is 750m north-west of the Aqueduct of Valens, on Fevzi Paşa Caddesi. Catch a dolmuş from Aksaray or Taksim to the city hall (ask for the Belediye Sarayı, behl-eh-DEE-yeh sar-rah-yuh) near the aqueduct and walk five blocks; or you can catch any bus or dolmuş that has 'Fatih' or 'Edirnekapı' listed on its itinerary board.

The Fatih Camii was the first great imperial mosque to be built in İstanbul following the Conquest. For its location,

Sultan Mehmet the Conqueror chose the hilltop site of the ruined Church of the Apostles. The mosque complex, finished in 1470, was enormous, set in extensive grounds, and included in its külliye 15 charitable establishments – religious schools, a hospice for travellers, a caravanserai etc. The mosque you see, however, is not the one he built. The original stood for nearly 300 years before toppling in an earthquake in 1766. It was rebuilt, but destroyed by fire in 1782. The present mosque dates from the reign of Abdül Hamit I, and is on a completely different plan. The exterior of the mosque still bears some of the original decoration; the great doors have been beautifully restored; the interior is of less interest, though there is a simple but beautiful mihrab and plentiful fine stained glass.

Directly behind (south-east of) the mosque are two tombs, the tomb of Mehmet the Conqueror and that of his wife Gülbahar, who is rumoured to have been a French princess.

Places to Eat If you need refreshment, cross Fevzipaşa Caddesi and walk southeast one block to the *Dilek Pastanesi*. The glass cases are a pastry-lover's sweet dream come true. There are other eateries here as well.

Fener

Fener (fehn-EHR; from *Phanar*, the Greek word for lantern or lighthouse) was the centre of Greek life in Ottoman İstanbul, and is still the seat of the Ecumenical Orthodox patriarchate.

Ecumenical Orthodox Patriarchate The Ecumenical patriarch is a ceremonial head of the Orthodox churches, though most of the churches – in Greece, Cyprus, Russia and other countries – have their own patriarchs or archbishops who are independent of İstanbul. Nevertheless, the 'sentimental' importance of the patriarchate, here in the city which saw the great era of Byzantine and Orthodox influence, is considerable.

In the eyes of the Turkish government, the patriarch is a Turkish citizen of Greek descent nominated by the church and appointed by the government as an official in the Directorate of Religious Affairs. In this capacity he is the religious leader of the country's Orthodox citizens and is known officially as the Greek Patriarch of Fener (Fener Rum Patriği).

The patriarchate (*patrikhane*, ☎ 212-527 0323), has been in this district since 1601. To find it, go inland from the Fener ferry dock on the Golden Horn, and ask the way. It's a good idea to telephone in advance if you want to enter the compound.

The **Church of St George**, within the patriarchate compound, is a modest place, built in 1720, but the ornate patriarchal throne may date from the last years of Byzantium. In 1941 a disastrous fire destroyed many of the buildings but spared the church.

Selimiye Camii Between the Fatih and Fener districts is the Mosque of Yavuz Selim (Selim I, 1512-20), or Sultan Selim 'the Grim'.

Approaching the mosque along Sultan Selim Caddesi, you pass the huge Roman **Çukur Bostan** or Cistern of Aspar, built by a Gothic general in the Roman army in the 400s AD. After it ceased being used as a cistern, a Turkish village grew up sheltered in its depths. That was recently swept away to make room for spacious sports-grounds and parkland.

Renovations are being carried out at the Selimiye at this writing, though it's still possible to visit the mosque.

From the Selimiye you can descend easily to the Fener district on the Golden Horn by going down the steps on the northern side of the mosque gardens by the toilets.

Church of St Stephen of the Bulgars
The Church of St Stephen of the Bulgars, which is between Balat and Fener on the Golden Horn, is made completely of cast iron, as is most of its interior decoration. The building is unusual, and its history even more so.

The church is not normally open for visits, but well-dressed visitors arriving during or after services on Sunday morning may well be invited in for a look round.

During the 19th century the spirit of ethnic nationalism swept through the Ottoman Empire. Each of the many ethnic

---

Selim 'the Grim'

Sultan Selim 'the Grim' (1512-20) laid the foundations of Ottoman greatness for his son and successor, Süleyman the Magnificent.

Though he ruled for a very short time, Selim greatly expanded the empire's territory, solidified its institutions and filled its treasury. He came to power by deposing his father, Beyazıt II (1481-1512), who died 'mysteriously' soon after.

To avoid any threat to his power, and thus the sort of disastrous civil war which had torn the empire apart in the days before Mehmet the Conqueror, Selim had all his brothers put to death, and in the eight years of his reign he had eight grand viziers beheaded.

But his violence was in the interests of empire-building, at which he was a master. He doubled the empire's extent during his short reign, conquering part of Persia and all of Syria and Egypt. He took from Egypt's decadent, defeated rulers the title Caliph of Islam, which was borne by his successors until 1924. In his spare time he wrote poetry in Persian, the literary language of the time.

groups in the empire wanted to rule its own affairs. Groups identified themselves on the basis of language, religion and racial heritage. This sometimes led to problems, as with the Bulgars.

The Bulgars, originally a Turkic-speaking people, came from the Volga in about 680 AD and overwhelmed the Slavic peoples living in what is today Bulgaria. They adopted the Slavic language and customs, and founded an empire which threatened the power of Byzantium. In the 9th century they were converted to Christianity.

The Orthodox Patriarch, head of the Eastern church in the Ottoman Empire, was an ethnic Greek; in order to retain as much power as possible, the patriarch was opposed to any ethnic divisions within the Orthodox church. He put pressure on the sultan not to allow the Bulgarians, Macedonians and Rumanians to establish their own religious groups.

The pressures of nationalism became too great, however, and the sultan was finally forced to recognise some sort of autonomy for the Bulgars. He established not a Bulgarian patriarchate, but an 'exarchate', with a leader supposedly of lesser rank, yet independent of the Greek Orthodox patriarch. In this way the Bulgarians would get their desired ethnic recognition and would get out from under the dominance of the Greeks, but the Greek Patriarch would allegedly suffer no diminution of his glory or power.

St Stephen's is the Bulgarian exarch's church. The Gothic structure was cast in Vienna, shipped down the Danube on 100 barges, and assembled in İstanbul in 1871. A duplicate church erected in Vienna, the only other copy, was destroyed by aerial bombing during WWII.

Edirnekapı (Map 8)

Mihrimah Sultan Camii When you're finished at the Fatih mosque, go back to Fevzi Paşa Caddesi and catch a bus or dolmuş headed north-west towards Edirnekapı. Get out just before the city walls at the Mihrimah Sultan Camii, a

mosque built by Süleyman the Magnificent's favourite daughter, Mihrimah, in the 1560s. Mihrimah married Rüstem Paşa, Süleyman's brilliant and powerful grand vizier (his little tile-covered mosque is down by the Egyptian Market).

The architect of the Mihrimah Camii was Sinan, and the mosque, a departure from his usual style, is among his best works. Visit in the morning to get the full effect of the light streaming through the delicate stained-glass windows on the east side. The interior space is very light, with 19 windows in each arched tympanum. Virtually every other surface is painted in arabesques, creating a delicate feminine effect. The inevitable earthquakes worked their destruction in 1766 and 1894, and the building is again under restoration, though still visitable, at this writing.

Cross the road from the Mihrimah Camii and, still inside the walls, head north towards the Golden Horn. You'll see signs, and children pointing the way, to the Kariye Müzesi.

Kariye Müzesi If we translate the original name, Chora Church, of this building, it would be called 'Church of the Holy Saviour Outside the Walls' or 'in the Country', because the first church on this site was indeed outside the walls built by Constantine the Great. But just as London's church of St Martin-in-the-Fields is hardly surrounded by bucolic scenery these days, the Church of the Holy Saviour was soon engulfed by Byzantine urban sprawl. It was enclosed within the walls built by the Emperor Theodosius II in 413, less than 100 years after Constantine. So the Holy Saviour in the Country was 'in the country' for about 80 years, and has been 'in the city' for 1550 years.

It was not only the environs of the church which changed: for four centuries it served as a mosque (Kariye Camii), and is now a museum, the Kariye Müzesi (☎ 212-523 3009). It is open daily from 9 am to 4 pm, closed Wednesday; admission costs US$3.

You reach it by taking any Edirnekapı bus along Fevzi Paşa Caddesi.

The building you see is not the original church-outside-the-walls. Rather, this one was built in the late 11th century, with repairs and restructuring in the following centuries. Virtually all of the interior decoration – the famous mosaics and the less-renowned but equally striking mural paintings – dates from about 1320. Between 1948 and 1959 the decoration was carefully restored under the auspices of the Byzantine Society of America.

The **mosaics** are breathtaking, and follow the standard Byzantine order. The first ones are those of the dedication, to Christ and to the Virgin Mary. Then come the offertory ones: Theodore Metochites, builder of the church, offering it to Christ. The two small domes of the inner narthex have portraits of all Christ's ancestors back to Adam. A series outlines the Virgin Mary's life, and another, Christ's early years. Yet another series concentrates on Christ's ministry. Various saints and martyrs are depicted in the interstices.

In the nave are three mosaics: of Christ, of the Virgin as Teacher, and of the Dormition (Assumption) of the Blessed Virgin – turn around to see this one, it's over the main door you just entered. The 'infant' in the painting is actually Mary's soul, being held by Jesus, while her body lies 'asleep' on its bier.

South of the nave is the parecclesion, a side chapel built to hold the tombs of the church's founder and his relatives, close friends and associates. The frescoes appropriately deal with the theme of death and resurrection. The striking painting in the apse shows Christ breaking down the gates of Hell and raising Adam and Eve, with saints and kings in attendance.

Places to Eat The *Café Kariye* in the plaza in front of the museum serves drinks and snacks. For a full meal, try the *Asitane restaurant* in the adjoining Kariye Oteli, where a three-course meal might cost US$10 to US$15.

Tekfur Sarayı From Kariye, head west to the city walls, then north again, and you'll soon come to the Tekfur Sarayı (Palace of Constantine Porphyrogenetus; tehk-FOOR sar-rah-yuh). It's nominally open on Wednesday, Thursday and Sunday from 9 am to 5 pm, but you can usually just wander in on any day. The caretaker may appear and sell you a ticket for US$0.25.

Though the building is only a shell these days, it is remarkably preserved for a Byzantine palace built in the 14th century. Sacred buildings often survive the ravages of time because they continue to be used even though they may be converted for use in another religion. Secular buildings, however, are often torn down and used as quarries for building materials once their owners die. The Byzantine palaces that once crowded Sultanahmet Square are all gone; so is the great Palace of Blachernae, which adjoined the Tekfur Sarayı. Only this one remains.

Climb the rickety ladder up to the walls for a view of the palace, the city walls, the Golden Horn and much of the city.

City Walls Since being built in the 5th century, the city walls have been breached by hostile forces only twice. The first time was in the 13th century, when Byzantium's 'allies', the armies of the Fourth Crusade, broke through and pillaged the town, deposing the emperor and setting up a king of their own. The second time was in 1453 under Mehmet the Conqueror. Even though Mehmet was ultimately successful, he was continually frustrated during the siege as the walls withstood admirably even the heaviest bombardments by the largest cannon in existence.

The walls were kept defensible and in good repair until about a century ago, when the development of mighty naval guns made such expense pointless: if İstanbul was going to fall, it would fall to ships firing from the Bosphorus, not to soldiers advancing on the land walls.

During the late 1980s, the city undertook to rebuild the major gates for the delight of tourists. Debates raged in the Turkish newspapers over the style of the reconstruction. Some said the restorations were too theatrical, while others said that if the walls never actually did look like that, perhaps they should have. The gates which have been completed include the Topkapı, Mevlanakapı and Belgratkapı (Map 1).

For a look at the most spectacular of the defences in the walls see the Yedikule section later in this chapter.

Heading North or East Heading north, you can make your way on foot to the Golden Horn (see the Fener entry earlier in this section) at Balat or Ayvansaray and then take a bus, dolmuş or ferry to Eyüp. To walk to the Fethiye Camii from the Kariye Müzesi (eight to 10 minutes), walk back toward Fevzipaşa Caddesi, but just past the Kariye Oteli turn left downhill on Neşler Sokak, then left at the bottom of the hill around a little mosque, then straight on along a level street and uphill on Fethiye Caddesi. At the top of the slope most traffic goes right, but you go left toward the church, which is visible from this point.

Fethiye Camii Fethiye Camii, or Mosque of the Conquest, was built in the 12th century as the Church of the Theotokos Pammakaristos or Church of the Joyous Mother of God.

The original monastery church was added to several times over the centuries, then converted to a mosque in 1591 to commemorate Sultan Murat III's victories in Georgia and Azerbaijan. Before its conversion it served as the headquarters of the Ecumenical Orthodox Patriarch (1456-1568); Mehmet the Conqueror visited to discuss theological questions here with Patriarch Gennadios not long after the conquest of the city. They talked things over in the side chapel known as the pareclesion, which has been restored to its former Byzantine splendour; the rest of the building remains a mosque. Unfortunately, the pareclesion is not currently open to visitors, and the church itself is something

of a disappointment inside, though the exterior still bears some inscriptions in Greek on the south side.

From the Fethiye Camii you can continue your explorations by walking south-east to the Selimiye Camii, or north-east to the seat of the Ecumenical Orthodox Patriarchate (see the Fener entry earlier in this section). For the Selimiye Camii, continue uphill on Fethiye Caddesi for five minutes, then turn sharp left around the Çarşamba Polis Karakolu (police station) onto Sultan Selim Caddesi, with the mosque visible ahead.

Balat

The quarter on the Golden Horn called Balat (Map 1) used to house a large portion of the city's Jewish population. Spanish Jews driven from their country by the judges of the Spanish Inquisition found refuge in the Ottoman Empire in the late 15th and early 16th centuries. As the sultan recognised, they were a boon to his empire: they brought news of the latest western advances in medicine, clock making, ballistics and other means of warfare. The refugees from the Inquisition set up the first printing presses in Turkey. Like all other religious 'nations' within the empire, the Jewish community was governed by its supreme religious leader, the Chief Rabbi, who oversaw their adherence to biblical law and who was responsible to the sultan for their good conduct.

Balat used to have dozens of **synagogues**, of which two remain for worship: the recently restored **Ahrida** and the nearby **Yanbol**. Admission is by guided tour only. Contact a travel agent (see the Getting There & Away chapter) or İstanbul's Chief Rabbinate (☎ 212-243 5166, 293 8794, fax 244 1980), Yemenici Abdüllatif Sokak 23, two minutes walk north of Tünel Square.

Eyüp

The district of Eyüp (Map 1), once a village outside the city walls, is named after the standard-bearer of the Prophet Muhammed. Eyüp Ensari (Ayoub al-Ansari) had been a

Ayoub al-Ansari

Ayoub al-Ansari (Eyüp Ensari in Turkish), a friend of the Prophet's and a revered member of Islam's early leadership, fell in battle outside the walls of Constantinople while carrying the banner of Islam during the Arab assault and siege of the city in 674-78. He was buried outside the walls and, ironically, his tomb later came to be venerated by the Byzantine inhabitants of the city.

When Mehmet the Conqueror besieged Constantinople in 1453, Eyüp's tomb was no doubt known to him. He undertook to build a grander and more fitting structure to commemorate it.

A legend persists, however, that the tomb had been lost and was miraculously rediscovered by Mehmet's Şeyh-ül-İslam (Supreme Islamic Judge), an event seen by the Turkish armies as a sign from heaven that they would be victorious.

Perhaps both stories are true. If the tomb was known to Mehmet and his leadership but not to the common soldiers, its 'rediscovery' may well have inspired the troops for the holy war in which they were engaged.

friend of the Prophet and a revered member of Islam's early leadership. His tomb and the adjoining **Eyüp Sultan Camii**, or Mosque of the Great Eyüp, are sacred places for most Muslims, ranking after Mecca, Medina and Jerusalem.

Mehmet the Conqueror had a mosque built here within five years of his victory. His mosque was levelled by an earthquake in 1766, and a new mosque was built on the site by Sultan Selim III in 1800.

Take bus No 55 (Taksim to Eyüp Üçşehitler) or bus No 99 (Eminönü to Alibeyköyü) and get off at the 'Eyüp' stop. There are also dolmuşes: Edirnekapı to Eyüp, Topkapı to Eyüp, Aksaray to Eyüp, or Aksaray to Alibeyköyü. The mosque opens long hours every day and entry is free; avoid visiting on Friday or on other Muslim holy days. For a snack or lunch, there are little pastry shops and snack stands on Kalenderhane Caddesi across from the mosque.

Visiting the Eyüp Sultan Camii & Tomb
From the open space next to the complex, enter the great doorway to a large courtyard, then to a smaller court shaded by a huge ancient plane tree. Note the wealth of brilliant İznik tile work on the walls. To

the left, behind the tiles and gilded grillework, is Eyüp's tomb; to the right is the mosque. Be careful to observe the Islamic proprieties when visiting: decent clothing (no shorts) and modest dresses for women, who should also cover head, shoulders and arms. Take your shoes off before entering the small tomb enclosure, rich with silver, gold, crystal chandeliers and coloured tiles. Try not to stand in front of those at prayer; be respectful; don't use a camera (and especially not a flash!).

During your visit you may see boys dressed up in white satin suits with spangled caps and red sashes emblazoned with the word 'Maşallah'. These lads are on the way to their circumcision and have made a stop beforehand at this holy place.

Across the court from the tomb is the mosque, where for centuries the Ottoman princes came for the Turkish equivalent of coronation: to gird on the Sword of Osman, signifying their power and title as *padişah* (king of kings); or sultan.

As the Eyüp Sultan Camii is a sacred place, many important people including lots of grand viziers wanted to be buried in its precincts. Between the mosque-and-tomb complex and the Golden Horn lies a virtual 'village' of octagonal tombs. Even those who were not to be buried here left their marks. The Valide Sultan Mihrişah, Queen Mother of Selim III, built important charitable institutions such as schools, baths and soup kitchens. Sokollu Mehmet Paşa, among the greatest of Ottoman grand viziers, donated a hospital, which still functions as a medical clinic to this day.

Pierre Loti Café Up the hill to the north of the Eyüp mosque is a cafe where French novelist Pierre Loti is said to have come for inspiration.

Loti loved İstanbul, its decadent grandeur, and the fascinating late-medieval customs of a society in decline. When he sat in this cafe, under a shady grapevine sipping çay, he saw a Golden Horn busy with caiques, schooners and a few steam vessels. The water in the Golden Horn was still clean enough for boys to swim in, and the vicinity of the cafe was given over to pasture.

The cafe which today bears his name may not have any actual connection to Loti, but it occupies a spot and offers a view which he must have enjoyed. It's in a warren of little streets on a promontory surrounded by the Eyüp Sultan Mezarlığı, or Cemetery of the Great Eyüp, just north of the Eyüp mosque. The surest way to find it is to ask the way to the cafe via Karyağdı

Sokak. Walk out of the mosque enclosure, turn right, and walk around the mosque complex keeping it on your right to the north side of the mosque until you see the street going uphill into the cemetery marked by a marble sign, 'Maraşal Fevzi Çakmak'. Hike up the steep hill on Karyağdı Sokak for 15 minutes to reach the cafe. If you take a taxi, it will follow a completely different route because of one-way streets. A few snacks and sandwiches are served as well as drinks, and all are relatively expensive.

YEDİKULE

If you arrived in İstanbul by train from Europe, or if you rode in from the airport along the seashore, you've already had a glance at Yedikule, the Fortress of the Seven Towers, looming over the southern approaches to the city.

The fortress is open every day from 9.30 am to 5 pm; admission costs US$1.

History

Theodosius I built a triumphal arch here in the late 4th century. When the next Theodosius (408-50) built his great land walls, he incorporated the arch. Four of the fortress' seven towers were built as part of Theodosius II's walls; the other three, inside the walls, were added by Mehmet the

---

Pierre Loti

Louis-Marie Julien Viaud (1850-1923), aka Pierre Loti, pursued a distinguished career in the French navy, and at the same time became his country's most celebrated novelist. Though a hard-headed mariner, he was also an inspired and incurable romantic who fell in love with the graceful and mysterious way of life he discovered in Ottoman İstanbul.

Loti set up house in Eyüp for several years and had a love affair, fraught with peril, with a married Turkish woman whom he called Aziyadé (the title of his most romantic and successful novel). He was transferred back to France and forced to leave his mistress and his beloved İstanbul, but he decorated his French home in Ottoman style and begged Aziyadé to flee and join him. Instead, her infidelity was discovered and she 'disappeared'.

Pierre Loti's romantic novels about the daily life of İstanbul under the last sultans introduced millions of European readers to Turkish customs and habits, and helped to counteract the politically inspired Turkophobia then spreading through Europe.

Conqueror. Under the Byzantines, the great arch became known as the **Golden Gate**, and was used for triumphal state processions into and out of the city. For a time, its gates were indeed plated with gold. The doorway was sealed in the late Byzantine period.

In Ottoman times the fortress was used for defence, as a repository for the imperial treasury, a prison and a place of execution. Diplomatic practice in Renaissance times included chucking into loathsome prisons the ambassadors of countries with which yours didn't get along. For foreign ambassadors to the Sublime Porte, Yedikule was that prison. Latin and German inscriptions still visible in the Ambassadors' Tower bring the place's history to light. It was also here that Sultan Osman II, a 17-year-old youth, was executed in 1622 during a revolt of the janissary corps. The kaftan he was wearing when he was murdered is now on display in Topkapı Sarayı's costumes collection.

Visiting Yedikule & the Walls

The best view of the city walls and of the fortress is from the **Tower of Sultan Ahmet** III, near the gate in the city wall. It is possible to walk along the land walls from the Sea of Marmara past Yedikule, even making some of the walk atop the walls. The district is not the safest, however, and I know of at least one robbery attempt, so it's best to go in a group and to take the normal precautions.

Right down at the shoreline, where the land walls meet the Sea of Marmara, you will find the **Marble Tower**, once part of a small Byzantine imperial seaside villa.

Getting There & Away Yedikule is a long way from most other sights of interest in İstanbul and involves a special trip. Situated where the great city walls meet the Sea of Marmara, it's accessible by cheap train from Sirkeci. Take any *banliyö* train and hop off at Yedikule, then walk around to the enterance in teh north-east. You can take bus No 80 ('Yedikule') from Eminönü (on the west side of the Yeni Cami), but the ride may take over an hour if the traffic is heavy.

Places to Stay

Turkey's tourism boom of the 1980s and 1990s saw the construction of hundreds of hotels in İstanbul. The accommodation situation is good, with plenty of hotels in all price ranges, though the city is now such a popular tourist destination that many of the best hotels fill up early in the day, even out of season.

If you want a room in a particular hotel described below, reserve it in advance.

SULTANAHMET (MAP 7)

The Sultan Ahmet Camii (Blue Mosque) gives its name to the quarter surrounding it. This is İstanbul's premier sightseeing area, so the hotels here, and in the adjoining neighbourhoods to the east (Cankurtaran), west (Küçük Ayasofya) and north (Binbirdirek), are supremely convenient. Unless otherwise noted, the postal code for these hotels is 34400 Sultanahmet.

Budget

Some budget hotels in this area are run by carpet merchants, who can be tedious in their efforts to get you into the ground-floor shop to buy a rug. If you're interested, don't let yourself be pressured as you look and ponder.

Cankurtaran This quiet residential district south-east of Aya Sofya and the Sultan Ahmet Camii is accessible on foot from Sultanahmet (ask for the Four Seasons Hotel on Tevkifhane Sokak), or by *banliyö treni* (commuter train) from Sirkeci to the Cankurtaran station.

Side Pansiyon (*☎/fax 212-517 6590, Utangaç Sokak 20*) has two buildings: the older Side Pansiyon with rooms for US$20/25/35 a single/double/triple with sink, and US$30/35/45 with private shower; and the new Side Hotel with quite nice rooms for US$40/50/60 with bath and balcony – as good as rooms costing much more. It also has two small apartments with cooking facilities for rent in the basement starting at US$50, good for families.

Continue down Tevkifhane Sokak to Kutlugün Sokak and turn left.

Mavi Guesthouse (*☎ 212-516 5878, fax 517 7287, Kutlugün Sokak 3*), at the end of the street and not to be confused with the expensive Mavi Ev nearby, charges only US$8 for a dorm bed, or US$20 for a waterless double room, with breakfast – right next door to the Four Seasons Hotel. Other identically priced options only two blocks away include the *Troy Hostel* (*☎ 212-516 8757, fax 638 6450, Yeni Saraçhane Sokak 6*) and the *Konya Pansiyon* (*☎ 212-638 3638, Terbıyık Sokak 15*) where there are also a few rooms with private bath for US$35. If the Konya is full, try the *İlknur* across the street.

Around the corner, the *Orient Youth Hostel* (*☎ 212-518 0789, fax 518 3894, email orienthostel@superonline.com, www.hostels.com/orienthostel, Akbıyık Caddesi 13*) has been renovated and the service improved. Beds cost US$6.50 in dorms, US$7 in quad rooms and a bit more in double rooms; all rooms have at least a sink. Services include Internet access, belly-dancing shows three times a week, hookahs twice a week and a rooftop bar with good views. There's a street market on Akbıyık Caddesi on Wednesday.

Across the street, the *Star Pansiyon* (*☎ 212-638 2302, fax 516 1827, Akbıyık Caddesi 18*) has tidy doubles with shower and breakfast for US$35, and a public laundry as well. The nearby *Alaaddin Guest House* (*☎ 212-516 2330, fax 638 6059, Akbıyık Caddesi 32*) is similar, if a bit more expensive. The *Sultan Tourist Hostel* (*☎ 212-516 9260, 517 1626, Terbıyık Sokak 3*) is cheaper, with waterless rooms going for US$25.

Terrace Guesthouse (*☎ 212-638 9733, fax 638 9734, email terrace@escortnet.com, Kutlugün Sokak 39*) has only a few rooms,

Where to Find Lodging

Here are some rules of thumb for finding lodgings in the price range you prefer. Keep in mind that the appearance of a hotel's lobby tells you little about its rooms. Look at several rooms if possible, and choose the best. If the first one you see won't do, ask *Başka var mı* (BAHSH-kah VAHR-muh, Are there others?).

Camping İstanbul's camping areas are ranged along the shore in Florya, Yeşilköy and Ataköy near the airport, about 20km from Aya Sofya. They have good sea-view locations and average prices of US$8 for two people in a tent. All are served by the frequent commuter trains, which run between Sirkeci train station and the western suburb of Halkalı for less than a dollar.

Student Hostels In July and August, several university dormitories open their doors to foreign students. These dorms tend to be extremely basic and cheap, charging only a few dollars per night for a dorm bed. They're not for all tastes, and the great majority of visitors prefer the cheap hotels in Sultanahmet which cost just slightly more for much greater comfort, convenience and privacy. If you want to look into student dorms, ask for the latest information from the Tourism Information Office in Sultanahmet, right at the northern end of the Hippodrome.

Backpacker Hotels Some bottom-end hotels provide you with a dormitory bed for as little as US$6 or US$8 per person, others offer double rooms with private toilet, sink and hot-water shower for as much as US$50. Mostly though, these places have simple but adequate double rooms (with a sink or private shower for US$25 to US$40).

Mid-Range Hotels Mid-range hotels, usually newer buildings constructed during the past two decades, vary in size from 30 to 80 rooms and charge from US$40 to US$100 for a double with private shower and/or bath; many include breakfast in the price. Most rooms fall in the range of US$50 to US$75. Except for a few hotels in Sultanahmet and Taksim, virtually all of

but they're cheerful, with tiny baths, balconies and sea views for US$40 to US$45 a double with breakfast served in the rooftop dining room.

Around the corner, the **Hotel Şebnem** (☎ *212-517 6623, fax 638 1056, Adliye Sokak 1*) is clean and fairly quiet with double rooms priced at US$40 to US$50 in summer, private shower and breakfast included.

Off Yerebatan Caddesi The *Yücelt Interyouth Hostel* (☎ *212-513 6150, fax 512 7628, email yucelthostel@escortnet.com, www.travelturkey.com/yucelt.html, Caferiye Sokak 6/1*) is literally across the street from the front (west) door of Aya Sofya. Though

called a hostel, it's a cheap hotel with restaurant, bulletin board, TV room, terrace, email, travel service, coin-operated laundry and Turkish bath. Doubles with sink cost US$18, rooms with three or four beds go for US$8 per person, and dormitory beds (eight to a room) cost US$6 each. Some readers enjoy this place, others complain.

A few other cheap hotels are a short walk north-west from Aya Sofya along Yerebatan Caddesi to Salkımsöğüt Sokak, on the right. This area is not as quiet or desirable as Cankurtaran, but still serviceable.

Hotel Ema (☎ *212-511 7166, fax 512 4878, Salkımsöğüt Sokak 18)* is friendly, simple and not too noisy for US$20 a

Where to Find Lodging

these places are rated at two or three stars by the Ministry of Tourism, which means they can be depended upon to have lifts, restaurants and bars (though often empty), and staff who speak a smattering of foreign languages. Many rooms are equipped with TV, and some also have minibars.

Ottoman-Style Hotels The Cankurtaran and Kadırga districts, near Sultanahmet, are the place to find these charming 'boutique' hotels made from restored Ottoman mansions, with rooms from US$60 to US$125.

Upper Mid-Range Hotels Taksim Square has many comfortable four-star hotels with double rooms from US$80 to US$125. It's an interesting area with lots to do.

Top Hotels In İstanbul's luxury hotels of an international standard, prices range from US$125 to US$300 and higher for a double, but most rooms cost from US$140 to US$200. Try not to pay the 'normal' published rates (rack rates), which are quite high. Often these hotels offer special packages; ask when you make reservations. The big international chains usually allow children of any age to share a double room with their parents at no extra charge or, if two rooms are needed, they charge only the single rate for each room.

Long-Term Stays İstanbul does not yet have lodgings aimed at travellers wanting to stay for several months. Visitors staying more than a few days customarily make arrangements with a suitable hotel, and receive a discount on the room and some meals for a longer period.

Despite its status as the European low-price leader, prices for housing in Turkey are not low, and any apartment in İstanbul with a water view commands a premium rate.

Available apartments *(kiralık daireler)* and brokers *(emlakçı)* are advertised in the newspapers. Those in the *Turkish Daily News* are aimed at foreigners, which means that you'll have fewer difficulties with language, but may pay a premium price.

waterless double, or US$30 with private shower. The neighbouring *Elit Hotel* (☎ 212-526 2549, fax 512 4878, Salkımsöğüt Sokak 14) has 12 clean, slightly fancier rooms with private facilities above a carpet shop. Prices can go as high as US$30/50 a single/double in summer, but the hotel is ready to bargain.

Down Salkımsöğüt Sokak a few more steps on the right is the *Hotel Anadolu* (☎ 212-512 1035) at No 3. It's possibly the oldest hotel in the quarter, but also the cheapest and quietest. By the front door are a few little tables overlooking a car park, a good place to sip a tea or write a letter. The rooms are tiny, and in summer prices can go

as high as US$20 for a double room with a sink, or US$30 for one with shower, but hot showers are free, and there's no carpet shop.

Binbirdirek Just uphill west of the Hippodrome is the district of Binbirdirek, named after the Byzantine cistern of that name.

Türkmen Hotel & Pansiyon (☎ 212-517 1355, fax 638 5546, Dizdariye Çeşmesi Sokak 27) is a modern nondescript but friendly place on a quiet back street a bit out of the way. Double rooms in the pension have private showers, but no toilets, and are priced at US$18; in the hotel, nicer rooms with toilet, sink and shower are US$35 in high summer.

Küçük Ayasofya This neighbourhood is downhill from the south-western end of the Hippodrome.

Just off the Hippodrome is the *Hotel Best Hipodrom (☎/fax 212-516 0902, Üçler Sokak 9)*. It offers excellent value: decent rooms with shower, TV and breakfast for US$35 a double.

Can Pansiyon (☎ 212-638 6608, Şehit Mehmet Paşa Yokuşu, Liman Caddesi, Kaleci Sokak 2), just downhill from the Hotel Sokullu Paşa, is very simple and basic, but very cheap at US$5 per person in waterless rooms. More expensive but also more comfortable is the *Seagull Pension (☎ 212-517 1142, fax 516 0972, Küçük Ayasofya Caddesi, Aksakal Sokak 22)*, charging US$18 for a double with private bath.

Divan Yolu The *Arsenal Youth Hostel (☎ 212-513 6407, Dr Emin Paşa Sokak 12)*, by the Tarihi Park Hamamı, is cramped and rundown but central. Dorm rooms with four beds each cost US$8 per bed, with showers down the hall.

The *Sipahi Otel (☎ 212-527 9261, fax 527 3402, Divan Yolu, Türbedar Sokak 20)*, up from the Press Museum, is an old but relatively quiet building popular with Turkish tradesmen travelling on a budget. Its 57 rooms are conveniently located midway between Sultanahmet and the Kapalı Çarşı. Rates are US$18 a double in rooms with sink, US$22 with shower. Breakfast costs extra.

Mid-Range

Mid-range hotels in Sultanahmet are either historic buildings with character – even Ottoman-style mansions – or comfortable but characterless modern buildings.

Ottoman-Style Hotels The lobby of the small *Hotel Empress Zoe (☎ 212-518 2504, 518 4360, fax 518 5699, email emzoe@ibm.net, www.emzoe.com, Akbıyık Caddesi, Adliye Sokak 10)* is in a Byzantine cistern

next to an old Ottoman *hamam*. The small rooms above, reached by a narrow staircase, are simply decorated with taste and character. The rooftop bar-lounge-terrace affords fine views of the sea and the Sultan Ahmet Camii; the pleasant 'secret garden' is a flower-bordered haven. Prices are US$50/70/85 a single/double/triple (US$5 discount for cash), a good breakfast included. Run by American expatriate Ann Nevans, it's a fine choice for single women.

A block away, the *Hotel Poem (☎/fax 212-517 6836, Terbıyık Sokak 12)* is two buildings with a small glass-covered restaurant in between, and rooms (some with sea views) for US$50/75 a single/double, breakfast included. There's a poem in each room; this is among the quietest of options. The *Hotel Acropol (☎ 212-638 9021, fax 518 3031, Akbıyık Caddesi 25)* is one of the newest and most comfortable hotels in this quarter, with 26 fully equipped rooms going for US$70/90, and fine views from the penthouse restaurant.

For maximum Ottoman ambience, the award goes to the *Hotel Turkuaz (☎ 212-518 1897, fax 517 3380, Cinci Meydanı 36, Kadırga)* at the bottom of the hill from the south-western corner of the Hippodrome, somewhat out of the way. The rooms, furnishings, Turkish bath and Turkish folk-art lounge in this period house are the real thing, not posh modern imitations. When you stay in the 'Sultan's Room', you feel the part. The 14 double rooms, all with private shower, cost between US$40 and US$80, breakfast included.

Just around the corner, the *Hotel Sidera (☎ 212-638 3460, fax 518 7262, Kadırga Meydanı, Dönüş Sokak 14, Kumkapı)* is the modern version of an Ottoman mansion, quiet and comfortable. It charges US$55/85 for its bath-equipped rooms in summer, less in the off season.

Go east (downhill) from the Hippodrome along Mehmet Paşa Yokuşu and Suterazisi Sokak to find the *Hotel Yeni Ayasofya (☎ 212-516 9446, fax 518 0700, Küçük Ayasofya Caddesi, Demirci Reşit Sokak 28)*. This is another nicely renovated house in a quiet residential area. It charges US$70/95 for rooms with shower, and the staff are ready to haggle with you for lower rates.

Nearby ***Ottoman House (☎ 212-517 4203, fax 517 3512, Kadırga Limanı Caddesi 85)***, on the north side of the park, posts an outrageous price of US$90 a double, but charges barely half that for so-so modern rooms.

Up the hill a few steps off the Hippodrome, the ***Hotel Turkoman (☎ 212-516 2956, fax 516 2957, Asmalı Çeşme Sokak, Adliye Yanı 2)*** is a recently renovated, 19th-century building with the feeling of a private club. The 12 bath-equipped rooms have names, not numbers, are simply but tastefully decorated, and cost US$70/85/100 a single/double/triple. Take your breakfast (included in the rates) on the roof terrace with fine views of the Hippodrome, Sultan Ahmet Camii and the Museum of Turkish & Islamic Arts, which is next door.

Right behind the Turkoman is the small, simple and mostly modern ***Hotel İbrahim Paşa (☎ 212-518 0349, fax 518 4457, email pasha@ibm.net, www//all-hotels.com/a /tkpasha/tkpasha.htm)***. It has a lift and 18 small shower-equipped rooms, which are a bit too pricey at US$80/95 a single/double, breakfast included, but the location is quietish and convenient and the management friendly and accommodating.

Best Western Hotel Sokullu Paşa (☎ 212-518 1790, fax 518 1793, email Sokullu@superonline.com, Mehmet Paşa Sokak 5/7, Küçük Ayasofya) is a restored Ottoman house with its own small terrace and hamam. Get one of the light, airy, high-ceilinged rooms such as No 306 or 308 for US$65/90, breakfast included; some other rooms are not as good. The hotel will cut the price quickly if it's not full.

Hotel Sümengen (☎ 212-517 6869, fax 516 8282, Amiral Tafdil Sokak 21) is an Ottoman town house with its own marble-covered Turkish bath (US$10 extra) and an airy, light dining room and open-air rooftop terrace with views of the Sea of Marmara. The 30 guest rooms are small with tiny

showers and twin or double beds. A few of the rooms have views of the sea, but many rooms open only onto corridors, giving their inhabitants little privacy. Rates are a bit too high at US$90/110/120 a single/double/triple, breakfast included.

The ***Hotel Historia (☎ 212-517 7472, fax 516 8169, Amiral Tafdil Sokak 23)***, just to the right of the Sümengen, is Ottoman on the outside but more modern on the inside, though there is a marble-clad hamam. Some of the 27 rooms have short bathtubs as well as showers, and all cost US$70/90/110, lower if they're not full. Corner rooms such as Nos 401 and 501 are choice.

The ***Hotel Avicenna (☎ 212-517 0550, fax 516 6555, email avicenna@superonline .com, www.avicenna.com.tr, Amiral Tafdil Sokak 31-33)***, to the right of the Historia, is also Ottoman on the outside but modern on the inside, with satellite TV, a roof-terrace cafe-bar, and 49 small though pleasant rooms for US$90/110 (bargainable), breakfast included.

Pensions ***Guesthouse Berk (☎ 212-516 9671, fax 517 7715, Kutlugün Sokak 27)*** is family-run and a good choice for single women, though comparatively expensive. The half-dozen rooms all have private bath and cost US$40 to US$70 a single, US$50 to US$90 a double.

Barut's Guesthouse (☎ 212-516 5256, fax 516 2944, İshakpaşa Caddesi 8) is a 23-room pension run by artists Hikmet and Füsun Barut (Hikmet Bey specialises in the old Turkish craft of paper marbling – look at the fine examples in the lobby). Guest rooms are quite basic and simple, but the family atmosphere makes up for them. Rates are $40/50/60/70 for a single/double/triple/quad.

Modern Hotels ***Hotel Halı (☎ 212-516 2170, fax 516 2172, Klodfarer Caddesi 20, Çemberlitaş)***, uphill to the north-west of the Hippodrome, is another good modern choice at a lower price: US$48/65 a single/double, breakfast included. There's a bit more street noise here. The simpler but acceptable

Gülşah Otel (☎ *212-516 2760, fax 516 2172, Piyerloti Caddesi 6)* is a cheaper choice at US$42/45 a single/double, but without the Halı's views.

The *Hotel Piyer Loti* (☎ *212-518 5700, fax 516 1886, Piyerloti Caddesi 5, Çemberlitaş)*, is a modern building with a popular glass-covered sidewalk cafe-restaurant on Divan Yolu two blocks west of the Hippodrome. The simple, modern rooms cost US$60/75 a single/double, a great price for such a convenient location. A half-block south, the three-star *Hotel Antea* (☎ *212-638 1121, fax 517 7949, Piyerloti Caddesi 21)* is fancier and more expensive at US$70/100/130.

The friendly *Hotel Nomade* (☎ *212-511 1296, fax 513 2404, Divan Yolu, Ticarethane Sokak 15)* is just a few steps off busy Divan Yolu. French is spoken here, and the price is a comparatively expensive US$45/60 a single/double with private shower and breakfast. It's a good place for single women.

Top End

The Turkish Touring & Automobile Association (Turing) has restored historic buildings throughout the city, including several Ottoman mansions next door to Aya Sofya and the Sultan Ahmet Camii.

Yeşil Ev (☎ *212-517 6785, fax 517 6780, Kabasakal Caddesi 5)* is an Ottoman house rebuilt by Turing with 22 rooms furnished with period pieces and antiques in fine taste; it's the classiest of the restored Ottoman mansion hotels. Behind the hotel is a lovely shaded garden-terrace restaurant. It costs US$115/150/195 a single/double triple or US$240, breakfast included, for the Pasha's Room, with its own private Turkish bath.

Mavi Ev (or 'Blue House', ☎ *212-638 9010; fax 638 9017, email bluehouse@ istanbulhotels.com,www.istanbulhotels.com/ bluehouse .htm, Dalbastı Sokak 14)*, opened in 1997, has comfortable rooms, a supremely convenient location and excellent morning views of the Sultan Ahmet Camii from its rooftop restaurant. The cost is US$110/130 a single/double, which includes breakfast.

Hotel Arcadia (☎ *212-516 9696, fax 516 6118, Dr İmren Öktem Caddesi 1)*, on the north-west side of the modern Adliye Sarayı (law courts), is a modern mid-rise hotel with comfortable rooms for a somewhat high US$120/140, breakfast included. The location is excellent – quiet and convenient – and the afternoon views of the Sultan Ahmet Camii, Aya Sofya, Topkapı Sarayı and the Sea of Marmara from the upper-floor rooms and rooftop restaurant are nothing short of spectacular.

On the north side of Aya Sofya against the walls of Topkapı Palace is a row of Ottoman houses, now the *Ayasofya Pansiyonları* (☎ *212-513 3660, fax 513 3669, email ayapans@escortnet.com.tr, Soğukçeşme Sokak)*, which have also been rebuilt and refitted by Turing. The 58 rooms with private baths are in 19th-century Ottoman style with brass or antique wooden beds, glass lamps, Turkish carpets and period wall hangings. Prices are from US$80 to US$90 a single, US$100 to US$120 a double, US$160 a triple, breakfast included. The cheaper rooms, at the back, get less light; front rooms look right onto Aya Sofya.

Across the street, the *Konuk Evi (same numbers as Ayasofya Pansiyonları)* was rebuilt by Turing in 1992 to duplicate a historic mansion which stood on this site during the reign of Sultan Abdül Hamit. It now has a garden, conservatory-restaurant and 20 guest rooms with all mod cons priced as at the Yeşil Ev (above).

The Four Seasons Hotel Istanbul (☎ *212-638 8200, fax 638 8210, email Huluer@fshr.com, www.fshr.com, Tevkifhane Sokak 1)* is Istanbul's top hotel in every respect: location, accommodation, design, furnishings and service. With only 65 rooms and a staff of around 200, this perfectly restored Ottoman building literally in the shadow of the Sultan Ahmet Camii and Aya Sofya has only one problem: there aren't enough rooms for everyone who wants one, even at the lofty price of US$220 to US$350 a single, US$250 to US$380 a double, plus 15% tax (breakfast extra).

The *Hotel Armada* (☎ 212-638 1370, fax 518 5060, Ahırkapı Sokak), very near the Cankurtaran suburban train station, is a few steps from the Bosphorus shore and only a 10-minute walk uphill to Sultanahmet. The 110 rooms have all the modern conveniences and many luxuries, and are priced at US$125/150 a single/double.

The *Best Western President Hotel* (☎ 212-516 6980, fax 516 6999, Tiyatro Caddesi 25, 34490 Beyazıt, Map 6), only a block from the Kapalı Çarşı, is the place for inveterate shoppers. Though it's on a narrow street, you're in good company here, with the Ministry of Finance's shiny granite-clad guesthouse directly opposite. The President has most luxury services, and moderate (for luxury) prices of US$130/170 a single/double, breakfast included.

TAKSİM SQUARE (MAP 3)

The heart of modern İstanbul is also a good place to stay, with lots of restaurants, theatres, cinemas, nightclubs and shops nearby. Airline offices, foreign banks and luxury hotels are mostly near Taksim Square. The postal code is 80090 Taksim.

Budget

A few inexpensive hostelries exist amidst the banks, airline offices, nightclubs and towering luxury hotels of Taksim Square.

One such place is the *Otel Avrupa* (☎ 212-250 9420, fax 250 7399, Topçu Caddesi 32, Talimhane), at Şehit Muhtarbey Caddesi. It's a converted apartment house with an entrance at street level, a cheerful breakfast room one flight up, and guest rooms of varying sizes priced at US$36/45 a single/double with private bath and breakfast.

Also take a look at the old-fashioned *Hotel Plaza* (☎ 212-245 3273, fax 293 7040, Aslanyatağı Sokak 19-21), off Sıraselviler Caddesi by the Alman Hastanesi (German Hospital). Although it's a bit difficult to find it's quiet and has some fine Bosphorus views. It charges US$40 a double for its aged rooms with bath and breakfast.

For Families

Two lodging places might appeal especially to families:

Family House (☎ 212-249 7351, fax 249 9667, Kutlu Sokak 53; see Map 3) has five small four-room apartments for rent in a quiet building. The owner-manager, Mr Atıl Erman, a retired teacher, is available to answer any question or solve any problem. He can even arrange your transport from the airport to Family House for US$25. Apartments have two single beds and one double bed, telephone, colour TV, kitchen with refrigerator, two-burner gas cooker and utensils. In summer it's US$96 per day, US$600 per week for up to four people. To find Family House, walk down İnönü Caddesi from Taksim, turn right, walk beneath the large red Chinese gate and down the steps, then down another flight, following the Family House signs. Ask him about his guesthouse in rural Göynük.

The *Virginie Apart-Hotel* (☎ 212-251 7856, fax 251 0184, İstiklal Caddesi 100; see Map 3), at Sakızağacı Caddesi, has five little apartments overlooking the trendy street for US$75/100/120 single/double/triple.

Mid-Range

The area also has nearly a dozen modern four-star hotels charging US$90 to US$150 for comfortable double rooms with private bath, TV, minibar and air-conditioning, breakfast included. All are fairly quiet and have lifts, bars and restaurants, 24-hour room service (of sorts) and English-speaking personnel. You should be granted a discount if you stay for several days off season; be sure to ask about it. Most customers are here on business or organised tours.

Hotel Lamartine (☎ 212-254 6270, fax 256 2776, Lamartin Caddesi 25) has 58 rooms for US$90/110 a single/double.

Riva Otel (☎ 212-256 4420, fax 256 2033, Aydede Caddesi 8) charges US$80/100 a single/double and has its own currency-exchange office.

Eresin Taksim Hotel (☎ *212-256 0803, fax 253 2247, Topçu Caddesi 34*) is older but well maintained, with rooms for US$90/110/130 a single/double/triple.

The Madison Hotel (☎ *212-238 5460, fax 238 5151, Recep Paşa Caddesi 23*) is among the newest ones, with rates for its 108 rooms at US$85/110 a single/double. There's a hamam, sauna and small indoor swimming pool.

Hotel İstanbul Kervansaray (☎ *212-235 5000, fax 253 4378, Şehit Muhtar Caddesi 61*), just around the corner from the Eresin, has a quiet location and charges US$90/110 a single/double for its rooms.

Feronya Hotel (☎ *212-238 0901, fax 238 0866, Abdülhak Hamit Caddesi 70-72*) is among the newer hotels, nominally charging US$100/140, but I was quoted US$100 for a double in the off season.

Nippon Hotel (☎ *212-254 9900, fax 250 4553, Topçu Caddesi 10*) has 94 rooms, is a bit more expensive, and is often filled by tour groups paying US$90/110.

Top End

Except for the Marmara Hotel facing Taksim, the district's luxury hotels are on and off Cumhuriyet Caddesi (Map 4), a few blocks north of the square.

The ***Divan Oteli***, dee-VAHN, (☎ *212-231 4100, fax 248 8527, Cumhuriyet Caddesi 2, Elmadağ*) is a small European-style hotel with excellent cuisine and personal service by well-trained multilingual staff. Rooms cost US$170/205 a single/double, tax included. Breakfast is an alarming US$18 extra.

Two blocks north is the ***İstanbul Hilton*** (☎ *212-231 4650, fax 240 4165*), set in a 5.6-hectare park overlooking the Bosphorus, with tennis courts, swimming pool and rooms from US$200 to US$275 a single, US$235 to US$295 a double.

The 360-room ***Hyatt Regency Istanbul*** (☎ *212-225 7000, fax 225 7007, Taşkışla Caddesi*) has the feel of a vast Ottoman mansion – but with a popular jazz bar, an

Italian restaurant and swimming pool. It charges US$210 to US$270 for a single, US$240 to US$300 for a double.

The 390-room ***Ceylan Inter-Continental Istanbul*** (☎ *212-231 2121, fax 231 2180, www.interconti.com*) towers above Taksim Gezi Parkı, with fine views from its upper floors, and even some from the outdoor swimming pool. Rates rise along with the rooms, costing US$282/317 on the lower floors, US$317/351 on upper floors.

The Marmara (☎ *212-251 4696, fax 244 0509, see Map 3*) towers over busy Taksim Square, affording splendid views of the Old City, Beyoğlu and the Bosphorus from its upper floors. The 432 guest rooms are priced from US$175 to US$200 a single, US$200 to US$250 a double, buffet breakfast included.

TEPEBAŞI (MAP 3)

Between Galatasaray Square and Tünel Square, west of İstiklal Caddesi, is the district called Tepebaşı (TEH-peh-bah-shuh), which was the first luxury hotel district in the city.

The main road through Tepebaşı is Meşrutiyet Caddesi. To get there from Taksim, take the restored tram along İstiklal Caddesi to Galatasaray, or go by taxi or dolmuş; you may have to use a dolmuş that goes past Tepebaşı (say, to Aksaray) and pay the full fare. You can catch a bus along Tarlabaşı Bulvarı (TAHR-la-bash-uh), just out of Taksim near the Air France ticket office. Coming from Karaköy, take the Tünel to the top station and walk the several blocks to the hotels.

Mid-Range

The four-star ***Yenişehir Palas*** (☎ *212-252 7160, fax 249 7507, email newcity@comnet .com.tr, Meşrutiyet Caddesi, Oteller Sokak 1-3*) is a hotel of eight floors and few views, but it's in a convenient location. Its 138 comfortable rooms come with bath, TV and minibar, and go for US$75 to US$100 a single, US$100 to US$130 a double, breakfast included.

Büyük Londra Oteli (☎ 212-245 0670, fax 245 0671, *Meşrutiyet Caddesi 117*) dates from the same era as the Pera Palas Oteli, but has much smaller rooms and bathrooms, and is a bit the worse for wear. But it does preserve some of the Victorian-era glory (in the public rooms at least) at a price which includes a significant nostalgia mark-up, but is nonetheless lower than the Pera's. A room with shower costs US$60 with one double bed, US$80 with two beds, breakfast included, but they'll come down in price if business is slow.

Next to the British Consulate is the modern, four-star *Hotel Emperyal* (☎ 212-293 3955, fax 252 4370, *Meşrutiyet Caddesi 38*), offering good value for money at US$80/100/130.

Top End

Hotel Richmond (☎ 212-252 5460, fax 252 9707, *İstiklal Caddesi 445*), next to the palatial Russian consulate, is one of the few hotels on İstiklal. Behind and around its 19th-century facade, the Richmond is all modern, quite comfortable and well run, with 101 full-service rooms priced at US$135/165, breakfast included. Most guests are American.

The *Hotel Mercure* (☎ 212-251 4646, fax 249 8033, *Meşrutiyet Caddesi*) is a modern 22-storey tower across the street from the Pera Palas. All 200 simple rooms have satellite TV and minibar, and some have splendid views of the Golden Horn, the Old City and the Bosphorus, for US$150/190, breakfast included.

KARAKÖY (MAP 4)

Between the Galata Tower and Karaköy Square, the *Galata Konutları Apart Hotel* (☎ 212-252 6062, fax 244 2323, *Bankalar Caddesi, Hacı Ali Sokak, Karaköy*) is a historic building once owned by the wealthy Kamondo family. As the Felek Han, it was an apartment house, then a school of the Alliance Israelite Universelle. It's now a comfortable apartment-hotel charging US$150 per night, breakfast included, with discounts for longer stays. Buried in Galata's maze of narrow streets, it's difficult to find by car, but fairly convenient to Karaköy and Tünel on foot.

AKSARAY & LALELİ

The districts of Aksaray and Laleli, 2.5km west of Sultanahmet, are packed with one to three-star hotels at decent prices. Most of the patrons are eastern European traders shopping for Turkish-made apparel, especially blue jeans and leather goods. If

---

The Pera Palas

The **Pera Palas Oteli**, *PEH-ra pa-LAHS*, (☎ 212-251 4560, fax 251 4089, *Meşrutiyet Caddesi 98-100, Tepebaşı, see Map 3*) fills up regularly with independent and package tourists looking to relive the great age of Constantinople. The public salons and bar amply fulfil the nostalgia need, though the sometimes indifferent service and mediocre restaurant are strong reminders that things were better here a century ago.

The Pera's 145 rooms vary from high-ceilinged chambers, with period furnishings and bathrooms to match, to cramped upper-floor servants' quarters and uninspiring annexe rooms. Rooms with bath and breakfast are US$120/180 a single/double in the hotel, US$70/100 in the annexe. You're paying a substantial premium for nostalgia here, much of which you can enjoy at huge savings just by having a coffee in the grand salon or a drink at the bar.

The Pera Palas' ingenious promoters claim that Agatha Christie stayed in room 411 when she visited İstanbul, though reliable sources affirm that she stayed at the once prime but now long-gone Tokatliyan Hotel on İstiklal Caddesi.

However, there is no disputing that the great Atatürk preferred room 101, a vast suite, which, kept just as he used it, is now a museum (ask at the reception desk for admission).

you're not in the garment trade, you may find the constant bustle of shoppers and the huge bundles of goods stacked in hotel lobbies, hallways and lifts a bit tedious. If hoteliers here speak a foreign language, it's most probably Polish, Serbo-Croat, Romanian or Russian. Other hotels in this area are filled by foreign groups on incredibly cheap tours who are expected to shop early and often in shops attached to the hotel in order to swell the hotel's coffers.

THE BOSPHORUS (MAP 1)

There are several luxury hotels north-east of Taksim Square. While they enjoy fine views of the Bosphorus, their location out of the centre requires you to take taxis everywhere as few attractions are within walking distance.

Conrad International Istanbul (☎ 212-227 3000, fax 259 6667, Yıldız Caddesi, Beşiktaş) has earned a reputation for having well-trained staff. Off Barbaros Bulvarı just west of Yıldız Palace, the Conrad's 625 rooms and suites have fine Bosphorus views and all the luxuries. Hotel services run the gamut from indoor and outdoor swimming pools to in-room faxes (on request) and a casino. Rates range from US$195 to US$295 a single, US$235 to US$310 a double, tax included.

Swissôtel Istanbul The Bosphorus (☎ 212-259 0101, fax 259 0105, Bayıldım Caddesi 2, Maçka) capitalises upon its magnificent Bosphorus views: the lobby, restaurant and rooms all benefit. Lavish use of marble gives it a luxury feel, and all services give it luxury for real. Rates for the 600 rooms range from US$195 to US$320 a single, US$215 to US$350 a double, tax included.

Çirağan Palace Hotel Kempinski İstanbul (☎ 212-258 3377, fax 259 6687, Çirağan Caddesi 84, Beşiktaş) is a modern 291-room luxury hotel annexe built next to the historic Çirağan Palace, on the shore at the foot of the Yıldız Palace park. Destroyed by fire in 1911, the rebuilt marble palace holds meeting rooms, VIP suites, a ballroom, restaurants and boutiques. East-facing rooms enjoy fine Bosphorus views, but west-facing 'park-view' rooms look onto a stone wall. All luxury services are available, and prices are İstanbul's highest: from US$220 to US$340 a single, and from US$255 to US$380 a double, tax included.

NEAR THE AIRPORT

İstanbul's Atatürk airport (see the Greater İstanbul map) is 24km from Sultanahmet or Taksim. It's far more interesting to stay in the city centre than to stay near the airport. Though morning and evening rush-hour traffic can double or triple the time needed to reach the airport from the city centre, there is usually no difficulty in getting to the airport for an early morning flight as traffic is light at that time. Even so, some situations make it advisable to stay within a quick taxi ride of the airport.

Camping

İstanbul's camping areas are ranged along the Sea of Marmara in Florya, Yeşilköy and Ataköy near the airport, about 20km from Sultanahmet. They have good sea-view locations and average prices of US$10 for two persons in a tent. All are served by frequent banliyö treni, which run between Sirkeci train station and the western suburb of Halkalı for less than US$1.

Ataköy Mokamp (☎ 212-559 6000, fax 559 6007), in the Ataköy Tatil Köyü (holiday village) complex, has a bar, restaurant, swimming pools and other services and charges US$10 for two in a tent (try to get a site – sahile yakın, sah-heel-EH yah-kuhn – near the shore and away from the highway). Ataköy is accessible by banliyö treni from Sirkeci and by Eminönü-Ataköy and Taksim-Ataköy buses. Coming from the airport, the Havaş bus does not stop here; the closest stop is several kilometres farther east at Bakırköy, so it's best to take a 10-minute taxi ride for US$3.

Florya Turistik Tesisleri (☎ 212-574 0000), on the shore road south of the airport and west of Yeşilköy, is over 20km from the city centre, but more pleasant because of it. Two-person tent sites cost US$9. Transport is by banliyö treni (the station is 500m away), or by Taksim-Florya bus.

Londra Kamping (☎ 212-560 4200) is on the south side of the Londra Asfaltı highway between the airport and Topkapı gate across from the Süt Sanayi (milk factory). Right on the highway is a truck fuel and service station, but behind it, farther off the road, are grassy plots with small trees. You won't escape the noise and pollution completely here, but it's not an impossible location. To reach it you must be going eastward from the airport towards Topkapı gate and turn into the *servis yolu* (service road); watch carefully for the sign. About 300m after the turn, the camping ground is on the right-hand side.

Top End

The hotels near the airport tend to be top-end places, though they do offer good value for money in that price range.

The Holiday Inn has two hotels in its Ataköy beach and shopping complex on the Sea of Marmara shore 8km south-east of the airport. The five-star *Holiday Inn Crowne Plaza (☎ 212-560 8100; fax 560 8155, Sahil Yolu, Ataköy)* is a 298-room high-rise tower offering all luxury facilities for US$139 to US$200 per room, full breakfast included. The cheaper, four-star, 170-room *Holiday Inn İstanbul Ataköy Marina (☎ 212-560 4110, fax 559 4905, Sahil Yolu, Ataköy)* charges US$119 for its rooms, breakfast included, and allows its guests to use the more lavish facilities at the neighbouring Crowne Plaza.

The five-star *İstanbul Polat Renaissance Hotel (☎ 212-663 1700, fax 663 1755, Sahil Caddesi, Yeşilyurt)*, 4km south of the airport, is a tall tower of reflective glass with 383 luxury rooms priced very reasonably at US$115 a double, breakfast included. A shuttle van takes you to the city centre.

The four-star, 214-room *Çınar Hotel (☎ 212-663 2900, fax 663 2921, email reservation@www.cinarotel.com, Yeşilköy)* is only 4km from the airport. It's been here for over three decades, but has been renovated and updated. Guest rooms come in a variety of styles, and price ranges from US$70 to US$110 a double.

PLACES TO STAY

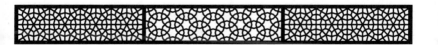

Places to Eat

The Ottoman Empire encompassed dozens of peoples and culinary traditions, and provided every sort of provision needed for a sophisticated cuisine.

Modern Turkish cuisine is the heir to the Ottoman tradition. Many of its recipes are deceptively simple, with no complex sauces. Spices are used in most dishes but simply; it is a rare dish which has more than one herb plus salt and pepper. With simple recipes, the quality of ingredients and the care of preparation are crucial.

For a listing of cafe-bars good for a drink, a snack and light meals, see the Entertainment chapter. For help in reading the menu, recognising foods and ordering meals in a restaurant, see the Turkish Language Guide at the back of this book.

SULTANAHMET (MAP 7)
Budget
The most obvious restaurants in Sultanahmet, those along Divan Yolu, offer decent food in pleasant surroundings, but prices are high by Turkish standards because this is the epicentre of touristic İstanbul.

Köftecis Divan Yolu's *köftecis* were traditionally where the district's workers ate cheap, filling, tasty lunches. Now 'famous' (*meşhur*), their prices have risen a bit, but the *köfte* (grilled lamb meatballs) and *şiş kebap* are still good, and the clientele a mix of locals and foreigners.

The *Meşhur Sultanahmet Köftecisi*, on Divan Yolu opposite the Firuz Ağa Camii and the tram stop, is about the cheapest. As if the length of its name determined its prices, the *Meşhur Tarihi Halk Köftecisi Selim Usta* (Chef Selim, Famous Historic Popular Köfte-Maker), Divan Yolu 12/A, is somewhat more expensive. The *Sultanahmet Meşhur Meydan Köftecisi*, just to the left (west) of the Sultan Pub, is in the middle as far as price is concerned.

Hazır Yemek Restaurants Divan Yolu has numerous steam-table restaurants and grills, all priced higher than equivalent restaurants outside the tourist zone. Most do not serve alcoholic beverages.

The cheap favourite is *Doy-Doy* (Fill up! Fill up!). At the south-eastern end of the Hippodrome, walk downhill to Şifa Hamamı Sokak 13, to find this simple, cheap restaurant busy with locals and backpackers. *Kuru fasulye* (broad beans in tomato sauce), pilav (rice), bread and a soft drink costs about US$2, other meals not much more.

The famous *Pudding Shop*, where the drop-out generation of the 1960s was kept alive and happy on inexpensive puddings, is still in operation, though it has become self-conscious and gone upmarket. A meal taken for nostalgia's sake might cost US$5 to US$8, a sandwich and soft drink less. Breakfast is also expensive.

A few doors down Divan Yolu, overlooking the small park atop Yerebatan Saray, is the *Sultan Pub* (☎ 212-526 6347, *Divan Yolu 2*). The upper floor holds a middle-range restaurant, but the ground-floor cafe serves sandwiches and drinks for US$5 or so. It's a favourite place to meet and talk.

Up the street from the Pudding Shop is the *Can Restaurant*, a cafeteria-style place with better food and lower prices than the Pudding Shop. It's also generally more popular than the nearby *Vitamin*, VEE-tahmeen (☎ 212-526 5086, *Divan Yolu 16*), at which you must check your bill carefully. *Baran 2 Lokantası*, at Divan Yolu 54, is another decent choice.

Going off the beaten track only a block gets you more value for money.

At the south-western end of the Hippodrome, walk up Peykhane Sokak to the *Yeni Birlik Lokantası* (☎ 212-517 6465), at No 46, a large restaurant (with ready-cooked food) favoured by lawyers from

Turkish Restaurants

Restaurants are everywhere, and most are open early in the morning until late at night.

Köftecis, serving grilled lamb meatballs, and *kebapçıs*, serving a variety of grilled meats (şış kebap, lamb chops, spiced ground lamb etc) are usually simple places. At an *ocakbaşı* grill, there are seats right at the grill so you can watch the cook at work. Order your main meat course by the *porsyon* (portion): *bir porsyon* (BEER porss-yohn, one portion) if you're not overly hungry; *bir buçuk porsyon* (BEER boo-CHOOK, one and a half) if you are, and *duble porsyon* (DOOB-leh, double) if you're ravenous. An order of köfte or kebap, a plate of salad, bread and a glass of *ayran* (a yoghurt drink) should cost around US$4 to US$5.

Hazır yemek restaurants are small places serving 'ready-made food' – soups, stews, pilavs etc – kept warm in steam tables. Sometimes they have some roast meats as well. Often called *lokanta*, they charge from US$2 to US$3 for a simple main-course lunch to perhaps US$5 or US$6 for a several-course tuck-in. They do not normally serve alcoholic beverages.

Mid-range restaurants with white tablecloths, waiters and alcoholic beverages charge from US$8 to US$20 for a three-course meal with wine, beer or *rakı*.

Though meals costing more than US$20 per person used to be rare in Turkey, this is changing. Chic cafe-restaurants with designer decor and innovative menus are attracting a well-heeled local and foreign clientele willing to pay US$25 to US$35 and higher per person, and the growing scarcity of seafood has also driven up the cost of meals at luxury seafood restaurants.

the nearby law courts. Meals are available for US$2.50 to US$4; alcohol is not available.

Across the street from the Yeni Birlik, *Gaziantep Kebap ve Lahmacun* will serve you a full meal of roast meat, salad and soft drink for US$5 or US$6, or a snack of *lahmacun* (Arabic pizza) for half that.

The *Karadeniz Pide ve Kebap Salonu*, a cheap, simple place on Hacı Tahsin Bey Sokak a half block north of Divan Yolu, does a good business sending out meals to local shopkeepers. Have stuffed cabbage leaves, rice pilav, bread and a drink for less than US$3. The upstairs dining room is nicer than downstairs, and both are open on Sunday. A few steps away, the *Hotel Akdeniz Lokantası* is similar.

Cafes *Cafe Mesale* on the Hippodrome, with outdoor tables, nightly Turkish music and roadside flares, is surprisingly atmospheric for its position. *Çiğdem Patisserie* (*Divan Yolu 62/A*) gets top marks for its ex-

cellent though pricey (US$2) cappuccinos. The cakes are pretty good, too.

The *Sultan Sofrası*, a cafe-restaurant facing the Hippodrome on its north-west side, is good for a snack or sandwich and soft drink (US$2.50), and people-watching.

If you prefer shade to sun, seek out the *Derviş Aile Çay Bahçesi* (Dervish Family Tea Garden), Kabasakal Caddesi 2/1, west of the Yeşil Ev Hotel. Stimulants and small sandwiches (US$1) are served in the cool, dark shadows cast by great plane trees. Try *peynirli tost*, a cheese sandwich mashed in a vice-like cooker.

Mid-Range

Darüzziyafe (☎ 212-518 1351, Meydanı 27) on the Hippodrome to the right (south) of the Sultan Ahmet Camii, serves good Ottoman cuisine. A full lunch might cost US$10 to US$15. Though hardly as fancy as its namesake by the Süleymaniye Camii (see that section in the Things to See & Do chapter), it is much more conveniently located.

PLACES TO EAT

A nearby favourite is **Rami** (☎ 212-517 6593, Utangaç Sokak 6), in a restored house behind the Sultan Ahmet Camii. The several dining rooms are decorated with impressionist-style paintings by Turkish painter Rami Uluer (1913-1988), but the favoured spot is the rooftop terrace. In fine weather, phone for advance reservations to get a table with the full view of the Sultan Ahmet Camii, then order some of the Ottoman specialties such as Hünkâr Beğendi (grilled lamb and rich aubergine purée) or kağıt kebap (lamb and vegetables cooked in a paper pouch). With drinks, a meal costs about US$20 to US$30 per person. The rooftop terrace has fine views of the Sultan Ahmet Camii.

Two hotel restaurants have good views of the Sultan Ahmet Camii as well. Try the one at the **Mavi Ev**, near Rami. The restaurant of the **Hotel Arcadia** has a truly breathtaking view of the Sultan Ahmet Camii late in the afternoon, and full meals for US$12 to US$25. See the Places to Stay chapter.

Hanımeli Yemek Salonu (Klodfarer Caddesi 31), to the left of the Hotel Olivier, has home-style Turkish cooking (mantı on Tuesday and Friday). Prices are moderate, and there's a quiet little garden at the back.

The indefatigable Turkish Touring & Automobile Association has established four restaurants within a few steps of Aya Sofya. The **Yeşil Ev** hotel's garden restaurant has perhaps the prettiest setting of any restaurant in the area, and moderate prices.

The Ottoman-Victorian dining rooms of the **Ayasofya Pansiyonları,** on Soğukçeşme Sokak, feature a Turkish menu with grilled aubergine, lamb chops, mutton stews and veal cutlets. Full meals cost around US$14 to US$18.

At the intersection of Caferiye and Soğukçeşme sokaks is the **Taverna-Restaurant Sarnıç** (☎ 212-512 4291), set up in a vast old Roman cistern. The baronial fireplace hardly belongs in a sunken stone cistern, but the rosy glow is welcome on rainy evenings. The menu is a blend of continental and Ottoman. Meals cost from US$20 to US$30 per person with drinks, tax and tip. It's open Wednesday to Sunday from 11.30 am to 11 pm.

Just across the street from the Sarnıç, next to the Konuk Evi hotel, is its **Conservatory Restaurant** (☎ 212-513 3660), a glass greenhouse with an open-air terrace serving light meals and snacks. Have a beer and a cheese plate (US$6), assorted böreks (flaky cheese pastries; US$3.50) or an omelette (US$4).

The obvious **Sultan Pub** (☎ 212-526 6347, Divan Yolu 2), between the Pudding Shop and the small park atop Yerebatan Saray, has a cafe-bar on the ground floor and a nicer restaurant one flight up. A full meal upstairs, with wine or beer, costs between US$12 and US$18.

Buhara Ocakbaşı (☎ 212-513 7424, Nuruosmaniye Caddesi 7), off Yerebatan Caddesi near the Cağaloğlu Hamamı, is a neighbourhood grill with good mezes (Turkish hors-d'oeuvres), lamb grills and alcoholic beverages. A big, full dinner with drinks usually costs around US$10 or US$12 per person.

Top End

For ambience, food and service, the **Rumeli Café** (Map 7, ☎ 212-512 0008, Ticarethane Sokak 8), a few steps off Divan Yolu, gets top marks. Haydar Sarıgül, the congenial owner, had his friend Nikos from Athens design the cafe with cool stone walls for hot days and three fireplaces in the four tiny dining rooms for chilly evenings. Classical music or cool jazz plays quietly; there's similar live music at weekends. The menu lists updated Ottoman classics, and a three-course meal with drinks might cost US$15 to US$30 per person.

Café Magnaura (☎ 212-518 7622, Akbıyık Caddesi 27), right in the midst of the Cankurtaran hotel area, serves European-American dishes with Turkish accents to a clientele that's 99% foreign on three floors of a romantically antiqued house. The atmosphere is good (there's romantic Greek and Turkish music), as is the food. A full meal of soup, main course and a half-

feel no embarrassment in opening the bill, redoing the addition, and questioning any items, including obscure *kuver* (cover) and *servis* (service) charges. If you don't get an itemised bill, by all means ask for one.

Restaurant Hints

In any restaurant in Turkey, whether fancy or simple, there is a convenient sink (*lavabo*) so that you can wash your hands before eating. Just say the word and the waiter will point it out.

If you're a woman or are travelling with a woman, ask for the *aile salonu* (family dining room, often upstairs) which will be free of the sometimes oppressive all-male atmosphere to be found in many cheap Turkish eateries.

Many Turkish waiters have the annoying habit of snatching your plate away before you're finished with it. This may be due to a rule of Eastern etiquette which holds that it is impolite to leave a finished plate sitting in front of a guest. If a waiter engages in plate-snatching, say *Kalsın* (kahl-SUHN, 'Let it stay').

Preparing the evening's menu.

Breakfast

In a hotel or pastry shop, breakfast (*komple kahvaltı,* kohm-PLEH-kahvahl-TUH) consists of fresh, delicious *ekmek* (ek-MEHK, Turkish bread) with jam or honey, butter, salty black olives, sliced tomatoes and cucumbers, white sheep's milk cheese, sometimes also a slice of mild yellow *kaşar peynir* cheese, and *çay* (CHAH-yee, tea). A wedge of processed cheese may be added or substituted for one of the other cheeses. In my experience, Turkish bread and tea are usually fresh and good, but the other ingredients are often of poor quality or stale. You won't know until you sit down to breakfast.

You can always order an egg (*yumurta,* yoo-moor-TAH). Soft-boiled is *üç dakikalık* (EWCH dahk-kah-luhk), hard-boiled is *sert* (SEHRT), and fried eggs are *sahanda yumurta* (sah-hahn-DAH yoo-moor-tah). Bacon is difficult to find as any pork product is forbidden to Muslims. You may find it in the big hotels in the biggest cities. Sometimes your bread will come toasted (*kızarmış,* kuh-zahr-MUSH). This is the standard breakfast for tourists. If you order an egg or another glass of tea, you may be charged a bit extra.

Hot, sweetened milk (*sıcak süt,* suh-JAHK sewt) is a traditional breakfast drink, replaced in winter by *sahlep* (sah-LEHP), which is hot, sweetened milk flavoured with tasty orchid-root (*Orchis mascula*) powder and a sprinkle of cinnamon.

Lunch

The midday meal (*öğle yemeği*) can be big or small. In summer, many Turks wisely prefer to eat a big meal at midday and a light supper in the evening. You might want to do this, too.

Dinner

The evening meal (*akşam yemeği*) can be a repeat of lunch, a light supper or a sumptuous repast. In fine weather the setting might be outdoors.

Turkish Delight

For a traditional Ottoman treat, walk through the archway to the left of the Yeni Cami in Eminönü, and turn left onto Hamidiye Caddesi. One short block along, on the right-hand (south) side of the street near the corner with Şeyhülislam Hayri Efendi Caddesi, is the original shop of *Ali Muhiddin Hacı Bekir* (☎ 212-522 0666), inventor of Turkish delight.

History notes that Ali Muhiddin came to İstanbul from the Black Sea mountain town of Kastamonu and established himself as a confectioner in the Ottoman capital in the late 18th century. Dissatisfaction with hard candies and traditional sweets led the impetuous Ali Muhiddin to invent a new confection that would be easy to chew and swallow. He called his soft, gummy creation *rahat lokum*, the 'comfortable morsel'. Lokum, as it soon came to be called, was an immediate hit with the denizens of the imperial palace, and anything that goes well with the palace goes well with the populace.

Ali Muhiddin elaborated on his original confection, as did his offspring (the shop is still owned by his descendants), and now you can buy lokum made with various fillings: *cevizli* (JEH-veez-LEE, with walnuts), *şam fıstıklı* (SHAHM fuhss-tuhk-LUH, with pistachios), *portakkallı* (POHR-tah-kahl-LUH, orange-flavoured), or *bademli* (BAH-dehm-LEE, with almonds). You can also get *çeşitli* (CHEH-sheet-LEE, assortment). Price is according to weight; one kilogram costs US$3 to US$9, depending upon variety. Ask for a free sample by indicating your choice and saying *Deneyelim!* (DEH-neh-yeh-LEEM, 'Let's try it').

During the winter, a cool-weather speciality is added to the list of treats for sale. *Helva*, a crumbly sweet block of sesame mash, is flavoured with chocolate or pistachio nuts or sold plain. Ali Muhiddin Hacı Bekir has another, more modern shop on İstiklal Caddesi between Taksim Square and Galatasaray next to Vakko.

KAPALI ÇARŞI
Budget

Within the Kapalı Çarşı (Covered Market), the *Sevim Lokantası*, on Koltuk Kazazlar and Kahvehane sokaks, was founded (a sign states proudly) in 1945. Take a seat in the little dining room or sit at a table set out in one of the little streets and order one or two plates of food. The bill shouldn't exceed US$4 or US$5.

Similar meals are available for the same price at the *Köşk Restaurant*, on Keseciler Caddesi just off Kuyumcular Caddesi.

Even cheaper? Leave the bazaar by the Nuruosmaniye door, turn left just outside the door and walk downhill one block to the *Subaşı Restaurant,* on the right, a ready-food place full of locals, not foreigners. The food is a bit better, the prices a bit lower, and there's additional seating upstairs.

For the full bazaar experience, try the little cookshops set up in many of the hans on the bazaar's periphery. Don't be afraid to stroll into one and sit down for a döner kebap sandwich or a plate of stew or pilav. Like the Sevim, this is where the bazaar merchants eat.

You will no doubt pass the *Şark Kahvesi* (SHARK kahh-veh-see, Oriental Cafe), at the end of Fesçiler Caddesi, which is always filled with locals and tourists. The arched ceilings betray its former existence as part of a bazaar street; some enterprising *kahveci* (coffeehouse owner) walled up several sides and turned it into a cafe. On the grimy walls hang paintings of Ottoman scenes and framed portraits of sultans and champion Turkish freestyle wrestlers. A cup of Turkish coffee, a soft drink or a glass of tea costs less than US$1.

Mid-Range

Though most Kapalı Çarşı eateries are low budget, at the *Havuzlu Lokantası* (☎ 212-527 3346, Gani Çelebi Sokak 3) prices are in the moderate range of US$8 to US$14 for a meal. The food is about the same as at the low-budget places in this area, but you get a lofty dining room made of several bazaar streets walled off for the purpose long ago, and a few tables set out in front of the entrance by a little stone pool (*havuzlu* means 'with pool'), which I suspect was a deep well centuries ago. Waiter service here is more polite and unhurried, though slow when there are tour groups. To find the Havuzlu, follow the yellow-and-black signs and ask for the PTT, which is next door.

Cafe Colheti is set up in the former auction hall (Sandal Bedesteni), a pleasant, spacious place to sit for restful refreshment. Soft drinks cost US$1, coffee US$2, a light lunch about US$5 or US$6.

TAKSİM SQUARE (MAP 3)
Budget

The cheapest eats in Taksim are at the *büfes* right between Sıraselviler and İstiklal caddesis. Look out for the prominent *Çetin Restaurant*, at İstiklal 1, and the büfes are just to the left. They serve fresh-squeezed fruit juices, döner sandwiches (both lamb and chicken) etc for about US$1 each. The Çetin, by the way, specialises in rotisserie chicken, and rows of spitted birds can be seen slowly revolving. The upstairs terrace is the place to dine in fair weather.

A few steps down İstiklal from the Çetin is the *Pehlivan Restaurant*. This bright, plain place has the standard cafeteria line, steam tables and decent prices. Don't take too much; three dishes is plenty. Fill up at lunch or dinner for US$4. *Taksim Sütiş*, to the right, specialises in sweets, but serves light meals as well.

The local *McDonald's* hamburger restaurant, always packed, is on the east side of Cumhuriyet Caddesi near the Turkish Airlines office and the PTT, along with *Pizza Hut* and several street cafes. Try the 'McBörek' – only in Turkey!

Mid-Range

Hacı Baba Restaurant, ha-JUH bah-bah, (☎ 212-244 1886, *İstiklal Caddesi 49*) has a pleasant terrace with tables overlooking the courtyard of the Aya Triada Greek Orthodox Church next door. The menu is long and varied, the food good and service usually competent; some English is spoken.

Have a look in the kitchen to help you choose your meal. You'll pay from US$10 to US$20 per person for a full lunch or dinner with wine or beer.

Three other good, full-service restaurants are a short walk from the square, down the hill on İnönü Caddesi by the Atatürk Cultural Centre.

Top End (Map 2)

The better restaurants are north of Taksim on the way to Nişantaşı. The posh *Boğaziçi Borsa Restaurant* (☎ 212-232 4201), just north of the Istanbul Hilton in the Lütfi Kırdar Kongre ve Sergi Salonu (convention centre), serves creatively updated Ottoman specialties and new-wave Turkish cuisine in deluxe surroundings at reasonable prices. A three or four-course meal with wine need cost only US$15 to US$30 per person.

The dining room at the *Divan Oteli* (☎ 212-231 4100) on Cumhuriyet Caddesi at Asker Ocağı Caddesi serves excellent continental and Turkish cuisine in posh surroundings and at decent prices – about US$35 to US$50 per person for a fine meal, all included. *Divan Pub*, adjoining, is still fairly fancy but significantly cheaper. The specialty here is Turkish döner kebap.

In Nişantaşı proper, *Hasır* (☎ 212-261 6005, *Valikonağı Caddesi 65*) is a local favourite. The menu is Turkish, the food and service are excellent and the prices reasonable. The better dining room is the one upstairs.

Just out of Taksim near the top of İnönü Caddesi on the right-hand side is a large Chinese gateway and beyond it, down the stairs, is the *Great Hong Kong Restaurant* (☎ 212-252 4268, *İnönü Caddesi 12/B*), a small but quite nice restaurant serving an assortment of Chinese dishes. Full meals cost US$20 to US$30 per person with drinks. It's open daily for lunch (11 am to 3 pm) and dinner (6 to 11.30 pm).

İSTİKLAL CADDESİ (MAP 3)
Budget

Borsa Fast Food Kafeteryası (*89 İstiklal*) is modern, bright and popular with Turkish

PLACES TO EAT

youths – especially the *dondurma* (ice cream) kiosk. Grills (US$2 to US$3) are the specialty, and beer is served.

Continuing along İstiklal Caddesi, Büyük Parmak Kapı Sokak holds many eating and drinking possibilities, including the cheap *Ada Restaurant*, at No 25, where you can fill up for US$3 to US$5. *Nature & Peace*, at No 21, serves vegetarian soups (US$1.50), salads (US$2 to US$3) and main courses (US$3), plus a few chicken dishes, at lunch and dinner (closed Sunday). Around the corner on Çukurlu Çeşmesi Sokak, *Hala* serves *mantı* (Turkish ravioli) and other home-cooking favourites. Look for the traditionally-clad woman rolling out mantı dough in the window.

For meat-eaters, *Sohbet Ocakbaşı* (*Mis Sokak 9*) specialises in Kozan kebap, a spicy Arab-influenced şiş from south-eastern Turkey. Full meals cost under US$10, and there's sidewalk dining in fine weather. Behind (south of) the Ağa Camii on Mahyacı Sokak, the *Meşhur Sultanahmet Köftecisi* serves grilled lamb meatballs, lahmacun and pide at prices below those on İstiklal.

Atlas Restaurant & Cafe (*İstiklal Caddesi 251*), in the Örs İş Merkezi building directly across from the Çiçek Pasajı, was built by an Armenian architect in 1815. Once the residence of Mr Fethi Okyar, first prime minister of the Turkish Republic (1930s), it's now a favourite lunch place for students at the British Council (in the same building) who come for the good, daily, three-course, set-price lunch for just US$3.

Just north of Galatasaray is the Balık Pazar (Fish Market), actually a complete food market spread out in two little streets, Sahne and Duduodaları, next to the touristy Çiçek Pasajı. The cheapest and simplest place to eat here is *Mercan* – you can't miss its bright white-and-red-tiled façade – specialising in *midye tavası* (mussels deep-fried on a skewer) for about US$0.30 and a bit more if they're served in a *sandviçli* (in bread); the favoured beverage is draught beer.

The Balık Pazar is a prime area for picnic assembly, with greengrocers, *şarküteri* (char-

cuterie, delicatessen) shops and bakeries offering cheeses, dried meats such as *pastırma*, pickled fish, olives, jams and preserves, and several varieties of bread including wholegrain. *Şütte* (☎ *212-244 9292, Duduodaları Sokak 21*) is regarded by many as the best of the delis.

Afacan Pizza & Burger Restaurant (*331 İstiklal*), just south of the big red brick Church of San Antonio di Padua, is popular for its namesake dishes and low prices.

Teras Secret Garden, in the Beyoğlu İş Merkezi building at Istiklal Caddesi 365/19, lives up to its intriguing name by providing a peaceful terrace dining area overlooking the historic Palais de France. Drinks, snacks, light and more substantial meals are served in good weather at moderate prices. To find it, walk down Nuruziya Sokak a half block, enter on the right and walk straight until you must turn, then turn left.

Mid-Range

Hacı Abdullah (☎ *212-293 8561, Sakızağacı Caddesi 17*), beside the Ağa Camii (İstiklal Caddesi's only mosque), is a Beyoğlu institution, having been in business a century. Its dining rooms are simple but tasteful, its Turkish and Ottoman cuisine outstanding, with a varied menu of traditional dishes otherwise rarely found in restaurants. Service is friendly, single women are welcomed and a full meal with soft drink (no alcohol is served) costs US$9 to US$15.

At Galatasaray, 700m along, on the north side at İstiklal Caddesi 172, is an entrance to the *Çiçek Pasajı* (Flower Passage), a collection of taverna-restaurants open long hours every day in the courtyard of a historic building.

This used to be a jolly place where locals gathered for drinking, singing and good, cheap food. It has now been tarted up for tourists, and while the food can still be good, prices and the hassle factor have increased dramatically. Prices are twice as high as elsewhere, overcharging and un-ordered items are commonplace. If you must eat here (and it *can* be enjoyable), ask prices, don't accept unordered items, and be cautious with locals who chat you up and propose outings or nightclubs, which may turn into rip-offs (see the Nightlife Rip-Offs boxed text in the Entertainment chapter).

The locals who used to eat in the Çiçek Pasajı have moved on to the *meyhanes* (taverns) deeper in the market. Walk along Sahne Sokak to the first street on the right, Nevizade Sokak. There are at least eight restaurants here and they have pavement tables in fine weather. They charge about US$1.50 to US$2.25 for plates of meze, about twice that for kebaps; ask the prices of fish before you order. Alcohol is served enthusiastically.

The **Tarihi Cumhuriyet Meyhanesi** is one of the nicest ones. The **Çağlar Restaurant** (☎ 212-249 7665) is at No 6, and **Kadri'nin Yeri** (☎ 212-243 6130) nearby. My favourite, however, is the **İmroz Restaurant** (☎ 212-249 9073, *Nevizade Sokak 24*), down at the end of the row on the right. Run by a Turk and a Greek from the island of İmroz (Gökçeada, Imbros), it specialises in fish and other island dishes. Be prepared to look in the kitchen, and to use sign language, which should (and must) suffice.

TEPEBAŞI & TÜNEL (MAP 3)
Budget

Near the Pera Palas Oteli and the US Consulate-General, **Şemsiye** (*'umbrella'*, ☎ 292 2046, *Şeyhbender Sokak 18*), serves vegetarian meals (US$5 to US$9) at lunch and dinner, with at least one or two meat, fowl or fish dishes as well. It's popular with diplomats and young professionals, who also come for **Yağmur** (*'rain'*), the cybercafe upstairs.

For a light lunch or snack near the Pera Palas and Mercure hotels, go to the **Karadeniz Pide Salonu** behind and to the left of the Mercure, where you can get a fresh pide with butter and cheese for US$1.25. No alcohol is served.

Mid-Range

Popular with the diplomatic set at lunchtime is the **Four Seasons** (*Dört Mevsim*, ☎ 212-293 3941, *İstiklal 509*), almost in Tünel Square. Under Turkish and English management, it is well located to draw diners from the US, UK, Dutch, Russian and Swedish consulates. The food is continental with several delicious concessions to Turkish cuisine; preparation and service are first-rate. Lunch is served from noon to 3 pm, dinner from 6 pm to midnight; it's closed Sunday. If you order the fixed menu at lunch, you might pay US$10, drink and tip included. Ordering from the regular menu at dinner may bring your bill to US$20 or US$25 per person.

Çatı Restaurant (☎ 212-251 0000, *İstiklal Caddesi, Orhan Adli Apaydın Sokak 20/7*) is on the 7th (top) floor of a building on a small side street that runs between İstiklal and Meşrutiyet caddesis. Though the view is vestigial at best, the greenhouse-style dining room is pleasant, the food quite good and not expensive. Try the Çatı Böreği for an appetiser; it's halfway between a Turkish börek and a turnover, made with cheese. Main courses are mostly Turkish, with a few European specialties. Expect to spend from US$12 to US$18 per person. If you don't like syrupy organ music, come early for dinner. It's open for lunch and dinner every day.

Yakup 2 Restaurant, yah-KOOP ee-KEE, (☎ 212-249 2925, *Asmalımescit Sokak 35/37*) is popular with local artists, musicians, actors and academics. It hasn't been fancied up for tourists, so the decor is minimal, but the food is quite good and moderately priced. Strike up a conversation with those at a neighbouring table; they may well speak a foreign language. Full meals with wine, beer or *rakı* cost about US$8 to US$15. It's open every day for dinner, and for lunch daily except Sunday.

KUMKAPI (MAP 6)

In Byzantine times, the fishers' harbour called Kontoscalion was due south of Beyazıt. The gate into the city from that port came to be called Kumkapı (Sand Gate) by the Turks. Though the gate is long gone, the district is still filled with fishers who moor their boats in a more modern

PLACES TO EAT

Seasonal Fish

A menu is of no use when ordering fish (*balık, bah-LUHK*). You must ask the waiter what's fresh, and then ask the approximate price. The fish will be weighed, and the price computed at the day's per-kilogram rate. Sometimes you can haggle. Buy fish in season (*mevsimli, mehv-seem-LEE*), as fish out of season are very expensive.

From March to the end of June is a good time to order *kalkan* (turbot), *uskumru* (mackerel), and *hamsi* (fresh anchovies), but from July to mid-August is spawning season for many species, and fishing them is prohibited. In high summer, these are the easiest to find in the markets and on the restaurant tables: *çinakop* (a small bluefish), *lüfer* (medium-size bluefish), *palamut* (bonito), *tekir* (striped goatfish: *Mullus surmuletus*), *barbunya* (red mullet: *Mullus barbatus*), and *istavrit* (scad, horse mackerel).

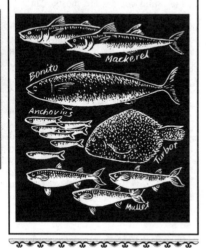

version of the old harbour. Each afternoon and evening the streets of the neighbourhood resound to the footsteps of people hungry for fish. In fine weather restaurant tables crowd the narrow streets, and happy diners clatter plates and cutlery between bolts of pungent rakı.

In recent years the scene has become a bit too hectic for some visitors, with touts pushing menus at you as you approach. Ignore them, find a seat, order carefully (and don't accept anything you haven't ordered), and you'll enjoy yourself. Expect to part with US$20 to US$40 per person for the meal, appetisers, salads, drink, sweet, tax and tip all included.

You can get to Kumkapı by one of three methods. Walk from Laleli, Beyazıt or the Kapalı Çarşı. Just opposite the Beyazıt Camii in Beyazıt Square, on the south side of Yeniçeriler Caddesi, is the beginning of Tiyatro Caddesi. Follow this street south for 10 short blocks (for the last block, it veers to the left), and you'll find yourself in Kumkapı's main square.

You can also take a taxi, but it may be a bit expensive as the driver might choose to cruise all the way around the old city in order to enter this congested district from the sea side; figure on US$4 or so from Sultanahmet, US$6 or US$7 from Taksim.

The cheapest way to go is by train from Sirkeci station. Enter the station, bear to the right and buy a ticket at one of the kiosks marked 'Banliyö' for US$0.40, and board any of the electric commuter trains on the right-hand platforms. Most will be for Halkalı, but in fact any train will do, as they all pass Kumkapı. You can also board the train at the Cankurtaran station. The trains are run down, but the ride is short.

You will round Saray Burnu (Seraglio Point), offering marvellous views of the Sea of Marmara and Topkapı Sarayı, and stop briefly at Cankurtaran train station before pulling into Kumkapı train station. Leave the train and the station, and walk down the most prominent street, which is Ördekli Bakkal Sokak (Grocer with a Duck St), to reach the restaurants.

Restaurant Suggestions

Kumkapı has dozens of seafood restaurants, many operated by Turkish citizens of Greek or Armenian ancestry. Among the favourite

Typical hotel, Yerebatan Caddesi, Sultanahmet

The well-lit cafe of the Kybele Hotel

The sumptuous main salon of Pera Palas Oteli

The Pera Palas Oteli, built in the 1890s

The Four Seasons Hotel in Sultanahmet, formerly an Ottoman-era prison

Boatmen selling quick-cooked fish in fresh bread, near the Eminönü end of the Galata Bridge.

Çiçek Pasajı tavernas, Beyoğlu

Spice shop in the Mısır Çarşısı (Egyptian Bazaar)

Fruit stand in Türbe Souk, Sultanahmet

dishes to order is *kılıç şiş* (swordfish şiş kebap), chunks of fresh fish skewered and grilled over charcoal, but there are also fish soups and stews, fish poached with vegetables, pan-fried fish and pickled fish.

Typical of Kumkapı's seafood eateries is *Minas*, MEE-nahss, (☎ 212-522 9646, Samsa Sokak 7), facing the square. Minas is not one of the cheaper places; you can dine for a lot less elsewhere. If you're not in the mood for seafood but would like to explore Kumkapı in any case, come for a kebap, and you'll spend a mere US$8 or so.

Also facing the square is *Köşem Cemal Restaurant* (☎ 212-520 1229, Samsa Sokak 1) with similar prices, cuisine and advantages. Here there are white tablecloths, good careful service and a mixed clientele of Turks and tourists.

Ördekli Bakkal Sokak runs from the train station to Kumkapı Meydanı, the neighbourhood square. The street has another half-dozen good seafood restaurants, including *Üçler Balık Restaurant* (☎ 212-517 2339), at No 3 just off the square. The *Deniz Restaurant* (☎ 212-528 0858), at No 12/A, seems to make it difficult for customers to find out prices in advance. Yet other side streets hold more restaurants. Two recommendations are the *Yengeç Balık Lokantası* (☎ 212-516 3227, Telli Odalar Sokak 6) and the *Kumkapı Restaurant* (☎ 212-522 6590, Üstat Sokak 7).

THE BOSPHORUS

Restaurant suggestions for dining on the Bosphorus are given in the Excursions chapter under the heading for the town in which the restaurant is found. Look particularly at the Tarabya and Sarıyer sections.

PLACES TO EAT

Entertainment

For many first-time visitors, the name 'İstanbul' conjures up Hollywood-Baroque images of mysterious intrigues in dusky streets, sultry belly dancers undulating in smoky dens and dangerous liaisons from the sublime to the taboo. As with most stereotypes, the reality is quite different.

Yes, you can find titillation here, as you can in most big cities, but what will be of more interest are the festivals of music, film and dance, the sound-and-light performances, and the simple, inexpensive evening pleasure of a ferry ride on the Bosphorus.

Information

News of performances and concerts is carried in the *Weekend* supplement to the *Turkish Daily News'* Friday edition, and its *Arts & Culture* section on Sunday.

Venues

İstanbul's major venues for concerts and performances of dance and opera are the *Atatürk Kültür Merkezi*, or Atatürk Cultural Centre (☎ 212-251 5600, fax 245 3916), in Taksim Square (Map 3); the *Cemal Reşit Rey Konser Salonu* (☎ 212-240 5012), a 'concert salon' on Gümüş Sokak east of the Askeri Müzesi (Military Museum; Map 2); and the *Aya İrini*, or Hagia Eirene Church, in the First Court of Topkapı Sarayı (Map 7).

Outdoor venues for summer performances include the *Açık Hava Tiyatrosu*, or Open-Air Theatre, just north of the İstanbul Hilton (Map 2), and *Rumeli Hisar* (see the Greater İstanbul map), north of Bebek on the Bosphorus. For really big shows, it's the *İnönü Stadyumu*, a stadium just inland from Dolmabahçe Sarayı (Map 2).

MUSIC FESTIVALS

The *International İstanbul Music Festival* (office: ☎ 212-260 4533, 260 9072, fax 261 8823, İstanbul Kültür ve Sanat Vakfı, Yıldız Kültür ve Sanat Merkezi, 80700 Beşiktaş,

İstanbul) is the most prominent entertainment event in İstanbul. It begins in mid-June and continues to mid-July. World-class performers – soloists and virtuosos, orchestras, dance companies, rock and jazz groups – give recitals and performances in numerous concert halls, historic buildings and palaces. The highlight is Mozart's *Abduction from the Seraglio*, performed in Topkapı Sarayı, with the sultan's private Gate of Felicity as the backdrop. Contact the festival office or check at the box offices in the Atatürk Kültür Merkezi for schedules, ticket prices and availability.

The *Akbank International Jazz Festival*, 10 days of concerts, seminars, video screenings and art shows, is held in early October.

FOLK DANCE & MUSIC

Turks are enthusiastic folklore fans, and many are still close enough in tradition to their regional dances to jump in and dance along at a performance. University groups, good amateur companies and professionals all schedule performances throughout the year.

There are regular concerts of Turkish traditional music scheduled at the *Cemal Reşit Rey Konser Salonu* (Map 2), near the İstanbul Hilton.

CLASSICAL MUSIC & BALLET

There are symphony, opera and ballet seasons, and occasional tour performances of world-renowned artists. Many but not all of these performances are given in the Atatürk Kültür Merkezi in Taksim Square.

THEATRE

The Turks are enthusiastic theatre-goers, and seem to have a special genius for dramatic art. The problem for the foreign visitor, of course, is language. If you're a true theatre-buff you might well enjoy a performance of a familiar classic, provided you know the play well enough to follow

ENTERTAINMENT

the action without the benefit of dialogue in your native language.

Theatres are concentrated in Beyoğlu (Map 3) along İstiklal Caddesi and near Taksim Square; many others are in the suburbs. The International İstanbul Theatre Festival, with performances by Turkish and foreign casts, takes place in mid-May. Contact the İstanbul Kültür ve Sanat Vakfı (see Music Festivals, earlier).

CINEMA

The İstanbul International Film Festival is held annually from mid-April to early May. Tickets are sold at the Atatürk Kültür Merkezi.

İstiklal Caddesi (Map 3) between Taksim and Galatasaray is the centre of İstanbul's cinema *(sinema)* district, with many foreign films being shown. The advent of television put many cinemas out of business; some of the survivors screen the racier movies, plus the much-beloved Turkish melodramas. For all movie listings, see the *Turkish Daily News'* Friday *Weekend* supplement.

Many first-run foreign feature films make it to İstanbul, and you will be able to enjoy them at discount prices.

Ask at the box office to see if the film is in the original language, *Orijinal* (ohr-zhee-NAHL), or dubbed in Turkish, *Türkçe*.

When possible, buy your tickets a few hours in advance. Tickets cost from US$3 to US$5. Also, the usher will expect a small tip for showing you to your seat.

Beyoğlu (Map 3)

Look for these cinemas along İstiklal Caddesi:

Aksanat Kültür Merkezi (Aksanat Cultural Centre, ☎ 212-252 3500, *İstiklal Caddesi 16-18)*, in the Akbank building on İstiklal Caddesi just out of Taksim; it shows movies as well as films of musical and theatrical performances

Alkazar Sinema Merkezi (☎ 212-293 2466 *İstiklal Caddesi 179)*

Atlas (☎ 212-252 8576, *İstiklal Caddesi 209, Kuyumcular Pasajı)*

Emek (☎ 212-293 8439, *İstiklal Caddesi Yeşilçam Sokak 5)*

Fitaş & Fitaş Cep (☎ 212-249 0166, *İstiklal Caddesi 24-26, Fitaş Pasajı)*; four cinemas in one

Sinepop (☎ 212-251 1176, *İstiklal Caddesi, Yeşilçam Sokak 22)*

Çemberlitaş (Map 7)

There's a seven-screen cinema in the *Darüşşafaka Sitesi (*☎ 212-516 2660) with tickets costing about US$3 for English-language films.

CAFE-BARS
Sultanahmet (Map 7)

Many of Sultanahmet's cafe-restaurants such as the *Rumeli Café* on Ticarethane Sokak, the *Sultan Pub* on Divan Yolu, *Cafeterya Medusa* on Yerebatan Caddesi, and the many small places along Hoca Rüstem Sokak (between Divan Yolu and Yerebatan Caddesi) have cool music and outdoor tables that are very pleasant in good weather. Check prices before you order.

Beyoğlu (Map 3)

The narrow side streets leading from İstiklal Caddesi are lined with lively little cafes, bars and bistros, each filled with loyal clientele. An evening's stroll here, looking for good music, drinks and snacks, is among this city's best diversions.

Two nice little mod-intellectual cafe-bars are *Kaktüs (*☎ 212-249 5979, *İmam Adnan Sokak 4)*, a half-block north off İstiklal, and *Cadde-i Kebir*, directly across the street. Kaktüs is lighter, noisier, more active, with a longer menu. Cadde-i Kebir is quieter; snacks *(çerez)* and light meals are served. At either place, beer is US$1.75, rakı US$2.50. Both have pavement tables.

On the other (south-east) side of İstiklal, Büyükparmakkapı Sokak has another half-dozen evening haunts to choose from. Check out the *Hayal Kahvesi (*☎ 212-244 2558, *Büyükparmakkapı Sokak 19)*, where gilded local youths come to drink, dine and listen to live music most nights.

Nearby at the *Nature & Peace Café* (☎ 212-252 8609), at No 21, the decor is strictly old Pera in contrast to the 1960s name and pricey vegetarian/health food menu; it's closed on Sunday. *Sal Café-Bar,*

Bar, at No 18, features Turkish *saz* (folk) music. Next along, the *Umut Café-Bar* is downstairs. It's followed by *Vivaldi* (☎ *212-293 2599),* at No 29/1, which serves a variety of drinks, along with hot and cold hors d'oeuvres the accompaniment of Turkish and pop music and the occasional Vivaldi track. A small terrace is opened in good weather.

There are more cafe-bars on Hasnun Galip Sokak, off Büyükparmakkapı Sokak, including *Yörem* (☎ *212-252 1428),* which is decked out with Anatolian carpets and kilims and serves traditional village food and alcoholic beverages. Lively Turkish folk music can be heard most evenings.

Just before coming into Galatasaray Square, turn south onto Turnacıbaşı Sokak, then right onto Kartal Sokak to find *Urban* (☎ *212-252 1325),* a trendy cafe-bistro where you're virtually guaranteed to be the only tourist. Classical music or cool jazz greets you as you enter past a rack of periodicals in a half-dozen languages. Various caffeine and alcoholic stimulants are served along with sandwiches and omelettes (US$3), salads (US$4) and a few meat dishes (US$6). The stonewalled rear room was once a Byzantine cistern.

Two-thirds of the way along İstiklal toward Tünel, right next to the Odakule office building, is *Garibaldi* (☎ *212-249 6895),* an upmarket restaurant-bar with live music (jazz or Turkish pop) starting most nights around 8.30 pm. The speciality here is steak and there's an extensive salad bar.

Just north of the Hilton is *Pub Avni* (☎ *212-246 1136, Cumhuriyet Caddesi 239),* a neighbourhood bar with a nightly crowd of middle-aged regulars, American and European recorded music, and a variety of snacks and full meals; it's closed on Sunday.

NIGHTCLUBS

Nightclubs with entertainment are mostly in Beyoğlu and along the Bosphorus shores. Near Sultanahmet and Beyazıt there are several Ottoman theme restaurants, which offer dinner and an 'Ottoman' show, including belly dancers and folk troupes. The

Nightlife Rip-Offs

Foreigners, especially single foreign males, are targets for a classic İstanbul rip-off that works like this:

You're a single male out for a stroll in the afternoon or evening. A well-spoken, well-dressed Turk strikes up a conversation, and says he knows 'a good place where we can have a drink and chat' or 'a great nightspot' etc. You enter, sit down, and immediately several women move to your table and order drinks. When the drinks come, you're asked to pay – anywhere from US$100 to however much money you have with you. It's a mugging, and if you don't pay up they take you into the back office and take it from you.

An exotic variation is a single foreign male having a drink and a meal at the Çiçek Pasajı. Several Turkish friends strike up a conversation, then suggest you all take a taxi to another place. In the taxi, they forcefully relieve you of your wallet.

How do you avoid such rip-offs? As most Turks are generous, hospitable, curious and gregarious, it's difficult to know when an invitation is genuine (as it most often is) or the prelude to a mugging. Tread carefully if there's any reason for suspicion. As for nightclub recommendations, take them from a trusted source, such as your hotel clerk.

larger, more expensive clubs are tame – and hardly authentic – but safe, as are the clubs in the big hotels. You may get ripped off in some of the smaller clubs.

Kervansaray (☎ *212-247 1630, Cumhuriyet Caddesi 30, Harbiye),* on the north side of the İstanbul Hilton arcade (Map 2), is a good club of long standing with decent food and drinks and a good show at top prices of around US$35 to US$60 per person. It's popular with foreign tour groups.

A similar club, but with a largely Turkish clientele, is *Maksim Gazino* (☎ *212-293*

Originally associated with religious worship, at times regarded as scandalous, the ancient and sensual art of belly dancing survives today as both a means of selfexpression and a form of entertainment.

4110, Sıraselviler Caddesi 37), just out of Taksim to the right of the Savoy Hotel. Maksim has a set menu (US$50), which includes dinner and a show (8.30 or 11.30 pm).

DISCOS & ROCK CLUBS (MAP 3)

Most discos and rock clubs are near Taksim Square.

Other music-and-dance clubs are along Sıraselviler Caddesi, south of Taksim. For rock, try *Kemancı*, in the Taksim Sitesi building at Sıraselviler Caddesi 69, a block south of Taksim on the left-hand (east) side. Andon Dancing, open from 9.30 pm to 2 am, is part of the popular *Andon Pera* cafe-

bar *(☎ 212-251 0222, Sıraselviler Caddesi 89/2)*, a short walk farther along.

Cadde-i Kebir Kültür ve Eğlence Merkezi (Grand Avenue Culture & Amusement Centre) on İmam Adnan Sokak just down from the Cadde-i Kebir (see Cafe-Bars, earlier) often has bands and special events.

JAZZ BARS

The *Kehribar (☎ 212-231 4100)* in the Divan Oteli (Map 2) is smooth and luxurious, with excellent music and expensive drinks. Next door in the Hyatt Regency Istanbul is *Harry's Jazz Bar (☎ 212-225 7000)*, with a similar reputation. Also try the *Tepe Lounge Bar (☎ 212-251 4696)* at the Marmara Hotel (Map 3) in Taksim, where there's jazz from 10.30 pm to 1 am.

For Turkish jazz music, try the friendly *Jasmine* cafe-bar *(☎ 212-252 7266, Akarsu Sokak 10)* off İstiklal Caddesi between Taksim and Galatasaray (Map 3). It's open from 3 pm to 2 am.

GAY & LESBIAN VENUES

An online guide to Turkey's gay venues is at www.qrd.org/qrd/www/world/europe/turkey. Despite the low profile of homosexuality in İstanbul, there are a number of venues that cater to a gay and lesbian crowd. Try *Kemancı (☎ 212-245 3048, Sıraselviler Caddesi 69, Taksim)*, which has both gay and straight patrons. The cruisy *Han Cafe* on Cumhuriyet Caddesi, Taksim Square, is also worth a visit. *Club 14 (☎ 212-256 2121, Abdülhak Hamit Caddesi, Belediye Dükkanları 14, Taksim)* is another popular place, which also operates a radio station – Radio 2019 at 90.6 MHz. See the Gay & Lesbian Travellers section in the Facts for the Visitor chapter for information on local attitudes.

NIGHT CRUISES

One of the cheapest, yet most enjoyable, night-time activities in İstanbul is to take a Bosphorus ferry somewhere. It doesn't really matter where, as long as you don't

ENTERTAINMENT

end up on the southern coast of the Sea of Marmara or on the Kızıl Adalar. Catch one over to Üsküdar or any town up the Bosphorus and enjoy the view, the twinkling lights, the fishing boats bobbing on the waves, the powerful searchlights of the ferries sweeping the sea lanes. Have a glass of tea (a waiter will offer you some). Get off anywhere, and take a taxi to your hotel if you can't catch a ferry back directly.

Perhaps the easiest ferry to catch for this purpose is the one from Eminönü to Üsküdar. Just go to Eminönü, buy two jetons (for the voyages out and back), and walk on board. From Üsküdar, just come back; or wait for one of the frequent ferries to Beşiktaş or Kabataş, from where you can catch a bus or dolmuş back to your part of town.

A similar ride is the one from Karaköy to Haydarpaşa or Kadıköy. Return boats bring you right back to Karaköy. The voyage takes 20 minutes in each direction and costs US$1 for a round-trip.

TURKISH BATHS

A visit to the *hamam* (Turkish steam bath) can be wonderful: they are cleansing, refreshing, relaxing and sociable.

The tradition of the steam bath was passed from the Romans to the Byzantines, and from them to the Turks, who have fostered it ever since. Islam's emphasis on personal cleanliness resulted in the construction of hundreds of hamams throughout İstanbul. Many of these survive and continue their historic function.

In İstanbul, the price for the entire hamam experience can be US$3 or US$4 in a local bath if you bring your own soap, shampoo and towel, and bathe yourself; from US$8 to US$10 for an assisted bath; from US$16 to US$25 at a 'historic' touristy bath, including a perfunctory massage. Tips will be expected.

The bath leaves you utterly relaxed and hyperclean in body, mind and spirit.

Bath Procedure

Upon entry you are shown to a dressing cubicle. Store your clothes, wrap the cloth *(peştemal)* that's provided around you, and slip into the sandals. An attendant leads you through the *frigidarium* (cool room) and the *tepidarium* (warm room) to the *caldarium* (hot room), where you sit and sweat for a while, relaxing and loosening up. You can have a massage here, perhaps on the central, raised platform *(göbektaşı)* atop the heating source. Haggle with a masseur or masseuse on a price before beginning.

Soon you will be half-asleep and as soft as putty from the steamy heat. The cheapest bath is the one you do yourself, having brought your own soap, shampoo and towel. But the real Turkish-bath experience is to have an attendant wash and massage you.

If you have opted for the latter, an attendant leads you to the warm room, douses you with warm water, then lathers you with a sudsy swab. Next you are scrubbed with a coarse cloth mitten loosening dirt you never suspected you had. Then comes a shampoo, another dousing with warm water, followed by one with cool water.

When the scrubbing is over, head for the cool room, there to be swathed in Turkish towels and then led back to your cubicle for a rest or a nap. Here you can order tea, coffee, a soft drink or a bottle of beer. If you want to nap, tell the attendant when to wake you.

Modesty

Traditional Turkish baths have separate sections for men and women, or have only one set of facilities and admit men or women at different times. Bath etiquette requires that men remain clothed with the bath-wrap at all times. During the bathing, they wash their private parts themselves, without removing the modesty wrap. In the women's section modesty is less in evidence. Sexual activity of any kind has no place in the traditional bath ritual.

In touristy areas, some baths now accept that foreign men and women like to bathe together. The prices are raised substantially for the privilege, and some questionable practices have emerged. No Turkish woman

particularly in and around İstanbul's Kapalı Çarşı (Covered Market or Grand Bazaar). So much leather clothing is turned out that a good deal of it will be badly cut or carelessly made, but there are lots of fine pieces as well.

The traditional leather apparel centre is the Kürkçüler Çarşısı section of the Kapalı Çarşı, but there are many other shops on and off Fesçiler Caddesi, the street leading in from the entrance by the Beyazıt Camii. Leather shops also fill street after street in the Beyazıt, Laleli and Aksaray districts.

The best way to be assured of quality is to shop around, trying on garments in several shops. Look especially for quality stitching and lining, sufficient fullness of sleeve and leg, and care taken in the small things such as attaching buttons and zippers.

Made-to-order garments can be excellent or disappointing, as the same tailor who made the ready-made stuff will make the ordered stuff; and will be making it fast because the shopkeeper has already impressed you by saying 'No problem. I can have it for you tomorrow'. It's better to find something off the rack that fits than to order it, unless you can order without putting down a deposit or committing yourself to buy (this is often possible).

Fashions & Silk

İstiklal Caddesi in Beyoğlu, once known as the Grand Rue de Péra, has reclaimed some of its Ottoman chicness, and is now lined with shops selling upmarket clothing, fashions, leather apparel, furs and silks. For silk scarves, try İpek (☎ 212-249 8207), İstiklal Caddesi 230/7-8, just south of Galatasaray.

Handicrafts

The Kapalı Çarşı has lots of general tourist ware, but a few shops specialise in high-quality handicrafts. One such is Selvi El Sanatları (see the Kapalı Çarşı map in the Things to See & Do chapter; ☎ 212-527 0997, fax 527 0226), Yağlıkçılar Caddesi 54, Kapalı Çarşı. The speciality here is Kütahya faïence, and not just the *turist işi*

(tourist ware) sold in most shops. Many of the tile panels, vases, plates and other items here are fine, artistic work.

İstanbul Sanatlar Çarşısı (Handicrafts Market) is in the 18th-century Cedid Mehmed Efendi Medresesi, restored by Turing on the southern side of the Yeşil Ev hotel on Kabasakal Caddesi, between Aya Sofya and the Blue Mosque. Local artisans ply their traditional Turkish arts and crafts here, and sell their products.

Antiques

Turkey has a lot of fascinating stuff left over from the empire: rustic peasant jewellery, water-pipe mouthpieces carved from amber, old Korans and illuminated manuscripts, Greek and Roman figurines and coins, tacky furniture in the Ottoman Baroque style.

The grand Ottoman-era houses of Beyoğlu and Old İstanbul have given up a wealth of antique furniture, glassware, paintings and art objects, most of them interesting, some precious, others pretty awful. The shops in the so-called Old Bazaar at the centre of the Kapalı Çarşı specialise in antiques and jewellery, but there are other, less obvious places to prowl in search of the perfect Ottoman knick-knack.

However, *it is illegal to buy, sell, possess or export any antiquity*, and you can go to prison for breaking the law. All antiquities

---

Antiquities & the Law

When shopping for antiques, it's important to remember that *antiquities* – objects from Turkey's Hittite, Greco-Roman, Byzantine and classical Ottoman past – may not be sold, bought, or taken out of the country under penalty of law. A century-old painting, lampshade or carpet usually poses no problems, but a Roman statuette, Byzantine icon or 17th-century İznik tile means trouble, and quite possibly jail time.

must be turned over to a museum immediately upon discovery.

Çukurcuma (Map 3) On the prowl for antiques, most İstanbullus in the know will tell you to head for Çukurcuma, a district lost in the maze of back-street Beyoğlu south-east of Galatasaray. Start from Galatasaray and follow Turnacıbaşı Sokak south-east off İstiklal Caddesi. At the far end of Turnacıbaşı Sokak is the Tarihi Galatasaray Hamamı. Go left, then right, around the bath and continue downhill on Çapanoğlu Sokak and Acıçeşme Sokak to Faik Paşa Sokak (also called Faik Paşa Yokuşu) and, just beyond it, Çukurcuma Caddesi.

Of the shops here, Chez Byzance (☎ 212-251 6636), Faik Paşa Sokak 37-A, has its collection of Ottoman furniture and artefacts set up in a Byzantine basement. Hikmet & Pınar (☎ 212-243 2400), at No 36, has an eclectic, even fascinating mix of old things. Other shops worth a look include Resto (☎ 212-245 7454), at Nos 41 and 69, and Şamdan (☎ 212-244 3681) at 32-A.

On Çukurcuma Caddesi, look for Aslı Tunca (☎ 212-249 5123) at No 67-B, selling mostly furniture.

Kuledibi (Map 3) Perhaps even more obscure is the small collection of shops in the Kuledibi ('foot of the tower') district, right near the Galata Tower in Beyoğlu. Look for Kybele Antiques (☎ 212-243 6022) at Camekan Sokak 4, just south of the tower, and, nearby, the Kuledibi Bit Pazarı (flea market), a narrow row of shops sheltering objects that are antique, old or merely out of date.

Tünel & Sofyalı Sokak (Map 3) At the southern end of İstiklal Caddesi, directly across from the upper station of the Tünel, is the Tünel Pasajı, one of those old İstanbul shopping passages with sturdy metal gates which could be chained and locked at night. Within the passage are several antiquarian bookshops and antique shops, including

Artrium (☎ 212-251 4302), specialising in old books, prints and frames.

Walk out the northern end of the passage (ie away from the Tünel station) on Sofyalı Sokak, a narrow back street which has begun to see the opening of other old book, frame and antique shops.

At its northern end, Sofyalı Sokak meets Asmalımescit Sokak which runs between İstiklal Caddesi and the Pera Palas Oteli. It, too, has a few fusty antique shops.

Nişantaşı Choice antiques at top prices may be found in some shops in Nişantaşı. See the Nişantaşı section later in this chapter.

Old Books, Maps & Prints
Librairie de Péra (☎ 212-245 4998), Galip Dede Caddesi 22, Tünel, just south of the Galata Mevlevihanesi (Whirling Dervish Hall), is a good antiquarian shop with old books in Turkish, Greek, Armenian, Arabic, French, German, English and more.

Eren (☎ 212-251 2858), Sofyalı Sokak 34, Tünel, has old and new history and art books and maps.

Sahaflar Çarşısı (see under Where to Shop, Old Book Bazaar, following), the used-book bazaar just west of the Kapalı Çarşı across Çadırcılar Caddesi, in the shadow of the Beyazıt Camii, is best for browsing and not bad for buying. The Üniversiteli Kitabevi (☎ 212-511 3987, fax 216-345 9387), at No 5, is among the best shops, with a modern outlook and the most current books published in Turkey. Zorlu Kitabevi (☎ 212-511 2660, fax 526 0495), at No 22, specialises in books about İstanbul, old documents and maps. Dilmen Kitabevi (☎ 212-527 9934), at No 20, has a good selection of titles on Turkey and Turkish history in English.

Beyoğlu Anabala Han Sahafları is a passage lined with dusty shops selling whatever old printed materials fall into their hands: books in all languages, Turkish and foreign magazines, movie posters, stock and bond certificates, even some 45rpm vinyl records. From Galatasaray, follow

Turnacıbaşı Sokak to No 23, just past the İlyada art and crafts shop.

Follow Turnacıbaşı Sokak further on, turn right onto Faikpaşa Sokak and among the antiques shops here and along Çukurcuma Caddesi to the east are some which stock old prints and maps, and a few picture books. The finest is perhaps Galeri Alfa (☎ 212-251 1672, fax 243 2429), Faikpaşa Sokak 47.

Alabaster

A translucent, fine-grained variety of either gypsum or calcite, alabaster is pretty because of its grain and colour, and because light passes through it. You'll see ashtrays, vases, chess sets, bowls, egg cups, even the eggs themselves carved from the stone.

Copper

Gleaming copper vessels will greet you in every souvenir shop you peep into. Some are old, sometimes several centuries old. Most are handsome, and some are still eminently useful. The new copperware tends to be of a lighter gauge; that's one of the ways you tell the new from old. But even the new stuff will have been made by hand.

'See that old copper water pipe over there?' my friend Alaettin asked me once. We were sitting in his impossibly cluttered, closet-sized shop on İstanbul's Çadırcılar Caddesi, just outside the Covered Market. 'It dates from the time of Sultan Ahmet III (1703-30), and was used by the *Padişah* (sultan) himself. I just finished making it yesterday.'

Alaettin was a master coppersmith, and had made pieces for many luminaries, including the late Nelson Rockefeller. His pieces might well have graced the sultan's private apartments – except that the sultanate was abolished in 1922. He charged a hefty price for his fine craftwork but not for the story, which was the gift-wrapping, so to speak.

Copper vessels should not be used for cooking in or eating from unless they are tinned inside: that is, washed with molten tin which covers the toxic copper. If you intend to use a copper vessel, make sure the interior layer of tin is intact, or negotiate to have it *kalaylamak* (tinned). If there is a *kalaycı* shop nearby, ask about the price of the tinning in advance, as tin is expensive.

Inlaid Wood

Cigarette boxes, chess and *tavla* (backgammon) boards and other items will be inlaid with different coloured woods, silver or mother-of-pearl. It's not the finest work, but it's pretty good. Make sure there is indeed inlay. These days, alarmingly accurate decals exist. Also, check the silver: is it silver, or aluminium or pewter? And what about that mother-of-pearl, is it in fact 'daughter-of-polystyrene'?

Jewellery

İstanbul is a wonderful place to buy jewellery, especially antique. None of the items may meet your definition of 'chic', but window-shopping is great fun. In the Kapalı Çarşı (Covered Market), a blackboard sign hung above Kuyumcular Caddesi (Jewellers St) bears the daily price for unworked gold of so-many carats. Serious gold-buyers should check this price, watch carefully as the jeweller weighs the piece in question, and then calculate what part of the price is for gold and what part for labour.

Silver is another matter. There is sterling silver jewellery (look for the hallmark), but nickel silver and pewter-like alloys are much more common. Serious dealers don't try to pass off alloy as silver.

Meerschaum

If you smoke a pipe, you know about meerschaum. For those who don't, meerschaum ('sea foam' in German; *lületaşı* in Turkish) is a hydrous magnesium silicate, a soft, white, clay-like material which is porous but heat-resistant. When carved into a pipe, it smokes cool and sweet.

Over time, it absorbs residues from the tobacco and turns a nut-brown colour. Devoted meerschaum pipe smokers even have special gloves for holding the pipe as they smoke, so that oil from their fingers won't sully the fine, even patina of the pipe.

The world's largest and finest beds of meerschaum are found in Turkey, near the city of Eskişehir. Miners climb down shafts in the earth to bring up buckets of mud, some of which contain chunks of the mineral. Artful carving of this soft stone has always been done, and blocks of meerschaum were exported to be carved abroad as well. These days, however, the export of block meerschaum is prohibited because the government realised that exporting uncarved blocks was the same as exporting the jobs to carve them. So any carved pipe will have been carved in Turkey.

You'll marvel at the artistry of the Eskişehir carvers. Pipes portraying turbaned paşas, wizened old men, fair maidens and mythological beasts, as well as many pipes in geometrical designs, will be on view in any souvenir shop.

Pipes are not the only things carved from meerschaum these days. Bracelets, necklaces, pendants, earrings and cigarette holders all appear in souvenir shops.

When buying, look for purity and uniformity in the stone. Carving is often used to cover up flaws in a piece of meerschaum. For pipes, check that the bowl walls are uniform in thickness all around, and that the hole at the bottom of the bowl is centred. Purists buy uncarved, plain pipe-shaped meerschaums that are simply but perfectly made.

Prices for pipes vary, but should be fairly low. Abroad, meerschaum is an expensive commodity, and pipes are luxury items. Here in Turkey meerschaum is cheap, the services of the carver are low-priced, and nobody smokes pipes. If you can't get the pipe you want for US$10 to US$20, or at least only half of what you'd pay at home, then you're not working at it hard enough.

WHERE TO SHOP

İstanbul's Kapalı Çarşı (Covered Market) in Beyazıt and the Mısır Çarşısı (Egyptian Market) in Eminönü are the first places you'll want to go shopping. Though not exclusively patronised by tourists, many of the shops in the Kapalı Çarşı are aimed at the tourist trade. Other İstanbul shopping areas are almost completely Turkish, however. My favourite of these is Uzunçarşı Caddesi and Tahtakale, through which you can make an interesting walking tour.

Kapalı Çarşı

İstanbul's Covered Market (Grand Bazaar; see the Kapalı Çarşı map in the Things to See & Do chapter) consists of 4000 shops and several kilometres of streets, as well as mosques, banks, police stations, restaurants and workshops. It's open daily except Sunday from 8.30 am to 6.30 pm. These days it is very touristy, with touts badgering bus tour groups and eastern European clothing merchants everywhere.

Starting from a small *bedesten* (warehouse) built in the time of Mehmet the Conqueror, the bazaar grew to cover a vast area as neighbouring shopkeepers decided to put up roofs and porches so that commerce could be conducted comfortably in all weather. Rich merchants built *hans* (caravanserais) at the edges of the bazaar so that caravans could bring wealth from all parts of the empire, unload and trade right in the bazaar's precincts. Finally, a system of locked gates and doors was provided so that the entire minicity could be closed up tight at the end of the business day.

Though tourist shops now crowd the bazaar, it is still a place where an İstanbullu may come to buy a few metres of printed cloth, a gold bangle for a daughter's birthday gift, an antique carpet or a fluffy sheepskin. Whether you want to buy or not, you should see the bazaar (remember that it's closed on Sunday). Guard your belongings in the bazaar's crowded streets, and beware the occasional pickpocket or bag slasher.

If you're walking up Divan Yolu from Sultanahmet, turn right off Divan Yolu at the Çemberlitaş (Burnt Column) and walk north down Vezirhanı Caddesi (Map 7).

The big mosque before you is **Nuruos-maniye Camii**, or Light of Osman Mosque, built between 1748 and 1755 by Mahmut I and his successor Osman III, in the style known as Ottoman Baroque. It's one of the earliest examples of the style.

Turn left through the mosque gate. The courtyard of the mosque is peaceful and green, but with a constant flow of pedestrian traffic heading to and from the bazaar.

On the other side of the courtyard is Çarşıkapı Sokak (Bazaar Gate St) and one of several doorways into the bazaar. The gold emblem above the doorway is the Ottoman armorial emblem with the sultan's monogram.

The street inside the bazaar is called **Kalpakçılarbaşı Caddesi** and it's the closest thing the bazaar has to a main street. Most of the bazaar is on your right (north) in the maze of tiny streets and alleys, though the **Kürkçüler Çarşısı** (Furriers Bazaar) is to the left and up a few steps. It now houses shops selling leather clothing and other goods, but it's still an interesting corner of the bazaar.

Street names refer to trades and crafts: Jewellers St, Pearl Merchants St, Fez-makers St. Though many trades have died out, moved on or been replaced, there are several areas that you should see. **Kuyum-cular Caddesi**, the second street on the right as you walk along Kalpakçılarbaşı Caddesi, is Jewellers St, aglitter with gold and gems.

You should of course have a look in the **Old Bazaar** at the centre of the market, dating from the 15th century. This is sometimes called the Cevahir Bedesteni (Jewellery Warehouse). I'd also recommend explorations into one or more of the hans which adjoin the bazaar. A particularly pretty one is the **Zincirli Han** at the far (northern) end of Kuyumcular Caddesi, on the right.

By the way, no one will mind if you wander into any of these hans for a look around. In fact, you may well be invited to

rest your feet, have a glass of tea and exchange a few words.

If it's lunchtime and you're peckish, see the Places to Eat chapter for restaurant recommendations.

Old Book Bazaar

Leave the Kapalı Çarşı by the Hacı Hüsnü Kapısı (gate) at the western end of Kalpakçılarbaşı Caddesi, or the Fesçiler Kapısı at the end of Fesçiler Caddesi. Just across Çadırcılar Caddesi is the entrance to the Sahaflar Çarşısı, or Old Book Bazaar (see the Kapalı Çarşı map in the Things to See & Do chapter). Go up the steps and along to the shady little courtyard. Actually, the wares in the shops here are both new and old. It's unlikely that you'll uncover any underpriced antique treasures, but you can certainly find books on İstanbul and Turkish culture in several languages, old engravings and a curiosity or two.

The book bazaar dates from Byzantine times. Today, many of the booksellers are members of a dervish order called the Halveti after its founder, Hazreti Mehmet Nureddin-i Cerrahi-i Halveti. Their *sema* (religious ceremony) includes chanting from the Koran, praying, and rhythmic dancing and breathing to the accompaniment of classical Turkish liturgical music. As with all dervish orders, the sema is an attempt at close knowledge of and communion with God. The Mevlevi dervishes attempt it by their whirling dance, the Halveti through their circular dance and hyperventilation. Don't, however, expect to wander into a den of mystics. What you'll see are normal Turkish booksellers who just happen to be members of this dervish order.

Just beyond the northern gate of the Sahaflar Çarşısı is a **daily flea market** specialising in old coins, seals, stamps, watches, jewellery and Ottoman knick-knacks. On Sunday the flea market expands and fills Beyazıt Square with hawkers selling everything from TV aerials to electric-blue socks.

TURKISH CARPETS

NEIL WILSON

Turkey is famous for its beautiful carpets and kilims and wherever you go you'll be spoilt for choice as to what to buy. Unfortunately, the carpet market is very lucrative and the hard-sell antics of some dealers and their shills have tended to bring it into disrepute, putting many visitors off venturing into the shops. Also, with the tourism boom, carpet prices in Turkey have risen so much that it may actually be cheaper to buy your Turkish carpet at home. Indeed, we've heard one story of a man who bought up old kilims in the Paris flea market, had them cleaned, then brought them to Turkey to sell to tourists at high prices – creative recycling!

If you have it in mind to buy a carpet, browse in your local shop before coming to Turkey. This will give you some idea of prices and will acquaint you with the various designs so you can shop more knowledgeably when in Turkey.

An Age-Old Art

Turkish women have been weaving carpets for a very long time. These beautiful, durable, eminently portable floor coverings were a nomadic family's most valuable and practical 'furniture', warming and brightening the clan's oft-moved homes.

The oldest known carpet woven in the Turkish double-knotted *Gördes* style dates from between the 4th and 1st centuries BC.

It is thought that hand-woven carpet techniques were introduced to Anatolia by the Seljuks in the 12th century. Thus it's not surprising that Konya, the Seljuk capital, was mentioned by Marco Polo as a centre of carpet production in the 13th century.

Traditional Patterns

Traditionally, village women wove carpets for their own family's use, or for their dowry. Knowing they would be judged on their efforts, the women took great care over their handiwork, hand-spinning and dyeing the wool, and choosing what they judged to be the most interesting and beautiful patterns.

The general pattern and colour scheme of old carpets was influenced by local traditions and the availability of certain types of wool and colours of dyes. Patterns were memorised, and women usually worked with no more than 18 inches of the carpet visible. But each artist imbued her work with her own personality, choosing a motif or a colour based on her own artistic preferences, and even events and emotions in her daily life.

In the 19th century, the European rage for Turkish carpets spurred the development of carpet companies. The companies, run by men, would deal with customers, take orders, purchase and dye the wool according to the customers' preferences, and contract local women to produce the finished product. The designs might be left to the women, but more often were provided by the company based on the customers' tastes. Though well made, these carpets lost some originality and spirit of the older work.

Even carpets made today often use the same traditional patterns and incorporate all sorts of symbols which can be 'read' by those in the know. At a glance two carpets might look identical, but closer examination reveals the subtle differences that give each Turkish carpet its individuality and much of its charm.

Carpet Weaving Today

These days the picture is more complicated. Many carpets are made not according to local traditions, but to the dictates of the market. Weavers in eastern Turkey might make carpets in popular styles native to western Turkey. Long-settled villagers might duplicate the wilder, hairier and more naive *yörük* (nomad) carpets.

Village women still weave carpets but most of them work to fixed contracts for specific shops. Usually they work to a pattern and are paid for their final effort rather than for each hour of work. A carpet made to a fixed contract may still be of great value to its purchaser. However, the selling price should be lower than for a one-off piece.

Other carpets are the product of division of labour, with different individuals responsible for dyeing and weaving. What such pieces lose in individuality and rarity is often more than made up for in quality control. Most silk Hereke carpets are mass produced but to standards that make them some of the most sought-after of all Turkish carpets.

Fearing that old carpet-making methods would be lost, the Ministry of Culture now sponsors a number of projects to revive traditional weaving and dyeing methods in western Turkey. Some carpet shops will have stocks of these 'project carpets' which are usually of high quality with prices reflecting that fact.

Kilims, Sumaks & Cicims

A good carpet shop will have a range of pieces made by a variety of techniques. Besides the traditional pile carpets, they may offer double-sided flat-woven mats such as kilims. Some traditional kilim motifs are similar to patterns found at the prehistoric mound of Çatal Höyük, testifying to the very ancient traditions of flat-woven floor coverings in Anatolia. Older, larger kilims may actually be two narrower pieces of similar but not always identical design stitched together. As this is now rarely done, any such piece is likely to be fairly old.

Other flat-weave techniques include *sumak,* a style originally from Azerbaijan in which coloured threads are wrapped around the warp. *Cicims* are kilims with small, lively patterns embroidered on top of them.

Carpets From Other Countries

As well as Turkish carpets, many carpet shops sell pieces from other countries, especially from Iran, Afghanistan and from the ex-Soviet Republics of Azerbaijan, Turkmenistan and Uzbekistan. If it matters that yours is actually from Turkey, bear in mind that Iran favours the single knot and Turkey the double knot. Turkish carpets also tend to have a higher pile, more dramatic designs and more varied colours than their Iranian cousins. Some Iranian sumaks are decorated with naive animal patterns, encouraging shopkeepers to call them 'Noah's Ark carpets' although they have absolutely nothing to do with the Bible story.

A CARPET BUYER'S PRIMER

The bad news is that there are no short cuts when it comes to learning about carpets. To ensure you get a good buy, you'll have to spend time visiting several shops and compare prices and quality. It's also worth taking a look in the department stores at home before you leave. That way, you'll know what's available and for what prices at home.

That said, when deciding whether to buy a particular carpet, it might help to follow some of the guidelines below.

A good-quality, long-lasting carpet should be 100% wool (*yüz de yüz yün*): check the warp (the lengthwise yarns), weft (the crosswise yarns) and pile (the vertical yarns knotted into the matrix of warp and weft). Is the wool fine and shiny, with signs of the natural oil? More expensive carpets may be of a silk and wool blend. Cheaper carpets may have warp and weft of mercerised cotton. You can tell by checking the fringes at either end – if the fringe is of cotton or 'flosh' (mercerised cotton) you shouldn't pay for wool. Another way to identify the material of the warp and weft is to turn the carpet over and look for the fine, frizzy fibres common to wool, but not to cotton. But bear in mind that just being made of wool doesn't guarantee a carpet's quality. If the dyes and design are ugly, even a 100% woollen carpet can be a bad buy.

Check the closeness of the weave by turning the carpet over and inspecting the back. In general, the tighter the weave and the smaller the knots, the higher the quality and durability of the carpet. The oldest carpets sometimes had thick knots, so consider the number of knots alongside the colours and the quality of the wool.

Compare the colours on the back with those on the front. Spread the nap with your fingers and look at the bottom of the pile. Are the colours brighter there than on the surface? Slight colour variations could occur in older carpets when a new batch of dye was mixed, but richer colour deep in the pile is often an indication that the surface has faded in the sun. Natural dyes don't fade as readily as chemical dyes. There is nothing wrong with chemical dyes, which have a long history of their own, but natural dyes and colours tend to be preferred and therefore fetch higher prices. Don't pay for natural if you're getting chemical.

New carpets can be made to look old, and damaged or worn carpets can be rewoven (good work, but expensive), patched or even painted. There's nothing wrong with a dealer offering you a patched or re-painted carpet provided they point out these defects and price the piece accordingly, but it would be dishonest to offer you cheap goods at an inflated price. But some red Bokhara carpets will continue to give off colour even though they're of better quality than cheap woollen carpets which don't.

Look at the carpet from one end, then from the other. The colours will differ because the pile always leans one way or the other. Take the carpet out into the sunlight and look at it there. Imagine where you might put the carpet at home, and how the light will strike it.

In the end the most important consideration should be whether or not you like the carpet. It's all very well to pluck some fibres and burn

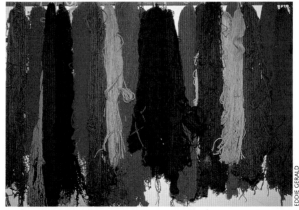

Top: A kaleidoscope of colours waiting to be turned into the finest of Turkish carpets.

Middle: Wool stocked in cupboard of rug mender, Sultanahmet area.

Bottom: Rug mender, Sultanahmet area

EDDIE GERALD

Many Turkish carpets are made not according to local traditions, but to the demands of the market.

When buying a carpet, take your time and shop around. Wherever you go you'll be spoilt for choice.

Top: Carpet shop owners in Turkey are always willing to show you their wares.

Middle: A cosy place for a catnap at the Kapalı Çarşı (Grand Bazaar), İstanbul.

Bottom: A woman presides over a carpet shop in Side on the Mediterranean Coast.

them to see if they smell like wool, silk, or nylon or to rub a wet handkerchief over the carpet to see if the colour comes off, but unless you know what you're doing you're unlikely to learn much from the exercise – and you may well end up with a irate carpet seller to deal with!

Pricing & Payment

When it comes to buying, there's no substitute for spending time developing an 'eye' for what you really like. You also need to be realistic about your budget. These days carpets are such big business that true bargains are hard to come by unless there's something (like gigantic size) that makes them hard to sell for their true value.

Prices are determined by age, material, quality, condition, demand in the market, the enthusiasm of the buyer, and the debt load of the seller. Bear in mind that if you do your shopping on a tour or when accompanied by a guide, the price will be hiked by up to 35% to cover somebody's commission.

It may be wiser to go for something small but of high quality rather than for a room-sized cheapie. Another way to make the money stretch further is to opt for one of the smaller items made from carpet materials: old camel bags and hanging baby's cradles opened out to make rugs; sofras or rugs on which food would be eaten; decorative grain bags; cushion covers; even the bags which once held rock salt for animals.

Some dealers will take personal cheques, but all prefer cash. An increasing number of shops take credit cards but some require you to pay the credit card company's fee and the cost of the phone call to check your creditworthiness. A few dealers will let you pay in instalments.

All this is a lot to remember, but it'll be worth it if you get a carpet you like at a decent price. It will give you pleasure for the rest of your life.

SHOPPING

Uzunçarşı Caddesi & Tahtakale (Map 4)

Among the most interesting walking tours in the city is this one which takes you through the heart of İstanbul's central market districts.

Start from within the Kapalı Çarşı (see the Kapalı Çarşı map in the Things to See & Do chapter). Near the western end of Kalpakçılarbaşı Caddesi, Sipahi Sokak heads north, changes name to become Feraceciler Sokak (Cloakmakers St), then becomes Yağcılar Caddesi (Oil Merchants St). You'll see the Şark Kahvesi on your left, then some steps up to a small mosque *(mescit)*. Continue straight on, past shops and han entrances to Örücüler Kapısı (Gate of the Darners). Cross a main street named Mercan Caddesi (to the left) and Çakmakçılar Yokuşu (to the right), and continue downhill on Uzunçarşı Caddesi.

This takes you to the very untouristy Tahtakale market district, unpenetrated by bus tours. Turn right at the Rüstem Paşa Camii and follow Hasırcılar Caddesi to the Mısır Çarşısı and the Galata Bridge.

Uzunçarşı Caddesi 'Longmarket St' lives up to its name: one long market of woodturners' shops, luggage merchants, shops selling guns and hunting equipment, plastic toys, freshly baked *simits* (sesame rolls), secondhand clothing, backgammon sets and the like. A few blocks downhill from the Kapalı Çarşı is the market district of Tahtakale, synonymous with buying and selling anything and everything, including the bizarre and the illegal.

At the foot of the hill, near the Mısır Çarşısı and Galata Bridge, Uzunçarşı Caddesi runs straight to the small, exquisite Rüstem Paşa Camii.

Hasırcılar Caddesi Going south-east from the Rüstem Paşa Camii is Hasırcılar Caddesi, or Mat Makers' Street. Shops along it sell fresh fruits, spices, nuts, condiments, knives and other cutlery, coffee, tea, cocoa, hardware and similar retail necessities. The colours, smells, sights and sounds make this one of the liveliest and most interesting streets in the city. A 10-minute stroll brings you right to the Mısır Çarşısı.

Mısır Çarşısı (Map 4)

The Egyptian Market is also called the Spice Bazaar because of its many spice shops. It's open daily except Sunday from 8.30 am to 6.30 pm.

The market was constructed in the 1660s as part of the Yeni Cami mosque complex, the rents from the shops going to support the upkeep of the mosque and its charitable

---

Maşallah!

In İstanbul's Mısır Çarşısı (Egyptian Market) you may see a shop which specialises in the white outfits boys wear on the day (usually Sunday) of their circumcision *(sünnet)*. The white suit is supplemented with a spangled hat and red satin sash emblazoned with the word *Maşallah* (MAH-shah-lah, 'What wonders God has willed!').

Circumcision, or the surgical removal of the foreskin on the penis, is performed on a Turkish Muslim lad when he is nine or 10 years old, and marks his formal admission into the faith, as does confirmation in Christianity and bar mitzvah in Judaism.

On the day of the operation the boy is dressed in the special suit, visits relatives and friends, and leads a parade – formerly on horseback, now in cars – around his neighbourhood or city, attended by musicians and merrymakers. You may come across these lads while visiting the Eyüp Sultan Camii, one of Islam's holiest places, where they often stop on their way to circumcision.

The simple operation, performed in a hospital or clinic in the afternoon, is followed by a celebration with music and feasting. The newly circumcised lad attends, resting in bed, as his friends and relatives bring him gifts and congratulate him on having entered manhood.

activities. These included a school, baths, hospital and public fountains.

Strolling through the market, the number of shops selling tourist trinkets is increasing annually, though there are still some shops which sell spices *(baharat)* and even a few which specialise in the old-time folk remedies. More to the point for anyone on a walking tour are the shops selling nuts, dried and candied fruits, chocolate and other snacks. Try some figs *(incir)* or Turkish delight *(lokum)*. Fruit pressed into sheets and dried (looks like leather) is called *pestil*. It's often made from apricots or mulberries, and is delicious and relatively cheap. The shop right at the juncture of streets within the bazaar (look for the picture of Atatürk formed of pistachio nuts) usually has it. Buy 50 or 100g for a sample.

Between the Mısır Çarşısı and the Yeni Cami is the city's major outdoor market for flowers, plants, seeds and songbirds. There's a toilet *(tuvalet)* down a flight of stairs, subject to a small fee. Across the courtyard near the mosque is the **tomb of Valide Sultan Turhan Hatice**, the lady who completed construction of the Yeni Cami. Buried with her are no fewer than six sultans, including her son Mehmet IV, plus dozens of imperial princes and princesses.

Mahmutpaşa Yokuşu (Map 7)

Mahmutpaşa Yokuşu is the street which descends the hill from the Nuruosmaniye Camii, on the eastern side of the Kapalı Çarşı, to the Mısır Çarşısı, the Tahtakale district and Eminönü. This is where ordinary Turkish shoppers come to find inexpensive clothing, yard goods, buttons and sewing materials, toys, accessories, luggage and more.

Shops line both sides of the street, and itinerant vendors fill most of the roadway. The good-natured throng of shoppers jostles and lurches along through the maze, frequently parting (under duress) to allow an overloaded pick-up truck to squeeze through.

You're unlikely to find anything here that you can't live without, and you'll almost certainly get lost, but it's good fun, and a real slice of İstanbul life. When you get lost,

ask directions to either the Kapalı Çarşı (kah-pah-LUH char-shuh, Covered Market) or Mısır Çarşısı (MUH-suhr char-shuh-suh, Egyptian Market), from which you can easily find your way onward.

İstiklal Caddesi (Map 3)

The one-time Grande Rue de Péra has reclaimed some of its former glory in recent years. When cars were banned, strollers and window-shoppers flooded in, encouraging the shops to stay and new ones to open.

For fashionable apparel, try the following shops, all of them along İstiklal Caddesi.

The Olgunlaşma Enstitüsü, at No 48, is a girls' technical school specialising in exquisite embroidery worked on clothing and accessories. If you admire delicate handwork, be sure to have a look.

Beymen, at No 68, is a very successful Turkish upmarket clothier for both men and women. In fact, Beymen also runs Turkey's Benetton outlets.

Vakko, at No 125, has been in business for at least half a century, and is noted for its high style and quality. Its Vakkorama subsidiary, on the other hand, has hip, chic, youthful clothing and gear.

Nişantaşı (Map 2)

Nişantaşı, just north of the İstanbul Hilton, has many more upmarket shops. Walk north from the hotel for a few minutes and bear right onto Valikonağı Caddesi. The first street on the right, Mim Kemal Öke Caddesi, has several carpet and antique shops. The next street on the right, Abdi İpekçi Caddesi, has the top names (and prices) for everything from kids' wear and bathing costumes to night dresses, lingerie and home furnishings.

Next along Valikonağı Caddesi is the busy intersection with Rumeli and Teşvikiye caddesis. The intersection is marked at its eastern corner by a small obelisk, the Nişan Taşı (memorial) which gave this district its name.

Turn left (north-west) onto Rumeli Caddesi for three blocks of clothing shops packed close together: upmarket infant apparel, wedding gowns, lingerie, sportswear and equipment, and shoes for both men and women.

Back at the Nişan Taşı intersection, turn right into Teşvikiye Caddesi where the assortment of apparel and accessories shops continues.

Akmerkez

Akmerkez (☎ 212-282 0170) gets top buzz among İstanbul's upmarket shoppers. Located in Etiler, well north of Taksim and west of Bebek, it's an authentic posh US-style shopping mall with all the well-known, world-class names (Polo-Ralph Lauren, Pierre Cardin, Benetton) and the best of the Turkish chains (Beymen, Tiffany & Tomato, Yargıcı) as well as numerous boutiques. When you get tired of shopping, take sustenance in any of the cafes or restaurants, or from the supermarket, or relax in one of the cinemas.

Except during morning and evening rush hours, you can get there by taxi in 15 minutes from Taksim. In the evening rush, the trip can take an hour.

Galleria Ataköy

İstanbul's first US-style shopping mall was the Galleria (gah-LEHR-ree-yah, ☎ 212-559 9560), on the Marmara shore road at Ataköy, west of the city walls (see the Greater İstanbul map). Now somewhat upstaged by the Akmerkez, Galleria is nonetheless still active. As with Akmerkez, access is best by taxi.

Excursions

İstanbul makes an excellent base for day trips and overnight excursions to several places in Trakya (Thrace), the Marmara region, and even farther afield.

For more detailed information on all of these excursions, refer to Lonely Planet's *Turkey*, which covers the entire country in detail. Travel agencies in İstanbul can arrange any of these excursions for you (see Travel Agencies under Organised Tours in the Getting Around chapter).

The Bosphorus

The forces of history have travelled up and down the Bosphorus, affecting empires and the great imperial capital of İstanbul as they came and went. The strait, which connects the Black Sea and the Sea of Marmara, is 32km long, from 500m to 3km wide and 50 to 120m (average 60m) deep. An excursion up the Bosphorus is an essential part of any visit to İstanbul.

In Turkish, the strait is the İstanbul Boğazı, from *boğaz*, throat or strait, or Boğaziçi (*iç*, inside or interior: 'within the strait').

The Bosphorus provides a convenient boundary for geographers. As it was a military bottleneck, armies marching from the east tended to stop on the eastern side, and those from the west on the western. So the western side was always more like Europe, the eastern more like Asia. Though the modern Turks think of themselves as Europeans, it is still common to say that Europe ends and Asia begins at the Bosphorus.

Except for the few occasions when the Bosphorus froze solid, crossing it always meant going by boat – until 1973. Late in that year, the Bosphorus Bridge, the fourth-longest suspension bridge in the world, was opened to travellers. For the first time in history there was a firm physical link across the straits from Europe to Asia. (Plans had been drawn up for a bridge during the late

years of the Ottoman Empire, but it was never built.)

Traffic was so heavy over the new bridge that it paid for itself in less than a decade. Now there is a second bridge, the Fatih Bridge (named after Mehmet the Conqueror, Mehmet Fatih), just north of Rumeli Hisarı. A third bridge, even farther north, is planned, as is a railway tunnel connecting Haydarpaşa station in Asia with the European line at Yenikapı, but don't hold your breath until these very ambitious projects become reality.

History

Ancient myth lives on in the name of the Bosphorus. *Bous* is cow in ancient Greek, and *poros* is crossing place, so 'Bosphorus' is the place where the cow crossed. The cow was Io, a beautiful lady with whom Zeus, king of the gods, had an affair. When his wife Hera discovered his infidelity, Zeus tried to make up for it by turning his erstwhile lover into a cow. Hera, for good measure, provided a horsefly to sting Io on the rump and drive her across the strait. (Notice that Zeus got off with no punishment!)

From earliest times the Bosphorus has been a maritime road to adventure. It is thought that Ulysses' travels brought him through the Bosphorus. Byzas, founder of Byzantium, explored these waters before the time of Jesus. Mehmet the Conqueror built two mighty fortresses at the strait's narrowest point so as to close it off to allies of the Byzantines. Each spring, enormous Ottoman armies would take several days to cross the Bosphorus on their way to campaigns in Asia. At the end of WWI, the defeated Ottoman capital cowered under the guns of Allied frigates anchored in the strait. When the republic was proclaimed, the last sultan of the Ottoman Empire snuck quietly down to the Bosphorus shore, boarded a British man-of-war and sailed away to exile.

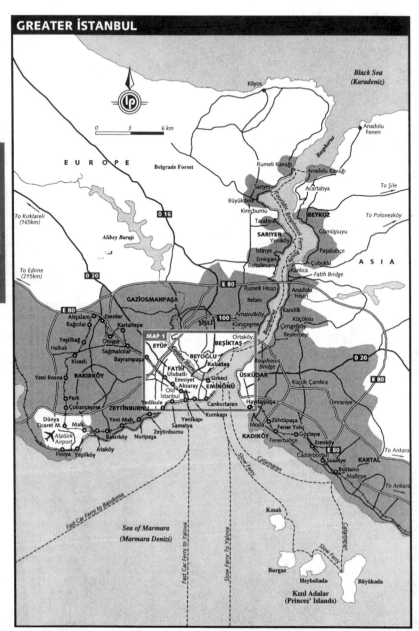

TOURING THE BOSPHORUS

You could spend several days exploring the sights of the Bosphorus (see the Greater İstanbul Map): there's five Ottoman palaces, four castles, Üsküdar and other Asian suburbs, and several interesting small towns. However, one day will do in a pinch.

The essential feature of any Bosphorus tour is a cruise along the strait. A trip combining travel by both land and sea is best. Begin your explorations with a ferry cruise for a general view, then visit selected sites by bus, dolmuş and taxi.

A Bosphorus Cruise

Though tour agencies and luxury hotels have private boats for cruises on the Bosphorus, it's considerably cheaper to go on one of the daily excursion ferries.

Special Bosphorus cruise trips are operated twice daily on summer Saturdays and weekdays, and five times a day on summer Sundays and holidays. If you can't afford the time for the whole trip, you can get off at one of the stops en route.

As you approach the docks in Eminönü, ignore the touts shouting 'Bosphorus! Bosphorus!' They want to sell you a ticket at two or three times the normal price.

Eminönü-Kavaklar Boğaziçi Özel Gezi Seferleri (Eminönü-Kavaklar Bosphorus Special Touristic Excursions) depart from Eminönü daily at 10.35 am, 12.35 and 2.10 pm each weekday, stop at Beşiktaş on the European shore, Kanlıca on the Asian shore, Yeniköy, Sarıyer and Rumeli Kavağı on the European shore, and Anadolu Kavağı on the Asian shore (the turn-around point). Times are subject to change.

The ferries go all the way to Rumeli Kavağı and Anadolu Kavağı (1¼ hours), but you may want to go only as far as Sarıyer, then take a dolmuş, bus or seabus back down, stopping at various sights along the way. Arrival at Sarıyer on the European shore about three quarters of the way up the Bosphorus, is at 11.50 am, 1.50 and 3.30 pm respectively. Departures from Sarıyer for the trip back down the Bosphorus are at 2.20, 3.10 and 5.50 pm on weekdays.

Trips are added o
with boats departing
and 11 am, noon, 1.3

The weekday rou
half-price on Saturda
are printed on all tic
ticket; you need to sh   ... re-board the boat for the return trip. The boats fill up early in summer – on weekends particularly – so buy your ticket and walk aboard at least 30 or 45 minutes prior to departure to get a seat.

Cross-Bosphorus Ferries

At several points along the Bosphorus, passenger ferries run between the European and Asian shores, often following a ring route among three docks and allowing you to cross easily from one side to the other. If you can't catch one of these ferries, you can often hire a boater to motor you across the Bosphorus for a few dollars.

Southernmost are the routes from Eminönü, Kabataş and Beşiktaş in Europe to Üsküdar in Asia.

Another ring route is from Kanlıca to Anadolu Hisarı on the Asian shore, then across the Bosphorus to Bebek on the European shore. Departures from Kanlıca are at 8.30, 9.30, 10.30 and 11.30 am, and 12.30, 2.30, 4, 5.15 and 6.15 pm. The voyage to Bebek takes 25 minutes and costs US$0.50.

Other ring routes are from İstinye on the European side to Beykoz and Paşabahçe on the Asian side. Yet another ring route is from Sarıyer and Rumeli Kavağı in Europe to Anadolu Kavağı in Asia, with 17 ferries a day (at least one every hour) from 7.15 am to 11 pm.

Touring by Land

Starting from Sultanahmet, take the tram to Eminönü to catch the ferry. If you'd like to see the sights on land as you go north up the Bosphorus and then return on the ferry going south, take bus No 210 (Sultanahmet-Emirgan, two tickets), which departs every two hours from a stop just east of the Tourism Information Office in Sultanahmet.

minönü, bus No 25E 'Eminönü-' goes all the way up the Bosphorus along the European shore, but shore road traffic is slow (particularly on weekends) so allow several hours for the trip. The bus leaves from 2 Nolu Peron (the 2nd bus rank) in the lot just west of the Yeni Cami.

From Taksim, the downhill walk along İnönü Caddesi to Dolmabahçe Sarayı is short (about 10 minutes) and pleasant with views of the Bosphorus and the palace. On the right-hand side of İnönü Caddesi just out of Taksim are dolmuşes going to Beşiktaş, which will drop you at Dolmabahçe if you want to ride. There are also dolmuş minibuses to Sarıyer from Mete Caddesi west of the Hotel Gezi.

SIGHTS ON THE EUROPEAN SHORE

Here are the sights to look for as you head north up the Bosphorus from Dolmabahçe.

Deniz Müzesi

The Deniz Müzesi (Maritime Museum; Map 1) is on the Bosphorus shore just south of the flyover in Beşiktaş. Among its exhibits are an outdoor display of cannon (including Selim the Grim's 21-tonne monster) and a statue of Barbaros Hayrettin Paşa (1483-1546), the famous Turkish admiral known also as Barbarossa who conquered North Africa for Süleyman the Magnificent. The admiral's tomb, designed by Sinan, is close by.

History Though the Ottoman Empire is most remembered for its conquests on land, its maritime power was equally impressive. During the reign of Süleyman the Magnificent (1520-66), the eastern Mediterranean was virtually an Ottoman lake. The sultan's navies cut a swath in the Indian Ocean as well. Sea power was instrumental in the conquests of the Aegean coasts and islands, Egypt and North Africa. Discipline, well-organised supply and good ship design contributed to Ottoman victories.

However, during the later centuries the navy, like the army and the government,

lagged behind the west in modernisation. The great battle which broke the spell of Ottoman naval invincibility was fought in 1571 at Lepanto, in the Gulf of Patras off the Greek coast. (Cervantes fought on the Christian side, and was badly wounded.) Though the Turkish fleet was destroyed, the sultan quickly produced another, partly with the help of rich Greek shipowners who were his subjects.

Admission The museum is open daily (except Wednesday and Thursday) from 9.30 am to 12.30 pm and from 1.30 to 5 pm. Admission costs US$1.

Exhibits The sleek, swift imperial barges in which the sultan would speed up and down the Bosphorus from palace to palace are over 30m in length but only 2m wide. With 13 banks of oars, the barges were the speed boats of their day. The ones with latticework screens were for the imperial ladies. There's also a war galley with 24 pairs of oars.

You may also be curious to see a replica of the *Map of Piri Reis*, an early Ottoman map (1513), which purports to show the coasts and continents of the New World. It's assumed that Piri Reis (Captain Piri) got hold of the work of Columbus for his map. The original map is in Topkapı Sarayı; this one is on the wall above the door as you enter the Bosphorus section. Copies are on sale.

Ihlamur Kasrı

Sheltered in a narrow valley inland to the north of Dolmabahçe Sarayı and the Deniz Müzesi is a park containing the Ihlamur Kasrı (UHH-lah-moor kahss-ruh), or Kiosk of the Linden Tree (☎ 212-261 2991). The park is surrounded by a maze of twisting streets. The two small ornate imperial kiosks that constitute the pavilion are open from 9.30 am to 4 pm every day except Monday and Thursday. Admission to the park and kiosks costs US$0.75, or US$0.25 if you just want to stroll through the park. The fee for using a camera is US$6.

Try to imagine what it must have been like when these two miniature palaces stood here alone, in the midst of a forest. Near the entry gate the park is open and formal, with grassy lawns, ornamental trees and a quiet pool.

As you enter the grounds, look across the pool to find the **Merasim Köşkü**, or Sultan's Kiosk, built on the orders of Sultan Abdül Mecit between 1849 and 1855 by Nikogos Balyan, of the family of imperial architects. As you enter, a guide will approach to offer you a free guided tour.

Up the marble stairway and through the ornate door is the Hall of Mirrors, with crystal from Bohemia and vases from France. The Baroque decor includes patterns of shells, flowers, vines, fruits and lots of gold leaf.

The music room which is to the right of the entrance has precious Hereke fabrics on the chairs and an enamelled coal-grate fireplace painted with flowers. Similarly beautiful fireplaces ornament the other rooms; the music room's walls are faux-marble.

The main appliance in the Imperial Water Closet is of the traditional flat Turkish type, demonstrating that in here even the sultan was dethroned.

The room to the left of the entrance was a reception salon with a sofa-throne and faux-marble decoration of plaster with gold flecks. The tour ends downstairs, where displays of photographs show details of the restoration work carried out in the 1980s.

The **Maiyet Köşkü**, or Retinue Kiosk, was for the sultan's suite of attendants, guests or harem. It's now a teahouse serving tea, coffee and snacks (for around US$2). Downstairs are toilets and a bookshop.

To the right behind the Maiyet Köşkü the gardens are more rustic, shady and cool, with naturalistic spring-like fountains.

Getting There & Away The easiest way to find this place is to take a taxi, which from Dolmabahçe or Beşiktaş should cost only US$1 or so. Bus No 26 – Dikilitaş (DEE-kee-lee-tahsh) to Eminönü – makes a

return trip from Eminönü stopping at Karaköy, Dolmabahçe and Beşiktaş, before heading inland to the Ihlamur stop and continuing to Dikilitaş, which is not far past Ihlamur. Other buses include Nos 26A, 26B and 26C.

Çirağan Sarayı

Not satisfied with the architectural exertions of his predecessor at Dolmabahçe, Sultan Abdülaziz (1861-76) built his own grand residence at Çirağan on the Bosphorus shore only 1km north of Dolmabahçe, replacing an earlier wooden palace. The architect was the self-same Balyan who designed Dolmabahçe.

The sultan was deposed, however, and later died in Çirağan under mysterious circumstances. His mentally unstable nephew Murat came to the throne, but was deposed within a year by his brother Abdül Hamit II, who kept Murat a virtual prisoner in Çirağan. Much later (1909) it was the seat of the Ottoman Chamber of Deputies and Senate, but in 1910 it was destroyed by fire under suspicious circumstances.

From the Deniz Müzesi and the flyover in Beşiktaş, you can walk north for 10 minutes, or catch a bus or dolmuş heading north along the shore (get out at the Yahya Efendi stop), to reach the entrance to the Çirağan complex. The palace has been restored as part of the luxury Çirağan Palace Hotel Kempinski Istanbul, and is now used for meetings and functions. If you're decently dressed, feel free to enter the grounds, wander around, admire the view and perhaps have refreshments, although prices are breathtaking, even for five-star places.

Just a minute's walk north of Çirağan is the entrance, on the left, to Yıldız Park.

Yıldız Sarayı & Park

Sultan Abdül Hamit II (1876-1909), who succeeded Murat V, also had to build his own palace. He added considerably to the structures built by earlier sultans in Yıldız Park (Map 1), on the hillside above Çirağan.

The park is open from 9 am to 6 pm every day; admission costs US$1.75 for cars (including taxis); it's free to pedestrians. If you come to the park by taxi, have it take you up the steep slope to the Şale Köşkü. You can visit the other kiosks on the walk down. A taxi from Taksim Square to the top of the hill might cost around US$5 or US$6.

The park, with its kiosks, had become derelict, but was beautifully restored by the Turkish Touring & Automobile Association (Turing) in the 1980s, under lease from the city government. In 1994 the newly elected city government declined to renew the lease, and took over operation of the park.

The park began life as the imperial reserve for Çirağan Sarayı, but when Abdül Hamit built the Şale Köşkü, largest of the park's surviving structures, the park served that palace. Under Abdül Hamit, the park was planted with rare and exotic trees, shrubs and flowers, and was provided with carefully tended paths and superior electric lighting and drainage systems.

Çadır Köşkü & Malta Köşkü As you toil up the hill along the road, near the top of the slope to the left you'll see the Çadır Köşkü (Pavilion Kiosk, ☎ 212-258 9020), an ornate kiosk built between 1865 and 1870 as a place for the sultan to enjoy the view, rest from a walk, and have a cup of tea or coffee. It still serves coffee, tea, soft drinks and snacks, and is the prettiest place in the park for refreshments.

To the right (north) as you hike up the road from the gate are two greenhouses, the **Kış Bahçesi** (Winter Garden) and the **Yeşil Sera** (Green Nursery), and the Malta Köşkü (Malta Kiosk, ☎ 212-258 9453). Restored in 1979, the kiosk is now a cafe serving refreshments and light meals, but no alcoholic beverages. The view from here is the best in the park, much better than that at the Çadır Köşkü. If you sit down to a plate of grilled lamb and then finish up with something sweet, your bill will add up to US$8 to US$12.

Also to the right is the **Yıldız Porselen Fabrikası**, or Yıldız Porcelain Factory, constructed to manufacture dinner services for the palace. It still operates and is open to visitors.

Yıldız Şale At the very top of the hill, enclosed by a lofty wall, is the Yıldız Şale (Yildiz Chalet), a 'guesthouse' put up in 1882 and expanded in 1898 by Abdül Hamit for use by Kaiser Wilhelm II of Germany during a state visit. You must pay a separate admission fee of US$4 (plus US$8 for a camera or US$16 for a video camera) to see the chalet (☎ 212-258 3080), which is open from 9.30 am to 5 pm, closed Monday and Thursday.

I expect the Kaiser had enough space to move in, as the chalet has 64 rooms. After his imperial guest departed, the sultan became quite attached to his 'rustic' creation, and decided to live here himself, forsaking the more lavish but less well-protected palaces on the Bosphorus shore.

Abdül Hamit was paranoid, and for good reason. Fate determined that his fears would come true. When eventually deposed, he left this wooden palace in April 1909 and boarded a train that took him to house arrest in Ottoman Salonika (today Thessaloniki, in Greece). He was later allowed by the Young Turks' government to return to İstanbul and live out his years in Beylerbeyi Sarayı, on the Asian shore of the Bosphorus.

This place was to be associated with more dolorous history. The last sultan of the Ottoman Empire, Mehmet V (Vahideddin), lived here until, at 6 am on 11 November 1922, he and his first chamberlain, bandmaster, doctor, two secretaries, valet, barber and two eunuchs accompanied by trunks full of jewels, gold and antiques, boarded two British Red Cross ambulances for the secret journey to the naval dockyard at Tophane. There they boarded the British battleship HMS *Malaya* for a trip into exile, ending the Ottoman Empire forever. On the way to the quay one of the tyres on the sultan's ambulance went flat; while it was being changed, the 'Shadow of God on Earth' quaked, fearing that he might be discovered.

In the republican era, the Yıldız Şale has served as a guesthouse for visiting heads of state, including Charles de Gaulle, Pope Paul VI and the Empress Soraya of Iran. As you enter the palace, a guide will approach and give you the tour, which is required.

The first section you visit was the original chalet, built in 1882. The first room on the tour was used by Abdül Hamit's mother for her religious devotions, the second was her guest reception room, with a very fine mosaic tabletop. Then comes a women's resting room, and afterwards a tearoom with furniture marked with a gold star on a blue background, which reminds one that this is the 'star' *(yıldız)* chalet.

In 1898 the chalet was expanded, and the older section became the harem (with steel doors), while the new section was the *selamlık* (male quarters). In the selamlık are a bathroom with tiles from the Yıldız Porcelain Factory, and several reception rooms, one of which has furniture made by Abdül Hamit himself, an accomplished woodworker. The grand hall of the selamlık is vast, its floor covered by a 7½-tonne Hereke carpet woven just for this room. So huge is the rug that it had to be brought in through the far (north) wall before the building was finished and the wall was closed.

Merasim Köşkü Other buildings at Yıldız include the Merasim Köşkü, or Ceremonial Kiosk and barracks. Part of the kiosk was restored in 1988 and opened as the **İstanbul Şehir Müzesi** (İstanbul City Museum), open daily except Thursday from 9 am to 4.30 pm; admission costs US$1. It's reached from Barbaros Bulvarı, the road running along the south side of the park, not from within the park itself.

Yıldız Sarayı Müzesi The carpentry shop *(marangozhane)* at Yıldız, where Sultan Abdül Hamit II liked to lay down the burdens of rank and office, pick up chisel and mallet and make furniture, is now a museum (☎ 212-258 3080, extension 280; closed Monday and Tuesday). It houses rare porcelain vases and urns, and some of the sultan's joinery projects.

Onward Transport After seeing Yıldız, you can take a bus or dolmuş north to Bebek and Rumeli Hisarı, or return to Beşiktaş to catch a shuttle ferry over to Üsküdar, on the Asian side, in order to continue your sightseeing. The ferries operate every 15 or 20 minutes in each direction, from 6 am to midnight. There are also boats between Üsküdar and Eminönü. Ferries going to Eminönü may bear the sign 'Köprü' or 'Bridge', meaning the Galata Bridge.

Ortaköy

Literally 'middle village', this Bosphorus suburb has an interesting ethnic history in which church, synagogue and mosque coexist peacefully in its narrow streets. Today it is a trendy gathering-place for the young and hip, with art galleries, chic cafebars, and boutiques selling antiques, carpets and jewellery. On warm Sundays, artisans display their wares in the narrow streets in an impromptu art-and-craft show.

Get out of the bus or dolmuş at Osmanzade Sokak, near the doorway to the Etz Ahayim Synagogue. The synagogue has been here since 1660, though the current building dates from 1941, when the old one was destroyed by a disastrous fire. The Church of Hagios Phocas (1856) is a short distance north of it.

Walk east from the synagogue (toward the Bosphorus). *The Wall*, against the wall of the synagogue, is a cafe-bar with dancing and beer for US$1.50, local drinks for US$3. *İlhami'nin Yeri* (İlhami's Place) is a full-service restaurant specialising in seafood. Meat, fish and *kalamar* (squid) dishes are usually available for about US$4 to US$8 each. Osmanzade Sokak has other cafe-bar-restaurants as well, including the *Vito Internet Café* (☎ 212-227 6598, Osmanzade Sokak 13).

The streets near Osmanzade Sokak have more browsing, eating and drinking possibilities. On Yelkovan Sokak, look for the *Çardak Café*, which sometimes has live music, and *Café-Bar Maria*, which serves cappuccino at outdoor tables in summer, sıcak şarap (mulled wine) in winter.

Alaturka (☎ 212-258 7924, Hazine Sokak 8) is Ortaköy's most popular cafe-restaurant, serving light meals for about US$4 to US$6, full meals for around US$8 to US$10.

At the water's edge by the ornate mosque called the **Ortaköy Camii** are terrace cafes (the *Çadır* is most popular), their open-air tables enjoying views of the Bosphorus and the mosque. Officially named the Büyük Mecidiye Camii, the eclectic-Baroque mosque is the work of Nikogos Balyan, architect of Dolmabahçe Sarayı, who designed it for Sultan Abdül Mecit in 1854. Within the mosque hang several masterful examples of Arabic calligraphy executed by the sultan, who was an accomplished calligrapher.

Fast food follows the crowd, and it has come to Ortaköy in the form of *Burger King*, in a garish yellow building, and *McDonald's*. Next to the McDonald's on Mecidiye Köprüsü Sokak is a row of snack stands selling *kumpir*, big baked potatoes topped with various sauces and condiments; *gözleme*, Turkish crêpes; and *midye tavası*, stuffed mussels which can be the equivalent of gastroenteritic hand grenades.

Bebek & Rumeli Hisarı

Bebek (see the Greater İstanbul Map) is a prosperous suburb of İstanbul with a surprising foreign and academic presence because of Boğaziçi Üniversitesi (Bosphorus University). A ring ferry service here joins Bebek with Kanlıca and Anadolu Hisarı on the Asian shore.

About 1.5km north of Bebek centre is Rumeli Hisarı, the Fortress of Europe. The fortress is open from 9.30 am to 5 pm daily; closed on Monday. Admission costs US$2.50, half-price on Sunday and holidays. Within the walls are park-like grounds, an open-air theatre and the minaret of a ruined mosque. Stairs lead up to the ramparts and towers.

Here at the narrowest part of the Bosphorus, Mehmet the Conqueror had this fortress built in a mere four months during 1452, in preparation for his planned siege of Byzantine Constantinople. To speed its completion in line with his impatience to conquer Con-

stantinople, Mehmet the Conqueror ordered each of his three viziers to take responsibility for one of the three main towers. If the tower's construction was not completed on schedule, the vizier would pay with his life, or so legend has it. Not surprisingly, the work was completed on time, with Mehmet's three generals competing fiercely with one another to finish.

Once completed, Rumeli Hisarı, in concert with Anadolu Hisarı on the Asian shore just opposite, controlled all traffic on the Bosphorus, and cut the city off from re-supply by sea from the north.

The mighty fortress's useful military life lasted less than one year. After the conquest of Constantinople, it was used as a glorified Bosphorus toll booth for a while, then as a barracks, later as a prison, and finally as an open-air theatre, but never again as a fortress.

Above the town you'll notice the New England 19th-century-style architecture of the **Boğaziçi Üniversitesi** (Bosphorus University) on a hilltop above the town of Bebek. Founded as Robert College in the mid-19th century by the American Board of Foreign Missions, the college had an important influence on the modernisation of political, social, economic and scientific thought in Turkey. Though donated by the board to the Turkish Republic in the early 1970s, instruction is still in English and Turkish.

Places to Eat On the shore just north of Rumeli Hisarı is the *Karaca Fish Restaurant (☎ 212-265 2968, Yahya Kemal Caddesi 10)*, with fine Bosphorus views, excellent fish and squid and a plethora of mezes; avoid shrimp, which are, as everywhere in Turkey, very expensive for what you get. Expect to pay US$12 to US$24 per person with *rakı*. Cheaper alternatives – snack stands and pastry shops – are nearby.

Emirgan & Yeniköy

Each spring a **tulip festival** takes place in Emirgan, a wealthy suburb north of the Fatih Bridge. North of Emirgan, at İstinye, is a cove with a dry dock. A ring ferry service a stop 600m inland along Sular Caddesi. The trip takes less than half an hour.

Heading south, it's easy enough to get back to Taksim Square by dolmuş (the stop is on Sular Caddesi 500m inland from the mosque); other dolmuş services also head south along the shore for a few kilometres before turning inland, like the Taksim service, at Büyükdere, Tarabya or İstinye to reach their destinations. Thus they are of little use if you want to stop at Rumeli Hisarı, Bebek, Ortaköy, Yıldız Parkı or Çırağan Sarayı on your trip south.

Bus No 25A, 'Rumelikavağı-Beşiktaş', and Bus No 25E, 'Sarıyer-Eminönü', are the exceptions, driving along the shore road via Bebek and Rumeli Hisarı back to the Golden Horn in a few hours. But this shore service is infrequent compared to the inland services, as the narrow shore road, busy with traffic, takes much longer than the inland route.

If you're in doubt as to whether a vehicle follows the shore all the way south, say 'Sahilden mi gidiyor?' (sah-heel-DEHN mee gee-dee-yohr, 'Does it go along the shore?') to the driver. If he says 'Yukarıdan' (yoo-kah-ruh-DAHN, 'Via the heights') you'll know it goes inland, not along the shore.

Rumeli Kavağı

This, the village farthest north on the European shore (see the Greater İstanbul Map), is a sleepy place that gets most of its excitement from the arrival and departure of the ferry. There is a little public beach named **Altınkum** near the village. North of Rumeli Kavağı is a military zone, off limits to casual visitors.

Dolmuşes for Rumeli Kavağı leave from Sular Caddesi in Sarıyer, 500m inland from the mosque.

Kilyos

İstanbul's coastal resort of Kilyos (see the Greater İstanbul Map) is a favourite place for a swim in the chilly waters of the Black Sea, or a leisurely meal at any time of year. You can even stay overnight if you like.

Dolmuşes and buses from Sarıyer make the trip over the hills to Kilyos in less than a half hour, passing little impromptu open-air roadside restaurants featuring *kuzu çevirme* (spit-roasted lamb).

Kilyos' best beach is the fenced one in front of the Turban Kilyos Moteli, open daily in warm weather from 8 am to 6 pm for US$3.50 per person. It gets very crowded on summer weekends, but it's not bad during the week. Parking costs US$2, so if you drive, park elsewhere in the village and walk to the beach.

Note that there can be a deadly undertow on Black Sea beaches. Swim only in protected areas or where there is an attentive lifeguard, don't swim alone, and be on guard against undertow and riptide.

Places to Stay & Eat On summer weekends all Kilyos lodgings are likely to be filled from advance reservations. You will have a better chance of finding a room if you plan your visit for the middle of the week, reserve ahead, or visit outside the high season (which lasts from mid-July to the end of August). Many of these hotels are adjuncts to their more popular restaurants; all offer two-star comforts, and charge around US$35 for a double room with private bath and breakfast in summer. The restaurants are all genteel, offering good food and drink for US$10 to US$20 per person.

Walk uphill from the bus and dolmuş stops to find the *Yuva Motel & Restaurant* (☎ 212-201 1043, Kale Caddesi 28). All rooms have little porches, but the rooms on the sea side are preferable.

Though its name means 'abundance' in Turkish, the two-star 42-room *Gurup Hotel* (☎ 212-201 1194, fax 201 1266, Kale Caddesi 21/1) is also often filled by British holiday groups (its other Turkish meaning) who like its swimming pool and jacuzzi.

The *Erzurumlu Otel Restaurant* (☎ 212-201 1003, fax 201 1108, Kale Caddesi 77) is next up the hill, and also has rooms with splendid views.

The modernised 35-room *Kilyos Kale Hotel* (☎ 212-201 1818, fax 201 1823, Kale

Caddesi 78) has a swimming pool as well as comfortable rooms with sea views.

The **Yonca Hotel** *(☎ 212-201 1018, Kale Caddesi 32)* has some old fashioned but tidy rooms to rent, but its main business is its seafood restaurant.

For cheaper food, look down in the village. *Mustafa'nın Yeri Karadeniz Pide,* on the left as you walk from the bus stop to the beach, serves fresh pide; the *Çimen Lokantası,* a bit farther along, has a variety of dishes, and *Hünkâr Börek,* right by the beach entrance, serves the flaky pastry that makes such a good and cheap filling snack.

Getting There & Away Kilyos is 35km north of the Galata Bridge, and can take several hours to reach in moderately heavy traffic. All public transport comes through Sarıyer; see Getting There & Away in that section (earlier) for details.

SIGHTS ON THE ASIAN SHORE

The Asian shore of the Bosphorus has a number of possibilities for interesting excursions, with the advantage that you will meet far fewer tourists than in European İstanbul.

Crossing the Bosphorus

To reach the Asian shore, hop on the Üsküdar ferry from Eminönü, which runs every 15 or 20 minutes between 6 am and midnight, even more frequently during rush hours, for US$0.50. A similarly frequent ferry service operates between Beşiktaş and Üsküdar. From Kabataş, just south of Dolmabahçe Sarayı, ferries run to Üsküdar every 30 minutes on the hour and half-hour from 7 am to 8 pm. There are also city buses and dolmuşes departing from Taksim Square for Üsküdar, but the ferries are faster and more enjoyable.

If you take the ferry to Üsküdar, you'll notice **Kız Kulesi** (the Maiden's Tower, and also known as Leander's Tower in English; Maps 1 & 9) to the south just off the Asian mainland. The tower was a toll booth and defence point in ancient times; the Bosphorus could be closed off by means of a chain

stretching from here to Seraglio Point. The tower has nothing to do with Leander, who was no maiden, and who swam not the Bosphorus but the Hellespont (Dardanelles), 340km from here.

The tower is subject to the usual legend: oracle says maiden will die by snakebite; concerned father puts maiden in snake-proof tower; fruit vendor comes by boat, sells basket of fruit (complete with snake) to maiden, who gets hers. The legend seems to crop up wherever there are offshore towers and maidens, and then we've got to repeat them in guidebooks.

Another landmark is the tall spear of a television tower on Büyük Çamlıca a hilltop lookout you can visit from Üsküdar.

A landmark especially for travellers is the German-style **Haydarpaşa station**, south of Üsküdar, the city's terminal for Asian trains. During the late 19th century, when Kaiser Wilhelm was trying to charm the sultan into economic and military cooperation, he gave him the station as a little gift.

You will also notice the large **Selimiye Kışlası** (Selimiye Barracks, Map 1), a square building with towers at the corners. It dates from the early 19th century, when Selim III and Mahmut II re-organised the Ottoman armed forces along European lines. Not far away is the **Selimiye Camii** (1805) and the storybook Ottoman rest home for ageing palace ladies, which is now used by Marmara University.

Üsküdar (Map 9)

Üsküdar (ER-sker-dahr) is the Turkish form of the name Scutari. Legend has it that the first ancient colonists established themselves at Chalcedon, the modern Kadıköy, south of Üsküdar. Byzas, bearing the oracle's message to found a colony 'Opposite the blind', thought the Chalcedonites blind to the advantages of Seraglio Point as a town site, and founded his town on the European shore. Still, people have lived on this, the Asian shore, longer than they've lived on the European side.

Ortaköy Camii beneath the Bosphorus Bridge.

EDDIE GERALD

Houses overlooking the Bosphorus.

PETER PTSCHELINZEW

One of many harbours along the Bosphorus.

KIMBERLY GRANT

Selimiye Camii, Mimar Sinan's masterpiece, as seen from the Tunca River Bridge, Edirne.

signed by Sarkis Balyan for Sultan Abdül Mecit. There had been imperial kiosks here for centuries. In 1833, the Ottoman and Russian empires signed a historic peace treaty here which took its name, the Treaty of Unkiar Skelessi, from the place. The peace lasted 20 years.

From Beykoz, a road heads eastward towards the Polish village of Polonezköy and the Black Sea beach resort of Şile (see the Şile section later in this chapter). Much of the land along the Bosphorus shore north of Beykoz is in a military zone, and you may be denied entry. You can, however, reach the village of Anadolu Kavağı by ferry, either on the Bosphorus touristic cruise from Eminönü or from Sarıyer and Rumeli Kavağı on the European shore.

Polonezköy

What's a Polish village doing in İstanbul? Polonezköy is a quaint and dying anachronism, a relic of 19th-century politics and the Crimean War.

Founded in 1842, it was originally named Adampol after Prince Adam Jerzy Czartoryski (1770-1861), who was once the Imperial Russian foreign minister and later head of a short-lived Polish revolutionary government (1830-31). When the revolution failed, he bought land in the Ottoman Empire for some of his former soldiers. In 1853 Russia provoked war with the Ottoman Empire; Britain, France and Sardinia joined the Ottomans in battling the Russians in the Crimea. The men of Adampol organised a regiment of Ottoman Cossacks and fought with such bravery that Sultan Abdül Mecit exempted them and their heirs from taxation.

A generation ago, Polish was still the lingua franca in the village, but with modern media, the language and customs of old Poland are dying out. Once Poles in a time warp, the people of Polonezköy are now Turkish citizens of Polish ancestry. Even so, the 'Polish Pope', John Paul II, visited the village in 1979.

For more than a century, city people would come here for authentic Polish farm food: wild mushrooms, wild boar, omelettes with eggs from free-range chickens and excellent fruit. Farmhouses provided simple lodgings as well as meals, and this attracted another, non-culinary clientele: lovers who, unable to show a marriage licence, could not shack up in İstanbul's hotels.

Alas, Polonezköy has lost much of its charm. Simple meals and lodgings are still available, but at relatively high prices; lovers still make up a hefty segment of the trade. Transport is also a problem; it's only easily reached if you have your own vehicle. If you do, stop and take a turn through the village, have a look at the tiny church and ponder the vicissitudes of history.

Şile

Seaside getaways from İstanbul tend to be disappointing. Ataköy and Florya, on the Sea of Marmara, are crowded and citified. Kilyos is small and crowded. But Şile, 72km north-east of Üsküdar on the Black Sea coast, has long sand beaches and a fairly laid-back atmosphere – at least on weekdays.

Buses (US$2.50) depart from the western side of Üsküdar's main square on the hour from 9 am to 4 pm for the two-hour journey.

Known as Kalpe in classical times, Şile was a port of call for ships sailing east from the Bosphorus. As an important port, it was visited by Xenophon and his Ten Thousand on their way back to Greece from their disastrous campaign against Artaxerxes II of Persia in the 4th century BC. Unable to find ships to sail them to Greece, Xenophon and his men marched to Chrysopolis (Üsküdar) along the route now followed by the modern road.

Şile's other claim to fame is *Şile bezi*, an open-weave cotton cloth with hand embroidery, usually made up into shirts and blouses, which are wonderfully cool in the summer heat.

Numerous hotels provide accommodation, with higher prices on weekends. The ***Kumbaba Hotel*** (☎ *216-711 1038*), 2km south of town, is among the oldest, yet still the most congenial. There are 40 rooms, for

US$50 to US$70 a double, and a camping ground as well. The similarly priced two-star **Değirmen Hotel** (☎ 216-711 5048, fax 711 5248, Plaj Yolu 24) has two stars, 76 rooms, restaurants and bars, and overlooks the beach. The aptly-named **Resort Hotel** (☎ 216-711 3627, fax 711 4003, Uzunkum, Ağlayan Kaya Mevkii) is a four-star lodging.

As İstanbul expands, so do the getaway spots on its outskirts. If Şile is too busy for you, hop on the bus to the village of **Ağva**, less than an hour eastward on the coast. Accommodation is limited, but there are good possibilities for camping – and peace and quiet.

Kızıl Adalar

Kızıl Adalar (Red Islands) is the Turkish name for what in English are known as the Princes' Islands. Most İstanbullus, however, get along with Adalar (The Islands) as it's the only archipelago around. The islands lie about 20km south-east of the city in the Sea of Marmara.

In Byzantine times, refractory princes, deposed monarchs and others whose bodies had outlived their roles were interned here. A Greek Orthodox monastery and seminary on Heybeliada turned out Orthodox priests until the 1970s.

In the 19th century the Ottoman business community of Greeks, Jews and Armenians favoured the islands as summer resorts. Many of the fine Victorian villas built by these wealthy Ottomans survive, and make the larger islands, Büyükada and Heybeliada, charming places.

When you visit the islands, bear in mind that there's no naturally occurring fresh water here. Use water sparingly as all water must be brought from the mainland.

Touring the Islands

At least 10 ferries (US$1.30) run to the islands each day from 7 am to 11.30 pm, departing from Sirkeci's 'Adalar İskelesi' dock, east of the dock for car ferries to Harem. On weekdays there are additional boats for commuters. On summer week-ends, board the vessel and seize a seat at least half an hour before departure time unless you want to stand the whole way.

You can also take a fast catamaran from Eminönü or Kabataş to Bostancı, then another from Bostancı to Büyükada, but you save little time, and the cost is much higher.

·The ferry steams away from Sirkeci, out of the Golden Horn and around Saray Burnu, offering fine views of Topkapı Sarayı, Aya Sofya and the Sultan Ahmet Camii on the right, and Üsküdar, Haydarpaşa and Kadıköy to the left. After about 45 minutes, the ferry reaches Kınalı, the first small island; another half hour brings you to Heybeli, the second-largest island, and another 15 minutes to Büyükada, the largest. Some express ferries go directly to Büyükada, from which there are occasional ferries to Heybeli, and fast catamarans to Bostancı on the Asian shore.

Büyükada

The 'Great Island's' splendid Victoriana greets you as you approach by sea, its gingerbread villas climbing up the slopes of the hill and the bulbous twin domes of the Splendid Otel providing an unmistakable landmark.

Only a few minutes after landing, you'll realise Büyükada's surprise: there are no cars! Except for the necessary police, fire and sanitation vehicles, transportation is by bicycle, horse-drawn carriage and foot, as in centuries past.

Walk from the ferry to the clock tower in İskele Meydanı (Dock Square). The market district is to the left along Recep Koç Caddesi. For a stroll up the hill and through the lovely old houses, bear right onto 23 Nisan Caddesi. If you need a goal for your wanderings, head for the Greek Monastery of St George, in the 'saddle' between Büyükada's two highest hills. Bicycles are available for rent (kiralık bisiklet) in several shops, and shops on the market street can provide the wherewithal for picnics, though food is obviously cheaper on the mainland.

Just to the left of the square by the clock tower is the waiting area for horse-drawn sunflowers, grown for their seeds and cooking oil, and for Edirne.

Edirne (eh-DEER-neh), 235km (2½ hours) north-west of İstanbul along the fast Trans European Motorway (TEM), is the traditional way station on the road from the Bosphorus to Europe. Edirne was the second capital city (after Bursa) of the Ottoman Empire, and an important staging-point for the sultan's annual military campaigns in Europe. As such it was graced with fine mosques, baths and caravanserais, including the serene Selimiye Camii, masterwork of the great Sinan.

History

The Roman emperor Hadrian founded Edirne in the 2nd century as Hadrianopolis. The town's name was later shortened by Europeans to Adrianople, and later by the Turks to Edirne.

The Ottoman state, an emirate founded around 1288 in north-west Anatolia, used Bursa as its capital. By the mid-1300s, the Ottomans had grown substantially in power and size, and were looking for new conquests. The mighty walls of Constantinople were beyond their powers, but they crossed the Dardanelles and captured Adrianople in 1363, making it their new capital.

For almost 100 years, this was the city from which the Ottoman sultan set out on his campaigns to Europe and Asia. When at last the time was ripe for the final conquest of the Byzantine Empire, Mehmet the Conqueror rode out from Edirne on the Via Ignatia to Constantinople.

When the Ottoman Empire disintegrated after WWI, the Allies granted all of Trakya to the Greek kingdom. In the summer of 1920, Greek armies occupied Edirne, but several years later Atatürk's republican armies drove them out, and the Treaty of Lausanne left Edirne and eastern Trakya to the Turks.

Orientation

The centre of town is Hürriyet Meydanı, or Freedom Square, at the intersection of the two main streets, Saraçlar/Hükümet Cad-

desi and Talat Paşa Caddesi. Just north-east of the square is the Üçşerefeli Cami. Going east along Talat Paşa Caddesi and north-east along Mimar Sinan Caddesi will bring you to Edirne's masterpiece, the Selimiye Camii. On the way to the Selimiye, you'll pass the Eski Cami. South of Hürriyet Square is the Ali Paşa Çarşısı, Edirne's largest covered bazaar.

The *otogar* (bus station) is 2km south-east of the Eski Cami on the old highway (D 100) to Istanbul. The main dolmuş station downtown is behind (east of) the Hotel Kervansaray.

Information

The Ministry of Tourism's Office (☎ 284-225 1518, 213 9208, fax 225 2518), Hürriyet Meydanı 17, is just off the main square, a half-block south-west of the Üçşerefeli Cami.

Kaleiçi

The Old Town, called Kaleiçi (Within the Fortress), was the original medieval town with streets laid out on a grid plan. The area is bounded by Saraçlar Caddesi in the east, Talat Paşa Caddesi to the north and the railway line to the south.

Walk south along Maarif Caddesi, the street beside the tourism office, past the Anıl, Park and Efe hotels to pass some fine if fragile old Ottoman wooden houses, designed in an ornate style known as *Edirnekâri,* and some abandoned churches. Continue on and at the southern end of Maarif Caddesi you will come to Edirne's great synagogue. Though presently a sad reminder of vanished grandeur, the synagogue is scheduled for restoration by Thracian University. There are other fine old houses along Cumhuriyet Caddesi, which crosses Maarif Caddesi north of the synagogue.

Fragments of Byzantine city walls are still visible on the edges of Kaleiçi, down by the Tunca River.

Üçşerefeli Cami

The name means 'mosque with three galleries (balconies)'. Actually it's one of the mosque's four minarets that has the three balconies. The minarets, built at different times, are all quite different.

Construction was begun in 1440 and finished by 1447. Its design shows the transition from the Selçuk Turkish-style mosques of Konya and Bursa to a truly Ottoman style, which would be perfected later in İstanbul. In the Selçuk style, smaller domes are mounted on square rooms. At the Üçşerefeli, the wide (24m) dome is mounted on a hexagonal drum and supported by two walls and two pillars. Keep this transitional style in mind as you visit Edirne's other mosques which reflect earlier or later styles.

The courtyard, with its central *şadırvan* (ablutions fountain), was an innovation in mosque architecture which came to be standard in the great Ottoman mosques. The architect's genius is best appreciated if you enter the mosque across the courtyard from the west, but the courtyard is presently closed for restoration, and the mosque itself will continue to be filled with scaffolding for years to come.

Across the street from the mosque is the **Sokollu Mehmet Paşa Hamamı** or Turkish baths, built in the late 1500s and still in use. Designed by the great Mimar Sinan for Grand Vizier Sokollu Mehmet Paşa, it is a *çifte hamam* (twin baths) with identical but separate sections for men *(erkekler kısmı)* and women *(kadınlar kısmı)*. Opening hours are from 6 am to 10 pm. Simple admission costs US$2, washing by an attendant US$3, a massage US$4.

Eski Cami

From Hürriyet Meydanı, walk east on Talat Paşa Asfaltı to the Eski Cami or Old Mosque. On your way you'll pass the *bedesten* (covered market for the sale of valuable goods) across the park on your right. Dating from 1418, it's now known as the **Bedesten Çarşısı**, or Bedesten Bazaar, and is still filled with shops. Behind it to the east is the Rüstem Paşa Hanı, a grand caravanserai built 100 years after the bedesten.

The Eski Cami (1414) exemplifies one of two principal mosque styles used by the Ot-

tomans in their earlier capital, Bursa. Like Bursa's great Ulu Cami, the Eski Cami has rows of arches and pillars supporting a series of small domes. Inside, there's a marvellous mihrab and huge calligraphic inscriptions on the walls. The columns at the front of the mosque were lifted from some Roman building, a common practice over the centuries.

Selimiye Camii

Up the hill to the north-east past the Eski Cami stands the Selimiye Camii (1569-1575), the finest work of the great Ottoman architect Mimar Sinan – or so the architect himself believed (see the special section on Ottoman Mosques in the Facts about İstanbul chapter). Constructed for Sultan Selim II (1566-74) and finished just after the sultan's death, this mosque is smaller than Sinan's earlier (1557), tremendous Süleymaniye Camii in İstanbul, but more elegant and harmonious. Crowning its small hill, it was meant to dominate the town and be easily visible from all approaches across the rolling Thracian landscape.

To fully appreciate its excellence you should enter it from the west as the architect intended. Walk up the street and through the courtyard rather than through the park and the *arasta* (shops), a financially necessary but obtrusive later addition made during the reign of Murat III.

The harmony and serenity of this most symmetrical of mosques surrounds you as you enter. The broad, lofty dome – at 31.5m, wider than that of Istanbul's Ayasofya by a few centimetres – is supported by eight pillars, as well as arches and external buttresses. The interior is surprisingly spacious and the walls, because they bear only a portion of the dome's weight, can be filled with windows, thus admitting plentiful light to the wide, airy central space.

Beneath the main dome is the *kürsü*, or prayer-reader's platform, and beneath that is a fountain, which gives a soothing sound of running water to the quiet interior.

As you might expect, the interior furnishings of the Selimiye Camii are exquisite, from the delicately carved marble mimber (pulpit) to the outstanding İznik faïence in and around the mihrab.

In contrast to its many 'twinnings' (pairs of windows, columns etc), the north side of the mosque (near the Türk-İslam Eserleri Müzesi) has playful groupings of three – arches, domes, niches etc; and even triads of pairs (windows).

Part of the Selimiye's excellent effect comes from its four slender, very tall (71m) minarets, fluted to emphasise their height. You'll notice that each is *üçşerefeli*, or built with three balconies – Sinan's respectful acknowledgment, perhaps, to his predecessor, the architect of the Üçşerefeli Cami.

Museums

The Selimiye's *medrese* (theological seminary) now houses the **Türk-İslam Eserleri Müzesi** (Turkish & Islamic Arts Museum), open daily except Monday from 8 am to noon and 1 to 5 pm, for US$1. Collections, labelled in Turkish only, are eclectic and inclusive, from weapons and chain mail through dervish arts and crafts to the Balkan Wars, locally made stockings and kitchen utensils.

The **Arkeoloji ve Etnoloji Müzesi** (Archaeological & Ethnological Museum) is across the street from the Selimiye Camii, a few steps north-east of the Türk-İslam Eserleri Müzesi. It's open from 8 am to noon and 1 to 5 pm, for US$1.

Ali Paşa Çarşısı

The covered market called the Ali Paşa Çarşısı, east of Maarif Caddesi near Sarac Caddesi, was designed by Sinan, built in 1569, restored in 1805, 1867 and 1947, destroyed by fire in 1992 and again restored in 1994-97. There's an entrance off Hürriyet Meydanı to the left of the tourism office.

River Walks

Follow Saraçlar Caddesi south and out of town, under the railway line and across an Ottoman stone humpback bridge spanning the Tunca River. A longer Ottoman bridge crosses the Meriç to the south. In between

the two are several restaurants, tea gardens and bars good for an outdoor drink or a meal in good weather (see Places to Eat).

On the south side of the Meriç bridge are even better, more scenic restaurants and tea gardens such as the *Emirgan*, opposite the restored Ottoman *çeşme* (fountain) of Hacı Adil Bey, with welcome shade and fine sunset views of the river and bridge.

Muradiye Camii

A short walk (10 to 15 minutes) north-east of the Selimiye along Mimar Sinan Caddesi brings you to the Muradiye Camii, a mosque built on the orders of Sultan Murat II. Finished in 1436, it was once the centre of a Mevlevi (Whirling Dervish) lodge. The small cupola atop the main dome is unusual. The mosque's T-shaped plan with twin *eyvans* (niche-like rooms) is reminiscent of the Yeşil Cami in Bursa, and its fine İznik tiles, especially in the mihrab, remind one that Bursa (near İznik) was the first Ottoman capital and Edirne, the second. Turkish mosque architecture would change dramatically after the Turks conquered Constantinople (1453) and studied the Aya Sofya.

Sarayiçi

Clearly visible from the Muradiye's hilltop perch is the grassy lowland swath of **Sarayiçi** (Within the Palace). This scrub-covered island, once the sultans' hunting preserve, is the site of the famous annual Kırkpınar oiled wrestling matches.

Next to the rather drab modern stadium is a stone tower with a pointed roof, the **Kasr-i Adalet** (Justice Hall, 1561), dating from the time of Süleyman the Magnificent, with two stones in front of it. On one stone, the *Seng-i Hürmet* (Stone of Respect), petitioners would put their petitions to the sultan to be collected by his staff. On the other, the *Seng-i İbret* (Stone of Warning), would be displayed the heads of high court officers who had lost the sultan's confidence in a major way.

Not far away are the ruins of the **Eski Saray** (Old Palace). Begun by Sultan Beyazıt

II in 1450, this palace once rivalled İstanbul's Topkapı in luxury and size. Today, little is left but a few ruins: a kitchen, a hamam etc, some of which is off limits in a military zone.

Walk west along the raised flood-control levee (cars can follow a curving paved road) to the Beyazıt II Külliyesi, the imperial mosque of Sultan Beyazıt II (1481-1512).

Beyazıt II Külliyesi

Building mosque complexes was the way the Ottomans populated and expanded their cities. A site would be chosen on the outskirts of a populated area and workers employed for construction. Many of the workers and their families would settle near the mosque construction, thereby attracting necessary services (grocers, cookshops, tailors etc) on which they would spend their pay. The scheme seems not to have worked for the İkinci Beyazıt Külliyesi, built from 1484 to 1488, remains on Edirne's outskirts, unpopulated and little used.

The architect of the complex, one Hayrettin, did a creditable job, though he was obviously no Sinan. The mosque's style is between that of the Üçşerefeli and the Selimiye, moving back a bit rather than advancing: its large prayer hall has one large dome, as do Bursa's mosques, but it has a courtyard and şadırvan like the Üçşerefeli Cami's. Though of a high standard, Hayrettin's work can't compare with the Selimiye, built less than a century later.

The mosque's külliye is extensive and includes a *tabhane* (hostel for travellers), medrese, bakery, *imaret* (soup kitchen), *tımarhane* (insane asylum) and *darüşşifa* (hospital). These buildings were fully restored in the late 1970s, though time has obviously been at work since then.

Places to Stay

Behind the tourism office, the *Otel Anıl* (☎ 284-212 1782, *Maarif Caddesi 8*) is a grand old Edirne townhouse now rundown. Clean beds cost US$4 per person in waterless rooms. The *Konak* (☎ 284-212 1348) next door is under restoration.

A block south of the tourism office, the *Park Hotel* (☎ 284-225 4610, fax 225 4635, *Maarif Caddesi 7*) charges US$22/30 a single/double with bath, TV and breakfast. A few metres south at No 13, the cheaper *Efe Hotel* (☎ 284-213 6166, fax 212 9446) has newish rooms with shower and TV (but no air-con) for US$18/26.

The *Otel Şaban Açıkgöz* (☎ 284-213 1404, fax 213 4516, *Tahmis Meydanı Çilingir Caddesi 9*) is near the park next to the Eski Cami, with decent rooms for US$16/23 with shower, TV and breakfast.

The top hotel, right in the centre, is the two-star, 83-room *Sultan Oteli* (☎ 284-225 1372, fax 225 5763, *Talat Paşa Caddesi 170*), a half-block west of the tourism office. Rooms with shower, TV, good reading lamps and a good breakfast cost US$30/45. There's plentiful parking in the hotel's rear car park.

Places to Eat

Edirne has many small eateries, especially *köftecis* (serving grilled lamb meatballs) and *ciğercis* (serving fried liver). Among the brightest and best is the *Serhad Köftecisi* on Saraçlar Caddesi just off Hürriyet Meydanı, where köfte with yoghurt, salad, bread and drink costs US$3.

The *Gaziantep Kebapçısı*, almost next to the tourism office, is as good a place as any for grilled kebaps and salads (no alcohol) for around US$3 or US$4 per meal. Even nicer, and not much more expensive, is the *Modern Park Restaurant* on the ground floor of the Park Hotel at Maarif Caddesi 7, just around the corner and a block down the street.

A row of small restaurants faces a tiny park west of the Rüstempaşa Kervansarayı by the Hotel Şaban Açıkgöz. The *Serhad 1 Köftecisi* is the nicest of the four köftecis here; the *Polat Lokantası* is best for stews, but serves grilled meats as well.

Facing these places, the name is the menu at the *Edirne Lahmacun Döner Pide*, a more modern place.

For fancier meals with alcoholic drinks, try the *Çatı Lokantası* across Talat Paşa

Caddesi from the Sultan Oteli, or the *Aile Restaurant*, Saraçlar Caddesi, on the upper floor in the Belediye İş Hanı, just south of the PTT. The entrance is on the side street by the PTT. Kebaps, stews and other traditional Turkish dishes are served for US$5 or US$7 per meal.

More atmospheric, and only slightly more expensive, are the restaurants a five-minute walk south of the centre by the rivers. The *Gazi Baba II*, between the two Ottoman stone bridges on the road to the Greek border, has white tablecloth formality at moderate prices. The *Emirgan Aile Çay Bahçesi*, at the southern end of the Meriç bridge, serves snacks and light meals as well as soft drinks and the ubiquitous çay. Restaurants upriver from it – the *Villa* and *Lalezar* – serve more substantial meat as well as fish dishes outdoors in warm weather, for US$10 or US$12 per person, all inclusive.

Getting There & Away

From İstanbul, take a bus from Taksim, or the Metro from Aksaray to the otogar stop in Esenler, to reach the İstanbul international bus terminal (Uluslararası İstanbul Otogar), from which buses depart for Edirne every 20 minutes or so throughout the day, taking about 2½ hours to make the 235km journey. Tickets cost US$6. Once you reach Edirne's Otobüs Garajı (bus station), take a city bus, dolmuş or taxi for the final 2km to the Eski Cami or Hürriyet Meydanı in the city centre.

Trains between Edirne and İstanbul are slow, infrequent and inconvenient.

İznik & Bursa

Two historic cities on the south shore of the Sea of Marmara are within a few hours' pleasant travel of İstanbul.

İznik, the ancient city of Nicaea, is a beautiful lakeside farming town surrounded on all sides by huge Byzantine walls. At its heart are several beautiful mosques and historic buildings, one of them the great church in which two ecumenical church councils were held.

Bursa, the first Ottoman capital city, is famed for its early Ottoman architecture, its savoury lamb kebaps, its fresh fruit and chestnuts, and its modern industrial might.

Although fast catamarans and jet ferryboats whisk you from İstanbul south to the Sea of Marmara port town of Yalova in only an hour, it's very difficult to see both İznik and Bursa in a single day. Choose one or the other for a day trip, or plan to stay the night in Bursa if you want to see both. For transport details see Getting There & Away at the end of the Bursa section later.

İZNİK

The road from Yalova to İznik (population 18,000) runs along fertile green hills punctuated by tall, spiky cypress trees, passing peach orchards, cornfields and vineyards. The journey of 60km takes about one hour.

As you approach İznik you may notice fruit-packing plants among the orchards. You will certainly have admired the vast İznik Gölü (İznik Lake). Watch for the great Byzantine city walls: one entrance to the city is through the old İstanbul Kapısı (İstanbul Gate) on Atatürk Caddesi, which leads directly to the centre and the ruined Aya Sofya (Sancta Sophia Church), now a museum.

History

This ancient city may have been founded around 1000 BC. We know that it was revitalised by one of Alexander the Great's generals in 316 BC. Another of the generals, Lysimachus, soon got hold of it and named it after his wife Nikaea. By 74 BC the entire area had been incorporated into the Roman Empire.

Nicaea flourished under Rome; the emperors built new walls, temples, theatres and baths. But invasions by the Goths and the Persians brought ruin by 300 AD.

With the rise of Constantinople, Nicaea took on a new importance. In 325 AD, the First Ecumenical Council was held here to condemn the heresy of Arianism. During Justinian's reign, Nicaea was grandly refurbished and embellished with new buildings

EXCURSIONS

and defences, which served the city well a few centuries later when the Arabs invaded.

In 787 AD another Ecumenical Council, the seventh, was held in Nicaea's Sancta Sophia Church. The deliberations solved the problem of iconoclasm: henceforth it would be church policy not to destroy icons. Theologians who saw icons as 'images', prohibited by the Bible, were dismayed. But Byzantine artists were delighted, and went to work on their art with even more vigour.

Nicaea and Constantinople did, however, fall to the crusaders. During the period from 1204 to 1261 when a Latin king sat on the throne of Byzantium, the true Byzantine emperor Theodore Lascaris reigned over the 'Empire of Nicaea'. When the crusaders cleared out, the imperial capital moved back to Constantinople.

The Selçuk Turks had a flourishing empire in Central Anatolia before 1250, and various tribes of nomadic warriors had circulated near the walls of Nicaea during those times. In fact, Turkish soldiers had served as mercenaries in the interminable battles that raged among rival claimants to the Byzantine throne. At one point, a Byzantine battle over Nicaea ended with a Turkish emir as its ruler.

It was Orhan, son of Osman and first true sultan (1326-61) of the Ottoman Empire, who conquered İznik on 2 March 1331.

Sultan Selim I (1512-20) the Grim, rolled his armies over Azerbaijan in 1514 and took the Persian city of Tabriz. Packing up all of the region's artisans, he sent them westward to İznik. They brought with them a high level of expertise in the making of coloured tiles. Soon İznik's kilns were turning out faïence unequalled even today. The great period of İznik faïence continued almost to 1700. At one point, artisans were sent to Tunisia, then an Ottoman possession, to begin a high-quality faïence industry there.

The art of coloured tile-making is being revived in İznik today. Though new tiles make good purchases, 17th and 18th-century İznik tiles are considered antiquities, and cannot legally be exported from Turkey.

Orientation

Aya Sofya (known for centuries as Sancta, or Hagia Sophia), at the very centre, is a good vantage point from which to consider the town's Roman layout: two dead-straight boulevards, north-south (Atatürk Caddesi) and east-west (Kılıçaslan Caddesi), leading to the four principal gates *(kapı)* in the city walls. To the north is the İstanbul Kapısı, to the south the Yenişehir Kapısı, to the east Lefke Kapısı and to the west, the Göl Kapısı.

The otogar is a few blocks south-east of Aya Sofya.

Information

The Tourism Information Office (☎/fax 224-757 1933), Kılıçaslan Caddesi 130, is a block north-east of Aya Sofya, just before the Hotel Babacan, on the 2nd floor. Hours are from 9 am to noon and from 1 to 5.30 pm every day in the warm months, with shorter hours (and no hours on weekends) off season.

Aya Sofya

The present Aya Sofya, the Church of the Divine Wisdom, is the ruin of three different buildings. Inside is a mosaic floor and a mural of Jesus with Mary and John the Baptist which dates from the time of Justinian (during the 6th century). That original church was destroyed by earthquake in 1065 but later rebuilt. Mosaics were set into the walls at that time. With the Ottoman conquest (1331), the church became a mosque. A fire in the 16th century ruined everything, but reconstruction was carried out under the expert eye of Mimar Sinan, who added İznik tiles to the decoration.

Aya Sofya is open from 9 am to noon and from 2 to 5 pm daily, closed on Monday. If there's no-one about when you visit, continue with your tour. The key is probably at the museum. After visiting there, ask to be let into the church.

Behind Aya Sofya is the **II. Murat Hamamı**, also called the Hacı Hamza Hamamı, a Turkish bath constructed during the reign of Sultan Murat II, in the first half of the 15th century, and still in operation.

The Main Street

İznik's main street, Kılıçaslan Caddesi, leads eventually to the Lefke Kapısı (Lefke Gate). Walking from Aya Sofya, on the left is the Belediye Sarayı or Municipality office, with a sign out the front that reads (in Turkish) 'Our motto is, Clean City, Green City'. The motto is carried out in the small but agreeable park with its big poplars shading the commercial district from the hot summer sun.

A bit farther along on the left is the Hacı Özbek Camii, one of the town's oldest mosques, dating from 1332.

Walk one block south along Gündem Sokak, opposite the Hacı Özbek Camii, to reach the Süleyman Paşa Medresesi. Founded by Sultan Orhan shortly after he captured Nicaea, it has the distinction of being the very first college (actually a theological seminary) founded by a member of the Ottoman dynasty.

Back on the main street, continue eastward and soon, to the left, you can see the tile-covered minaret of the Yeşil Cami.

Yeşil Cami

Built in the year of Columbus' first voyage to America (1492), the Yeşil Cami, or Green Mosque, has Selçuk Turkish proportions influenced more by Persia (the Selçuk homeland) than by İstanbul. The green-glazed bricks of the minaret foreshadowed the tile industry that arose a few decades after the mosque was built.

Nilüfer Hatun İmareti

Across the road from the Yeşil Cami is the Nilüfer Hatun İmareti, or Soup Kitchen of Lady Nilüfer (1388), now set up as the town's archaeological museum. Opening hours are from 8.30 am to noon and 1 to 5 pm, closed Monday (usually). Admission costs US$1.25.

Begun in 1388, it was built by Sultan Murat I for his mother, Nilüfer Hatun, who was born a Byzantine princess but was married off to Orhan, second sultan of the Ottoman state, to cement a diplomatic alliance.

The front court is filled with marble statuary, bits of cornice and column, and similar archaeological flotsam and jetsam. In the lofty, cool halls are exhibits of İznik faïence, Ottoman weaponry, embroidery and calligraphy, and several items from the city's Roman past. Many of the little signs are in French and English, but you'll need to know the word *yüzyıl* (century), as in XVI Yüzyıl (16th century).

While at the museum, inquire about a visit to the Yeraltı Mezar (underground tomb), a Byzantine tomb on the outskirts. You must have a museum official accompany you with the key; there is a small charge for admission, and the official should receive a small tip. Also, you will have to haggle with a taxi driver for a return-trip price.

The little tomb, discovered by accident in the 1960s, has delightful Byzantine murals covering the walls and ceiling. There is another tomb nearby, but it's not really worth the bother or expense to see.

Across the road to the south of the museum is the Şeyh Kutbettin Camii (1492), in ruins.

City Walls

Return to Kılıçaslan Caddesi and continue east to the Lefke Kapısı. This charming old monument is actually three gates in a row, all dating from Byzantine times. The middle one has an inscription, which tells us it was built by Proconsul Plancius Varus in 123 AD. It's possible to clamber up to the top of the gate and the walls here, a good vantage point for inspecting the ancient walls.

Outside the gate is an **aqueduct** and the **tomb of Çandarlı Halil Hayrettin Paşa** (late 1300s), with the graves of many lesser mortals nearby.

Lefke, now a small town called Osmaneli, was a city of considerable size in Byzantine times.

Re-enter the city through the Lefke Kapısı, and turn left. Follow the walls south and west to a gate called the **Yenişehir Kapısı**. On the way you will pass near the ruined **Church of the Koimesis**, on the west side of Kaymakam S Taşkın Sokak, which dates from about 800 AD. Only some bits of the foundation remain, but it is famous as the burial place of the Byzantine emperor Theodore I Lascaris. When the crusaders took Constantinople in 1204, Lascaris fled to Nicaea and established his court here.

Lascaris built Nicaea's outer ring of walls, supported by over 100 towers and protected by a wide moat. No doubt he didn't trust the crusaders, having lost one city to them. The emperor died and was buried here, and when the court finally returned to the city on the Bosphorus in 1261, it was under the leadership of Michael VIII Palaeologus. Lascaris never made it back to his beloved capital.

Half a block east of the church is an *ayazma* or **sacred fountain** (it may also be referred to as a *yeraltı çeşme* or underground spring).

After admiring the Yenişehir Kapısı, start towards the centre along Atatürk Caddesi. Halfway to Aya Sofya, a road on the left leads to the ruins of a Roman theatre. Nearby is the **Saray Kapısı**, or Palace Gate, in the city walls. Sultan Orhan had a palace near here in the 1300s.

Places to Stay

The few hotels in İznik may fill up with locals from nearby cities on summer weekends, and you may need to reserve a room in advance. The hotel situation is better in Bursa, in any case.

Kaynarca Pansiyon (☎ 224-757 1753, fax 757 1723, Gündem Sokak 1), run by the irrepressible Ali Bulmuş, is clean, simple and central, charging US$10/14/19 a single/double/triple with bath, TV and breakfast.

Hotel Şener (☎ 224-757 1338, fax 757 2280, Belediye Arkası, H Oktay Sokak 7) prides itself on being the fanciest hotel in the centre, with a lift, lounge, restaurant, and comfortable rooms going for US$15/24/32 a single/double/triple with shower. You can sometimes haggle a lower rate.

Motel Burcum (☎ 224-757 1011), on the lakefront road near the western end of Kılıçaslan Caddesi, has verdant grounds and tidy rooms, some with views of the lake, for US$22 a double, breakfast included. Get a room on the 2nd or 3rd floor if you want that view. You can camp in the garden for a few dollars per night.

The *Çamlık Motel*, CHAHM-luhk (☎ 224-757 1631), at the southern end of the lakefront road, has good rooms and a restaurant, with prices identical to those at the Burcum. There is camping here as well, and it's perhaps a bit quieter.

Places to Eat

On Kılıçaslan Caddesi, look for the *Konya Etli Pide Salonu*, serving good, cheap, freshly made Turkish-style pizzas for US$1.50 to US$3, depending upon toppings. The *Konak Barbekü Izgara*, farther east along Kılıçaslan, is the fancy version of a Turkish grill, with a greater variety of lamb and chicken grills but only slightly higher prices.

For ready-made food, try the *Çini Restaurant* next to the Konya Etli Pide Salonu. Another option is the *Ottoman Restaurant* farther east.

Kırıkçatal (Broken Fork), north of the Motel Burcum by the lake, has a longstanding reputation.

There are also several *pastahanes* here, including the *Saray Pastanesi* east of Aya Sofya, good for breakfast, tea or a snack.

Getting There & Away

Buses run hourly to İznik from the docks in Yalova. From İznik, buses run hourly back to Yalova and others run to Bursa. Don't wait until too late in the day to start for Bursa, however, as the last bus heads out at 6 or 7 pm on the 1½-hour trip. A ticket costs from US$2 to US$2.75, depending on the company.

BURSA

Sprawled at the base of Uludağ, Turkey's biggest winter sports centre, Bursa was the first Ottoman capital. It retains several fine mosques and pretty neighbourhoods from early Ottoman times, as well as thermal springs famous since Roman times.

History

Called Prusa by the Byzantines, Bursa was founded by Prusias, king of Bithynia, before 200 BC. Bursa grew to importance in the early centuries of Christianity. It was Justinian (527-65) who really put Bursa on the map. Besides favouring the silk trade, he built a palace for himself and bathhouses in Çekirge.

With the decline of Byzantium, Bursa's location near İstanbul drew the interest of would-be conquerors, including the Arab armies (circa 700 AD) and the Selçuk Turks. The Selçuks, having conquered much of Anatolia by 1075, took Bursa with ease that same year, and planted the seeds of the great Ottoman Empire.

With the arrival of the First Crusade in 1097, Bursa reverted to Christian hands, though it was to be conquered and reconquered by both sides for the next 100 years. When the rapacious armies of the Fourth Crusade sacked Constantinople in 1204, the Byzantine emperor fled to İznik and set up his capital there. He succeeded in controlling the hinterland of İznik, including Bursa, until the capital was moved back to Constantinople in 1261.

Ertuğrul Gazi (died 1281), a Turkish warlord, formed a small state near Bursa. Under the rule of his son Osman Gazi (1281-1326) the small state grew to a nascent empire and took Osman's name (Osmanlı, 'Ottoman'). Bursa was besieged by Osman's forces in 1317 and was finally starved into submission on 6 April 1326 when it immediately became the Ottoman capital.

Osman was succeeded by Orhan Gazi (1326-61) who, from his base at Bursa, expanded the empire to include everything from what is now Ankara in Central Anatolia to Trakya (Thrace) in Europe. Orhan took the title of *sultan* (lord), struck the first Ottoman coinage and near the end of his reign was able to dictate to the Byzantine

emperors. One of them, John VI Cantacuzene, was Orhan's close ally and later even his father-in-law (Orhan married the Princess Theodora).

The Ottoman capital moved to Adrianople (Edirne) in 1402, but Bursa is still revered.

Orientation & Information

The city centre, with its banks and shops, is along Atatürk Caddesi between the Ulu Cami (Grand Mosque) to the west and the main square, Cumhuriyet Alanı, commonly called Heykel *(heykel* means 'statue'), to the east. The PTT is on the south side of Atatürk Caddesi across from the Ulu Cami. Çekirge, with its hot springs, is about 6km west of Heykel. Bursa's bus station ('terminal') is 10km north on the Yalova road, reached by special grey buses marked 'Terminal', which leave from Heykel (US$0.35).

You can get maps and brochures at the tourist office (☎ 224-251 1834) in the Orhangazi Altgeçidi subway, Ulu Cami Parkı, opposite the Koza Han (silk market).

Things to See & Do

The largest of Bursa's beautiful mosques is the 20-domed Selçuk-style **Ulu Cami** (Grand Mosque), built in 1399; it's on Atatürk Caddesi in the city centre.

North and east of the Ulu Cami are Bursa's great *hans* (caravanserais) and covered markets. Just north-east of the mosque, the **Emir Han** and, east of it the **Koza Han**, have been the centre of the city's silk trade for centuries. Great sacks of silkworm cocoons are still sold here each April.

Bursa's **Bedesten**, or Covered Bazaar, a good place to buy a souvenir silk scarf or other garment, is just north of the Emir Han. Originally built in the late 1300s by Yıldırım Beyazıt, the Bedesten was destroyed by the earthquake of 1855. The reconstructed Bedesten retains the look and feel of the original, though it is obviously much tidier. This is not a tourist trap; most of the shoppers are local people. As you wander around, look for the **Eski Aynalı Çarşı**, which, though now a market, was originally built as the Orhangazi Hamamı (1335), the Turkish bath of the Orhan Camii Külliyesi. The domed ceiling with many small lights shows this.

From the Ulu Cami, walk west and up Orhan Gazi (Yiğitler) Caddesi, a ramp-like street which leads up to the section known as Hisar (Fortress) or Tophane. Near a sign which reads 'İstiklal Savaşı Şehitler', are the **Osman Gazi ve Orhan Gazi Türbeleri** (tombs of sultans Osman and Orhan), founders of the Ottoman Empire. The original structures were destroyed in the earthquake of 1855 and rebuilt in Ottoman Baroque style by Sultan Abdülaziz in 1868.

In a pretty pedestrian zone about 1km east of Heykel is the early Ottoman **Yeşil Cami** (Green Mosque, built in 1424), which represents a turning point in Turkish architectural style. Before this, Turkish mosques such as Bursa's Ulu Cami echoed the Great Selçuk's style, which was basically Persian. However, in the Yeşil Cami a purely Turkish style emerges. Notice the harmonious façade and the beautifully carved marble work around the central doorway. As you enter, you will pass beneath the sultan's private apartments into a domed central hall. Greenish-blue tiles on the interior walls gave the mosque its name.

Behind the mosque is the beautifully tiled **Yeşil Türbe** (Green Tomb, open from 8 am to noon and 1 to 5 pm; free entry), resting-place of the Yeşil Cami's founder, Mehmet I (Çelebi), and his family.

The nearby **Türk İslam Eserleri Müzesi**, or Turkish & Islamic Arts Museum (open 8.30 am to noon and 1 to 5 pm; closed Monday; entry US$1.50), was once the Yeşil Cami's medrese, or theological seminary. Exhibits include the contents of an Ottoman *sünnet odası* (circumcision room), ceramics from the Selçuk period (12th and 13th centuries), İznik ware from the 14th to 18th century, more modern Kütahya ware (18th to 20th century), Karagöz shadow puppets, costumes, carpets, jewellery, metalwork, arms, a *dergah* (dervish-hall), musical instruments, turbans, illuminated Korans, carpet weaving and embroidery.

İskender Kebap

Roast lamb and mutton have been staples of the Turkish diet for millennia, and it does not take an overly fertile imagination to picture nomadic Turkish warriors skewering mutton on their swords and roasting it over a campfire 1500 years ago. Melted fat would drip into the fire causing flare-ups, smoking and burning the meat.

Along comes İskender Usta (Chef Alexander), a cook in Bursa. In 1867 he had the idea to build a vertical grill, fill it with hot coals, and stand the meat-packed sword on its point next to the grill. This way the fat would baste the meat rather than char it. He sliced the meat off in thin strips as it was cooked.

Like the Earl of Sandwich's revolutionary luncheon invention, İskender Usta's vertically grilled lamb was an instant success.

Today *döner kebap* (revolving roast) is Turkey's national dish, served everywhere from street corners to posh dining rooms. Many of the specially made döner grills even continue the symbolism of the sword, with a miniature hilt at the top.

İskender used lamb and mutton from sheep fed on the wild spices (especially thyme) of Uludağ. To compound his fame, he laid the slices of lamb on a bed of flat pide bread, and topped the whole with savoury tomato sauce and browned butter.

The dish's popularity has spread throughout the country and indeed the world, but it's still best in Bursa. The city's most prominent İskender kebapçıs claim direct descent – in both family and recipe – from the original İskender Usta.

A few hundred metres east of the Yeşil Cami is the Ottoman Rococo **Emir Sultan Camii** (1805). The setting, next to a large hillside cemetery surrounded by huge trees and overlooking the city and valley, is as pleasant as the mosque itself. To get there, take a dolmuş or bus No 18 (marked Emir Sultan) from Heykel.

The **mineral baths** are in the suburb of Çekirge. Most people coming to take the waters stay in hotels that have their own mineral bath facilities. The public baths are crowded on Friday, the Muslim holy day. For details on the ritual of the Turkish bath, see Turkish Baths in the Entertainment chapter.

The **Yeni Kaplıca** (☎ 224-236 6955), Mudanya Caddesi 10, on the north-west side of the Kültür Parkı, is a bath renovated in 1522 by Sultan Süleyman the Magnificent's grand vizier, Rüstem Paşa, on the site of a much older one built by Justinian. Besides the Yeni (New) baths, you'll find the Kaynarca (Boiling) limited to women, and the Karamustafa, which has facilities for family bathing. All baths in the complex are open from 6 am to 11 pm (last admission at 10 pm).

Perhaps the most attractive place is the **Eski Kaplıca** (☎ 224-233 9300) or Old Baths, right next door to the Kervansaray Termal Hotel on the eastern outskirts of Çekirge. Beautifully restored, the baths now cater to an upmarket clientele of business travellers, tourists and local notables who stay at or socialise in the hotel. Hours are daily from 7 am to 11 pm for men, from 7.30 am to 11 pm for women. There's an entry fee of US$6, and US$4 for a massage or to have an attendant wash you; the cost of soap is additional, so figure on spending US$20 for the works, including massage and tips. You can bring your own soap and wash yourself for little more than the basic entry fee.

To get to the Eski Kaplıca, take any bus or dolmuş marked 'SSK Hast(anesi)' or 'Sigorta', or a short taxi ride (US$3).

For a simpler, less expensive bath near the hotels in the centre of Bursa, try the Çakır Ağa Hamamı, at the corner of Atatürk Caddesi and Kazım Baykal (Temiz) Caddesi, just west of the Tahtakale/İnebey district. Posted prices are US$3 for a wash, another US$1.50 for soap and scrub, US$1 for a massage, US$3 for use of a resting cubicle, or the works for US$10 or so. The hamam is open from 7 am to 11 pm.

On a clear day it's worth going up Uludağ. From Heykel take bus Nos 3B, 3C etc or a dolmuş east to the *teleferik*, or cable car, which ascends the mountain (US$5 one way), or take a dolmuş (US$6) from Orhangazi Caddesi, the entire 22km to the top.

Places to Stay

In Tahtakale, south of the Ulu Cami, the *Otel Güneş* (☎ 224-222 1404, *İnebey Caddesi 75)* has serviceable, waterless singles/doubles for US$8/12. The neighbouring *Otel Çamlıbel* (☎ 224-221 2565, *İnebey Caddesi 71)* is fancier at US$20/30. Better value is the *Hotel İpekçi* (☎ 224-221 1935, *Çancılar Caddesi 38)*, in the market north of Heykel, with rooms at US$12/18.

The tidy, quiet *Hotel Çeşmeli* (☎ 224-224 1511, *Gümüşçeken Caddesi 6)*, just north of Heykel, is run by God-fearing Muslims and is conveniently located. It costs US$28/42/55 for a single/double/triple room with shower and breakfast. Though expensive, this is a good choice for women travellers.

Hotel Dikmen (☎ 224-224-1840, fax 224 1844, Maksem – Fevzi Çakmak – Caddesi 78), is farther west, then south. This 50-room, three-star hotel has rooms with bathtubs, TVs and mini bars for US$30/40 a single/double, slightly cheaper without the frills. Ask for *sakin bir oda* (a quiet room). The hotel is about 50m uphill on the street which begins beside the PTT.

The nominally three-star *Kent Hotel* (☎ 224-223 5420, fax 224 4015, Atatürk Caddesi 69) is right in the city centre. All 64 rooms have air-conditioning, private showers, mini bars and satellite TVs. Although posted prices may be as high as US$75/100 a single/double, I was quoted US$55 a double when I asked, so rates are negotiable.

Opposite the Osman and Orhan tombs, the *Safran Otel & Restaurant* (☎ 224-224 7216, fax 224 7219, Kale Sokak) is a restored Ottoman house in a historic neighbourhood containing many others. Rooms with private bathroom and TV cost US$55/80 a single/double, with breakfast included. The adjoining restaurant and Mavi Bar are good, too.

Staying in Çekirge, you get free mineral baths. The *Öz Yeşil Yayla Oteli* (*☎/fax 224-236 8026, Çekirge Caddesi, Selvi Sokak 6*), between the Boyugüzel and Yıldız II hotels at the upper end of the village, is old fashioned and simple – a living piece of 1950s Çekirge – and charges US$22 a double for rooms with a sink and free use of the mineral baths.

Next door, the *Boyugüzel Termal Otel* (*☎ 224-233 3850, fax 233 9999, Selvi Sokak*) charges US$22 for a double room with sink and toilet, with a half-hour mineral bath downstairs included each day.

The three-star *Termal Hotel Gönlü Ferah* (*☎ 224-233 9210, fax 233 9218, I. Murat Caddesi 24*) is in the very centre of the village. Some of the 62 rooms have fine views over the valley. The ambience here is 'European spa', the service good. Rates are US$70/90 a single/double with breakfast.

Next door, the four-star, 100-room *Hotel Dilmen* (*☎ 224-233 9500, fax 235 2568, I. Murat Caddesi*) is slightly more expensive.

Places to Eat

Bursa's culinary specialities include fresh fruit (especially peaches – *şeftali* – in season) and candied chestnuts (*kestane şekeri*), but its most famous meal is *Bursa kebap*, or *İskender kebap*, döner kebab laid on a bed of fresh pide bread and topped with savoury tomato sauce and browned butter. This is the thing to have for lunch on a day-trip to the city.

Cost differences among restaurants of the same class are small due to fixed municipal prices. A *bir porsyon* (one-serving) plate of Bursa kebap with yoghurt costs US$5 or US$6, soft drink included (alcohol is not normally served at *kebapçıs*). Add US$2 if you order *bir buçuk porsyon* (1½ portions). All these places are open seven days a week from 11 am until 9 or 10 pm.

The owners of *Kebapçı İskender* (*☎ 224-221 4615, Ünlü Cadde 7*), half a block south-east of Heykel, claim to be descended from the eponymous İskender Usta

himself. The elaborate Ottomanesque façade and semi-formal waiters belie moderate prices (US$6 to US$8 for Bursa kebap with yoghurt, plus a soft drink). İskender kebap and a few salads and sweets are all that is served.

Directly across Ünlü Caddesi is *Adanur Hacıbey* (*☎ 224-221 6440*), a simpler place where the Bursa kebap comes with a dab of smoky aubergine purée on the side. Don't begin eating your kebap until the waiter brings the tomato sauce and browned butter.

The original *Hacıbey Kebapçısı* (*☎ 224-222 6604, Taşkapı Sokak 4/11*) is just south of the Koza Parkı. Two floors of narrow rooms have marble floors, beautiful tiled walls and dark polished woodwork.

Bursa kebap was supposedly invented in a small restaurant now called *Kebabcı İskenderoğlu Nurettin* (İskender's Son) at Atatürk Caddesi 60, between Heykel and the Ulu Cami.

Çiçek Izgara (*☎ 224-221 6526, Belediye Caddesi 15*), a block from the Koza Parkı behind (north of) the half-timbered Belediye building, does not specialise in Bursa kebap, but serves excellent grills in a white tablecloth setting that's especially comfortable for single women. Prices range from US$2.50 for köfte to US$7 for the big mixed grill; a *bonfile* (small beef fillet steak) costs US$5.

Strolling around the Cultural Park is pleasant, and having a meal here is more so. The *Selçuk Restaurant* (*☎ 224-220 9695*), near the mosque, is good, quiet, shady, serves alcoholic beverages and is not overly expensive – three-course meals cost US$8 to US$15.

In Çekirge, the *Sezen Restaurant* (*☎ 224-236 9156*), on Çekirge Caddesi to the right of the Ada Palas Hotel, serves decent food for US$5 or US$6 for a full meal.

Getting There & Away

The best way to get to Bursa is by the fast (one hour) İstanbul-Yalova *deniz otobüsü* (catamaran; five a day, US$6), which departs the Kabataş docks just south of Dolmabahçe Sarayı; or the *jet feribot* from

Yenikapı (US$6) to Yalova, then a bus from Yalova to Bursa (every half-hour, 70 minutes, US$3).

Though the ferry connection at Yalova is the fastest and most enjoyable way to go, there are also direct buses between İstanbul and Bursa. Those designated *feribot ile* use the Topçular-Eskihisar ferry, which is quicker (2½ hours) than the land route *(karayolu ile)* round the Marmara (four hours, US$9).

An airport is under construction at Yenişehir, 40km east of Bursa. Flights from İstanbul will be quick, but when you add the time necessary to get to the airport, pass the security checks, check in, and do the same at the arrival airport, there is little time saving over the catamaran-and-bus route.

Getting Around

Buy BOI city bus tickets (US$0.40) at kiosks and shops. Most routes stop on Atatürk Caddesi. Bursa dolmuş with little 'D' plates on top charge US$0.45 or more for a seat. Those marked 'SSK Hastanesi' go to Çekirge, those marked 'Dev(let) Hast(anesi)' go to the Orhan & Osman tombs, those marked 'Yeşil' go to the Yeşil Cami (Green Mosque) area. Special grey 'Terminal' buses shuttle the 10km north to the bus station.

Gallipoli & Troy

The slender peninsula which forms the north-western side of the Çanakkale Boğazı (Dardanelles), across the water from the town of Çanakkale, is called Gelibolu in Turkish. The Gallipoli battlefields, a raging hell during WWI, are now peaceful places covered in scrubby brush, pine forests and farmers' fields.

It's possible to visit the battlefields of Gallipoli, the Dardanelles strait, Çanakkale and the ruins of Troy from İstanbul in a day if you charter a private plane and hire a car and driver. Failing that expensive method, the way to go is by rental car or bus, staying the night in Çanakkale and making it a two-day excursion. You can combine this excursion

with the trip to Edirne, making it a too-fast two-day or comfortable three-day trip.

GALLİPOLİ
History

With the intention of capturing the Ottoman capital and the road to Eastern Europe during WWI, Winston Churchill, British First Lord of the Admiralty, organised a naval assault on the straits. A strong Franco-British fleet tried first to force them in March 1915 but failed. Then, in April, British, Australian, New Zealand and Indian troops were landed on Gallipoli, and French troops near Çanakkale. Both Turkish and Allied troops fought desperately and fearlessly, and devastated one another. After months of ferocious combat with little progress, the Allied forces were withdrawn.

The Turkish success at Gallipoli was partly due to bad luck and bad leadership on the Allied side, and partly due to the timely provision of reinforcements coming to the aid of the Turkish side under the command of General Liman von Sanders. But a crucial element in the defeat was that the Allied troops happened to land in a sector where they faced Lieutenant-Colonel Mustafa Kemal (Atatürk).

He was a relatively minor officer, but he had General von Sanders' confidence. He guessed the Allied battle plan correctly when his commanders did not, and stalled the invasion by bitter fighting which wiped out his division. Though suffering from malaria, he commanded in full view of his troops and of the enemy, and miraculously escaped death several times. His brilliant performance made him a folk hero and paved the way for his promotion to pasha (general).

The Gallipoli campaign lasted for nine months, until January 1916, and resulted in a total of more than half a million Allied and Turkish casualties.

Touring the Battlefields

Gallipoli is a fairly large area to tour: it's over 35km as the crow flies from the northernmost battlefield to the southern tip of the peninsula. The principal battles took place on the western shore of the peninsula near Anzac Cove and Arıburnu, and in the hills just to the east.

With a car you can easily tour the major battlefields in a day and be in a Çanakkale hotel by nightfall. A morning or afternoon suffices to see the high points if you're in a hurry.

Several companies run four-hour minibus tours (US$14 to US$20) of Gallipoli from Çanakkale, Eceabat and Gelibolu. Most companies are allied with hotels or pensions, which may put pressure on you to take their tour. Ask other travellers which tour they've liked.

Troy-Anzac Tours (☎ 286-217 5849, fax 217 0196), Saat Kulesi Meydanı 6, facing the clock tower in Çanakkale, has been in business for decades.

If you're a hiker and you have lots of time, take a ferry from Çanakkale to Eceabat and a dolmuş or taxi to Kabatepe, and follow the trail around the sites described in a booklet sold at the visitor centre (Kabatepe Tanıtma Merkezi) there.

Gallipoli National Historic Park

Gallipoli National Historic Park (Gelibolu Tarihi Milli Park) covers much of the peninsula and all of the significant battle sites. Park headquarters is 2km south-west of Eceabat (5km north-east of Kilitbahir) at the Ziyaretçi Merkezi (Visitors Centre); there's a picnic ground here as well.

About 3km north of Eceabat a road marked for Kabatepe and Kemalyeri heads west.

Kabatepe Tanıtma Merkezi The Kabatepe Information Centre, 9km from Eceabat and 1km or so east of the village of Kabatepe, holds a small museum (US$0.50) with period uniforms, soldiers' letters, rusty weapons and other battlefield finds such as the skull of a luckless Turkish soldier with a ball lodged right in the forehead.

The road uphill to Lone Pine (Kanlı Sırt) and Chunuk Bair (Conkbayırı) begins 750m west of the Information Centre. Anzac Cove is 3.5km from the information centre.

Anzac Cove & Beaches Going west from the information centre, it's 3km to the **Beach Cemetery**, and another 90m to where a road goes inland to the Shrapnel Valley & Plugge's Plateau cemeteries.

Another 400m along is Anzac Cove (Anzac Koyu). The ill-fated Allied landing was made here on 25 April 1915, beneath and just south of the Arıburnu cliffs. The Allied forces were ordered to advance inland, but met with fierce resistance from the Ottoman forces under Mustafa Kemal (Atatürk), who had foreseen the landing here and, disobeying a direct order from his commanders to send his troops south to Cape Helles, was prepared for it. After this first failed effort, the Anzacs concentrated on consolidating and expanding the beachhead, which they did until June while awaiting reinforcements.

In August a major offensive was staged in an attempt to advance beyond the beachhead and up to the ridges of Chunuk Bair and Sarı Bair. It resulted in the bloodiest battles of the campaign, but little progress was made.

The Anzac Monument

Anzac Cove is marked by a Turkish monument that repeats the famous words uttered by Atatürk in 1934 for the Anzac troops:

Those heroes that shed their blood and lost their lives ... you are now lying in the soil of a friendly country. Therefore rest in peace. There is no difference between the Johnnies and the Mehmets to us where they lie side by side here in this country of ours ... You, the mothers, who sent your sons from far away countries, wipe away your tears; your sons are now lying in our bosom and are in peace. After having lost their lives on this land they have become our sons as well.

As a memorial reserve, the beach here is off-limits to swimmers and picnickers.

A few hundred metres beyond Anzac Cove is the **Arıburnu Cemetery** and, 750m farther along, the **Canterbury Cemetery**. Less than 1km farther along the seaside road are the cemeteries at **No 2 Outpost**, set back inland from the road, and the **New Zealand No 2 Outpost**, right next to the road. The **Embarkation Pier Cemetery** is 200m beyond No 2 Outpost.

Anzac Cove to Lone Pine Retrace your steps and follow the signs up the hill for Lone Pine (Kanlı Sırt), perhaps the most poignant and affecting of all the Anzac cemeteries. It's just under 3km from the junction with the beach road to Lone Pine, and another 3km uphill to the New Zealand Memorial at Chunuk Bair (Conkbayırı).

This area, which saw the most bitter fighting of the campaign, was later cloaked in pines, but a disastrous forest fire in 1994 denuded the hills. Reforestation efforts are under way.

At Lone Pine, 400m uphill from the Kanlı Sırt Kitabesi (Turkish monument), Australian forces captured the Turkish positions on the evening of 6 August. In the few days of the August assault 4000 men died here. The trees which shaded the cemetery were swept away by the fire in 1994, leaving only one: a lone pine planted as a memorial years ago from the seed of the original tree which had stood here during the battle. The small tombstones carry touching epitaphs: 'Only son', 'He died for his country' and 'If I could hold your hand once more just to say well done'.

Lone Pine to Quinn's Post As you progress up the hill, you quickly come to understand the ferocity of the battles. At some points the trenches were only a few metres apart. The order to attack meant certain death to all who followed it, and virtually all – on both the Ottoman and Allied sides – did as they were ordered.

At **Johnston's Jolly** (Kırmızı Sırt/125 Alay Cephesi), 200m beyond Lone Pine, at

Courtney's & Steele's Post, another 300m along, and especially at Quinn's Post (Bomba Sırt, Yüzbaşı Mehmet Şehitliği), another 400m uphill, the trenches were separated only by the width of the modern road. On the eastern side at Johnston's Jolly is the Turkish monument to the soldiers of the 125th Regiment who died here on 'Red Ridge'. At **Quinn's Post** is the memorial to Sergeant Mehmet, who fought with rocks and his fists after he ran out of ammunition; and the Captain Mehmet Cemetery.

57. Alay (57th Regiment) Just over 1km uphill from Lone Pine is another monument to 'Mehmetçik' (the Turkish equivalent of GI Joe) on the west side of the road and, on the east side, the cemetery and monument for officers and soldiers of the Ottoman 57th Regiment. As the Anzac troops made their way up the scrub-covered slopes toward Chunuk Bair on 25 April, divisional commander Mustafa Kemal (Atatürk) brought up the 57th Infantry Regiment and gave them his famous order: 'I order you not just to attack, but to die. In the time it takes us to die, other troops and commanders will arrive to take our places.' The 57th was wiped out, but held the line and inflicted equally heavy casualties on the Anzacs below.

The statue of an old man showing his granddaughter the battle sites portrays veteran Hüseyin Kaçmaz, who fought in the Balkan Wars, in the Gallipoli campaign and in the War of Independence at the fateful Battle of Dumlupınar. He died in 1994 at the age of 110.

Mehmet Çavuş & The Nek A hundred metres uphill past the 57th Regiment cemetery, a road goes west to the monument to Mehmet Çavuş (another Sergeant Mehmet) and The Nek. It was at The Nek on 7 August 1915 that the 8th (Victorian) and 10th (West Australian) regiments of the 3rd Light Horse Brigade vaulted out of their trenches into withering fire and certain death. They were doomed but utterly courageous.

Baby 700 Cemetery, on the site of the other object of the assault, is 300m farther uphill from Mehmet Çavuş.

Chunuk Bair At the top of the hill, 600m past the monument to Talat Göktepe, a forestry director who died battling the flames of the 1994 forest fire, is a 'T' intersection. A right turn takes you east to the spot where, having stayed awake for four days straight, Atatürk spent the night of 9 to 10 August, and to **Kemalyeri** (Scrubby Knoll), his command post. A left turn leads after 100m to **Chunuk Bair** (Conkbayırı), the first objective of the Allied landing in April 1915, and now the site of the New Zealand memorial.

Chunuk Bair was also at the heart of the struggle from 6 to 9 August 1915, when 28,000 men died on this ridge. The peaceful pine grove of today makes it difficult to imagine the blasted wasteland of almost a century ago, when bullets, bombs and shrapnel mowed down men and trees as the fighting went on day and night with huge numbers of casualties. The Anzac attack on 6-7 August, which included the New Zealand Mounted Rifle Brigade and a Maori contingent, was deadly, but the attack on the following day was of a ferocity which, according to Atatürk, 'could scarcely be described'.

On the western side of the road is the **New Zealand Memorial** and some **reconstructed Turkish trenches** *(Türk Siperleri)*. A sign indicates the spots at which Mustafa Kemal stood on 8 August 1915: where he gave the order for the crucial attack at 4.30 am (Atatürk'ün taarruz emrini verdiği yer); where he watched the progress of the battle (Savaş gözetleme yeri); and the spot where shrapnel would have hit his heart, but was stopped by his pocket watch (Atatürk'ün saatinin parçaladığı yeri).

To the east a side road leads up to the **Turkish Conkbayırı Memorial**, five gigantic tablets with inscriptions (in Turkish) describing the progress of the battle.

Beyond Chunuk Bair the road leads to Kocaçimentepe, less than 2km along.

Kabatepe to Seddülbahir A road goes south from near the Kabatepe Information Centre past the side road to **Kum Limanı**, where there is a good swimming beach and the *Hotel Kum and Kum Camping (☎ 286-814 1466, fax 814 1917)*, just over 6km south-west of the information centre. It has comfortable shower-equipped rooms for US$40 in summer, and camping places with some shade for US$6. This is the place to stop for a swim; if you're on a guided tour, you will probably do so.

From Kabatepe (Gaba Tepe) it's about 12km to the village of **Alçıtepe**, formerly known as Krythia or Kirte. In the village, signs point out the road south-west to **Twelve Tree Copse** and **Pink Farm** cemeteries, and north to the Turkish **Sargı Yeri cemetery** and **Nuri Yamut monument**.

Heading north, the road passes the **Redoubt Cemetery**. About 5.5km south of Alçıtepe, just south of the **Skew Bridge Cemetery**, the road divides, the right fork leading to the village of Seddülbahir and several Allied memorials. **Seddülbahir** (Sedd el Bahr), 1.5km from the intersection, is a sleepy farming village with a few small pensions, including the *Helles Panorama*, *Evim*, *Kale* and *Fulda*, a PTT, a ruined Ottoman/Byzantine fortress, army post and a small harbour.

Follow the signs for Yahya Çavuş Şehitliği to reach the **Helles Memorial**, 1km beyond the Seddülbahir village square.

The initial Allied attack was two-pronged, with the southern landing taking place here at the tip of the peninsula on 'V' Beach. Yahya Çavuş (Sergeant Yahya) was the Turkish officer who led the first resistance to the Allied landing on 25 April 1915, causing heavy casualties. The cemetery named after him (**Yahya Çavuş Şehitliği**) is between the Helles Memorial and 'V' Beach.

Lancashire Landing cemetery is off to the north along a road marked by a sign; another sign points south to **'V' Beach**, 550m downhill. Right next to the beach is the *Mocamp Seddülbahir*, with tent and caravan sites and a few pension-like rooms.

From the Helles Memorial there are fine views of the straits, with ships cruising placidly up and down. A half million men were killed, wounded or lost in the dispute over which ships should (or should not) go through.

Retrace your steps to the road division and go east following signs for Abide and/or Çanakkale Şehitleri Abidesi (Çanakkale Martyrs' Memorial) at Morto Bay. Along the way you pass the **French Memorial & Museum**. French troops, including a regiment of Africans, attacked Kumkale on the Asian shore in March 1915 with complete success, then reimbarked and landed in support of their British comrades-in-arms at Cape Helles.

At the foot of the Turkish monument hill is a fine pine-shaded picnic area. The monument, or **Çanakkale Şehitleri Abidesi**, commemorates all of the Turkish soldiers who fought and died at Gallipoli. It's a gigantic four-legged stone table (almost 42m high and surrounded by landscaped grounds) standing above a war museum (admission US$0.50).

Getting There & Away

See Getting There & Away in the Çanakkale section below for full transport details.

ÇANAKKALE

Çanakkale is a hub for transport to Troy and across the Dardanelles to Gallipoli. It was here that Leander swam across what was then called the Hellespont to his lover Hero, and here too that Lord Byron did his romantic bit and duplicated the feat. The defence of the straits during WWI led to a Turkish victory over Anzac forces on 18 March 1916, now a major local holiday.

Orientation & Information

The bus station (otogar) is 1km inland from the ferry docks, but many buses also stop at ticket offices nearer to the docks. The helpful tourist office (☎/fax 286-217 1187) and many cheap hotels and cafes are within a few steps of the docks, near the landmark clock tower (Saat Kulesi).

Things to See

The Ottoman castle of Çimenlik Kalesi, built by Sultan Mehmet the Conqueror in 1452, is now the **Army & Navy Museums**, set in a nice park. The park is open daily from 9 am to 10 pm; the museums are open daily except Monday and Thursday from 9 to 11 am and from 2.30 to 7.30 pm. Admission is free to the park, US$0.50 to the museums (half-price for students).

Just over 2km south of the ferry pier, the **Archaeological Museum** holds artefacts found at Troy and Assos. Opening hours are from 10 am to 5 pm (closed Monday). Admission costs US$2.

Places to Stay

Most small Çanakkale hotels and pensions have identical city-regulated prices (singles/doubles for US$6/10, or US$7/11 with shower). All are heavily booked in summer; the town is insanely crowded around Anzac Day, 24 April.

Anzac House (☎ 286-217 1392, Demiricioğlu Caddesi), right in the centre, has dorm beds for US$4, and singles/doubles for US$6/10. Look at the room first.

Hotel Efes (☎ 286-217 4687, Aralık Sokak 5), behind the clock tower, is bright and cheerful. *Hotel Akgün* (☎ 286-217 3049), across the street, is similar, as are the *Hotel Erdem* (☎ 286-217 4986) and *Hotel Umut* (☎ 286-217 6473), nearer to the clock tower.

Otel Aşkın (☎/fax 286-217 4956, Hasan Mevsuf Sokak 53), less than a block north of the bus station, charges US$16 a double with shower and breakfast. The nearby *Aşkın Pansiyon* (same phone), has waterless doubles for US$8.

The *Hotel Temizay* (☎ 286-212 8760, fax 217 5885, Cumhuriyet Meydanı 15) is central, clean and new, with singles/doubles/triples for US$20/30/45. The one-star *Hotel Kestanbol* (☎ 286-217 0857, fax 217 9173, Hasan Mevsuf Sokak 5), inland a few blocks and across the street from the Emniyet Sarayı (police station), has 26 rooms, all with bath, costing US$20/30 a single/double including breakfast.

You can't miss the two-star, 70-room *Otel Anafartalar* (☎ 286-217 4454, fax 217 2622, *İskele Meydanı*) a seven-storey high-rise on the north side of the ferry docks. The front rooms are good value with harbour views, bath and breakfast for US$31/42 a single/double.

The three-star *Büyük Truva Oteli* (☎ 286-217 1024, fax 217 0903, *Mehmet Akif Ersoy Caddesi 2*), on the waterfront 200m north of the docks, has 66 clean, serviceable rooms, many with sea views. Rates are US$40/50/65 a single/double/triple, breakfast included, for a room with TV, minibar and private shower or tub/shower combination.

The best in town is the high-rise, four-star *Hotel Akol* (☎ 286-217 9456, fax 217 2897, *Kordonboyu*), on the waterfront north of the docks. The 136 rooms with bath cost US$60/90 a single/double.

Places to Eat

The *Gaziantep Aile Kebap ve Pide Salonu*, behind the clock tower, serves good cheap pide and more substantial kebabs, while *Trakya Restaurant*, on the main square, always has lots of food ready and waiting 24 hours a day.

The most enjoyable places to dine are those facing the quay to the north and south of the ferry docks. *Rıhtım, Entellektüel* (Intellectuals' Restaurant) and *Çekiç* are all long standing places. A meal of an appetiser, fried or grilled fish, salad and a bottle of beer at any one of them might cost from US$10 to US$14. Be sure to ask prices, as bill-fiddling is not unknown, especially at busy times.

On the north side, the seaside restaurant at the *Otel Anafartalar* is quite popular, with prices posted prominently.

Getting There & Away

Çanakkale is the logical base for visits to the Gallipoli battlefields and/or Troy. Buses depart İstanbul's main otogar at Esenler hourly for Çanakkale (340km, six hours, US$9 to US$12).

A slightly shorter and more interesting route is to take an early morning catamaran or jet car ferry from İstanbul's Yenikapı docks to Bandırma, on the south shore of the Sea of Marmara, then a taxi 2km uphill to the bus station, then one of the 12 buses daily westward to Çanakkale (195km, three hours, US$7). The catamaran cruise is a pleasant alternative to six hours on a bus.

To cross the Dardanelles, there are ferries between Gelibolu and Lapseki; Eceabat and Çanakkale; and Kilitbahir and Çanakkale.

The Gelibolu-Lapseki car ferry departs from Gelibolu at 6.30, 7.30, 8.15, 9 and 11 am, and 1, 3, 5, 6, 7, 8, 9, 10, 11 pm and midnight. Departures from Lapseki are at 6.30, 7.30, 8.15 and 10 am, noon, 2, 4, 5, 6, 7, 8, 9, 10, 11 pm and midnight. The fare is US$0.60 per person, US$1.50 for a bicycle or moped, US$4.50 for a car. If you miss this boat, you can go south-west to Eceabat (45km, one hour) and catch the similar car ferry, or to Kilitbahir 7km beyond Eceabat and catch the small private ferry, which can take a few cars as well, and charges less than the other ferries.

TROY

The approach to Troy (Truva), 30km from Çanakkale, is across low, rolling grain fields, with villages here and there. This is the ancient Troad, or land of Troy, all but lost to legend until German-born Californian treasure-seeker and amateur archaeologist Heinrich Schliemann (1822-90) excavated it in 1871. The poetry of Homer was at that time assumed to be based on legend, not history, but Schliemann got permission from the Ottoman government to dig here at his own expense. He uncovered four superimposed ancient towns, more or less destroying three others in the process.

History

In Homer's *Iliad*, Troy was the town of Ilium. The Trojan War took place in the 13th century BC, with Agamemnon, Achilles, Odysseus (Ulysses), Patroclus and Nestor on the Achaean (Greek) side, and Priam with his sons Hector and Paris on the Trojan side. Rather than suggesting commercial rivalries as a cause for the war,

Frank Calvert, Discoverer of Troy

Heinrich Schliemann is usually given the credit for rediscovering Troy, but according to Dr Susan Heuck Allen it was Frank Calvert (1828-1908), a Malta-born British expatriate and sometime American consul at the Dardanelles, owner of much of the land around the site, who really rediscovered Troy.

In 1859 Calvert, an amateur archaeologist, published a pioneering excavation report on his work at Hanay Tepe, a prehistoric site near Troy. By 1863 he was convinced that the hill on his land called Hisarlık, identified in 1812 as the site of the Roman city of Ilium Novum, was the site of Troy.

Calvert applied to the British Museum for support in his excavations, but was turned down. He continued his excavations in a small way, but was hampered by financial difficulties and family responsibilities.

In 1868 Calvert was visited by Heinrich Schliemann, who had been excavating for Troy at nearby Pınarbaşı in vain. Convinced by the artefacts which Calvert had uncovered that this was Troy, Schliemann began to excavate on Calvert's land at Hisarlık. The two men later had a falling out, but Calvert continued to support Schliemann's work for the sake of science, and Schliemann continued to fund Calvert's own explorations elsewhere in exchange for the benefit of Calvert's knowledge.

Schliemann, a peerless self-promoter, saw to it that his name was inscribed in the history books as the discoverer of Troy, but it was Frank Calvert who made Schliemann's success possible. In the 20th century, Calvert's priceless collection of artefacts from Troy and nearby sites was dispersed to museums in Çanakkale, London, and Boston and Worcester, Massachusetts.

Homer claimed that Paris had kidnapped the beautiful Helen from her husband Menelaus, King of Sparta (his reward for giving the golden apple for most beautiful woman to Aphrodite, goddess of love), and the king asked the Achaeans to help him get her back.

During the decade-long war, Hector killed Patroclus and Achilles killed Hector. Paris knew that Achilles' mother had dipped her son in the River Styx to make him invincible. However, to do so she had had to hold him by his heel, the one part of his body that remained unprotected. Hence Paris shot Achilles in the heel and bequeathed a phrase to the English language.

When 10 years of carnage couldn't end the war, Odysseus came up with the idea of the wooden horse filled with soldiers, against which Cassandra warned the Trojans in vain. It was left outside the west gate for the Trojans to wheel inside the walls.

One theory has it that the earthquake of 1250 BC gave the Achaeans the break they needed, bringing down Troy's formidable walls and allowing them to battle their way into the city. In gratitude to Poseidon, the earth-shaker, they built a monumental wooden statue of his horse. So there may well have been a real Trojan horse, even though Homer's account is less than fully historical.

Excavations by Schliemann and others have revealed nine ancient cities, one on top of another, dating back to 3000 BC. The first people lived here during the early Bronze Age. The cities called Troy I to Troy V (3000-1700 BC) had a similar culture, but Troy VI (1700-1250 BC) took on a different character, with a new population of Indo-European stock related to the Mycenaeans. The town doubled in size and carried on a prosperous trade with Mycenae.

Troy VII lasted from 1250 to 1050 BC, then sank into a torpor for four centuries. It was revived as a Greek city (Troy VIII, 700-85 BC) and then as a Roman one (Troy IX, 85 BC-500 AD).

The Ruins of Troy

Half a kilometre before the archaeological site, the village of Tevfikiye has a hotel, drink stands, restaurants, souvenir shops and replicas of Schliemann's cabin and the Trojan treasure. The relics of two old restaurants opposite the Hotel Hisarlık are slated to become a museum in the future.

The window *(gişe)* where you buy your admission ticket (US$2, plus US$1 per car) is just past Tevfikiye, 500m before the site. The ruins are open from 8 am to 5 pm daily.

A huge replica of the wooden Trojan horse catches your eye as you approach Troy. The Kazı Evi (Excavation House) to the right of the path was used by earlier archaeological teams. Today it holds exhibits on work in progress. The models and superimposed pictures should help you understand what Troy looked like at different points in its history.

The identifiable structures at Troy are marked by explanatory signs. Notice especially the walls from various periods, including one of the oldest still standing in the world; the **bouleuterion** (council chamber) built at about Homer's time (circa 800 BC); the **stone ramp** from Troy II; and the **Temple of Athena** from Troy VIII, rebuilt by the Romans.

Don't miss the beautiful views of the Troad, particularly over towards the straits. On a clear day you can see the Çanakkale Martyrs' Memorial on the far shore, and ships passing through the Dardanelles. You can almost imagine the Achaean fleet beached on the Troad's shores, ready to begin a battle that would be remembered over 3000 years later.

Getting There & Away

In Çanakkale, walk straight inland from the ferry docks and turn right onto Atatürk

The eye-catching replica of the famous Trojan horse – a monument to the legend of Odysseus' conquest of Troy.

Caddesi, the Troy road; the dolmuş station for minibuses to Tevfikiye and Troy is several hundred metres along it next to a small bridge, about 1km from the docks. Dolmuşes go to Troy (30km, 35 minutes, US$1.50) every 30 to 60 minutes in high summer.

If you'd prefer to take a tour, contact Troy-Anzac Tours (☎ 286-217 5847, 217 5049, fax 217 0196), Saat Kulesi Meydanı 6, in Çanakkale. It's not a bad idea since a good guide can bring the sometimes confusing ruins of Troy to life in a way that's difficult for the casual visitor.

Another way to go is to haggle with a taxi driver for the trip to Troy, 60 to 90 minutes of waiting time, and the return ride.

Language

Turkish is the dominant language in the Turkic language group which also includes such less-than-famous tongues as Kirghiz, Kazakh and Azerbaijani. Once thought to be related to Finnish and Hungarian, the Turkic languages are now seen as comprising their own unique language group. You can find people who speak Turkish, in one form or another, from Belgrade all the way to Xinjiang in China.

In 1928, Atatürk did away with the Arabic alphabet and adopted a Latin-based alphabet much better suited to easy learning and correct pronunciation. He also instituted a language reform to purge Turkish of abstruse Arabic and Persian borrowings, in order to rationalise and simplify it. The result is a logical, systematic and expressive language which has only one irregular noun (*su*, 'water'), one irregular verb (*etmek*, 'to be') and no genders. It is so logical, in fact, that Turkish grammar formed the basis for the development of Esperanto, an artificial international language.

This language guide should help you in your travels around Turkey. For the meanings of common terms used through out this book, and Turkish words and phrases you might encounter on signs, please refer to the Glossary at the end of this book.

For a much more comprehensive guide to the Turkish language, get Lonely Planet's *Turkish Phrasebook*.

Turkish Language Cassettes

For a useful aid to learning correct pronunciation, and getting started with speaking a bit of Turkish, we can recommend a 90-minute audio cassette keyed to the words and phrases in this language guide. Send a cheque or money order payable to Tom Brosnahan for US$12 or UK£8 to *Turkish Cassette*, c/o Tom Brosnahan, PO Box 563, Concord, MA 01742-0563 USA. Mention that you'd like Cassette TSK06. Fast letter-mail ('1st-class') postage is included in the price. (This address is for audio cassette orders *only*. Please send all other correspondence to Tom Brosnahan via a Lonely Planet office; for addresses, see the back of the title page at the front of this book.)

Grammar

Word order and verb formation in Turkish are very different from what you'll find in Indo-European languages like English. This makes it somewhat difficult to learn at first, despite its elegant simplicity. A few hints will help you comprehend road and shop signs, schedules and menus.

Suffixes

A Turkish word consists of a root and one or more suffixes added to it. Though in English we have only a few suffixes ('-'s' for possessive, '-s' or '-es' for plural), Turkish has lots and lots of suffixes. Not only that, these suffixes are subject to an unusual system of 'vowel harmony' whereby most of the vowel sounds in a word are made in a similar manner. What this means is that the suffix might be -*lar* when attached to one word, but -*ler* when attached to another; it's the same suffix, though. Sometimes these suffixes are preceded by a 'buffer letter', a 'y' or an 'n'.

Here are some of the noun suffixes you'll encounter most frequently:

-a, -e	'to'
-dan, -den	'from'
-dır, -dir	emphatic (ignore it!)
-dur, -dür	
-(s)ı, -(s)i	object-nouns (ignore it!)
-(s)u, -(s)ü	
-(n)ın, -(n)in	possessive
-lar, -ler	plural
-lı, -li,	'with'
-lu, -lü	
-sız, -siz,	'without'
-suz, -süz	

Here are some of the common verb suffixes:

-ar, -er, -ır, -ir, **-ur, -ür**	simple present tense
-acak, -ecek, **-acağ-, -eceğ**	future tense
-dı, -di, -du, -dü	simple past tense
-ıyor-, -iyor-	continuous (like English '-ing', eg '... is eating')
-mak, -mek	infinitive ending

Nouns

Suffixes can be added to nouns to modify them. The two you'll come across most frequently are *-ler* and *-lar*, which form the plural: *otel* (hotel), *oteller* (hotels); *araba* (car), *arabalar* (cars).

Other suffixes modify in other ways: *ev* (house), *Ahmet* (Ahmet) but *Ahmet'in evi* (Ahmet's house). Similarly with *İstanbul* and *banka*: it's *İstanbul Bankası* when the two are used together. You may see *-i, -ı, -u* or *-ü, -si, -sı, -su* or *-sü* added to any noun. A *cami* is a mosque; but the *cami* built by Mehmet Pasha is the *Mehmet Paşa Camii*, with a double 'i'. Ask for a *bira* and the waiter will bring you a bottle of whatever type is available; ask for an *Efes Birası* and that's the brand you'll get.

Yet other suffixes on nouns tell you about direction: *-a* or *-e* means 'to': *otobüs* (bus), *otobüse* (to the bus) and *Bodrum'a* (to Bodrum). The suffix *-dan* or *-den* means 'from': *Ankara'dan* (from Ankara), *köprüden*, (from the bridge). Stress is on these final syllables *(-a* or *-dan)* whenever they are used.

Verbs

Verbs consist of a root plus any number of modifying suffixes. Verbs can be so complex that they constitute whole sentences in themselves, although this is rare. The standard example for blowing your mind is *Afyonkarahisarlılaştıramadıklarımızdanmısı nız?* (Aren't you one of those people whom we tried, unsuccessfully, to make resemble the citizens of Afyonkarahisar?). It's not the sort of word you see every day!

The infinitive verb form is with *-mak* or *-mek*, as in *gitmek* (to go) or *almak* (to take).

The stress in the infinitive is always on the last syllable ('geet-MEHK', 'ahl-MAHK').

The simple present form is with *-r*, as in *gider* (he/she/it goes), *giderim* (I go). The suffix *-iyor* has a similar meaning: *gidiyorum* (I'm going). For the future, there's *-ecek* or *-acak*, as in *alacak* (ah-lah-JAHK), he will take (it).

Word Order

The nouns and adjectives usually come first, then the verb; the final suffix on the verb is the subject of the sentence:

I'll go to İstanbul.	*İstanbul'a gideceğim.*
I want to buy (take) a carpet.	*Halı almak istiyorum.* (lit: Carpet to buy want I)

Pronunciation

Once you learn a few basic rules, you'll find Turkish pronunciation quite simple to master. Despite oddities such as the soft 'g' (**ğ**) and undotted 'i' (**ı**), it's a phonetically consistent language – there's generally a clear one-letter/one-sound relationship.

It's important to remember that each letter is pronounced; vowels don't combine to form diphthongs and consonants don't combine to form other sounds (such as 'th', 'gh' or 'sh' in English). Watch out for this! Your eye will keep seeing familiar English double-letter sounds in Turkish – where they don't exist. It therefore follows that **h** in Turkish is always pronounced as a separate letter; in English, we're used to pronouncing it when it's at the beginnings of words, but in Turkish it can appear in the middle or at the end of a word as well. *Always* pronounce it! Your Turkish friend *Ahmet* is 'ahh-MEHT' not 'aa-meht', and the word *rehber* (guide) is pronounced 'rehh-BEHR' not 're-ber'.

Here are some of the letters in Turkish which may cause initial confusion:

A, a	as in 'art' or 'bar'
â	a faint 'y' sound in preceding consonant, eg *Kâhta* (kih-YAHH-tah)

E, e	as in 'fell' or as the first vowel in 'ever'
İ, i	a short 'ee' sound; as in 'hit', 'sit'
I, ı	a neutral vowel; as the 'e' in 'glasses' or the 'a' in 'about'
O, o	between the 'o' in 'hot' and the 'aw' in 'awe'
Ö, ö	as the 'e' in 'her'; say it with pursed lips
U, u	as the 'oo' in 'moo'
Ü, ü	an exaggerated rounded-lip 'yoo'
C, c	as the 'j' in 'jet'
Ç, ç	as the 'ch' in 'church'
G, g	always hard as in 'get' (not as in 'gentle')
ğ	silent; lengthens preceding vowel
H, h	always pronounced; a weak 'h' as in 'half'
J, j	as the 'z' in 'azure'
S, s	always as in 'stress' (not as in 'ease')
Ş, ş	as the 'sh' in 'show'
V, v	soft, almost like a 'w'
W, w	same as Turkish 'v' (only found in foreign words)

USEFUL WORDS & PHRASES
Greetings & Civilities
Hello.
    Merhaba.
    MEHR-hah-bah
Good morning/Good day.
    Günaydın.
    gew-nahy-DUHN
Good evening.
    İyi akşamlar.
    EE ahk-shahm-LAHR
Good night.
    İyi geceler.
    EE geh-jeh-LEHR
Goodbye. (said only by one departing)
    Allaha ısmarladık.
    ah-LAHS-mahr-lah-duhk
Bon voyage. (said only by one staying ; lit: 'Go smiling')
    Güle güle.
    gew-LEH gew-LEH
Stay happy. (alternative to goodbye)
    Hoşça kalın.
    HOSH-cha KAH-luhn

May it contribute to your health! (said to one sitting down to a meal)
    Afiyet olsun!
    ah-fee-EHT ohl-soon
In your honour!/To your health!
    Şerefinize!
    sheh-rehf-ee-neez-EH

What's your name?
    Adınız ne?
    AH-duh-NUHZ neh
How are you?
    Nasılsınız?
    NAHS-suhl-suh-nuhz
I'm fine, thank you.
    İyiyim, teşekkür ederim.
    ee-YEE-yihm, tesh-ek-KEWR eh-dehr-eem
Very well.
    Çok iyiyim.
    CHOHK ee-YEE-yeem

Basics
Yes.
    Evet.
    eh-VEHT
No.
    Hayır.
    HAH-yuhr
Please.
    Lütfen.
    LEWT-fehn
Thanks.
    Teşekkürler. ederim
    teh-sheh-kewr-LEHR
Thank you very much.
    Çok teşekkür ederim.
    CHOHK teh-sheh-KEWR eh-deh-reem
You're welcome.
    Bir şey değil.
    beer SHEHY deh-YEEL
Pardon me.
    Affedersiniz.
    AHF-feh-DEHR-see-neez
Help yourself.
    Buyurun(uz).
    BOOY-roon-(ooz)

What?		
Ne?	NEH	
How?		
Nasıl?	NAH-suhl	
Who?		
Kim?	KEEM	
Why?		
Niçin, neden?	NEE-cheen, NEH-dehn	
When?		
Ne zaman?	NEH zah-mahn	
Which one?		
Hangisi?	HAHN-gee-see	
What's this?		
Bu ne?	BOO neh	
Where is ...?		
... nerede?	NEH-reh-deh	
At what time?		
Saat kaçta?	saht-KAHCH-tah	
How much/many?		
Kaç/Kaç tane?	KAHCH/tah-neh	
How many liras?		
Kaç lira?	KAHCH lee-rah	
How many hours?		
Kaç saat?	KAHCH sah-aht	
What does it mean?		
Ne demek?	NEH deh-mehk	
Give me ...		
... bana verin	... bah-NAH veh-reen	
I want ...		
... istiyorum	... ees-tee-YOH-room	
this		
bu(nu)	boo(NOO)	
that		
şu(nu)	shoo(NOO)	
the other		
o(nu)	oh(NOO)	
hot		
sıcak	suh-JAHK	
cold		
soğuk	soh-OOK	
big		
büyük	bew-YEWK	
small		
küçük	kew-CHEWK	
new/old		
yeni/eski	yeh-NEE/ehss-KEE	
open		
açık	ah-CHUHK	
closed		
kapalı	kah-pah-LUH	

not ...		
... değil	... deh-YEEL	
and		
ve	VEH	
or		
veya	veh-YAH	
good		
iyi	EE	
bad		
fenah	feh-NAH	
beautiful		
güzel	gew-ZEHL	

Countries (Informal Names)

Australia		
Avustralya	AH-voo-STRAHL-yah	
Austria		
Avusturya	AH-voo-STOOR-yah	
Belgium		
Belçika	BEL-chee-kah	
Canada		
Kanada	KAH-nah-dah	
Denmark		
Danimarka	DAH-nee-MAR-kah	
France		
Fransa	FRAHN-sah	
Germany		
Almanya	ahl-MAHN-yah	
Greece		
Yunanistan	yoo-NAH-nee-stahn	
India		
Hindistan	HEEN-dee-stahn	
Israel		
İsrail	EESS-rah-yeel	
Italy		
İtalya	ee-TAHL-yah	
Japan		
Japonya	zhah-POHN-yah	
Netherlands		
Holanda	ho-LAHN-dah	
New Zealand		
Yeni Zelanda	YEH-nee zeh-LAHN-dah	
Norway		
Norveç	nohr-VECH	
South Africa		
Güney Afrika	gur-NEY AH-free-kah	
Sweden		
İsveç	eess-VECH	
Switzerland		
İsviçre	eess-VEECH-reh	

UK
  İngiltere   EEN-geel-TEH-reh
USA
  Amerika   ah-MEH-ree-kah

Accommodation

Where is ...?
  ... nerede?
  NEH-reh-deh
Where is a hotel?
  Bir otel nerede?
  BEER oh-TEHL NEH-reh-deh?
Where is the toilet?
  Tuvalet nerede?
  too-vah-LEHT NEH-reh-deh?
Where is the manager?
  Patron nerede?
  pah-TROHN NEH-reh-deh?
Where is someone who
understands English?
  İngilizce bilen bir kimse nerede?
  EEN-geh-LEEZ-jeh bee-lehn beer
  KEEM-seh NEH-reh-deh?

To request a room, say:

I want ...
  ... istiyorum.
  ees-tee-YOH-room

a double room
  İki kişilik oda
  ee-KEE kee-shee-leek OH-dah
a twin-bedded room
  Çift yataklı oda
  CHEEFT yah-tahk-LUH OH-dah
room
  oda
  OH-dah
single room
  bir kişilik oda
  BEER kee-shee-leek OH-dah
double room
  iki kişilik oda
  ee-KEE kee-shee-leek OH-dah
room with one bed
  tek yataklı oda
  TEHK yah-tahk-LUH OH-dah
room with two beds
  iki yataklı oda
  ee-KEEyah-tahk-LUH OH-dah

room with bath
  banyolu oda
  BAHN-yoh-LOO OH-dah
a quiet room
  sakin bir oda
  sah-KEEN beer oh-dah

It's very noisy.
  Çok gürültülü.
  CHOHK gew-rewl-tew-lew
What does it cost?
  Kaç lira?
  KAHCH lee-rah

cheaper	
daha ucuz	dah-HAH oo-jooz
better	
daha iyi	dah-HAH ee
very expensive	
çok pahalı	CHOHK pah-hah-luh
bath	
banyo	BAHN-yoh
Turkish bath	
hamam	hah-MAHM
shower	
duş	DOOSH
soap	
sabun	sah-BOON
shampoo	
şampuan	SHAHM-poo-AHN
towel	
havlu	hahv-LOO
toilet paper	
tuvalet kağıdı	too-vah-leht kyah-uh-duh
hot water	
sıcak su	suh-JAHK soo
cold water	
soğuk su	soh-OOH soo
clean	
temiz	teh-MEEZ
not clean	
temiz değil	teh-MEEZ deh-YEEL
air-conditioning	
klima	KLEE-mah
light(s)	
ışık(lar)	uh-SHUHK(-LAHR)
light bulb	
ampül	ahm-PEWL

Getting Around

Where is a/the ...?
  ... nerede?
  NEH-reh-deh

railway station
  gar/istasyon
  GAHR, ees-tah-SYOHN
bus station
  otogar
  OH-toh-gahr
toilet
  tuvalet
  too-vah-LEHT
restaurant
  lokanta
  loh-KAHN-tah
post office
  postane
  POHSS-tah-neh
policeman
  polis memuru
  poh-LEES meh-moo-roo
left luggage/checkroom
  emanetçi
  EH-mah-NEHT-chee
luggage
  bagaj
  bah-GAHZH
street/avenue
  sokak/cadde(si)
  soh-KAHK/JAHD-deh(see)

left
  sol   SOHL
right
  sağ   SAH
straight on
  doğru   doh-ROO
here
  burada   BOO-rah-dah
there
  şurada   SHOO-rah-dah
over there
  orada   OH-rah-dah
near
  yakın   yah-KUHN
far
  uzak   oo-ZAHK

a ticket to (İstanbul)
  (İstanbul'a) bir bilet
  (ih-STAHN-bool-AH) BEER bee-LEHT
map
  harita
  HAH-ree-TAH
timetable
  tarife
  tah-ree-FEH
ticket
  bilet
  bee-LEHT
reserved seat
  numaralı yer
  noo-MAH-rah-LUH yehr
1st class
  birinci sınıf
  beer-EEN-jee mehv-kee
2nd class
  ikinci sınıf
  ee-KEEN-jee mehv-kee
for today
  bugün için
  BOO-gewn ee-cheen
for tomorrow
  yarın için
  yah-ruhn ee-cheen
one-way trip
  gidiş
  gee-DEESH
round-trip
  gidiş-dönüş
  gee-DEESH-dew-NURSH
student (ticket)
  öğrenci (bileti)
  tah-leh-BEH
full-fare (ticket)
  tam (bileti)
  TAHM
daily
  hergün
  HEHR-gurn
today
  bugün
  BOO-gurn
tomorrow
  yarın
  YAHR-uhn

Arrivals & Departures

When does it ...?
Ne zaman ...?   NEH zah-mahn

depart
kalkar   kahl-KAHR
arrive
gelir   geh-LEER

early/late
erken/geç   ehr-KEHN/GECH
fast
çabuk   chah-BOOK
slow
yavaş   yah-VAHSH
next/last
gelecek/son   geh-leh-JEHK/SOHN

Air

aeroplane
uçak   oo-CHAHK
airport
havaalanı   hah-VAH-ah-lah-nuh
flight
uçuş   oo-CHOOSH
gate
kapı   kah-PUH

Boat

ship
gemi   geh-MEE
boat
tekne, motor   TEK-neh, moh-TOHR
rowboat
sandal   sahn-DAHL
ferry
feribot   FEH-ree-boht
dock
iskele   ees-KEH-leh
cabin
kamara   KAH-mah-rah
berth
yatak   yah-TAHK
class
mevki, sınıf   MEHV-kee, suh-nuhf

Bus

bus
otobüs, araba   oh-toh-BEWSS

bus terminal
otogar   OH-toh-gahr
direct (bus)
direk(t)   dee-REK
indirect
aktarmalı   ahk-tahr-mah-LUH

Car

air (tyres)
hava (lâstik)
hah-VAH (lyaass-TEEK)
brake(s)
fren
FREHN
car, truck
araba, kamyon
ah-rah-BAH, kahm-YOHN
diesel fuel
mazot, motorin
mah-SOHT, MOH-toh-reen
auto-electrician
oto elektrikçi
oh-TOH ee-lehk-TREEK-chee
exhaust (system)
egzos(t)
ehk-ZOHSS
headlamp
far
FAHR
highway
karayolu
kah-RAH-yoh-loo
hitchhike
otostop
OH-toh-stohp
motor oil
motor yağı
moh-TOHR yah-uh
petrol, gasoline
benzin
behn-ZEEN
regular
normal
nohr-MAHL
steering (-wheel)
direksiyon
dee-REHK-see-YOHN
super
süper
seur-PEHR

Highway Signs

GİRİLMEZ	No Entry
GİŞELER	Toll Booths
KATOTOPARK	Parking Garage
OTOYOL	Motorway/ Expressway
PARALI GEÇİŞ	Toll Highway
PARK ALANI	Rest Stop
PARK YERİ	Car Park/ Parking Lot
SERVİS ALANI	Service Area
ŞEHİR MERKEZİ	City Centre
TIRMANMA ŞERİDİ	Overtaking/ Passing Lane
ÜCRET ÖDEME	Toll Collection
ÜCRETLİ GEÇİŞ	Toll Highway
VERGİ KONTROLÜ	Tax Checkpoint (for trucks & buses)
YAĞIŞTA KAYGAN YOL	Slippery When Wet
YAVAŞLA	Slow Down

Note Motorway signs are green with white lettering; town signs are blue with white lettering; village signs are white with black lettering. Yellow signs with black lettering mark sights of touristic interest. Yellow signs with blue lettering mark village development projects.

tyre repairman
oto lâstikçi
oh-TOH lyass-TEEK-chee

Train
railway
demiryolu
deh-MEER-yoh-loo
train
tren
tee-REHN
railway station
gar, istasyon
GAHR, ees-tahs-YOHN

couchette
kuşet
koo-SHEHT
sleeping car
yataklı vagon
yah-tahk-LUH vah-gohn
dining car
yemekli vagon
yeh-mehk-LEE vah-gohn
no-smoking car
sigara içilmeyen vagon
see-GAH-rah eech-EEL- mee-yehn

Around Town
Post Office
post office (PTT)
postane, postahane
POHSS-tah-NEH
postage stamp
pul
POOL
by air mail
uçakla, uçak ile
oo-CHAHK-lah, oo-CHAHK-ee-leh
money order
havale
hah-vah-LEH
poste restante
postrestant
pohst-rehs-TAHNT
customs
gümrük
gewm-REWK
inspection (prior to mailing)
kontrol
kohn-TROHL
telephone token (large, medium, small)
jeton (büyük, orta, küçük)
zheh-TOHN (bew-YEWK, ohr-TAH, kew-CHEWK)

Bank
money
para	PAH-rah
Turkish liras
lira	LEE-rah
dollars
dolar	doh-LAHR
foreign currency
döviz	durr-VEEZ

cash		
efektif		eh-fehk-TEEF
cheque		
çek		CHEK
exchange		
kambiyo		KAHM-bee-yoh
exchange rate		
kur		KOOR
commission		
komisyon		koh-mees-YOHN
identification		
kimlik		KEEM-leek
cashier		
kasa, vezne		KAH-sah, VEHZ-neh
working hours		
çalışma saatleri		chal-ush-MAH sah-aht-leh-ree

Days of the Week

day		
gün		GEWN
week		
hafta		hahf-TAH
Sunday		
Pazar		pah-ZAHR
Monday		
Pazartesi		pah-ZAHR-teh-see
Tuesday		
Salı		sah-LUH
Wednesday		
Çarşamba		char-shahm-BAH
Thursday		
Perşembe		pehr-shehm-BEH
Friday		
Cuma		joo-MAH
Saturday		
Cumartesi		joo-MAHR-teh-see

Months of the Year

month		
ay		AHY
year		
sene, yıl		SEH-neh, YUHL
January	*Ocak*	oh-JAHK
February	*Şubat*	shoo-BAHT
March	*Mart*	MAHRT
April	*Nisan*	nee-SAHN
May	*Mayıs*	mah-YUSS
June	*Haziran*	HAH-zee-RAHN

July	*Temmuz*	teh-MOOZ
August	*Ağustos*	AH-oo-STOHSS
September	*Eylül*	ehy-LEWL
October	*Ekim*	eh-KEEM
November	*Kasım*	kah-SUHM
December	*Aralık*	AH-rah-LUHK

Health

handicapped		
özürlü/		ur-zuhr-LUR/
sakat		sah-KAHT
hospital		
hastane		hahss-tah-NEH
dispensary		
sağlık ocağı		saah-LUHK oh-jah-uh
I'm ill.		
Hastayım.		hahss-TAH-yuhm
My stomach hurts.		
Karnım ağrıyor.		kahr-NUHM aah-ruh-yohr
Help me.		
Yardım edin.		yahr-DUHM eh-den

Shopping

shop		
dükkan		dyook-KAHN
market		
çarşı		chahr-SHUH
price		
fiyat		fee-YAHT
service charge		
servis ücreti		sehr-VEES ewj-reh-tee
tax		
vergi		VEHR-gee
cheap		
ucuz		oo-JOOZ
expensive		
pahalı		pah-hah-LUH
very expensive		
çok pahalı		CHOHK pah-hah-luh
Which?		
Hangi?		HAHN-gee
this one		
bunu		boo-NOO
Do you have ...?		
... var mı?		VAHR muh
We don't have ...		
... yok		YOHK
I'll give you ...		
... vereceğim		VEH-reh-JEH-yeem

Children

child(ren)
    çocuk(lar)   CHO-jook-(LAHR)
baby
    bebek   beh-BEHK
diaper (nappy)
    bebek bezi   beh-BEHK beh-zee
nursery
    kreş   KRESH

Numbers

-½   *yarım*   YAH-ruhm
    (used alone, as in 'I want half')
-½   *buçuk*   boo-CHOOK
    (always used with a whole number,
    eg '1-½', *bir buçuk*)

0	*sıfır*	SUH-fuhr
1	*bir*	BEER
2	*iki*	ee-KEE
3	*üç*	EWCH
4	*dört*	DURRT
5	*beş*	BEHSH
6	*altı*	ahl-TUH
7	*yedi*	yeh-DEE
8	*sekiz*	seh-KEEZ
9	*dokuz*	doh-KOOZ
10	*on*	OHN
11	*on bir*	ohn BEER
12	*on iki*	ohn ee-KEE
13	*on üç*	ohn EWCH
20	*yirmi*	yeer-MEE
30	*otuz*	oh-TOOZ
40	*kırk*	KUHRK
50	*elli*	ehl-LEE
60	*altmış*	ahlt-MUSH
70	*yetmiş*	yeht-MEESH
80	*seksen*	sehk-SEHN
90	*doksan*	dohk-SAHN
100	*yüz*	YEWZ
200	*iki yüz*	ee-KEE yewz
1000	*bin*	BEEN
2000	*iki bin*	ee-KEE been
10,000	*on bin*	OHN been

one million
    milyon   meel-YOHN

Ordinal numbers consist of the number plus the suffix *-inci*, *-ıncı*, *-uncu* or *-üncü*, depending upon 'vowel harmony'.

first
    birinci   beer-EEN-jee
second
    ikinci   ee-KEEN-jee
sixth
    altıncı   ahl-TUHN-juh
13th
    onüçüncü   ohn-ew-CHEWN-jew

Emergencies

Help!
    İmdat!
    eem-daht
It's an emergency.
    Acil durum.
    ah-jeel doo-room
I'm ill.
    Rahatsızım.
    rah-haht-sih-zihm
Call the police!
    Polisi çağırın!
    poh-lee-see chah-ihr-rihn
Find a doctor!
    Doktoru arayın (pol)/ara! (inf)
    dohk-toh-roo ah-rah-yihn/ah-rah
(There's a) fire!
    Yangın var!
    yahn-gihn vahr
There's been an accident.
    Bir kaza oldu.
    beer kah-zah ohl-doo
Go away!
    Gidin (pol)/Git! (inf)
    gee-deen/geet
I've been raped/assaulted.
    Tecavüze/Saldırıya uğradım.
    teh-jah-vyu-zeh/sahl-dih-rih-yah
    oo-rah-dihm
I've been robbed.
    Soyuldum.
    sohy-ool-doom
I'm lost.
    Kayboldum.
    kahy-bohl-doom
Where are the toilets?
    Tuvalet nerede?
    too-vah-leht neh-reh-deh

Burma - Pistachio
Kadayıf = pastry (shredded)

FOOD
Basics
restaurant
  lokanta   loh-KAHN-tah
pastry-shop
  pastane   PAHSS-tah-neh
'oven' (bakery)
  fırın   FUH-ruhn
'pizza' place
  pideci   PEE-deh-jee
köfte restaurant
  köfteci   KURF-teh-jee
kebap restaurant
  kebapçı   keh-BAHP-chuh
snack shop
  büfe   bew-FEH

alcohol served
  içkili
  eech-kee-LEE
no alcohol served
  içkisiz
  eech-kee-SEEZ
family (ladies') dining room
  aile salonu
  ah-yee-LEH sah-loh-noo
no single men allowed
  aileye mahsustur
  ah-yee-LEH mah-SOOS-tuhr

breakfast
  kahvahltı
  KAHH-vahl-TUH
lunch
  öğle yemeği   ̶̶̶̶̶H veh-meh-yee
supper
  ̶̶̶̶̶̶vı
  ̶̶̶̶e

glass
  bardak   bahr-DAHK
bill, cheque
  hesap   heh-SAHP
service charge
  servis ücreti   sehr-VEES ewj-reh-tee
tax
  vergi   VEHR-gee
tip
  bahşiş   bah-SHEESH
error
  yanlış   yahn-LUSH
small change
  bozuk para   boh-ZOOK pah-rah

The Menu
This guide to restaurant words is arranged
(more or less) in the order of a Turkish menu
and a Turkish meal. Courses (*çorba, et* etc)
are listed in the singular form; you may see
them in the plural (*çorbalar, etler* etc).

Soup
balık çorbası   fish soup
  bah-LUHK
  chor-bah-suh
çorba   soup
  CHOHR-bah
domates çorbası   tomato soup
  doh-MAH-tess
  chor-bah-suh
düğün çorbası   egg & lemon soup
  dew-EWN
  chor-bah-suh
et suyu (yumurtalı)   mutton broth with egg
  EHT soo-yoo,
  yoo-moor-tah-LUH
ezo gelin çorbası   lentil & rice soup
  EH-zoh GEH-leen
  chor-bah-suh
haşlama   broth with mutton
  hahsh-lah-MAH
işkembe çorbası   tripe soup
  eesh-KEHM-beh
  chor-bah-suh
mercimek çorbası   lentil soup
  mehr-jee-MEHK
  chor-bah-suh
paça   trotter soup
  PAH-chah

sebze çorbası SEHB-zeh chor-bah-suh	vegetable soup
şehriye çorbası shehh-ree-YEH chor-bah-suh	vermicelli soup
tavuk çorbası tah-VOOK chor-bah-suh	chicken soup
yayla çorbası YAHY-lah chor-bah-suh	yoghurt & barley soup

Hors d'Oeuvres

Meze (MEH-zeh), or hors d'oeuvres, can include almost anything, and you can easily – and delightfully – make an entire meal of meze. Often you'll be brought a tray from which you can choose those you want.

beyaz peynir bey-AHZ pehy-neer	white cheese
börek bur-REHK	flaky pastry
etli eht-LEE	stuffed with lamb (hot)
kabak dolması kah-BAHK dohl-mah-suh	stuffed squash/marrow
patlıcan salatası paht-luh-JAHN sah-lah-tah-suh	aubergine or eggplant puree
pilaki, piyaz pee-LAH-kee	cold white beans vinaigrette
tarama salatası tah-rah-MAH sah-lah-tah-suh	red caviar in mayonnaise
yalancı dolması yah-LAHN-juh dohl-mah-suh	stuffed vine leaves
yaprak dolması yah-PRAHK dohl-mah-suh	stuffed vine leaves
zeytinyağlı zehy-teen-yah-LUH	stuffed with rice (cold)

Salads

Each of the following Turkish names would be followed by the word *salata* (sah-LAH-tah) or *salatası*. You may be asked if you prefer it *sirkeli* (SEER-keh-LEE), with vinegar or *limonlu* (LEE-mohn-LOO), with lemon juice; most salads (except *söğüş*) come with olive oil. If you don't like hot peppers, say *bibersiz* (BEE-behr-SEEZ), though this often doesn't work.

Amerikan/Rus ah-meh-ree-KAHN/ROOSS	mayonnaise, peas & carrots
beyin behy-EEN	sheep's brain
domates salatalık doh-MAH-tess sah-LAH-tah-luhk	tomato & cucumber salad
karışık (çoban) kah-ruh-SHUHK (choh-BAHN)	chopped mixed salad
marul mah-ROOL	romaine lettuce
patlıcan paht-luh-JAHN	roast aubergine/ eggplant puree
söğüş sur-EWSH	sliced vegetables, no sauce
turşu toor-SHOO	pickled vegetables
yeşil yeh-SHEEL	green salad

Fish

A menu is of no use when ordering fish (*balık*, bah-LUHK). You'll have to ask the waiter what's fresh, and then ask for the approximate price. The fish will then be weighed, and the price computed at the day's per-kg rate. Sometimes you can haggle. Buy fish in season (*mevsimli*, mehv-seem-LEE), as fish out of season are very expensive. From March to the end of June is a good time to order *kalkan* (turbot), *uskumru* (mackerel), and *hamsi* (fresh anchovies), but from July to mid-August is spawning season for many species, and fishing them is prohibited. In high summer, the following are the easiest to find in the markets and on the restaurant tables: *çinakop* (a small bluefish), *lüfer* (medium-size bluefish), *palamut* (bonito), *tekir* (striped goatfish: *Mullus surmuletus*), *barbunya* (red mullet: *Mullus barbatus*), and *istavrit* (scad, horse mackerel).

alabalık ah-LAH-bah-luhk	trout
barbunya bahr-BOON-yah	red mullet
dil balığı DEEL bah-luh	sole
hamsi HAHM-see	anchovy (fresh)
havyar hahv-YAHR	caviar
istakoz uhss-tah-KOHZ	lobster
kalkan kahl-KAHN	turbot
karagöz kah-rah-GURZ	black bream
karides kah-REE-dess	shrimp
kefal keh-FAHL	grey mullet
kılıç kuh-LUHCH	swordfish
levrek lehv-REHK	sea bass
lüfer lew-FEHR	bluefish
mercan mehr-JAHN	red coralfish
midye MEED-yeh	mussels
palamut PAH-lah-moot	tunny, bonito
pisi PEE-see	plaice
sardalya sahr-DAHL-yah	sardine (fresh)
tarama tah-rah-MAH	roe, red caviar
trança TRAHN-chah	Aegean tuna
uskumru oos-KOOM-roo	mackerel
yengeç yehn-GECH	crab

Meat & Kebap

In *kebap* (keh-BAHP), the meat (*et*, EHT) is always lamb, ground or in chunks; preparation, spices and extras (onions, peppers, bread) make the difference among the kebaps. Some may be ordered *yoğurtlu* (yoh-oort-LOO), with a side-serving of yoghurt.

If you don't eat meat, ask *Etsiz yemek var mı?* (eht-SEEZ yeh-mehk VAHR muh, Have you any meatless dishes?), or say *Hiç et yiyemem* (HEECH eht yee-YEH-mehm, I can't eat any meat). The word *vejeteryan* (vegetarian) is slowly gaining currency.

Adana kebap ah-DAH-nah keh-bahp	spicy-hot roast köfte
böbrek bur-BREHK	kidney
bonfile bohn-fee-LEH	small fillet beefsteak
bursa kebap BOOR-sah keh-bahp	döner with tomato sauce
çerkez tavuğu cher-KEHZ tah-voo	chicken in walnut sauce
ciğer jee-EHR	liver
çöp kebap CHURP keh-bahp	tiny bits of skewered lamb
dana DAH-nah	veal
domuz doh-MOOZ	pork (forbidden to Muslims)
döner kebap dur-NEHR keh-bahp	spit-roasted lamb slices
etli pide/ekmek eht-LEE PEE-deh, ehk-MEHK	flat bread with minced lamb
güveç gew-VECH	meat & vegetable stew

kağıt kebap kyah-UHT keh-bahp	lamb & vegetables in paper
karışık ızgara kah-ruh-shuk uhz-gah-rah	mixed grill (lamb)
koç yumurtası KOHCH yoo-moor-tah-suh	ram's 'eggs' (testicles)
köfte KURF-teh	grilled minced lamb patties
mantı mahn-TUH	ravioli (Turkish-style)
orman kebap ohr-MAHN keh-bahp	roast lamb with onions
pastırma pahss-TUHR-mah	sun-dried, spiced beef
patlıcan kebap paht-luh-JAHN keh-bahp	aubergine/eggplant & meat
piliç pee-LEECH	roasting chicken
pirzola peer-ZOH-lah	cutlet (usually lamb)
saç kavurma SAHTCH kah-voor-mah	wok-fried lamb
şatobriyan sha-TOH-bree-YAHN	chateaubriand
sığır suh-UHR	beef
şinitzel shee-NEET-zehl	wienerschnitzel
şiş kebap SHEESH keh-bahp	roast skewered lamb
(süt) kuzu (sewt) koo-ZOO	milk-fed lamb
tandır kebap tahn-DUHR keh-bahp	pit-roasted lamb
tas kebap TAHSS keh-bahp	lamb stew
tavuk tah-VOOK	boiling chicken

tavuk/piliç döner tah-VOOK/pee-LEECH dur-NEHR	spit-roasted chicken slices
tavuk/piliç şiş tah-VOOK/pee-LEECH sheesh	roast skewered chicken

There are numerous fancy kebaps, often named for the places where they originated. Best is *Bursa kebap* (BOOR-sah), also called *İskender kebap*, since it was invented in the city of Bursa by a chef named Iskender (Alexander). Of the other fancy kebaps, *Urfa kebap* comes with lots of onions and black pepper; *Adana kebap* is spicy hot, with red pepper the way the Arabs like it.

Sweets

aşure ah-shoo-REH	walnut, raisin & pea pudding
baklava bahk-lah-VAH	layered pastry with honey, nuts
burma kadayıf boor-MAH kah-dah-yuhf	shredded wheat with pistachios & honey
dondurma dohn-DOOR-mah	ice cream
ekmek kadayıf ehk-MEHK kah-dah-yuhf	crumpet in syrup
fırın sütlaç foo-roon SEWT-lach	baked rice pudding (cold)
güllaç gewl-LACH	flaky pastry, nuts & milk
helva hehl-VAH	semolina sweet
hurma tatlısı hoor-MAH	semolina cake in syrup
kabak tatlısı kah-BAHK TAHT-luh-suh	candied marrow/squash

kadın göbeği   'Lady's navel',
                   doughnut in syrup
   kah-DUHN
   gur-beh-yee
kazandibi   'bottom of the pot'
                   (cold baked pudding)
   kah-ZAHN-
   dee-bee
kek   cake
   KEHK
keşkül   milk & nut pudding
   kehsh-KEWL
komposto   stewed fruit
   kohm-POHSS-toh
krem karamel   baked caramel custard
   KREHM
   kah-rah-MEHL
krem şokolada   chocolate pudding
   KREHM shoh-
   koh-LAH-dah
lokum   Turkish delight
   loh-KOOM
meyve   fruit
   mehy-VEH
muhallebi   rice flour & rosewater
                   pudding
   moo-HAH-leh-bee
pasta   pastry
   PAHSS-tah
peynir tatlısı   cheese cake
   pehy-NEER
   TAHT-luh-suh
sütlaç   rice pudding
   sewt-LAHCH
tatlı   sweet, dessert
   taht-LUH
tavuk göğsü   sweet of milk, rice &
                   chicken
   tah-VOOK
   gur-sew
tel kadayıf   shredded wheat in
                   syrup
   TEHL kah-
   dah-yuhf
yoğurt tatlısı   yoghurt & egg
                   pudding
   yoh-OORT
   taht-luh-suh
zerde   saffron & rice sweet
   zehr-DEH

Other Dishes & Condiments

bal   honey
   BAHL
beyaz peynir   white (sheep's) cheese
   bey-AHZ pey-neer
biber   green pepper
   bee-BEHR
bisküvi   biscuits
   BEES-koo-VEE
börek (-ği)   flaky or fried pastry
   bur-REHK
buz   ice
   BOOZ
cacık   yoghurt & grated
                   cucumber
   jah-JUHK
dolma(sı) lahana   stuffed (vegetable)
                   cabbage leaves
   DOHL-mah(-suh)
   lah-HAH-nah
ekmek   bread
   ehk-MEHK
hardal   mustard
   hahr-DAHL
imam bayıldı   aubergine baked with
                   onions & tomatoes
   ee-MAHM
   bah-yuhl-duh
kabak   marrow/squash
   kah-BAHK
kara/siyah biber   black pepper
   kah-RAH/
karnıyarık   aubergine & lamb (hot)
   KAHR-nuh-
   yah-RUHK
kaşar peynir   mild yellow cheese
   kah-SHAHR
   pey-neer
limon   lemon
   lee-MOHN
makarna   macaroni, noodles
   mah-KAHR-nah
musakka   aubergine & lamb pie
   moo-sah-KAH
   see-YAH bee-behr
pasta   pastry (not noodles)
   PAHSS-tah
peynir   cheese
   pehy-NEER
pide   pizza, flat bread
   PEE-deh

reçel reh-CHEHL	fruit jam
sarmısak SAHR-muh-SAHK	garlic
şeker sheh-KEHR	sugar, candy, sweets
sigara see-GAH-rah	'cigarette' fritters
sirke SEER-keh	vinegar
spaket spah-KEHT	spaghetti
su SOO	water
tereyağı TEH-reh-yah	butter
tuz TOOZ	salt
yağ YAH	oil, fat
yalancı yah-LAHN-juh	vine leaves
yaprak yah-PRAHK	vine leaves
yoğurt yoh-OORT	yoghurt
zeytin zehy-TEEN	olives
zeytinyağı zehy-TEEN-yah-uh	olive oil

Cooking Terms

buğlama BOO-lah-MAH	steamed, poached
ezme(si) ehz-MEH(-see)	puree
fırın fuh-RUHN	baked, oven-roasted
haşlama hahsh-lah-MAH	boiled, stewed
iyi pişmiş ee-YEE peesh-meesh	well-done
ızgara uhz-GAH-rah	charcoal grilled
kızartma kuh-ZAHRT-mah	broiled
rosto ROHSS-toh	roasted

sıcak suh-JAHK	hot, warm
soğuk soh-OOK	cold
etli eht-LEE	with meat
kıymalı kuhy-mah-LUH	with ground lamb
peynirli pehy-neer-LEE	with cheese
salçalı sahl-chah-LUH	with savoury tomato sauce
soslu, terbiyeli sohss-LOO, TEHR-bee-yeh-LEE	with sauce
yoğurtlu YOH-oort-LOO	with yoghurt
yumurtalı yoo-moor-tah-LUH	with egg

Street Food

dürüm dur-RURM	grilled lamb roll-up
gözleme GURZ-leh-meh	Turkish crêpe
kuru yemiş koo-ROO yeh-MEESH	dried fruits
peynirli sandviç pehy-neer-LEE sahn-dveech	grilled cheese sandwich
simit see-MEET	sesame-covered circle roll

Fruit

Turkish fruits are superb, especially in mid-summer when the melon season starts, and early in winter when the first citrus crops start to come in.

armut ahr-MOOT	pear
ayva ahy-VAH	quince
çilek chee-LEHK	strawberries
elma ehl-MAH	apple

greyfurut	grapefruit
GREY-foo-root	
incir	fig
een-JEER	
karpuz	watermelon
kahr-POOZ	
kavun	yellow melon
kah-VOON	
kayısı	apricot
kahy-SUH	
kiraz	cherry
kee-RAHZ	
mandalin	tangerine, mandarin
mahn-dah-LEEN	
meyva, meyve	fruit
mehy-VAH	
muz	banana
MOOZ	
nar	pomegranate
NAHR	
portakal	orange
pohr-tah-KAHL	
şeftali	peach
shef-tah-LEE	
üzüm	grapes
ew-ZEWM	
vişne	morello (sour cherry)
VEESH-neh	

Vegetables

bamya	okra
BAHM-yah	
barbunye	red beans
bahr-BOON-yeh	
bezelye	peas
beh-ZEHL-yeh	
biber	peppers
bee-BEHR	
domates	tomato
doh-MAH-tess	
havuç	carrot
hah-VOOCH	
ıspınak	spinach
uhs-spuh-NAHK	
kabak	marrow/squash
kah-BAHK	
karnabahar	cauliflower
kahr-NAH-bah-hahr	

kuru fasulye	white beans
koo-ROO fah-sool-yah	
lahana	cabbage
lah-HAH-nah	
patates	potato
pah-TAH-tess	
salatalık	cucumber
sah-LAH-tah-luhk	
sebze	vegetable
sehb-ZEH	
soğan	onion
soh-AHN	
taze fasulye	green beans
tah-ZEH fah-sool-yah	
turp	radish
TOORP	

Cheese

Although there are some interesting peasant cheeses – such as *tulum peynir* (a salty, dry, crumbly goats' milk cheese cured in a goatskin bag) and a dried cheese which looks just like twine – they rarely make it to the cities and almost never to restaurant tables. What you'll find is the ubiquitous *beyaz peynir* (bey-AHZ pey-neer), white sheep's milk cheese. To be really good, it must be full-cream *(tam yağlı)* cheese, not dry and crumbly and not too salty or sour. You may also find *kaşar peynir* (kah-SHAHR pey-neer), a firm, mild yellow cheese, either fresh *(taze,* tah-ZEH) or aged *(eski,* ess-KEE).

DRINKS

İçki (eech-KEE) usually refers to alcoholic beverages, *meşrubat* (mehsh-roo-BAHT) to soft drinks. When waiters ask *İçecek?* or *Ne içeceksiniz?*, they're asking what you'd like to drink.

As for Turkish coffee (*kahve*, kahh-VEH) you must order it according to sweetness: the sugar is mixed in during the brewing, not afterwards. You can drink it *sade* (sah-DEH), without sugar; *az* (AHZ), if you want just a bit of sugar; *orta* (ohr-TAH), with a middling amount; *çok* or *şekerli* or even *çok şekerli* (CHOHK sheh-kehr-LEE), with lots of sugar. When the coffee arrives, the waiter may well have confused the cups, and you may find yourself exchanging with your dinnermates.

Nescafé is readily found throughout Turkey but tends to be expensive, often around 70c per cup.

Nonalcoholic Drinks

su	water
SOO	
maden suyu	mineral water
mah-DEHN	
soo-yoo	
maden sodası	fizzy mineral water
mah-DEHN	
soh-dah-suh	
menba suyu	spring water
mehn-BAH	
soo-yoo	
limonata	lemonade
lee-moh-NAH-tah	
meyva suyu	fruit juice
mey-VAH soo-yoo	
süt	milk
SEWT	
ayran	yoghurt drink
AH-yee-RAHN	
boza	thick millet drink
BOH-zah	
çay	tea
CHAH-yee	
çay bahçesi	tea garden
CHAH-yee	
bahh-cheh-see	
kahve(si)	coffee
kah-VEH(-see)	
Fransız	coffee & milk
frahn-SUHZ	
Amerikan	American coffee
ah-meh-ree-	
KAHN	

neskafe	instant coffee
NEHSS-kah-feh	
Türk kahvesi	Turkish coffee
TEWRK kahh-	
veh-see	
sahlep	hot milk & tapioca root
sah-LEHP	

Alcoholic Drinks

bira	beer
BEE-rah	
beyaz	light
bey-AHZ	
fıçı bira	draught ('keg')
fuh-CHUH	
bee-rah	
siyah	dark
see-YAH	
şarap	wine
shah-RAHP	
beyaz	white
bey-AHZ	
kırmızı	red
kuhr-muh-ZUH	
köpüklü	sparkling
kur-pewk-LEW	
roze	rose
roh-ZEH	
cin	gin
JEEN	
rakı	aniseed-flavoured brandy
rah-KUH	
viski	whisky
VEE-skee	
vermut	vermouth
vehr-MOOT	
votka	vodka
VOHT-kah	

Glossary

Here, with definitions, are some useful words and abbreviations. For an extensive list of translations for food and food-related words and menu items, see the Turkish Language section.

aile salonu – family room; for couples, families and single women in a Turkish restaurant
altgeçidi – pedestrian subway/underpass
arasta – row of shops near a mosque, the rent from which supports the mosque

banliyö treni/trenleri – suburban (or commuter) train/s
bebek – infant
bebek bezi – nappies (baby diapers)
bedesten – vaulted, fireproof market enclosure or warehouse where valuable goods are kept
bekçi – caretaker or guardian
Belediye Zabıtası – market inspector
boğaz – strait
bordro – exchange receipt

çalışma vizesi – work visa
çamaşır – laundry; underwear
cami(i) – mosque
çarşı – market, bazaar
cicim – embroidered kilim
çift – pair
çocuk/lar – child/ren

deniz – sea
deniz otobüsü – catamaran; sea bus
Dikkat! Yavaş! – Careful! Slow!
dolmuş – shared taxi (or minibus)
döviz bürosu – currency exchange office

eczane – chemist/pharmacy
emniyet – security
ezan – call to prayer

ferman – imperial edict
fiş – electricity plug

gazino – open-air Turkish nightclub (not for gambling)
gece – night
göbektaşı – hot platform in Turkish bath
gündüz – daytime

hamam(ı) – Turkish steam bath
han – caravanserai
harem – family/women's quarters of a residence
hat(tı) – route
hattat – Arabic calligraphy
hekimbaşı – chief physician to the sultan

ikamet tezkeresi – residence permit
imam – prayer leader; Muslim cleric; teacher
imaret(i) – soup kitchen for the poor
iskele(si) – landing-place, wharf, quay

jeton – token (for telephones)

kadın – wife
kafes – cage
kapı(sı) – door, gate
kasr – imperial lodge
kat – storey (of a building)
katma değer vergisi (KDV) – value-added tax (VAT)
kilise(si) – church
kızlarağası – chief black eunuch
köprü – bridge
köşk(ü) – pavilion, villa
köy(ü) – village
kreş – daycare
kule(si) – tower
külliye(si) – mosque complex including seminary, hospital, soup kitchen etc
kuru temizleme – dry cleaning

liman(ı) – harbour
lokum – Turkish delight

mahalli hamam – neighbourhood Turkish bath
mahfil – high, elaborate chair

Maşallah – Wonder of God! (said in admiration or to avert the evil eye)
medrese(si) – Muslim theological seminary
menba suyu – spring water
merkez postane – central post office
mescit – prayer room/small mosque
meydan(ı) – public square, open place
meyhane – wine shop, taverna
mevlevi – whirling dervish
mihrab – niche in a mosque indicating the direction of Mecca
mimber – pulpit in a mosque
minare(si) – minaret, tower from which Muslims are called to prayer
müezzin – cantor who sings the *ezan*, or call to prayer
müze(si) – museum

nargile – hookah, water pipe

oda(sı) – room
otel – hotel
otogar – bus terminal
otostop – hitchhike
otoyol – multi-lane toll highway

padişah – Ottoman emperor, sultan
pansiyon – pension, B&B, guesthouse
pazar(ı) – weekly market, bazaar
polis – police
PTT – Posta, Telefon, Telğraf: post, telephone and telegraph office

rakı – aniseed-flavoured grape brandy

şadırvan – fountain where Muslims perform ritual ablutions
saray(ı) – palace
saz – traditional Turkish long-necked string instrument
sebil – public fountain or water kiosk
sedir – low sofa
şehir – city; municipal
sema – Sufic religious ceremony
servis ücreti – service charge
servis yolu – service road
sıcak şarap – mulled wine
şile bezi – an open-weave cotton cloth with hand embroidery
sinema – cinema
Sufi – Muslim mystic, member of a mystic ('dervish') brotherhood
sultan – lord
sünnet odası – circumcision room

tarikat – a Sufic order
TC – Türkiye Cumhuriyeti (Turkish Republic), designates an official office or organisation
tekke(si) – dervish lodge(s)
telekart – telephone debit card
tuğra – sultan's monogram, imperial signature
türbe(si) – tomb, grave, mausoleum

valide sultan – queen mother

yalı – seaside villa
yardımcı – assistant
yıldız – star
yol(u) – road, way
yüzyıl – century

LONELY PLANET

Phrasebooks

onely Planet phrasebooks are packed with essential words and phrases to help travellers communicate with the locals. With colour tabs for quick reference, an extensive vocabulary and use of script, these handy pocket-sized language guides cover day-to-day travel situations.

- handy pocket-sized books
- easy to understand Pronunciation chapter
- clear & comprehensive Grammar chapter
- romanisation alongside script to allow ease of pronunciation
- script throughout so users can point to phrases for every situation
- full of cultural information and tips for the traveller

'... vital for a real DIY spirit and attitude in language learning'
– *Backpacker*

'the phrasebooks have good cultural backgrounders and offer solid advice for challenging situations in remote locations'
– *San Francisco Examiner*

Arabic (Egyptian) • Arabic (Moroccan) • Australian *(Australian English, Aboriginal and Torres Strait languages)* • Baltic States *(Estonian, Latvian, Lithuanian)* • Bengali • Brazilian • British • Burmese • Cantonese • Central Asia (Uyghur, Uzbek, Kyrghiz, Kazak, Pashto, Tadjik • Central Europe *(Czech, French, German, Hungarian, Italian, Slovak)* • Eastern Europe *(Bulgarian, Czech, Hungarian, Polish, Romanian, Slovak)* • Ethiopian (Amharic) • Farsi (Persian) • Fijian • French • German • Greek • Hebrew • Hill Tribes • Hindi & Urdu • Indonesian • Italian • Japanese • Korean • Lao • Latin American Spanish • Malay • Mandarin • Mediterranean Europe *(Albanian, Croatian, Greek, Italian, Macedonian, Maltese, Serbian, Slovene)* • Mongolian • Nepali • Pidgin • Pilipino (Tagalog) • Portugese • Quechua • Russian • Scandinavian Europe *(Danish, Finnish, Icelandic, Norwegian, Swedish)* • South-East Asia *(Burmese, Indonesian, Khmer, Lao, Malay, Tagalog Pilipino, Thai, Vietnamese)* • South Pacific Languages • Spanish (Castilian) *(also includes Catalan, Galician and Basque)* • Sri Lanka • Swahili • Thai • Tibetan • Turkish • Ukrainian • USA *(US English, Vernacular, Native American languages, Hawaiian)* • Vietnamese • Western Europe *(Basque, Catalan, Dutch, French, German, Greek, Irish, Italian, Portuguese, Scottish Gaelic, Spanish (Castilian), Welsh)*

LONELY PLANET

Guides by Region

Lonely Planet is known worldwide for publishing practical, reliable and no-nonsense travel information in our guides and on our Web site. The Lonely Planet list covers just about every accessible part of the world. Currently there are 16 series: Travel guides, Shoestring guides, Condensed guides, Phrasebooks, Read This First, Healthy Travel, Walking guides, Cycling guides, Watching Wildlife guides, Pisces Diving & Snorkeling guides, City Maps, Road Atlases, Out to Eat, World Food, Journeys travel literature and Pictorials.

AFRICA Africa on a shoestring • Cairo • Cairo City Map • Cape Town • Cape Town City Map • East Africa • Egypt • Egyptian Arabic phrasebook • Ethiopia, Eritrea & Djibouti • Ethiopian (Amharic) phrasebook • The Gambia & Senegal • Healthy Travel Africa • Kenya • Malawi • Morocco • Moroccan Arabic phrasebook • Mozambique • Read This First: Africa • South Africa, Lesotho & Swaziland • Southern Africa • Southern Africa Road Atlas • Swahili phrasebook • Tanzania, Zanzibar & Pemba • Trekking in East Africa • Tunisia • Watching Wildlife East Africa • Watching Wildlife Southern Africa • West Africa • World Food Morocco • Zimbabwe, Botswana & Namibia
Travel Literature: Mali Blues: Traveling to an African Beat • The Rainbird: A Central African Journey • Songs to an African Sunset: A Zimbabwean Story

AUSTRALIA & THE PACIFIC Auckland • Australia • Australian phrasebook • Australia Road Atlas • Bushwalking in Australia • Cycling Australia • Cycling New Zealand • Fiji • Fijian phrasebook • Healthy Travel Australia, NZ and the Pacific • Islands of Australia's Great Barrier Reef • Melbourne • Melbourne City Map • Micronesia • New Caledonia • New South Wales & the ACT • New Zealand • Northern Territory • Outback Australia • Out to Eat – Melbourne • Out to Eat – Sydney • Papua New Guinea • Pidgin phrasebook • Queensland • Rarotonga & the Cook Islands • Samoa • Solomon Islands • South Australia • South Pacific • South Pacific phrasebook • Sydney • Sydney City Map • Sydney Condensed • Tahiti & French Polynesia • Tasmania • Tonga • Tramping in New Zealand • Vanuatu • Victoria • Walking in Australia • Watching Wildlife Australia • Western Australia
Travel Literature: Islands in the Clouds: Travels in the Highlands of New Guinea • Kiwi Tracks: A New Zealand Journey • Sean & David's Long Drive

CENTRAL AMERICA & THE CARIBBEAN Bahamas, Turks & Caicos • Baja California • Bermuda • Central America on a shoestring • Costa Rica • Costa Rica Spanish phrasebook • Cuba • Dominican Republic & Haiti • Eastern Caribbean • Guatemala • Guatemala, Belize & Yucatán: La Ruta Maya • Havana • Healthy Travel Central & South America • Jamaica • Mexico • Mexico City • Panama • Puerto Rico • Read This First: Central & South America • World Food Mexico • Yucatán
Travel Literature: Green Dreams: Travels in Central America

EUROPE Amsterdam • Amsterdam City Map • Amsterdam Condensed • Andalucía • Austria • Baltic States phrasebook • Barcelona • Barcelona City Map • Belgium & Luxembourg • Berlin • Berlin City Map • Britain • British phrasebook • Brussels • Brussels, Bruges & Antwerp • Brussels City Map • Budapest • Budapest City Map • Canary Islands • Central Europe • Central Europe phrasebook • Corfu & the Ionians • Corsica • Crete • Crete Condensed • Croatia • Cycling Britain • Cycling France • Cyprus • Czech & Slovak Republics • Denmark • Dublin • Dublin City Map • Eastern Europe • Eastern Europe phrasebook • Edinburgh • Estonia, Latvia & Lithuania • Europe on a shoestring • Finland • Florence • France • Frankfurt Condensed • French phrasebook • Georgia, Armenia & Azerbaijan • Germany • German phrasebook • Greece • Greek Islands • Greek phrasebook • Hungary • Iceland, Greenland & the Faroe Islands • Ireland • Istanbul • Italian phrasebook • Italy • Krakow • Lisbon • The Loire • London • London City Map • London Condensed • Madrid • Malta • Mediterranean Europe • Mediterranean Europe phrasebook • Moscow • Mozambique • Munich • the Netherlands • Norway • Out to Eat – London • Paris • Paris City Map • Paris Condensed • Poland • Portugal • Portuguese phrasebook • Prague • Prague City Map • Provence & the Côte d'Azur • Read This First: Europe • Romania & Moldova • Rome • Rome City Map • Russia, Ukraine & Belarus • Russian phrasebook • Scandinavian & Baltic Europe • Scandinavian Europe phrasebook • Scotland • Sicily • Slovenia • South-West France • Spain • Spanish phrasebook • St Petersburg • St Petersburg City Map • Sweden • Switzerland • Trekking in Spain • Tuscany • Ukrainian phrasebook • Venice • Vienna • Walking in Britain • Walking in France • Walking in Ireland • Walking in Italy • Walking in Spain • Walking in Switzerland • Western Europe • Western Europe phrasebook • World Food France • World Food Ireland • World Food Italy • World Food Spain
Travel Literature: A Small Place in Italy • After Yugoslavia • Love and War in the Apennines • On the Shores of the Mediterranean The Olive Grove: Travels in Greece • Round Ireland in Low Gear

LONELY PLANET

Mail Order

L onely Planet products are distributed worldwide. They are also available by mail order from Lonely Planet, so if you have difficulty finding a title please write to us. North and South American residents should write to 150 Linden St, Oakland, CA 94607, USA; European and African residents should write to 10a Spring Place, London NW5 3BH, UK; and residents of other countries to Locked Bag 1, Footscray, Victoria 3011, Australia.

INDIAN SUBCONTINENT Bangladesh • Bengali phrasebook • Bhutan • Delhi • Goa • Healthy Travel Asia & India • Hindi & Urdu phrasebook • India • Indian Himalaya • Karakoram Highway • Kerala • Mumbai (Bombay) • Nepal • Nepali phrasebook • Pakistan • Rajasthan • Read This First: Asia & India • South India • Sri Lanka • Sri Lanka phrasebook • Tibet • Tibetan phrasebook • Trekking in the Indian Himalaya • Trekking in the Karakoram & Hindukush • Trekking in the Nepal Himalaya
Travel Literature: The Age of Kali: Indian Travels and Encounters • Hello Goodnight: A Life of Goa • In Rajasthan • A Season in Heaven: True Tales from the Road to Kathmandu • Shopping for Buddhas • A Short Walk in the Hindu Kush • Slowly Down the Ganges

ISLANDS OF THE INDIAN OCEAN Madagascar & Comoros • Maldives • Mauritius, Réunion & Seychelles
Travel Literature: Maverick in Madagascar

MIDDLE EAST & CENTRAL ASIA Bahrain, Kuwait & Qatar • Central Asia • Central Asia phrasebook • Dubai • Farsi (Persian) phrasebook • Hebrew phrasebook • Iran • Israel & the Palestinian Territories • Istanbul • Istanbul City Map • Istanbul to Cairo on a shoestring • Jerusalem • Jerusalem City Map • Jordan • Lebanon • Middle East • Oman & the United Arab Emirates • Syria • Turkey • Turkish phrasebook • World Food Turkey • Yemen
Travel Literature: Black on Black: Iran Revisited • The Gates of Damascus • Kingdom of the Film Stars: Journey into Jordan

NORTH AMERICA Alaska • Boston • Boston City Map • Boston Condensed • British Colombia • California & Nevada • California Condensed • Canada • Chicago • Chicago City Map • Deep South • Florida • Great Lakes • Hawaii • Hiking in Alaska • Hiking in the USA • Honolulu • Las Vegas • Los Angeles • Los Angeles City Map • Louisiana & The Deep South • Miami • Miami City Map • Montreal • New England • New Orleans • New York City • New York City City Map • New York City Condensed • New York, New Jersey & Pennsylvania • Oahu • Out to Eat – San Francisco • Pacific Northwest • Puerto Rico • Rocky Mountains • San Francisco • San Francisco City Map • Seattle • Southwest • Texas • Toronto • USA • USA phrasebook • Vancouver • Virginia & the Capital Region • Washington DC • Washington, DC City Map • World Food Deep South, USA • World Food New Orleans
Travel Literature: Caught Inside: A Surfer's Year on the California Coast • Drive Thru America

NORTH-EAST ASIA Beijing • Beijing City Map • Cantonese phrasebook • China • Hiking in Japan • Hong Kong • Hong Kong City Map • Hong Kong Condensed • Hong Kong, Macau & Guangzhou • Japan • Japanese phrasebook • Korea • Korean phrasebook • Kyoto • Mandarin phrasebook • Mongolia • Mongolian phrasebook • Seoul • Shanghai • South-West China • Taiwan • Tokyo • World Food – Hong Kong
Travel Literature: In Xanadu: A Quest • Lost Japan

SOUTH AMERICA Argentina, Uruguay & Paraguay • Bolivia • Brazil • Brazilian phrasebook • Buenos Aires • Chile & Easter Island • Colombia • Ecuador & the Galapagos Islands • Healthy Travel Central & South America • Latin American Spanish phrasebook • Peru • Quechua phrasebook • Read This First: Central & South America • Rio de Janeiro • Rio de Janeiro City Map • Santiago • South America on a shoestring • Santiago • Trekking in the Patagonian Andes • Venezuela
Travel Literature: Full Circle: A South American Journey

SOUTH-EAST ASIA Bali & Lombok • Bangkok • Bangkok City Map • Burmese phrasebook • Cambodia • Hanoi • Healthy Travel Asia & India • Hill Tribes phrasebook • Ho Chi Minh City • Indonesia • Indonesian phrasebook • Indonesia's Eastern Islands • Jakarta • Java • Lao phrasebook • Laos • Malay phrasebook • Malaysia, Singapore & Brunei • Myanmar (Burma) • Philippines • Pilipino (Tagalog) phrasebook • Read This First: Asia & India • Singapore • Singapore City Map • South-East Asia on a shoestring • South-East Asia phrasebook • Thailand • Thailand's Islands & Beaches • Thailand, Vietnam, Laos & Cambodia Road Atlas • Thai phrasebook • Vietnam • Vietnamese phrasebook • World Food Thailand • World Food Vietnam

ALSO AVAILABLE: Antarctica • The Arctic • The Blue Man: Tales of Travel, Love and Coffee • Brief Encounters: Stories of Love, Sex & Travel • Chasing Rickshaws • The Last Grain Race • Lonely Planet Unpacked • Not the Only Planet: Science Fiction Travel Stories • Lonely Planet On the Edge • Sacred India • Travel with Children • Travel Photography: A Guide to Taking Better Pictures

FREE Lonely Planet Newsletters

We love hearing from you and think you'd like to hear from us.

Planet Talk

Our FREE quarterly printed newsletter is full of tips from travellers and anecdotes from Lonely Planet guidebook authors. Every issue is packed with up-to-date travel news and advice, and includes:

- a postcard from Lonely Planet co-founder Tony Wheeler
- a swag of mail from travellers
- a look at life on the road through the eyes of a Lonely Planet author
- topical health advice
- prizes for the best travel yarn
- news about forthcoming Lonely Planet events
- a complete list of Lonely Planet books and other titles

To join our mailing list, residents of the UK, Europe and Africa can email us at go@lonelyplanet.co.uk; residents of North and South America can email us at info@lonelyplanet.com; the rest of the world can email us at talk2us@lonelyplanet.com.au, or contact any Lonely Planet office.

Comet

Our FREE monthly email newsletter brings you all the latest travel news, features, interviews, competitions, destination ideas, travellers' tips & tales, Q&As, raging debates and related links. Find out what's new on the Lonely Planet Web site and which books are about to hit the shelves.

Subscribe from your desktop: www.lonelyplanet.com/comet

Index

A

Abdül Hamit II, Sultan 17
accommodation, see places to
  stay
Ahmet I, Sultan 91
Ahmet III, Sultan 90
Ahrida Synagogue 119
air pollution 52
air travel 56-8
  airline offices 58-60
  security 56
  to/from Turkey 57-9
  within Turkey 56-7
Akbıyık Camii 97
Aksaray Square 103
alabaster 155
Alay Köşkü 95
Ali Paşa Çarşısı 187
Anadolu Hisarı 179-80
Anadolu Kavağı 179-80
Anthemius of Tralles 88-9
antiques 153-4, *153*
Anzac Cove 198-9
Aqueduct of Valens, see
  Bozdoğan Kemeri
Arkeoloji Müzeleri (Archaeo-
  logical Museum Complex)
  95-6
Armenian Church of Three
  Altars, see Üç Horan Ermeni
  Kilisesi
Armenians 21
arts 21-30
Askeri Müzesi 106-7
Atatürk 18
Atatürk airport 70
Atatürk Kültür Merkezi
  (Atatürk Cultural Centre)
  106
Atmeydanı, see
  Hippodrome
ATMs 38
Aya İrini Kilisesi 80
Aya Sofya 87-90, **88**
Aya Triyada Kilisesi 108
Ayasofya Pansiyonları 87
Aynalıkavak Kasrı 114
Ayoub al-Ansari 120

B

Bab-i Hümayun 87
Balık Pazar 109-10
Balat 119
ballet 146
Banded Stone Column, see
  Çemberlitaş
bargaining, see money
Basın Müzesi 98
Basil II, Emperor 11-12
Baths of Lady Hürrem, see
  Haseki Hürrem Hamamı
Bebek 172
Bedesten Çarşısı 186
Beyazıt Calligraphy Museum, see
  Beyazıt Hat Sanatları Müzesi
Beyazıt Camii 101
Beyazıt Hat Sanatları
  Müzesi 101
Beyazıt II Külliyesi 188
Beyazıt Square 101
Beykoz 180-1
Beylerbeyi Sarayı 178-9
Beyoğlu 104-12
Binbirdirek 97
Blue Mosque, see Sultan
  Ahmet Camii
boat travel 67-8
  to/from Turkey 68
  within İstanbul 74-6
  within Turkey 67
books 42-3, 154-5
bookshops 43
Bosphorus, The 132, 165-82
  Asian shore 176-82
  European shore 168-76
  ferries 167, 176
Bozdoğan Kemeri 102
British Consulate General 110
Burgaz 183
Burnt Column, see Çemberlitaş
Bursa 192-7
bus travel 59-62, 71
  to/from Turkey 60-2
  within İstanbul 71
  within Turkey 59-60
business procedures 54-5
business hours 52
Büyük Çamlıca 178
Büyükada 182-3
Büyükdere 173-4
Büyüksaray Mozaik
  Müzesi 92-3

C

Çadır Köşkü 170
cafe-bars 147-8
Cağaloğlu Hamamı 97
Cağaloğlu Square 97
calligraphy *22*
Çanakkale 201-2
car travel 35, 65-7, 72-5, see
  also motorcycle travel
  driving licence 35
  rental 72-5
  to/from Turkey 66
  within İstanbul 72
  within Turkey 65-8
carpets, see Turkish carpets
Carpet & Kilim Museum, see
  Halı ve Kilim Müzesi
Cartoon & Humour Museum,
  see İstanbul Karikatür ve
  Mizah Müzesi
Çemberlitaş 98
Çemberlitaş Hamamı 98
Çengelköy 179
children 50
Chora Church, see Kariye
  Müzesi
Christ Church 111
Church of Divine Peace, see
  Aya İrini Kilisesi
Church of Panaya Isodyon 110
Church of San Antonio di
  Padua 110
Church of St George 116
Church of St Mary Draperis
  110
Church of St Polyeuchtos 103
Church of St Stephen of the
  Bulgars 116-17
Çiçek Pasajı 109
cicims, see Turkish carpets
cinema 147
Çinili Cami 177, 178
Çinili Hamam 178
Çinili Köşk 96
Çırağan Sarayı 169
circumcision *162*
Cistern Basilica, see Yerebatan
  Saray
Cistern of Aspar, see Çukur
  Bostan
Cistern of Theodosius, see
  Şerefiye Sarnıcı
City Walls 118-19

Bold indicates maps.
Italics indicates boxed text.

classical music 146
conduct, see cultural
    considerations
Conqueror Monument Park,
    see Fatih Anıtı Parkı
Constantine VII Porphyrogene-
    tus, Emperor 94
copper vessels 155
Çorlulu Ali Paşa Medresesi 98
costs, see money
Covered Market, see Kapalı
    Çarşı
credit cards, see money
Crusade, Fourth 93
Crusades, The 13
Çukur Bostan 116
cultural considerations 30
Cumhuriyet Anıtı 106
currency, see money
customs 36

D
Dandolo, Enrico *90*
disabled travellers 50
discos 149
Divan Edebiyatı Müzesi 112
Divan Yolu 97-103
Dolmabahçe Sarayı 17, 107-8
dolmuş travel 72
driving, see car travel
Dutch Chapel 110

E
earthquakes 51
economy 19
Ecumenical Orthodox
    patriarchate 115-16
Edirne 183-9, **184**
    getting there & away 189
    history 185
    information 185
    museums 187
    places to eat 188-9
    places to stay 188
Edirnekapı 117-19, **Map 8**
electricity 46
email services 41
embassies 35
Eminönü 103-4, **Map 4**
Emir Sultan Camii 194
Emirgan 172-3
entertainment 146-51, *148*
environment 18
Eski Cami 186
Eski Kaplıca 195
Eski Şark Eserler Müzesi 95

etiquette, see cultural
    considerations
exchange offices, see money
exchange rates, see money
excursions 165-204
    Bosphorus, The 165-82
    Edirne 183-9
    Gallipoli & Troy 197-204
    İznik & Bursa 189-97
    Kızıl Adalar 182-3
Eyüp 119-21
Eyüp Sultan Camii 120

F
Fatih 115
Fatih Anıtı Parkı 102-3
Fatih Camii 115
fax services 41
Fener 115-16
ferry travel 149-50
festivals, see special events
Fethiye Camii 119
films 44
Firuz Ağa Camii 97
folk music 146
food, see places to eat
Fortress of the Seven Towers,
    see Yedikule
Forum of Theodosius 103
Fountain of Ahmet III, see
    Sultan III. Ahmet Çeşmesi
French Consulate General
    108-11

G
Galata, see Karaköy
Galata Bridge 103-4
Galata Kulesi (Tower) 113
Galata Mevlevihanesi 112
Galatasaray Square 109
Galipdede Caddesi 113
Gallipoli 197-204
gay travellers 49, *149*
Gazanfer Ağa Medresesi 103
geography 18
Golden Horn 103
government 19
Grand Bazaar, see Kapalı Çarşı
Great Palace Mosaic Museum,
    see Büyüksaray Mozaik
    Müzesi
Greek Orthodox Church of the
    Holy Trinity, see Aya
    Triyada Kilisesi
Greeks 20
Gülhane Park 94-5

H
Halı ve Kilim Müzesi 92
Hamamızade İsmail Dede
    Efendi Evi Müzesi 96-7
handicrafts 153
harem life 83
Haseki Hürrem Hamamı 91
Haseki Hürrem Sultan 94
Hasköy 114
health 46-9
Heybeliada 183
Hıdiv Kasrı 180
Hippodrome 93
history 10-18
    birth of the Ottoman Empire 14
    Byzantium 10
    Crusades 13-14
    founding of Constantinople 10
    Justinian, Emperor 11
    Ottoman conquest 14
    Ottoman decline 16
    Republican İstanbul 17
hitching 66-7
holidays, see public holidays
Hünkar Mahfili 90

I
İbrahim Paşa 94
Ihlamur Kasrı 168-9
Imperial Loge, see Hünkar
    Mahfili
inlaid wood 155
insurance 35
Internet
    access 41
    sites 42
Isidorus of Miletus 88-9
Islam 31
İstanbul **Map 1**
İstanbul Karikatür ve Mizah
    Müzesi 103
İstanbul University 101
İstiklal Caddesi 108-11, **Map 3**
İstinye 173
İznik 189-97
    getting there & away 192
    history 189-90
    information 190
    places to eat 192
    places to stay 192
İznik tiles 92, 104

J
janissaries *79*
jazz 149
jewellery 155

Jews 20
Justinian, Emperor 11, 88

K

Kabatepe Tanıtma Merkezi 198
Kaiser Wilhelm's fountain 93
Kanlıca 180
Kapalı Çarşı 98-101, 156-7, **99**
Karaköy 113-14
Kariye Müzesi 117-18
Kemal, Mustafa, see Atatürk
Kennedy Caddesi **Map 5**
Khedive's Villa, see Hıdıv Kasrı
kilims, see Turkish carpets
Kilyos 175-6
Kınalı 183
Kiosk of the Linden Tree, see
   Ihlamur Kasrı
Kız Kulesi 176
Kızıl Adalar 182-3
Küçük Aya Sofya Camii 96
Küçük Çamlıca 178
Küçüksu Kasrı 179
Kumkapı **Map 6**
Kurban Bayramı 54
Kurds 20

L

Laleli 103
Laleli Camii 103
laundry 46
Leander's Tower, see Kız Kulesi
leather goods 152-3
lesbian travellers 49
lese-majesty 51
libraries 50-1
Library of Ahmet III 85-6
literature, see books
'Little' Aya Sofya Mosque, see
   Küçük Aya Sofya Camii
Lone Pine 199
Loti, Pierre *121*
luggage storage 46

M

Mahmut II, Sultan 93-4
Maiden's Tower, see Kız Kulesi
Maiyet Köşkü 169
Malta Köşkü 170
maps 33
Marble Tower 122

Maritime Museum, see Deniz
   Müzesi
medical treatment, see
   health
Mecidiye Köşkü 87
meerschaum 155-6
Mehmet II, Sultan 14
Mehmet the Conqueror,
   Sultan 91
Merasim Köşkü 169, 171
metro travel 72
Mihrimah Sultan Camii 117,
   177
Military Museum, see Askeri
   Müzesi
Mimar Sinan 15
Mimar Sinan Çarşısı 177-8
Mısır Çarşısı 101, 162-3
money 36-40
mosaics 90, 118
Mosque of Süleyman the
   Magnificent, see Süley-
   maniye Camii
Mosque of Sultan Beyazıt II,
   see Beyazıt Camii
Mosque of the Conqueror,
   see Fatih Camii
Mosque of the Prince, see
   Şehzade Camii
Mosque of Yavuz Selim, see
   Selimiye Camii
motorcycle travel 65-7
Muradiye Camii 187
Murat III, Sultan 90
Museum of the Ancient
   Orient 95
Museum of Divan Literature,
   see Divan Edebiyatı
   Müzesi
Museum of Turkish & Islamic
   Arts 94
Museum of Turkish Musical
   Instruments 114
music festivals 146
musical instruments *24*
Mustafa Paşa Köşkü 87

N

Netherlands Consulate General
   110
Neve Shalom Synagogue
   113
newspapers 44-5
nightclubs 148
Nightingale, Florence *177*
Nilüfer Hatun İmareti 191

Nişantaşı **Map 2**
Nuruosmaniye Camii 100

O

Obelisk of Theodosius 93-4
Old Book Bazaar, see Sahaflar
   Çarşısı
organised tours 76
Orhan 14
Ortaköy 171-2
Osman Gazi ve Orhan Gazi
   Türbeleri 194

P

Paşabahçe 180-1
Palace of İbrahim Paşa 94
Palace of Antiochus 97
Palais de France 110
Palazzo Corpi 111
Palazzo di Venezia 110
Parade Kiosk, see Alay Köşkü
Pera *105*
Pera Palas Oteli *111*
photography 45
pipes 155-6
places to eat 134-45, *135*,
   138, *144*
   Bosphorus, The 145
   İstiklal Caddesi 141-42
   Kapalı Çarşı 140
   Kumkapı 143-44
   restaurants 135
   Sirkeci 137
   Sultanahmet 134-6
   Taksim 141
   Topkapı Sarayı 137
   Tünel 143
places to stay 123-33
   Aksaray 131-2
   Atatürk airport 132-3
   backpacker hotels 124
   Binbirdirek 125-6
   camping 124, 132-3
   Cankurtaran 123-4
   Divan Yolu 126
   family accommodation *129*
   Karaköy 131
   Küçük Ayasofya 126
   Laleli 131-2
   long-term stays 125
   Ottoman-style hotels 125,
      126
   student hostels 124
   Sultanahmet 123-7
   Taksim Square 129-30
   Tepebaşı 130-31

Bold indicates maps.
Italics indicates boxed text.

police 51
politics 19
Polonezköy 181
population 20
postal services 40
Press Museum 98
Princes' Islands, see Kızıl Adalar
public holidays 53

R

racism 52
radio 45
Rahmi M Koç Müzesi 114-15
Ramazan 53-4
religion 31
rental, see car travel
restaurant hints 139, see also
    places to eat
rock music 149
Roxelana, see Haseki Hürrem
    Sultan
Rumeli Hisarı 14, 172
Rumeli Kavağı 175
Russian Consulate General 111
Rüstem Paşa Camii 101, 104

S

Sahaflar Çarşısı 100-1
Sancta Sophia, see Aya Sofya
Sarayiçi 187-8
Sarıyer 174-5
Schliemann, Heinrich 203
Seferli Koğuşu 85-6
Şehzade Camii 102
Şehzadebaşı Caddesi 102
Şeker Bayramı 54
Selim 'the Grim', Sultan *116*
Selim III, Sultan 16
Selimiye Camii 116, 186-7
Şemsi Paşa Camii 177
senior travellers 50
Şerefiye Sarnıcı 98
shopping 152-64
Şile 181-2
silk goods 153
Soğukçeşme Sokak 87
Sokollu Mehmet Paşa Camii 96
Sokollu Mehmet Paşa Hamamı
    186
special events 50
Sphendoneh 96

Spice Bazaar, see Mısır Çarşısı
student cards 35
Sublime Porte 94-5
Süleyman the Magnificent 15
Süleymaniye Camii 101-2
sultans, see individual sultan's
    names
Sultan Ahmet Camii 91-3
Sultan III Ahmet Çeşmesi 87
Sultanahmet 78-122, **Map 7**
sumaks, see Turkish carpets
Swedish Consulate, Royal 111

T

taboos, see cultural
    considerations
Tahtakale 104
Taksim Gezi Yeri 106
Taksim Square 105-6
Tarabya 173
Tarihi Galatasaray Hamamı 108
taxes, see money
    departure tax 56
taxi travel 72
Tekfur Sarayı 118
telephone services 41
theatre 146-7
theft 51
Theodosius, Emperor 93-4
Tiled Kiosk, see Çinili Köşk
time 45
tipping, see money
toilets 46
Topkapı Sarayı 78-87,
    see map opposite 80
tourist offices 34
Tower of Sultan Ahmet 122
traffic accidents 51
train travel 61-5, *61*
    to/from Turkey 64-5
    within İstanbul
    within Turkey 61-5
travel insurance, see insurance
travellers cheques 38
travel with children, see
    children
Troy 202-4
Tünel 111-13
Tünel (underground train) 72
Türk ve İslam Eserleri Müzesi
    94
Turkish baths 150-1

Turkish carpets 152, 158-61
    buying carpets 160-1
Turkish cooking 138-9
Turkish delight *140*
Turks 20
TV 45

U

Üç Horan Ermeni Kilisesi 109
Üçşerefeli Cami 185-6
Üsküdar 176-8, **Map 9**
Uzunçarşı Caddesi 101

V

Valide Camii 103
visas 34-5
    extensions 35

W

walking 75
weights 46
women travellers 49
work 55

Y

Yanbol Synagogue 119
Yerebatan Caddesi 124-6
Yedikule 121-2
Yeni Cami 104
Yeni Kaplıca 195
Yeniköy 172-3
Yeni Valide Camii 177
Yerabatan Saray,
    see map opposite 96
Yeşil Cami 191
Yeşil Türbe 194
Yıldız Park 169-71
Yıldız Şale 170-1
Yıldız Sarayı 169-71
Yıldız Sarayı Müzesi 171
youth cards 35

Z

Zincirli Han 100
Zoe, Empress 12, 91

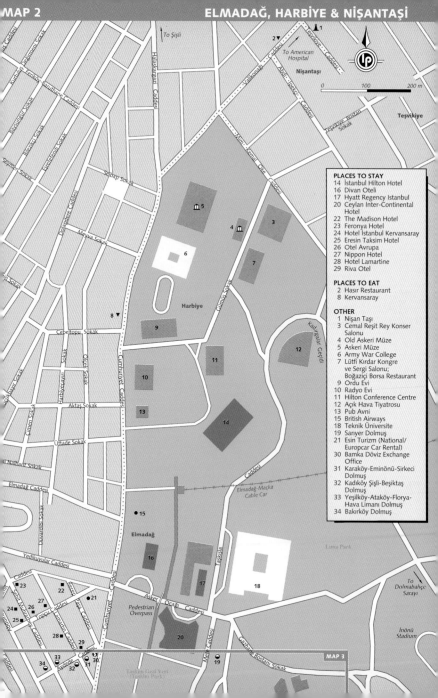

MAP 2   ELMADAĞ, HARBİYE & NİŞANTAŞI

To Şişli

Nişantaşı

To American Hospital

Teşvikiye

0   100   200 m

Harbiye

Kadırgalar Caydi

Ordu Evi

Elmadağ

Elmadağ-Maçka Cable Car

Luna Park

To Dolmabahçe Sarayı

Elmadağ

Pedestrian Overpass

İnönü Stadium

Taksim Gezi Yeri (Taşlık Park)

MAP 3

PLACES TO STAY
14 İstanbul Hilton Hotel
16 Divan Oteli
17 Hyatt Regency Istanbul
20 Ceylan Inter-Continental Hotel
22 The Madison Hotel
23 Feronya Hotel
24 Hotel Istanbul Kervansaray
25 Eresin Taksim Hotel
26 Otel Avrupa
27 Nippon Hotel
28 Hotel Lamartine
29 Riva Otel

PLACES TO EAT
2 Hasır Restaurant
8 Kervansaray

OTHER
1 Nişan Taşı
3 Cemal Reşit Rey Konser Salonu
4 Old Askeri Müze
5 Askeri Müze
6 Army War College
7 Lütfi Kırdar Kongre ve Sergi Salonu; Boğaziçi Borsa Restaurant
9 Ordu Evi
10 Radyo Evi
11 Hilton Conference Centre
12 Açık Hava Tiyatrosu
13 Pub Avni
15 British Airways
18 Teknik Üniversite
19 Sanyer Dolmuş
21 Esin Turizm (National/Europcar Car Rental)
30 Bamka Döviz Exchange Office
31 Karaköy-Eminönü-Sirkeci Dolmuş
32 Kadiköy Şişli-Beşiktaş Dolmuş
33 Yeşilköy-Ataköy-Florya-Hava Limanı Dolmuş
34 Bakırköy Dolmuş

Dolapdere Caddesi
Dilbaz Sokak
Soğancı
Düğün Sokak
Kıvanç
Kurtuluş Sokak
Kadıkol Sokak
Akkavak Sokak
Şirin Sokak
Dizçeki Sokak
Kasımpaşa Akarcası Sokak
Keramet Sokak
Tennure Sokak
Sıraselviler Ferhat Caddesi
Ömer
Ergün Sokak
Süngü Sokak
Çakar Sokak
Eski Çeşme
Kalyoncu Kulluk Sokak
Geniş Yokuş Sokak
Olcan Sokak
Zambak Sokak
Gümüş Küpe Sokak
Fiçici Sokak
Simitçi Sokak & Eski Çarşı
Nalbur Sokak
Dernek Sok
Cad
Emin Camii
Tarlabaşı
Bahriye Sokak
Firin Sokak
Sipahi Sokak
Aynalı Çeşme Caddesi
Meydanı
Arslan Sokak
Hamalbaşı Caddesi
Balık Sokak
Zil Sokak
Kameriye
Yeşilçam Sokak
Abanoz Sokak
Büyük
Topçekenler
Bayram Sokak
56
57
Yeşilçam
Aşıklar
Neva Sokak
Civici Sokak
Tepebaşı
Tepebaşı Caddesi
Çamaçan Sokak
Çatma Merdiven Sokak
Akarca Sokak
Gazköpman Mezarlık Sokak
Asmali Mescit
Tatlıbaş
Caddesi
Müstübiyet
62
63
64
65
66
67
68
69
70
71
72
73
74
75
76
77
78
79
80
81
82
83
84
85
86
87
88
89
90
91
92
93
94
95
96
97
98
99
100
101

Galatasaray

Tepebaşı

Kallavi Sokak
Eskiçiçekçi Sokak
Nuruziya Sokak
Tomtom Kaptan Sokak
Postacılar Sokak
Acar Sokak
Balyoz Sokak
Orhan Adli Apaydın Sokak
Gönül Sokak
Jumat Sokak
Soğal Sokak
Kumbaracı
Şimal Sokak
Sümbül Sokak
Tünel
Bedrettin Sokak
Müellif
Galipdede Caddesi
Tünel Square
Şişhane
Şişhane Square
Evliya Çelebi Caddesi
Lüleci
Yolcuzade İskender Caddesi
Şişhane Sokak
Büyük Hendek Caddesi
Küçük Hendek Sokak
Serdar-ı Ekrem Sokak
Boğazkesen Caddesi
Nazlı Hanım Sokak
Dik Sokak
Camcı Ormealtı Sokak

MAP 4

MAP 3

MAP 2

Gazhane Bostanı Sokak

Taksim Gezi Yeri
(Taşkim Park)

Taksim

5 🚶 ▼6

▼7

▼8

✉ 9

10
● 11
● 12
⊖ 13

To Dolmabahçe
& Kabataş

🛈 27

28
🛈

29

25

14

18 ●

19

❓ 20

Gümüşsuyu

📮 31

Kazancı Başı Camii Sokak

24

15

16 17

❓ 21

22

23

Kabataş

32

33

34

35

BEYOĞLU

Cihangir

İstanbul Boğazı
Bosphorus

Fındıklı

🔲 102

0   100   200 m

Tophane

MAP 5

İSTİKLAL CADDESİ

PLACES TO STAY
23 Family House
25 Marmara Hotel
35 Hotel Plaza
57 Virginie Apart-Hotel
63 Hotel Emperyal
76 Büyük Londra Oteli
86 Yenişehir Palas
87 Hotel Mercure
88 Pera Palas Oteli
95 Hotel Richmond; Patisserie Lebon

PLACES TO EAT
6 Pizza Hut
8 McDonald's
29 Çetin Restaurant; Büfe Snack Stands
30 Pehlivan Restaurant; Taksim Sütiş
37 Hacı Baba Restaurant
41 Borsa Fast Food Kafeteryası
45 Nature & Peace Café
46 Ada Restaurant
47 Hala
52 Sohbet Ocakbaşı
53 Cadde-i Kebir Café
54 Meşhur Sultanahmet Köftecisi
56 Hacı Abdullah Restaurant
58 Tarihi Cumhuriyet Meyhanesi; Other Tavernas
59 Mercan
61 Şütte Delicatessen
67 Çiçek Pasajı
68 Atlas Restaurant & Café; British Council
78 Afacan Pizza & Burger Restaurant
81 Teras Secret Garden
85 Çatı Restaurant
90 Karadeniz Pide Salonu
91 Şemsiye Restaurant; Yağmur Internet Café
92 Yakup 2 Restaurant
98 Dört Mevsim (Four Seasons) Restaurant

OTHER
1 Aksaray Dolmuş
2 Topkapı Dolmuş
3 Yapı Kredi Bankası
4 Air France Ticket Office
5 Türkiye İş Bankası
7 Turkish Airlines Ticket Office
9 PTT
10 Aeroflot Ticket Office
11 Hakiki Koç, İpek, İstanbul Seyahat (etc) Bus Ticket Office
12 Pamukkale Bus Ticket Office
13 Kadıköy-Bostancı Dolmuş
14 Atatürk Kültür Merkezi (Atatürk Cultural Centre)
15 Varan & Uludağ Bus Ticket Office
16 As Turizm & Hakiki Koç Bus Ticket Office
17 Kamil Koç; Metro Bus Ticket Office
18 Ulusoy & Bosfor Turizm Bus Ticket Office
19 Japanese Consulate
20 Yeni Adana, Mersin Seyahat (etc) Bus Ticket Office
21 German Consulate General
22 Beşiktaş-Dolmabahçe Dolmuş
24 Has, Köseoğlu, Set, Köksallar (etc) Bus Ticket Office
26 Cumhuriyet Anıtı (Republic Monument)
27 Toilets
28 Tourism Information Office
31 Maksim Gazino Nightclub; Taksim Sahnesi Theatre
32 Rumanian Consulate
33 Andon Pera Bar
34 Belgian Consulate
36 Aya Triyada Kilisesi (Greek Orthodox Church)
38 French Consulate
39 Akbank & Aksanat Kültür Merkezi
40 Türkiye İş Bankası
42 Fitaş Sineması

43 Ziraat Bankası
44 Pandora Bookshop
48 Vakko Department Store
49 Ali Muhiddin Hacı Bekir Confectionery
50 Yapı Kredi Bankası
51 Kaktüs Café
55 Ağa Camii
60 Üç Horan Ermeni Kilisesi (Armenian Church of Three Altars)
62 British Consulate General
64 Tourism Information Office
65 Galatasaray Square
66 PTT
69 Greek Consulate
70 Tarihi Galatasaray Hamamı
71 Toilets
72 Galatasaray Lycée
73 Telephone Centre
74 Yapı Kredi Bankası Gallery
75 Panaya İsodyon Greek Orthodox Church
77 Church of San Antonio di Padua
79 Odakule Office Building
80 Armenian Catholic Church of the Holy Trinity
82 Palais de France French Diplomatic Post
83 Robinson Crusoe Bookshop
84 Netherlands Consulate General
89 American Consulate General
93 Church of St Mary Draperis
94 Russian Consulate General
96 Dünya Aktüel Bookshop
97 Royal Swedish Consulate
99 Tünel (Underground Train)
100 Divan Edebiyatı Müzesi (Museum of Divan Literature)
101 Christ Church (Anglican)
102 Nusretiye Camii
103 Kılıç Ali Paşa Camii

View of the Old City from the Galata Kulesi.

The Sultan Ahmet Camii lights up as dusk descends.

View of Beyoğlu and the Galata Kulesi from Eminönü.

MAP 4

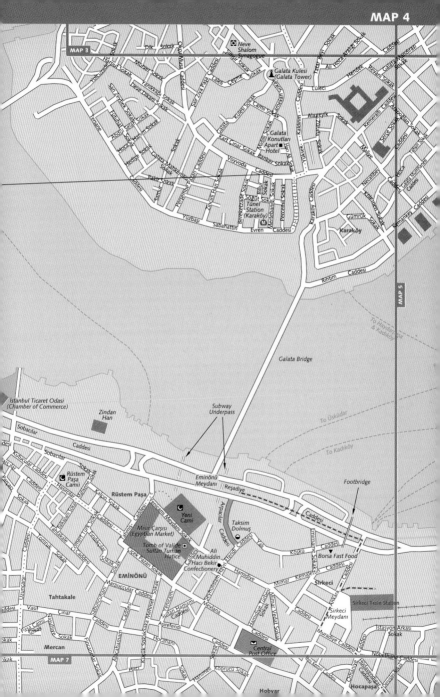

MAP 3
MAP 5
MAP 7

Neve
Shalom
Synagogue

Galata Kulesi
(Galata Tower)

Dik Sokak

Mumer Sokak

Galata Konutları
Apart Hotel

Voyvoda Caddesi

Tünel
Station
(Karaköy)

Karaköy

Karaköy Caddesi

Rıhtım Caddesi

Gümrük

Galata Bridge

İstanbul Ticaret Odası
(Chamber of Commerce)

Zindan
Han

Subway
Underpass

To Üsküdar

To Kadıköy

To Haydarpaşa
& Kadıköy

Footbridge

Sobacılar

Sobacılar Caddesi

Rüstem
Paşa Camii

Rüstem Paşa

Eminönü
Meydanı

Reşadiye

Taksim
Dolmuş

Caddesi

Yeni
Cami

Mısır Çarşısı
(Egyptian Market)

Tomb of Valide
Sultan Turhan Hatice

Ali
Muhiddin
Hacı Bekir
Confectionery

Borsa Fast Food

Sirkeci

EMİNÖNÜ

Sirkeci Train Station

Sirkeci
Meydanı

İstasyon Arkası
Sokak

Tahtakale

Mercan

Central
Post Office

Nöbethane Caddesi

Hobyar

Hocapaşa

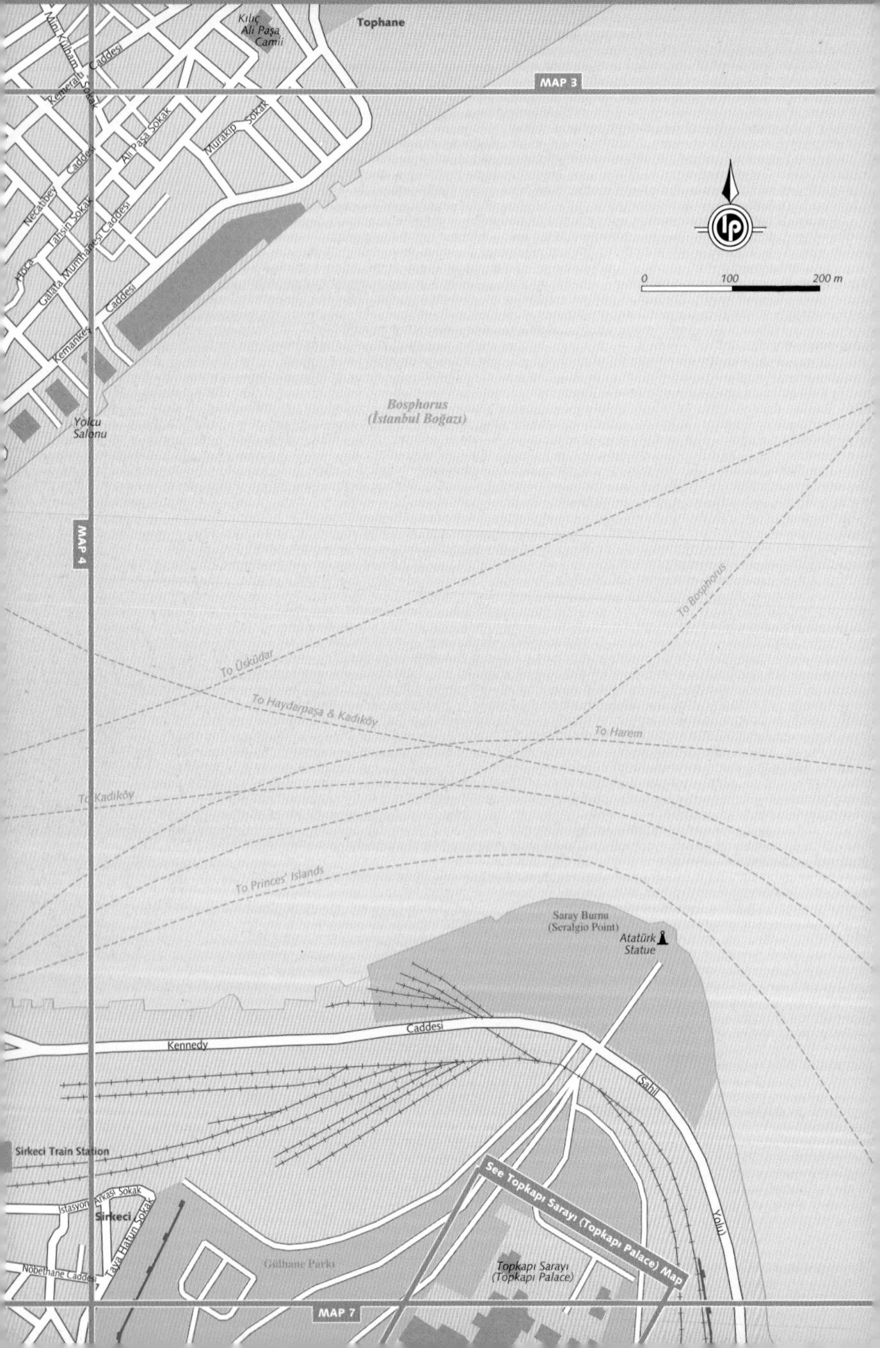

Tophane

MAP 3

Kılıç
Ali Paşa
Camii

Ali Paşa Sokak

Kurabiye Sokak

Necatibey Caddesi

Defterdar Sokak

Çavdar Mumhane Caddesi

Kemankeş Caddesi

Yolcu
Salonu

MAP 4

0   100   200 m

Bosphorus
(İstanbul Boğazı)

To Boğhorus

To Üsküdar

To Haydarpaşa & Kadıköy

To Harem

To Kadıköy

To Princes' Islands

Saray Burnu
(Seralgio Point)

Atatürk
Statue

Kennedy   Caddesi

Sahil

Sirkeci Train Station

İstasyon Arkası Sokak

Sirkeci

Kara Hamam Sokak

Nöbethane Caddesi

Gülhane Parkı

See Topkapı Sarayı (Topkapı Palace) Map

Yolu

Topkapı Sarayı
(Topkapı Palace)

MAP 7

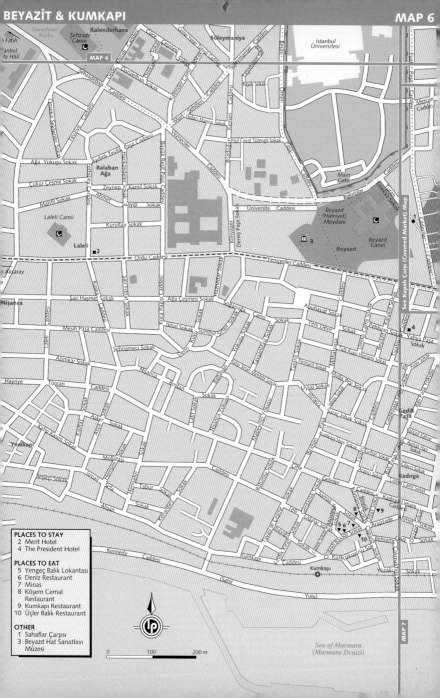

MAP 4

İstanbul
Üniversitesi

Beyazıt
(Hürriyet)
Meydanı

Beyazıt
Camii

Beyazıt

Sea of Marmara
(Marmara Denizi)

PLACES TO STAY
2 Merit Hotel
4 The President Hotel

PLACES TO EAT
5 Yengeç Balık Lokantası
6 Deniz Restaurant
7 Minas
8 Köşem Cemal
   Restaurant
9 Kumkapı Restaurant
10 Üçler Balık Restaurant

OTHER
1 Sahaflar Çarşısı
3 Beyazıt Hat Sanatlavı
   Müzesi

0   100   200 m

Mercan

Semaver Sokak

Mercan Caddesi

MAP 4

Hobyar

Hocapaşa

See Kapalı Çarşı (Covered Market) Map

Sururi

İstanbul Erkek Lisesi

İstanbul Vilayeti

Şeker Ahmet Paşa Sokak

Tayahatun

Bezciler Sokak

Ferdi Gökçay Sokak

Cağaloğlu Square

MAP 6

Kapalı Çarşı (Covered Market)

Aynacılar Sokak

Kılıççılar Sokak

Şeref Ef. Sokak

Nuruosmaniye Caddesi

4

3

5

6

2

Gazi Sinan

Himayeyi Eftal Sokak

Babıali

31

Yeniçeriler Caddesi

Çemberlitaş Tram Stop

34

33

32

Gazi Sinan

Çatal

28

27

24

Alemdar

30

25

İncili Çavuş

23 22 21 20

35

Emin Sinan

36

Divan

29

26

Sultanahmet Tram Stop

47

48

Doğramacı Sokak

39

37

Dr Şevkibey Sokak

Çemberlitaş

Binbirdirek

46

45

Gedik Paşa

38

42

43

Dostluk Yurdu Sokak

Law Courts

44

49

50

40

41

51

93

Piyerloti

94

92

91

88

Yahya Paşa Sokak

95

90

87

89

Sultan Ahmet Camii (Blue Mosque)

97

98

86

Küçük Ayasofya

96

105

Şehsuvarbey

Kadırga

108

99

104

107

100

103

102

106

101

Küçük Ayasofya

Sea of Marmara (Marmara Denizi)

MAP 7

Gülhane Parkı

MAP 5

Topkapı Sarayı
(Topkapı Palace)

🏛 11

🏛 10

12 🏛

Entrance

See Topkapı Sarayı (Topkapı Palace) Map

Tram
Stop

■ 8   ▼ 9

■ 16   ■ 15

13 🏛

🕇 14

17 ★

Aya Sofya
(Sancta Sophia)

See Aya Sofya (Sancta Sophia) Map

18

55

● 54

Sultanahmet
Square   ● 53

52 ▼

● 61
62

Sultanahmet

■ 60

56

57 C

58

■ 59

67 ■

● 63

65 ■   66 ■
64 ■   ■ 71

■ 68

■ 74

73 ■   69 ■

76 ●   ● 75   70 ■

▼ 77
● 78

Cankurtaran

Cankurtaran

■ 79

81 ■   ■ 80

C 82

84 🏛   83 ■

Ahırkapı

0   100   200 m

SULTANAHMET

PLACES TO STAY
5 Hotel Ema
6 Elit Hotel
7 Hotel Anadolu
8 Konuk Evi; Conservatory Restaurant
15 Ayasofya Pansiyonları
16 Yücelt Interyouth Hostel & Hobby Laundry
25 Hotel Nomade
28 Arsenal Youth Hostel
31 Sipahi Otel
36 Hotel Piyer Loti
37 Hotel Halı
38 Hotel Antea
40 Gülşah Otel
43 Hotel Arcadia
56 Mavi Guesthouse
58 Hotel Empress Zoe
59 Guesthouse Berk
60 Four Seasons Hotel
61 Yeşil Ev
63 Side Pansiyon
64 Alaaddin Guest House
65 Star Pansiyon; Laundry
66 Orient Youth Hostel
67 Barut's Guesthouse; Troy Hostel
68 Hotel Şebnem
69 İlknur Pansiyon
70 Hotel Poem
71 Konya Pansiyon
72 Sultan Tourist Hostel
73 Hotel Acropol
74 Terrace Guesthouse
76 Mavi Ev
79 Hotel Sümengen
80 Hotel Historia
81 Hotel Avicenna
83 Hotel Armada
90 Hotel Best Hipodrom
91 Hotel Turkoman
92 Hotel İbrahim Paşa
95 Türkmen Hotel & Pansiyon

98 Ottoman House
99 Hotel Sidera
100 Hotel Turkuaz
102 Can Pansiyon
103 Best Western Hotel Sokullu Paşa
104 Hotel Yeni Ayasofya
106 Seagull Pansiyon

PLACES TO EAT
1 Hoca Paşa Restaurants
3 Buhara Ocakbaşı
9 Taverna-Restaurant Sarnıç
20 Sultanahmet Meşhur Meydan Köftecisi & Sultan Pub.
21 Pudding Shop
22 Can Restaurant
23 Meşhur Tarihi Halk Köftecisi Selim Usta
24 Rumeli Cafe
26 Meşhur Sultanahmet Köftecisi
29 Karadeniz Pide ve Kebap Salonu; Hotel Akdeniz Lokantası
45 Sultan Sofrası
52 Derviş Aile Çay Bahçesi
77 Rami
87 Daruzziyafe
93 Gaziantep Kebap ve Lahmacun
94 Yeni Birlik Lokantası
107 Doy Doy

OTHER
2 Nuruosmaniye Camii
4 Cağaloğlu Hamamı
10 Eski Şark Eserler Müzesi
11 Çinili Köşk
12 İstanbul Arkeoloji Müzesi
13 İstanbul City Museum
14 Aya İrini (Hagia Eirene Church)
17 Tourism Police

18 Yerebatan Saray (Sunken Palace)
19 Cafeterya Medusa
27 Tarihi Park Hamamı
30 Tombs of Sultans
32 Basın Müzesi (Press Museum)
33 Çemberlitaş Hamamı
34 Atik Ali Paşa
35 Darüşşafaka Sitesi (Cinema Complex)
39 Şerefiye Sarnıçı (Cistern of Theodosius)
41 Keçicizade Fuat Paşa Camii
42 Binbirdirek (Philoxenes) Cistern
44 Türkve İslam Eserleri Müzesi
46 Palace of Antiochus Ruins
47 Firuz Ağa Camii
48 Tourism Information Office
49 Kaiser Wilhelm's Fountain
50 Obelisk of Theodosius
51 Tomb of Sultan Ahmet I
53 Haseki Hürrem Hamamı (Baths of Lady Hürrem, now a carpet shop)
54 Sultan III Ahmet Çeşmesi (Fountain of Ahmet III)
55 Imperial Gate, Topkapı Palace
57 İshak Paşa Camii
62 İstanbul Sanatlar Çarşışı (Handicrafts Market)
75 Magnaura Palace Restoration
78 Aypa Bookshop
82 Akbıyık Camii
84 Hamamzade İsmail Dede Efendi Evi Müzesi
85 Büyüksaray Mozaik Müzesi
86 Textile Museum
88 Spiral Column
89 Rough-Stone Obelisk
96 Sokollu Mehmet Paşa Camii
97 Kadırga Hamamı
101 Küçük Aya Sofya Camii
105 Sphendoneh
108 Tarihi Şifa Hamamı

Spend a day wandering through the Kapalı Çarşı and find hand-woven Turkish carpets and kilims ...

... belly dancing supplies ...

... souvenirs ...

... and embroidered hats and caps.

Krem Çeşme Sokak

Şişehane

Cebecibaşı

Meşatlık Sokak

Otakçıbaşı Sokak

Sarachane Caddesi

Edirnekapı

Hoçapaşır Caddesi

Edirnekapı

Hoçapaşır Caddesi

Ali Kuşçu Sokak

Eyüplü Sokak

**Mihrimah
Sultan Camii**

Viranodolar

**Hatice
Sultan**

Niyazi Mısri Sokak

Sarmaşık Sokak

Sokak Çeşme Sokak

Külâhlı

Sokak

Uzun Yol Sokak

Tüccan

Prof. Naci Şensoy Caddesi

Kovacı Sokak

Neslişah Sokak

Kariye Bostanı Sokak

Kariye Yağhane

Evliya Sokak

**Tekfur
Sarayı**

Avcı Bey

Caddesi

Marmaraze

Erikapı

Ece

Denizer Molla Yokuşu Sokak

Hasan Sokak

Kırkambar

Derviş Veli Ali

Demirhane Caddesi

Çınçınlı Çeşme Sokak

Şanbıdak Sokak

Sümmani El-Amun Sokak

Kasım Günani Camii

**Kasım
Gösim**

Vodina Caddesi

**Balat
Camii**

Gevgili Sokak

Hızır Çavi

**Koca
Mustafa**

Dükkân Sokak

Draman

**Yatağan
Camii**

Kesmekaya Caddesi

Miraç Sokak

Kalpakçı Çeşme

**Yazıcı
Camii**

**Katip
Muslihittin**

Draman

Hacı Hüreni Sokak

Fethiye Kapısı

**Fethiye
Camii**

Fethiye Caddesi

Manastağe

**Kariye Müzezi
(Chora Church)**

**Kariye
Oteli**

**Kariye-i
Atik**

Draman Caddesi

Tatlıcı

Fethiye Caddesi

Kasap Caddesi

Karanfil Sokak

Kefeli Sokak

Mürtüt Sokak

Karagümrük

**Draman
Camii**

Dilmen Sokak

**Yahyazade
Sokak**

Kollukçu

Sokak

Kasım Oğlan Sokak

Selma Yonnuk Sokak

Derviş Ali

Kasım Ağa Camii Caddesi

Paşa

Ekmekçi Sokak

Vefa Stadyumu

Kepderi Sokak

Beyceğiz

**Feda
Camii**

Nurettin Tekkesi Sokak

Todos Sokak

Zincirlikuyu Caddesi

Oflalı Bostan

Sarayi Akşar Sokak

Beyceğiz Caddesi

Cemali

Sokak

Hasan Fehmi Paşa Caddesi

Caddesi

Fatih Nişanca Caddesi

MAP 9

ÜSKÜDAR

1 Şemsi Paşa Camii
2 Mihrimah Sultan Camii
3 Şeyh Camii
4 Ağa Camii
5 Yeni Valide Camii
6 Mimar Sinan Çarşısı
7 Rumi Mehmet Paşa Camii
8 Ayazma Camii
9 İmrahor Camii
10 Kaptan Paşa Camii
11 Niyazibey İskender Kebapçı
12 Karakadı Alaattin Camii
13 Kara Davut Camii
14 Doğancılar Camii
15 Şehit Süleyman Camii
16 Ahmediye Camii
17 Nasuhi Camii
18 Atik Valide Camii
19 Çinili Camii

Bosphorus
(İstanbul Boğazı)

Kız Kulesi

MAP LEGEND

ROUTES & TRANSPORT

Freeway	
Highway	
Major Road	
Minor Road	
Unsealed Road	
City Freeway	
City Highway	
City Road	
City Street, Lane	

Pedestrian Mall	
Tunnel	
Train Route & Station	
Metro & Station	
Tramway	
Cable Car or Chairlift	
Walking Track	
Walking Tour	
Ferry Route	

HYDROGRAPHY

Coastline	
River	
Creek	
Lake	
Intermittent Lake	
Canal	

AREA FEATURES

Building	
Park, Gardens	

Market	
Cemetery	

Campus	
Hotel	

MAP SYMBOLS

✪ CAPITAL	National Capital	✈ Airport	◨	Petrol
◉ CAPITAL	State Capital	⊖ ATM, Bank	★	Police Station
● CITY	City	⚲ Castle or Fort	✉	Post Office
● Town	Town	✚ 🛈 Church	∴	Ruins
● Village	Village	◒ Embassy	❖	Shopping Centre
		◍ Hammam	🏛	Stately Home
■	Place to Stay	✛ Hospital	◙	Synagogue
▼	Place to Eat	⚑ Monument	☎	Telephone
⛻	Pub or Bar	◐ Mosque	◔	Toilet
		🏛 Museum	▣	Tomb
		← One Way Street	❶	Tourist Information
		🅿 Parking	◔	Transport

Note: not all symbols displayed above appear in this book

LONELY PLANET OFFICES

Australia
Locked Bag 1, Footscray, Victoria 3011
☎ 03 9689 4666 fax 03 9689 6833
email: talk2us@lonelyplanet.com.au

USA
150 Linden St, Oakland, CA 94607
☎ 510 893 8555 TOLL FREE: 800 275 8555
fax 510 893 8572
email: info@lonelyplanet.com

UK
10a Spring Place, London NW5 3BH
☎ 020 7428 4800 fax 020 7428 4828
email: go@lonelyplanet.co.uk

France
1 rue du Dahomey, 75011 Paris
☎ 01 55 25 33 00 fax 01 55 25 33 01
email: bip@lonelyplanet.fr
www.lonelyplanet.fr

World Wide Web: www.lonelyplanet.com *or* AOL keyword: lp
Lonely Planet Images: lpi@lonelyplanet.com.au